OTHER FROMM PAPERBACKS:

KALLOCAIN: A NOVEL
BY KARIN BOYE

AMERICAN NOTES: A JOURNEY
BY CHARLES DICKENS

BEFORE THE DELUGE: A PORTRAIT OF BERLIN IN THE 1920'S
BY OTTO FRIEDRICH

J. ROBERT OPPENHEIMER: SHATTERER OF WORLDS
BY PETER GOODCHILD

THE ENTHUSIAST: A LIFE OF THORNTON WILDER
BY GILBERT HARRISON

INDIAN SUMMER: A NOVEL
BY WILLIAM DEAN HOWELLS

A CRACK IN THE WALL: GROWING UP UNDER HITLER
BY HORST KRÜGER

EDITH WHARTON: A BIOGRAPHY
BY R. W. B. LEWIS

INTIMATE STRANGERS: THE CULTURE OF CELEBRITY
BY RICHARD SCHICKEL

BONE GAMES: ONE MAN'S SEARCH FOR THE ULTIMATE
ATHLETIC HIGH
BY ROB SCHULTHEIS

KENNETH CLARK: A BIOGRAPHY
BY MERYLE SECREST

ALEXANDER OF RUSSIA: NAPOLEON'S CONQUEROR
BY HENRI TROYAT

FROMM

ALSO BY DOUGLAS PORCH

ARMY AND REVOLUTION IN FRANCE, 1815-1848

(1974)

THE PORTUGUESE ARMED FORCES AND THE REVOLUTION

(1977)

THE MARCH TO THE MARNE:

THE FRENCH ARMY, 1871-1914

(1981)

THE CONQUEST OF MOROCCO

DOUGLAS PORCH

THE CONQUEST OF MOROCCO

FROMM INTERNATIONAL PUBLISHING CORPORATION
NEW YORK

Published in 1986 by

Fromm International Publishing Corporation

560 Lexington Avenue

New York, N.Y. 10022

Published by arrangement with Alfred A. Knopf, Inc.

THE CONQUEST OF MOROCCO

Copyright © 1982 by Douglas Porch.

Map Copyright © 1982 by David Lindroth.

All rights reserved

under International and Pan-American Copyright Conventions.

Published in the United States by Alfred A. Knopf, Inc., New York,

and simultaneously in Canada by Random House

of Canada Limited, Toronto. Distributed by

Random House, Inc., New York.

Published in Great Britain by Jill Norman

& Hobhouse, Ltd., London.

Grateful acknowledgement is made to the following

for permission to reprint from previously published material:

The Bodley Head: Excerpts from IN MOROCCO WITH GENERAL D'AMADE

by R. Rankin. Reprint with permission of the The Bodley Head.

John Murray Ltd.: Excerpts from WITH MOULAI HAFID AT FEZ

by Lawrence Harris, published by Smith Elder.

Library of Congress Cataloging in Publication Data

Porch, Douglas.

The conquest of Morocco.

Reprint. Originally published: New York: Knopf, 1983.

Bibliography: p. 317.

Includes index.

1. Morocco—History—20th century. I. Title.

[DT324.P6 1986]   964'.04   85-29340

ISBN 0-88064-057-X (pbk.)

Printed in the United States of America

FOR CHARLES

CONTENTS

The origins of this book lie in my interest in the French Army and, more specifically, a faction of it—the French Army in the colonies. In our own era, when so much of the world's disorder since 1945—in Algeria, black Africa, Afghanistan and the dreadful and tragic conflict which still continues in Indochina—has assumed the shape of the "war of the flea," a book that attempts to explain the origins of colonialism and the methods of its conquests may be relevant.

But history is not about parallels. It tells its own story, and that of the conquest of Morocco by France is a particularly compelling one. Morocco is a beautiful country and, in the early years of this century, it was still a wild and primitive one. Europeans were simultaneously drawn to Morocco and repelled by it, charmed by its savagery and, at the same time, the conscious if sometimes reluctant agents of its "civilization." The story of the conquest is that of the meeting of two cultures, Islamic and Christian. It is also about what contemporaries saw as the meeting of the modern age and the medieval world, of two peoples so distinct in mental, moral and physical condition as to belong not only to different continents but to separate historical epochs. I have attempted, through the use of documents and memoirs of the period, to convey something of the shock of that meeting. Where possible, I have offered the Moroccan point of view. But the documentary evidence is overwhelmingly European.

The French took ninety years to absorb Morocco, from the Battle of Isly in 1844 to the final submission of the Tafilalet in 1934. However, I have concentrated on the decade or so before the outbreak of the Great War. This offers a more manageable period, and one that includes the major events of the conquest. Before Lyautey's arrival in the South Oranais in 1903, the French advance had been spasmodic and unsustained. After 1914, when France proved that she could hold both on the Marne and in Morocco, all that remained to be accomplished, the Rif War apart, was to clean up a few pockets of "dissidence" in the mountains.

The actors in the drama were extraordinary people. The forty-three years of peace that began with the Treaty of Frankfurt in 1871 and ended abruptly in August 1914 appear in retrospect to be the last heroic age. This perhaps explains, at least in part, our current nostalgia for the world of Victoria and Edward. If our moral certainties appear to have disintegrated before forces too complex to understand, much less to counter, it is refreshing to step back into an era that appeared convinced of its values and confident of its future. It was this confidence in themselves and in their world that sustained the great figures of pre-1914 Europe, and that made subsequent generations of leaders, deprived of any basic set of beliefs in a world fragmented by war, economic chaos and political confusion, appear hesitant, shallow and opportunistic by comparison.

No one aspect of this period of European history was more obviously heroic than the exploration and conquest of Africa. The movement which made Livingstone and Stanley, Gordon and Kitchener, Marchand and Lyautey, household names has been regarded as the prime expression of the age. The more I study this period, however, the more I am convinced that colonial expansion, at least for the men who carried it out, was a countermovement, antiprogressive, a rejection of the age rather than an expression of it. Despite the talk of filling in the blank spaces on the map, of civilizing the natives, of providing markets and raw materials for European industry, Africa in fact offered an escape from a Europe in which technology was already allocating to everyone their minor tasks in an increasingly complex economic and social structure. Post-1871 Europe was changing rapidly. Men of strong religious conviction like Livingstone and Gordon, dissatisfied in a society devoted almost exclusively to increasing its material comfort, or, like Marchand, Lyautey, or any number of colonial soldiers, unhappy with the functionary's role assigned to them at home, sought asylum in Africa. "Renown," said Tacitus, "is easier won among perils." The explorers and conquerors of Africa were not so much thrown up by an expanding Europe as thrown out by it. Africa became a catchbag for European misfits, lionized abroad, unhappy and out of place at home.

Of no one was this more true than Hubert Lyautey. For the man whom Lloyd George called "the prince of proconsuls," whose name is indelibly linked with the conquest of Morocco, no good biography exists. Why has France—which cherishes her great men as servants of her civilization— deliberately chosen to ignore one of her greatest sons? The answer probably lies both in Lyautey's character and in the relationship of France with her colonies. Lyautey was both an eccentric and a colonial. While both characteristics earned for him, despite his rabid Anglophobia, a place in British esteem, in France they conspired to deflate his claims as a serious subject for biography. Colorful eccentricity has never enjoyed the acceptance in France which it can expect in Britain. But Frenchmen feel uncomfortable with Lyautey for reasons other than those connected with his personality. His ideas and politics cannot be slotted into a recognizable modern intellectual pattern, as can those even of other archreactionaries like Charles Maurras. Lyautey stands out as a loner, an individualist, a magnificent anachronism, a man with admirers perhaps but with no disciples. For French scholars, Lyautey is an isolated phenomenon, an intellectual cul-de-sac, a mere spectator who stands apart from the mainstream of French cultural life.

None of Lyautey's ideas was less fashionable, even in his own lifetime, than colonialism. While the empire was a source of pride in Britain, Frenchmen were at best ambivalent about the acres of desert, scrub and jungle brought under the flag by ambitious soldiers. The brutal methods of the colonizers frequently proved a source of scandal. While no particular opprobrium is attached to Lyautey's name, his association with an enterprise regarded by many in his country, then as now, as shameful is in part responsible for his being largely passed over by historians. Perhaps, too, the Marxist bias of much of French academic history, which tends to denigrate the influence of personality in favor of impersonal economic forces, has worked against Lyautey: why blow the penny whistle when one can summon up *le grand orchestre*?

The hazards of dealing with Lyautey are therefore numerous. There is no shortage of material. While he published little himself, he left numerous letters and reports. Even in these, one feels the magnetic strength of his personality, and it is difficult not to succumb to this "personnage." So many others have. I have tried to resist his spell, to remain objective in the face of his biased, if often entertaining, special pleading.

Since Vice-Admiral C. V. Usborne set down the military events of the conquest in a rather perfunctory manner in 1936, books on Morocco have fallen broadly into two categories. The first reflects the traditional interest in Morocco of modern diplomatic historians seeking the causes of the Great War. Their work concentrates on the crises that twice, in 1905 and 1911, brought Europe to the brink of war over that country. Since the end of the Second World War, a second school of historians led by Jean-Louis

Miège has written of French penetration as an episode of Moroccan history by tracing its effects on the economic, social and political structures of Moroccan society. My book is indebted to both of these groups.

Yet, there is a third viewpoint, which has been skirted by historians: that of the conquerors themselves. The conquest of Morocco was France's last great colonial enterprise. It involved a remarkable collection of soldiers—Lyautey, Charles Mangin, Henri Gouraud, Louis Franchet d'Esperey—who were to achieve fame in World War I. The conquest forms an important watershed in military history, for it saw the first systematic application of a strategy, central to any modern counterinsurgency operation, which has more recently been termed "the struggle for hearts and minds." How were these methods developed? How applied? How successful were they? Given the crucial role played by Lyautey in their popularization, in founding a "colonial" school of warfare, such questions have great relevance today. While seeking answers to them, I have attempted to give the conquest its Paris dimension by incorporating the remarkable research of Christopher Andrew and A. S. Kanya-Forstner on the colonial party active in metropolitan France.

Finally, historians of Morocco have been concerned primarily with explaining, in a logical manner, both the policy of the makhzan, the Moroccan government, and of the European powers. In this they have succeeded. But the story of the conquest is far more. It is a story of people, of chaos, villainy, glory, misery, violence, greed, avarice and maladministration. It is not a story for those who like their history neat.

THE CONQUEST OF MOROCCO

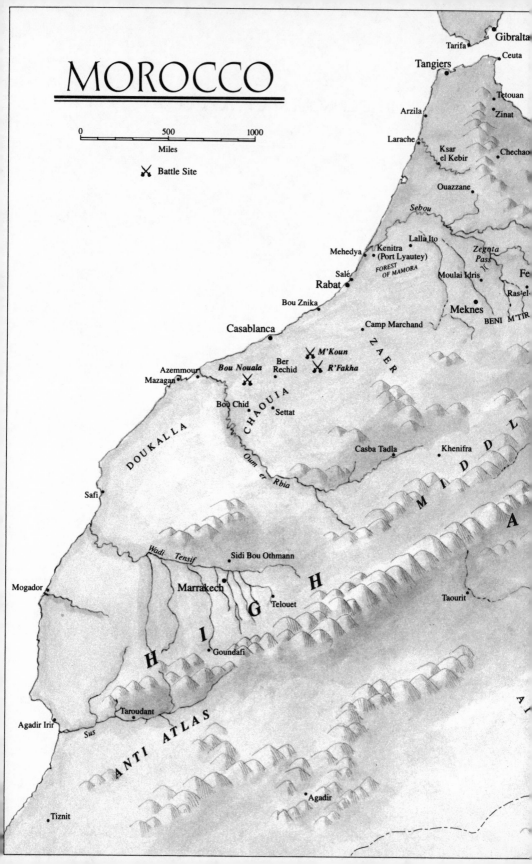

MOROCCO

0   500   1000

Miles

✗ Battle Site

Gibralta

Tarifa

Ceuta

Tangiers

Tetouan

Arzila

Zinat

Larache

Ksar
el Kebir

Chechao

Ouazzane

Sebou

Lalla Ito

Mehedya

Kenitra
(Port Lyautey)

*Zegota
Pass*

Salé

Moulai Idris

Fe

FOREST
OF MAMORA

Rabat

Ras·el-

Bou Znika

Meknes

BENI   M'TIR

Casablanca

Camp Marchand

✗ *M'Koun*

Z
A
E
R

Azemmour

Bou Nouala

Ber
Rechid

✗ *R'Fakha*

Mazagan

✗

Bou Chid

C
H
A
O
U
I
A

Settat

Oum er Rbia

Casba Tadla

Khenifra

M
I
D
D
L

DOUKALLA

A

Safi

Wadi   *Tensif*

Sidi Bou Othmann

H

Mogador

Marrakech

Telouet

Taourit

G

I

Goundafi

H

Taroudant

Agadir Irir

Sus

ANTI ATLAS

A

Tiznit

Agadir

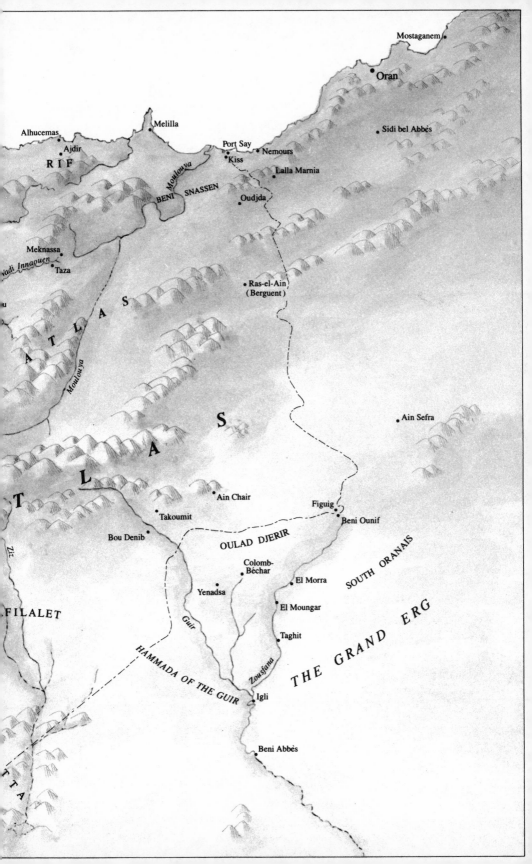

CHAPTER I

THE ROAD TO ZOUSFANA

Colonies can be conquered by accident. This may at first appear unlikely when we contemplate the immense colonial empires that Europe once possessed—such elaborate constructions must surely be the product of a policy, of a design, of economic calculation. But if you believe that, you may well be deceiving yourself. Algeria, to take one example, came to be the property of France by one of those flukes with which history abounds.

In 1828, Hussein, the dey of Algiers, struck the French consul, Pierre Deval, with his fly whisk in a fit of temper. The French government reacted in the classic fashion by sending an army. In fact, King Charles X of France hoped that by making a fuss over this "insult to the national honor" he might distract public attention from a series of planned domestic political measures that were bound to prove unpopular. In this, he was to be disappointed. In three bloody days in late July 1830, his government was overthrown and he was forced to flee for his life into exile, the last Bourbon king ever to rule France. But the French soldiers were already in Algiers. Stranded there without a government to issue orders, they behaved in the way soldiers often do when left to their own devices: they fought. Tribes and cities were gradually brought within the pale of French military administration and within fifteen years France had acquired, for better or worse, a colony.

By the turn of the century, French soldiers had in this same unplanned, ad hoc manner brought vast tracts of land in Africa and Indochina under the tricolor. However, one country had so far escaped their net: Morocco.

Morocco in 1900 was a country because the Sultan said it was. For Europeans who knew anything about the place, this claim appeared preposterous. Morocco was a land of tremendous contrasts—geographic, racial, linguistic—over much of which the Sultan exercised only nominal control. What gave it unity, at least on a map, was that it was virtually the only patch of Africa which had yet to be absorbed into one of those sweeping areas of pink, or yellow, or whatever color a European country used to delineate its empire. Morocco remained a cartographic anomaly, an untidy splash of noncolonial independence.

Morocco is dominated by its mountains. Those of the Rif rise out of the Mediterranean like an impenetrable barrier: "A naked, steep, savage-looking rocky wall," wrote the German explorer Gerhard Rohlfs, who visited Morocco in the 1860s. From the sea, the Rif appeared lifeless, "at the most, some lone cupola serving as the tombstone of a saint, shows that here human beings have lived and died." But its scrub-covered slopes were very much inhabited. Fierce Berber tribesmen kept the Rif both ungovernable and inaccessible. In 1888, Walter Harris, an English traveler who settled in Tangiers, claimed to be the first Christian to visit Chechaouèn, one of the chief towns of the Rif and certainly its most picturesque. Nestled at the foot of a six-hundred-foot rock precipice, the sloping red-tiled roofs of its houses give Chechaouèn an appearance far more Spanish than African, and one altogether unique in Morocco. But Harris enjoyed few of its charms. At the news that a Christian had infiltrated Chechaouèn, the streets filled with men intent on capturing the intruder, who was forced to hide in the house of one of his servants until nightfall, when he made his escape.

To the south, the stark, rocky spines of the Rif drop to the Taza corridor, the main passage between east and west Morocco, before the land again rises in successive ridges to the Middle Atlas. The large cedar forests and well-watered western slopes of this range make it one of the most pleasant regions of Morocco. It is here that the French conquerors would establish their best-known hill stations at Ifrane and Azrou, so that in summer wives and children could escape the baking heat of the plains below. These agreeable, tree-clad mountains rise to meet the High Atlas to the south. It is the snow-capped peaks of this range that curve majestically around the southern capital of Marrakech before they fall to the Atlantic above Agadir. The upper slopes of the High Atlas, which rise to over thirteen thousand feet, are virtually devoid of vegetation. Lower down, villages of square mud houses cling to the sides of precipitous valleys carved out by the melting snows.

Morocco's mountains divide the country both geographically and climatically. To the west, they cradle a well-watered land of plain and plateau, "as fertile as a garden," which stretches over three hundred miles from Marrakech in the south to the southern slopes of the Rif in the north. In the spring, this land is covered by a green felt of young wheat which ripens into a yellow carpet as summer progresses. Today, the light brown of the summer landscape is often broken by the blue-green groves of olive and the deeper green of citrus trees. Before the arrival of the French, however, the anarchy that ruled Morocco meant that this land was hardly cultivated, but given over almost exclusively to small herds of goats and sheep driven by nomadic tribesmen. This political instability placed severe limitations on the Moroccan economy, and on the Moroccan diet. Wheat ground into small grains of semolina which are then steamed formed the staple of the Moroccan diet — couscous. Couscous is served with mutton boiled together with any garden vegetables in season into a spicy stew. Chicken and eggs were also available in the small towns that served as markets, as was tea, which, in the nineteenth century, became the main beverage in Morocco, brewed with mint and highly sweetened. However, Morocco did have a well-established culinary tradition, which meant that the meals of the rich could be elaborate affairs indeed.

The lands to the east and south of the Atlas are far more wild and primitive than those to the west. The east has none of the large cities such as Fez, Meknes, Rabat or Tangiers, which provide both large markets and centers of government and Arab culture. Nor can eastern Morocco support them, for the mountains block the rain-laden westerly winds from the Atlantic and keep the annual rainfall in the east and south to under eight inches a year. This is the beginning of the steppe, the series of mountains and plateaux which run, arid and almost unbroken, across the Maghreb to Tunisia, bounded on the north by the Mediterranean and on the south by the sand wastes of the Sahara. Human habitation is concentrated along deep river valleys such as the Dra, the Guir and the Ziz in large, fortresslike buildings called *ksar*. Although dry for much of the year, these rivers nevertheless provide enough moisture for the date palms which thread the valleys and oases for the nomads who wander with their sheep, goats and camels over the near-barren land.

The mountains also divide the country culturally, into Arab and Berber. The term "Berber" commonly refers to the original, light-skinned inhabitants of the Maghreb who retreated into the mountains in the face of the two Arab invasions of the seventh and eleventh centuries. But the difference between Arab and Berber is far more linguistic or cultural than racial. The Berber population in the western lowlands was absorbed by the invaders, while the mountain folk resisted both Arabic and Islam, retaining in varying degrees their animist religious practices and their language, Shilha. The Arabs of the plain both despised and feared the warlike hill tribes: "Honey is not grease, durra is not food, Shilha is not a language," runs an Arab saying.

Finally, until the French conquest was completed in 1934, the Atlas complicated the whole question of who ruled Morocco. The government of Morocco is called the makhzan; the word literally means "storehouse" or "treasury," and is the origin of the English word "magazine." Before Lyautey settled the colonial administration in Rabat, Morocco had no capital as Europeans understood the term. The Sultan, surrounded by his viziers, or ministers, his harem, his soldiers and a small army of camp followers, scribes and merchants sometimes numbering thirty thousand souls, meandered between Fez, Meknes, Rabat and Marrakech, depending on the political situation in the country. As King of Morocco, the Sultan was able to impose his rule on those portions of his empire which his army could control— essentially the fertile crescent to the west of the Atlas. Elsewhere, his temporal authority was for all practical purposes ignored.

But the Sultan was a spiritual leader as well. A descendant of the Prophet and Commander of the Faithful, he was the object of great venera-tion even in those areas that refused to pay his taxes or accept his garrisons: they mentioned him rather than the Ottoman sultan in their Friday prayers, sent him embassies and presents. He was their caliph and the custodian of the *Dar el Islam*, the House of Islam, of which they were residents. They simply declined to pay the rent. The Moroccans had a name for the land whose inhabitants lived in this curious relationship with their lord: *bled el-siba*, or "land of dissidence."

The fact that the Sultan could not control the trans-Atlas regions should have made it easy for a country like France, which maintained a powerful army in neighboring Algeria, to move in. The difficulty lay in the fact that, around 1900, the governments of Europe found it expedient to recognize the makhzan as the legitimate government of Morocco—all of it. It was there-fore imprudent for France to begin military operations until she could gain the consent of her European neighbors. This they would not readily give. As a result, the future of Morocco provided one of the main sources of tension in European politics in the decade before the Great War.

Why had colonialists in France fixed their sights on Morocco? The answer to this question belongs more properly to the realm of psychology than that of economics. For Europeans, Morocco's economic importance was trifling—a few teapots and bolts of cloth were virtually all that Morocco bought from Europe, although there was a spirited market in contraband rifles. True, some spoke of Morocco's vast potential wealth in minerals, but these were dreamers, men who had not done their sums. Their visions were little more than hallucinations. The cost of conquering Morocco and of developing a transportation network beyond the few primitive tracks that existed in the interior would far exceed the profits from the few minerals that could be scratched from the soil.

For Europe, Morocco had only one value—strategic. Ironically, this proved the guarantee of Morocco's independence, with the result that the closest country in Africa to Europe was the last to fall in the mad scramble for African lands which had begun in the 1880s. Not because it was the least coveted: the French wanted to pull off a hat trick of takeovers in the Maghreb; Morocco would nicely complete the set which already included Algeria and Tunisia. In Paris and Algiers, the gnawing fear persisted that Morocco might, with foreign encouragement, become a staging post for an Islamic revolt that could throw France back across the Mediterranean and perhaps out of Africa altogether. Britain, for her part, was loath to see her major colonial rival installed across the strait from strategically vital Gibraltar, the first sentry post on the route to Suez and India. Spain feared foreign domination of the opposite shore. And events would soon bring Germany into contest for influence in Morocco. Mutual jealousies and suspicions thus kept each power at bay, postponed a takeover and preserved Morocco's fragile independence far beyond what should have been its natural life-span. Therefore, while in 1900 Morocco was still nominally independent, it was independent as a mouse surrounded by several hungry cats warily disputing who would carry off the dinner.

The stalemate over Morocco divided colonialists in France into two rival camps. The first group contained the diplomats led by Georges St.-René Taillandier, the French minister in Tangiers, and his boss, Foreign Minister Théophile Delcassé. All these men were acutely aware of the resistance to a French takeover of Morocco, both from Moroccans and from representatives of the other European powers. The colonialists in the Quai d'Orsay, the French foreign ministry, believed that a French protectorate must be carefully prepared, that hasty or ill-considered French military operations would provoke a violent reaction in Europe which might even lead to war.

St.-René and Delcassé believed that they had found a plan suited to the delicate international situation: Morocco would be suborned from within. The makhzan could be swallowed whole without the need to resort to force of arms. The Quai d'Orsay's "Program for military, economic and financial reconstruction of Morocco" would be France's Trojan horse left before the gates of an unsuspecting makhzan. Loans would be offered with strings attached—reform of the army and the civil service under French guidance, control of customs and of port police, a debt commission which would oversee Moroccan finances—until France held the Moroccan administration and economy by the throat. The French military mission in Fez would be expanded until its influence at court, and over the army, deprived the Sultan of any real independence. Delcassé's job was to prepare the ground in Europe. St.-René had the less enviable task of preparing it in Morocco.

For the second group of colonialists, made up of Algerian soldiers backed by the deputy for Oran and leader of the powerful colonial party in the Paris Chamber of Deputies, Eugène Etienne, the diplomats' plan was too clever by half. How could France suborn a country where the people were armed and prepared to resist? They saw more clearly than did the diplomats that the transparent conspiracy to reform and modernize a backward and conservative country like Morocco was bound to produce resistance and revolt. For the soldiers, the solution was at once more simple and more urgent: simple because a military invasion from Algeria would be a relatively easy affair to organize; urgent because French garrisons which manned the undefined frontier between Algeria and Morocco were failing in their attempts to contain the raiding parties from eastern Morocco which regularly struck into Algeria. The problem was especially acute in the southern section of the frontier region—the South Oranais. Here the Armée d'Afrique had established a series of posts running from Beni Ounif—which kept watch over the Moroccan oasis of Figuig—south along the Zousfana River through El Morra and Taghit to Beni Abbès, the last post before the real desert began. In these mud forts, built on promontories above the palm-fringed Zousfana, garrisons of foreign legionnaires, Algerian tirailleurs and French *bataillons d'Afrique* kept watch over a silent, empty landscape. However, they proved unable to prevent elusive Moroccan raiders from entering Algeria to plunder and steal. On the contrary, what made the soldiers especially angry was that they were themselves, more often than not, the victims of these successful hit-and-run raids. The supply columns that linked the isolated garrisons were an especially favored target. Paris, however, under pressure from the diplomats in Tangiers, expressly forbade retaliation, claiming that French incursions into territory claimed by the Sultan would anger the makhzan and set back their attempts to take over the country by peaceful means. So the army looked on helplessly as Moroccans ambushed its soldiers, lifted its livestock and weapons, and scurried back into the inviolate sanctuary of "Morocco."

For these reasons, the conquest of Morocco was to be a desperately complicated affair for France. Moroccan armed resistance was the least of her problems. She must also face the hostility of Europe, and this hostility had the effect of seriously dividing colonialists over questions of tactics. Each of the rival factions had its citadel: for the diplomats, this was Tangiers; for the soldiers, it was the line of posts along the Zousfana in the South Oranais. Their battles would be fought out in Paris as much as in Morocco.

CHAPTER II

EUROPEANS IN AFRICA

Scarcely thirty miles divide Gibraltar from Tangiers, and Morocco is clearly visible from Spain. In 1903, regular steamers from Gibraltar made the crossing in three hours. Yet there is an astonishing difference between the European and the African shores. Most visitors thought Gibraltar scarcely European. But nothing there prepared them for the total contrast of Tangiers.

For a town that was a hive of so much diplomatic activity, Tangiers at the turn of the century was remarkably unprepossessing. Despite its unique position at the entrance to the Mediterranean beside one of the world's most important crossroads, it had never developed as a commercial center. Since the site had first been settled in antiquity, successive generations of conquerors, including the British under Charles II, had discovered that the absence of a natural harbor and the inhospitable nature of the hinterland made Tangiers a prison rather than a gateway into the interior.

Seen from the sea, Tangiers was a tumble of flat-roofed buildings piled against the hillside. The old Moorish walls, the minarets, the Sultan's palace, were easily discernible. But what struck one immediately about Tangiers was its color: the water, the houses, stark white against the deep blue sky, tinted the town a transparent blue, very different from the yellow light that veiled Marrakech to the south.

Even from the sea, Morocco's quiet decay was apparent. The *Hassani*, flagship of the Sultan's three-boat navy, decorated the entrance to the bay. But the state of her boilers and the seamanship of her crew seldom permitted a voyage more adventurous than the annual trip to Gibraltar for repainting. As the Bay of Tangiers was too shallow for the few ships in the anchorage to approach the shore, the landing of passengers was effected by an armada of small boats and their porters, who swarmed over arriving steamers like pirates: "There is no question of 'Is this yours? Does this belong to you?' " wrote Grenadier Guards captain H. E. Colville. "Everything is seized and everything packed into one boat." To protest was futile. Passengers walked down the ship's steps and into small boats for the trip to shore, which, in boisterous weather, could be purgatory. Enormous black men waded into the surf to lift them the last few yards onto the beach.

The landing, exciting as it was, was simply the aperitif. For anyone unfamiliar with the East, the first impression on stepping through the customs shed into the twisting, dirty streets was usually one of revulsion: "My nostrils were assailed by a stench so powerful and nauseating as almost to be possessed of beauty, so description-defying as to relegate to a position of 'also smelt' the main drain of Pisa in summer," wrote Henry Selous, fresh from Cambridge to his first diplomatic posting in 1910. The narrow streets teemed with exotic figures whose origins were instantly recognizable to Walter Harris, Tangiers' best-known resident Englishman:

> The Genouah, from Timbuctoo, with their head-dresses of shells and strings and clanking cymbals; the Susi in dark blue linen, or black and brown jelabas; the mountaineers, tall and fair, many with bright blue eyes, and by far the handsomest of the Moorish peoples; the men from the Gharb, or fertile plains, enveloped in the numerous folds of coarse haiks, speaking with a strange accent; the Berbers, with thin guttural tongue, absolutely different from Arabic. . . . Amongst all this medley pass and repass the rich town Moors on horse or mule, gaudily caparisoned.

Mules and donkeys thrust their way through the crowd. Merchants sat cross-legged in shops hardly larger than packing crates calling out to passersby in an incomprehensible mélange of Arabic, Spanish and English. Over all lingered the persistent odor of "dung and dates."

Life in Tangiers revolved around the Grand Soko, a piece of bare hillside just outside the main gate which served as the terminal point for caravans from the south. A vast expanse of mud in winter and baked clay in summer, the Soko had a social life all its own: Camels with globulous eyes knelt among the crates and angular black tents chewing languidly, visibly relieved to have shed their burdens at last. Lower down, village women hawked the few poor products of the Rif—green food for horses, thistles for mules and donkeys, chickens, eggs and bread. Men and boys squatted in circles listening to storytellers, watching jugglers or perhaps a performing ape.

Occasionally, however, the oriental charm of the Soko could be shattered by the disturbing performance of a snake eater. A man whose hair hung in ringlets in the fashion of Victorian ladies ambled through the crowd swinging a poisonous reptile by the tail, now and then rushing the horrified but transfixed spectators who had began to gather. He then placed the head of the snake between his teeth and, taking the tail in both hands, he stretched it out beyond its full length until it broke off at the neck, leaving the head in his mouth. Then, having swallowed the head, he would continue to bite bits off the still-wriggling body.

Equally disturbing was the annual feast of the Isawa, the sons of Jesus, whose adherents flowed through the narrow streets like drunken men, entranced by the monotony of their koranic chant into an orgy of self-mutilation with whips and hatchets until their faces and bodies were a sticky crimson.

Tangiers was a microcosm of Morocco, and yet it was not a typical Moroccan town. Unlike the cities of the interior, Tangiers had no slave market, nor did it contain a mellah, or ghetto, such as Morocco's substantial population of city Jews was elsewhere required to live in. But what was most distinctive about Tangiers was its large population of Europeans.

Tangiers' European population fell broadly into two categories: the celestial and the criminal. The celestial contingent was provided by Christian missionaries. Tradition backed by treaties confined Catholic penetration of Morocco to a handful of Spanish Franciscans, originally admitted in the seventeenth century to minister to the significant number of Christian captives held in the Sultan's prisons. Their efforts to convert the local population were confined to ringing the church bells loudly each time the muezzin climbed the minaret to call the Moslem faithful to prayer. The French diplomat St.-Aulaire finally managed to crack the Spanish monopoly on Catholic worship by having six French nuns attached to the French hospital in Tangiers. As the rules of their order required that a chaplain accompany them, a French priest was thus smuggled into Morocco. This minor diplomatic triumph was especially appreciated by the Moslems: "Your Christian muezzin is truly a lord," St.-Aulaire's house servant told him. "He has six women all to himself."

Protestants, with more enthusiasm if less realism than their Catholic counterparts, attempted to carry Christ's word into the house of Islam, despite the fact that even a superficial knowledge of Morocco might have warned them that a country whose able-bodied male population was engaged mainly in cattle-stealing made stony ground for missionary work. Medical missionaries were most in demand, and they had their work cut out for them. Epidemics of cholera and smallpox periodically ravaged the country. It was reckoned that 75 percent of the population suffered from syphilis, while Morocco's incredible filth, which shocked even those familiar with the East, bred other endemic diseases such as ophthalmia. Moroccans were perfectly willing to accept medicines from the "Nazarenes," but declined the accompanying spiritual message. Indeed, missionary doctors lamented that the whole point of Christian charity seemed lost on the women who came to their surgeries to demand Spanish fly to stimulate the flagging interest of their husbands, or poison if they had an eye on the inheritance.

Missionaries met with setbacks enough to try the patience of Job. Moslems and Jews in coastal towns quickly lost interest in Christianity when they realized that the status of a protected person of a foreign embassy, which allowed them to escape Moorish justice and taxes, did not automatically follow upon conversion. Walter Harris told of one young missionary who arrived in Tangiers determined to preach a public sermon. His Moroccan interpreter demanded a large fee, stressing the dangers of preaching Christianity in the heartland of Islam. The sermon was duly delivered, translated sentence by sentence, to a large and attentive crowd in the Soko, which dispersed quietly at the end. Harris never had the heart to tell the Christian that his interpreter had simply repeated a tale from the *Arabian Nights*. The Presbyterian missionary Dr. Robert Kerr continually turned down offers from church publications for articles on "striking cases of conversion" because, he said, in thirty years of missionary work in Morocco he had never witnessed any. Edinburgh Presbyterians were briefly encouraged when a consignment of Bibles bound in "native style" with Morocco leather covers was snapped up by the Jews of Rabat. Conversions, however, failed to follow: the Jews, who had paid two reals per Bible, ripped out the pages and resold the leather bindings for five reals each, a profit margin of 150 percent.

In contrast to the Christians, Tangiers' criminal contingent flourished. The town had been a place of exile for political refugees since Napoleonic times. In 1900, Spanish anarchists and others who had finished on the wrong side of a *pronunciamento* kept this tradition alive. Most of Morocco's ten thousand or so Europeans at the turn of the century were Spaniards and most lived in Tangiers. The overwhelming majority were poor, driven from the Iberian Peninsula by drought or economic crisis, and earned their livings by smuggling, running low bars and cafés, or—and this especially offended Moorish sensibilities—raising pigs. "Here, there, everywhere can be seen Spaniards, many of them drunk, all of them objectionable," wrote Harris.

The mixture of Moorish and Spanish culture gave Tangiers a cosmopolitan atmosphere of a dowdy variety: "In the evening, if one passed through the tortuous labyrinth of alleys, one heard the scratching of guitars from behind the shutters, these languid rhythms which finish suddenly with a cry of mortal passion," wrote Madame St.-René. "This strange amalgamation where Moroccans, Spaniards and Jews lived together without ever mixing."

Not all of Tangiers' foreigners were "low adventurers." Unlike many European outposts in Africa, Tangiers had acquired a veneer of European civilization. A small diplomatic community had existed there since the eighteenth century, which swelled with the steady increase in trade and European interest in Africa over the next 150 years. As the Victorian era approached its end, the diplomats were joined by wealthy expatriates, mainly British, who came to Tangiers for reasons of health or, like Budgett Meakin's father, editor of the *Times of Morocco*—a newspaper noted for the inaccuracy of its information and the demented tone of its editorials—as an alternative to prison.

Life for this tiny *tout Tangiers* was far from unpleasant. The men devoted much time to polo or pig-sticking, a sport for which the British had acquired a taste in India and which had been developed in the scrubland behind the town by Sir John Drummond Hay, Britain's consul of forty years. The Frenchman St.-Aulaire found *le pig-sticking* something of a misnomer, as far more horses and men were stuck than pigs, especially by the enthusiastic but inept Gibraltar subalterns who took the packet boat over each weekend. As a consequence, he was far too concerned for the safety of his own skin to worry overmuch about planting his lance in the hide of a charging boar.

Ladies found Tangiers provincial, even restricting. Madame St.-René Taillandier catalogued the pleasures denied to a Parisian stranded in Africa: smoking, theater and concerts, talking of clothes (since every lady was as familiar with the wardrobe of her friends as she was with her own), or trips to shops or dressmakers, for none existed. The filthy condition of the streets meant that visits were never accomplished on foot but on the backs of donkeys, preceded by a guard who with guttural cries cleared a path through the crowds. Others, finding mules undignified and worried lest they spoil their toilette, had themselves carried on sedan chairs by Jews, if, that is, it was not Saturday: "No son of Mohammed would carry a Christian woman."

But Tangiers offered compensations: picnics, tennis, tea with the amusing Emily Keene, the English governess who had married the Sharif of

Ouezzane, the greatest spiritual figure in Morocco after the Sultan, but who left him when, contrary to his promise to her, he took a second wife; dinner at the sumptuous villa of Walter Harris, surrounded by peacocks and fierce Riffian guards ("Harris really knew how to live"), or with the American consul, Samuel R. Gummere, a tall, thin man with a mouth full of gold teeth who was proud owner of Tangiers' first phonograph, which he would play loudly enough at dinner parties to extinguish all conversation.

The cosmopolitan affability of Tangiers society was largely an illusion, however, for the national tensions which had begun to divide Europe into rival camps circumscribed relations between the representatives of different nations. The Spanish minister behaved as if Tangiers were already *terra nostra*. The French and British ministers, each of whom rightly suspected the other of entertaining designs on Morocco, cordially detested each other. The Germans, in the person of Richard von Kuhlmann, a future foreign minister of the Second Reich and by far the most charming and the most accomplished sticker of pigs in the diplomatic community, for the time being simply looked on. The Italians, while not interested in Morocco itself, were to support no country's claim until their own in Libya was recognized.

The atmosphere of Tangiers social life was, as a result, brittle, even tense. "There did not seem to be two people in the place who liked or trusted one another," one British visitor noted. The smiles and pleasantries barely camouflaged a fierce battle for prestige which transformed each reception and dinner party into a competition in which rival diplomats maneuvered for advantage in a game whose arcane rules were barely comprehensible to the outside world. National dignity was transposed to the personal level, intrigue and mistrust elevated to a way of life: "We had to be far more careful to avoid sensitive subjects than we would have been among our own compatriots," wrote Madame St.-René. "Nor was there any real intimacy, never the temptation to share a confidence, hardly to be humorous or joke. There was no backbiting for everything was repeated, no obvious preferences, never any of the subjects of conversation which create any real links of friendship among people who dine together twice weekly. "

The diplomats' task was made no easier by the attitude of Morocco's royal government, the makhzan, which sought by every means in its power to keep them at arm's length. And no wonder. Moroccans traditionally distrusted Europeans, and nothing in their relationship with Europe over the preceding half-century had done much to alter this attitude. After the Spanish-Moroccan War of 1860, the victorious Spaniards imposed an indemnity of

100 million pesetas on the makhzan, stipulating that it must be paid in foreign, not Moroccan, specie. As Morocco's gold and silver reserves drained away to Madrid, prices quadrupled to compensate for a now devalued currency, taxes were raised to maintain revenue, and a once stable economy was left in tatters. The monetary crisis was aggravated by the influx of cheap wheat, wool, hides and cloth from America and Europe which destroyed many traditional Moroccan craft industries. The newly acquired taste of Moroccans for tea and sugar increased the trade deficit. Unable to support themselves in the interior, Moroccans drifted to the coast in increasing numbers, pushed by famine and epidemics of cholera and smallpox, creating a landless, detribalized proletariat around the burgeoning coastal towns. There, many made contact for the first time with Europeans. The experience was seldom a happy one.

The government could do little about the arrival of Europeans on the coast. It did, however, do its best to keep them out of the interior. Moroccans close to power had long since abandoned Tangiers to the *roumi*; its royal palace had not housed a sultan for decades. The makhzan kept an official in Tangiers, Si Mohammed Torres, whose main duty was to handle complaints from European ministers and delay their requested visits to the court. When the ministers came to court, it was always to make mischief, for the main purpose of their visits was invariably to present claims involving protection.

For the makhzan, nothing better symbolized the nefarious influence of Christians in Morocco than the practice of protection. The eighteenth-century treaties which had established the system allowed each consul and commercial house with business in Morocco to name two of the Sultan's subjects as its "agents." These agents and their families fell under the protection of foreign flags, and so were exempted from taxes, Moroccan justice and other onerous local laws. This worked well enough in the beginning, but with the influx of Europeans into Morocco in the 1880s, abuses became the rule rather than the exception. Protection became a gold mine for a subspecies of chargés d'affaires, usually adventurers whose primary concern was to milk their office for all it was worth. The Italian minister was reckoned to have over a thousand protégés. The Portuguese and Brazilian ministers made substantial fortunes by selling patents of protection. The worst offender, however, was probably Felix A. Mattews (*né* Mateos), a onetime steward on the U.S.S. *Constitution* who worked his way into the good graces of the Republican Party and eventually into the American legation at Tangiers. His practices were so notorious that he was fired after the Tangiers diplomatic corps sent a formal complaint to the State Department. However, a change of administration in Washington saw him restored to his old position, and to his old tricks.

Coastal towns like Mogador virtually survived on the proceeds of protection: ". . . Almost every place where there was revenue sufficient to buy a flag and issue postage stamps for philatelists, had long ago sent consuls to Mogador," wrote the English traveler R. B. Cunninghame Graham. "Their flag staffs reared aloft looked like a mighty canebrake from the sea. Their banners shaded the streets . . . and half the population were consuls of some semi-bankrupt state." Or, on at least one occasion, of a nonexistent state:

> Araucania-Patagonia, even in Mogador, excited some surprise. . . . What struck their fancy most was the new oriflamme. Barred white and blue, a rising sun grinning across three mountain tops, a cap of liberty and a huanaco ruminant; an Araucanian Indian in his war paint in one corner, and here and there stars, daggers, scales and other democratic trademarks, made up a banner, the like of which had seldom been observed in all the much be-bannered town of Mogador.

It transpired that the new "consul," who called himself Abdul Kerim Bey, was in fact an Austrian named Geyling. But it took some time to convince the Moroccans, whose ignorance of the outside world was virtually total, that neither Araucania-Patagonia nor its King Orelie-Antoine actually existed.

But one did not need to wangle a diplomatic appointment, or found a new nation, to enjoy the fruits of protection. European "merchants" also benefited from the system which allowed them up to eight "agents" and fifty "agricultural associates." The practice was known as "farming in Morocco" and served to spread the abuses of protection beyond the small clique of consuls and ministers in Tangiers and other coastal towns. From the moment a "merchant" established himself in a coastal town like Larache or Safi, he received an endless stream of visits from Moroccans who, throwing themselves at his feet, begged to be taken on as agents. Ragged urchins emerged bearing bunches of chickens tied together by the legs, eggs, pots of butter and honey, while the supplicant, squatting before the "merchant's" desk, explained that he had cattle and land. It was a delicate task for the Moroccan, for he must convince the European that he was wealthy enough to pay his way but not so rich that the "merchant" would demand too large a price for his coveted patent of protection. The negotiations usually dragged on for several days while the European made inquiries and named his price—"two hundred dollars down and something when the certificate is renewed next year, besides which you would of course report yourself each quarter, and not come empty-handed. Animals and corn I can do best with, but I don't want any of your poultry." The Moroccan protested that this was too high a price: "I can't go any lower. There are scores of Moors who would give me that price. Do as you like. Good morning." And, of course, the Moor paid.

The makhzan looked on aghast as its wealthiest subjects stampeded to purchase protection and thus escape the government's authority altogether. But the government had only its own appalling rapaciousness to blame for the popularity of protection. Sir John Drummond Hay described Morocco as "a community of fishes, the giant fish feed upon those that are small, the smaller upon the least, and these again upon the worms." Extortion ruled the relationships between government and governed: The Sultan demanded revenue from his caids, who squeezed the richest men in their districts. They, in turn, extorted money from their retainers. Any hint of wealth was excuse enough to seize a man's property on some trumped-up pretext. "I have been in most oriental countries, but I have never seen such complete darkness as reigns here," wrote Sir Arthur Nicolson, British minister in Tangiers from 1895 to 1905. The instability of Moroccan politics made fortunes, even life itself, precarious. The fickleness of royal favor could overnight scatter a rich and great family and make a pauper of a powerful caid and of his elaborate network of clientele. At best, a Moroccan family might hope for three generations of relative comfort before being reduced once again to poverty. Islam taught its followers to accept such radical changes of fortune as the will of Allah. It was, defenders of tradition argued, proof of the "equality" and "hope" of Moroccan society—today a poor man, tomorrow a lord. But the popularity of protection, which for the first time offered Moroccans an insurance against utter destitution, suggests that oriental fatalism was more a product of circumstance than an ingrained state of mind.

Protection was not a completely dependable form of insurance, however. Its abuses did much to poison relationships between Moroccans and Europeans. It also led to a marked increase in anti-Semitism in the last quarter of the nineteenth century. As in other countries of the Maghreb, the status of the substantial minority of Moroccan Jews before the arrival of the European was precarious. Islam, like Christianity, regarded Jews as "the infidel in our midst," but their place in the Moroccan economy was far too important to permit their persecution to extinction—as goldsmiths, gunsmiths, traders and, above all, moneylenders (no caid was without his Jewish financier). Legally, Jews fell under the protection of the Sultan. A royal *dahir* of February 1864 stressed that they should be well treated, a sure indication that this was seldom the case.

Initially, the increasing European presence in Morocco threatened the livelihoods of many Jews, especially those who depended on the trans-Sahara trade in slaves, gold and ivory. The gunsmiths also found that their primitive muskets sold badly once the end of the American Civil War released onto the Moroccan market a trickle of modern arms which, with the end of the Franco-Prussian War in 1871 and the beginning of the arms race in Europe, soon became a torrent. Many Jews, however, supremely adaptable, drifted to the coastal towns, where a number of them insinuated themselves into the protégé network as vice-consuls, agents and interpreters. Others—several thousand in Fez alone—claimed Algerian nationality and automatically won French protection. Towns like Mogador, founded as an *entrepôt* of European commerce in the eighteenth century, virtually became Jewish settlements: "Jews, Jews and still more Jews possess the place," wrote Cunninghame Graham. ". . . They sit in shops, lean out of windows, lounge on the beach, walk about slowly as if they stepped on eggs, are kind in private life, cruel in business."

A small but extremely visible minority of Jews became the essential middlemen for the European penetration of Morocco, an invasion which most Moslems detested. They disapproved of the links between Jews and Europeans, links made obvious by the western clothes worn by some Jews and by the foreign languages taught in the Alliances Israélites, founded and funded by European Jews. Even more, Moroccans were angered by the arrogance of some Jews who no longer fell under the jurisdiction of the Moroccan authorities. But the involvement of Jews in the more unsavory practices of protection brought the hatred of Moslems down on the entire race.

For protection became a racket, and a very nasty one at that. And it was Moslems who most often suffered. To become an agent or "agricultural associate" of a European, the Moroccan was obliged to sign over half of his property to the European merchant. It was an indication of how desperate Moroccans often were to protect their modest fortunes that many did so. But even then they were by no means secure. "Merchants," seldom the cream of European society, were known to connive, often with the local caid, to imprison their associates and claim all their property. The method most often used was a bad debt. Islam forbade the lending of money and, outside of Fez, this religious injunction was largely respected. Moneylending became the virtual monopoly of Jewish protégés, who charged up to 400 percent interest on loans or even fabricated claims against Moslems for debts allegedly owed them. The consuls became the debt collectors for their protégés, with the passive assistance of the makhzan. As the government administration was usually too inefficient to verify these claims, the defendant—or his kin—was simply left to rot in prison until his relatives could scrape together the money to buy him out. In this way, Christian and Jew became associated with a system that was considered rotten even by Morocco's rather lax ethical standards: "God burn the Nazarenes, their wives and families, and all their ancestors!" Budgett Meakin was told by a man locked away as the result of a fraudulent claim placed by the Greek consul, acting on behalf of his Jewish protégé, against his brother. "They were never fit for aught but hell."

European diplomats oiled the machinery of protection. It was, therefore, hardly surprising that their reception in the interior was usually far from cordial, a fact which they hypocritically put down to the bigotry and ignorance of their hosts. Sir John Drummond Hay prided himself on his ability to make backwoods officials respect the dignity of his office:

> The following day, according to etiquette, I called on the [Governor of Azamor] at his residence. As I entered the porch, the "m'haznia" [military guard], about 40 in number, instead of being drawn up standing in line to receive me, were squatting on the ground, forming a double rank, reaching close to the kiosk in which the Governor was seated, thus leaving only a narrow passage for me to pass through. Some even had their legs sprawled out in my way. These I trod upon heavily, or kicked aside, much to their dismay.
>
> The Governor, who was seated, counting the beads of a rosary, on a small divan, remained seated as I approached, without attempting to rise or salute me; neither had he any chair or other resting-place to offer me, and merely held out his hand saying "You are welcome". Taking his hand with a firm grip, I lifted him gently from his divan and said, "I am glad to see you". When I got his astonished Excellency well on his legs, I wheeled him round suddenly and dropped on the middle of the divan where he had been seated, leaving him standing.
>
> Caid Ben Tahir looked bewildered, gazed first at me and then at his guards, and I think was still meditating whether to bolt or to call his

scowling attendants to seize and bastinado me, when I addressed him—"How thoughtful and attentive of you to have prepared this comfortable divan for me to sit upon without providing for yourself a chair or even a stool where you could sit to entertain me."

After this lesson in etiquette, the caid and the minister made friends, "so I told him I should not report the occurrence to his Lord and Master the Sultan."

In contrast to the hostility of local caids, the reception at court could be an elaborate affair. Walter Harris, who visited Marrakech with the British minister in 1887, described the scene:

Passing through two rather fine archways at each of which our approach was heralded by a blast of trumpets, we entered the great square of the Kasbah into which the palace looks. The square we found full of troops; on our right and in front of us the infantry, on our left the cavalry, of which each man was dismounted, standing at his horse's head. It seemed almost incredible to us that Morocco could turn out so many soldiers, for we learned afterwards from the most authentic of sources, that there were no less than 22,000 men present.

In the centre of these troops was left an open space, where already were the mules bearing presents from the British government, in front of which stood the small Shetland ponies, one led by Sir William's Albanian servant, the other by a Moor. In the centre of this open space we dismounted, took up our position while various court officials rushed around arranging minor details. . . . In front of us, some hundred yards' distance in the wall of the square, was the great green gateway that communicates with the palace, a fine example of a Moorish arch, and boasting much finish and decoration. Between us and the gateway, with their backs to us, and so facing the palace stood a row of courtiers, some 40 in all.

We had ample time to look around us before the ceremony of the day commenced, and this conclusion we all came to: be the Moors in other respects what they may, they are unrivalled in arranging effects. The great square, with its curious turreted walls and fine gateways; the thousands of troops all around us, the infantry in their scarlet and blue, the cavalry in white flowing haiks; and the long-robed courtiers before us all formed a wonderful picture. And if, then, we came to the conclusion that the Moors were "showmen", how much more did we do so when a blast of trumpets announced the Emperor, and, the great gates being thrown open, the procession began to appear. First, led by black slaves, came four magnificent horses—a black, a grey, a bay and a white—following which marched the Court-Marshall with a white wand, various officials, spear-bearers, and others; and finally the Sultan himself, mounted on a splendid horse, whose trappings of green and gold formed a strange contrast to the Emperor's plain white costume, which consisted of a jelaba and haik, both of which were drawn over his turbaned head, no doubt as protection from the sun, though this was scarcely needed, as high above him waved the Imperial umbrella, a marvellous structure of crimson and gold. On either side of his majesty walked men whose duty it was to keep the flies off his sacred person by continually flapping the air with long white silk scarves. Following the Sultan were more officials, and finally a green and gold brougham.

As the procession entered the square, all the troops fell down crying "Long Live the Sultan! Victory to the Sultan!", and a wonderful cry it was from 22,000 throats. As the Sultan approached the row of courtiers that I mentioned above as being between the palace and ourselves, they bowed themselves to the ground crying out, "It is the Sultan!", then suddenly turned round and fled in every direction, as though even the sight of his august majesty inspired fear.

This splendid reception must not be taken as an indication that European representatives were welcomed at court. On the contrary, the whole point of the ceremony was to emphasize the inferior status of the visitors, made to stand uncovered like tributaries before the Sultan, who was mounted on a splendid horse and shaded by a scarlet parasol. (In 1902, under pressure from the European powers, the ceremony was modified so that ambassadors could remain on horseback.)

The hospitality which followed was as splendid as the initial reception. In honor of the Europeans, the normal order of a Moroccan meal was often reversed, so that the sweet dishes were served last: "The menu was as follows," John Drummond Hay recorded of one court feast:

Roast pigeons, stuffed chicken, stewed lamb, turkey with almonds and highly flavoured siksu (a delicate paste, round in form, but being no larger than dust shot); olives in oil; oranges cut in sections and spiced, served as a vegetable; salad of olives and mint; eggs poached with olives and oil; chicken fricassée, with a rich egg sauce; chickens with red butter—a piquante sauce; stewed mutton with fried eggs; chickens stewed with almonds and sweetened.

Dry siksu; rice made up in a sort of porridge; bowls of new milk; almond tart, flavoured with musk; pastry dipped in honey.

Dessert: oranges, almonds, raisins, nuts, and 14 dishes of confectionery, including "kab ghazal", or gazelle hoofs, little cakes of that form, from which they take their name, made of pastry thickly iced and filled with a concoction of almonds.

A pleasant preparation of unripe figs, much resembling chutney, was served with the stewed lamb.

The only beverage was water, slightly flavoured with musk and essence of citron flowers.

Of this menu the turkey, the fricassées of chicken and the dry siksu, were pronounced excellent, but some of the other dishes were horrible concoctions.

The servants reported afterwards that as many dishes as had been served remained outside untasted; but that the steward, observing how little was eaten, promptly brought the banquet to a close and produced coffee, well made, but curiously flavoured.

Sumptuous entertainment and generous hospitality, which in European diplomatic circles was designed to ease and speed negotiations, in Morocco was meant to have the opposite effect. The Sultan's banquet was followed by the "friendly feasts," when the embassy was required to dine with each of the viziers in turn, prior to transacting official business. Picnics, sight-seeing and other outings were arranged which delighted the ladies who accompanied the embassies, but delayed affairs of state, as Sir John Drummond Hay discovered: "We have not made much progress in negotiations. We continue to be feasted and are rather bored thereby, for they fix on the late hour of 10 pm to commence festivities, and there is great monotony; illuminations, Moorish music, tea and cakes." After eight or ten days on a diet of couscous and sweetmeats saturated in butter and honey, the visitors' digestive functions were so upset that they required another week to recover sufficiently to transact business: "Meanwhile, the Sultan and his cabinet gain time, and enjoy themselves immensely at the expense of the mission."

Nothing in a traditional career prepared diplomats for their dealings with the Moroccan government. The makhzan was a combination of mosque and bureaucracy. The powers of the Sultan as king and Commander of the Faithful were vast and undefined, and his ministers obeyed his every whim. The cabinet consisted of five viziers or ministers, chief of whom was the grand vizier, whose task it was to impose taxes, nominate caids, regulate the religious fraternities and act as intermediary between the Sultan and his subjects. The remaining viziers dealt with foreign affairs, finance, war and the administration. In reality, this arrangement was even more primitive than it appears on paper. The "ministries" consisted of nothing more than small, cobwebbed rooms tucked away in a corner of the palace—or a tent if the makhzan were "on the road"—where the minister could be found sitting cross-legged behind a desk eighteen inches high flanked by two secretaries who made up the sum total of his administration. Cunning rather than competence was the primary quality of a vizier, while the ability to cite long passages from the Koran served as a sort of civil service examination for the secretaries. As Napoleon was the only European that these men had heard of, it was advisable to claim his acquaintance if one wanted to be thought important. Englishmen, however, could claim to have fought him or, in exceptional cases, might drop the name of Oliver Cromwell to achieve the desired effect.

The Sultan was seldom more worldly-wise than his ministers. The British journalist Lawrence Harris was admitted into the palace in Fez by a ragged old man, directed down a labyrinth of corridors, through a series of doors which slammed behind him with a clang as the rusty bolts slid back into place, to emerge into a vaultlike hall, at the end of which sat the Sultan cross-legged on a yellow divan. Harris presented Moulai Hafid with a copy of the *Daily Graphic* which bore the Sultan's picture and Harris's article about him on the front page. Hafid was delighted with the "magnificent and important journal" and asked Harris to explain the pictures. Those on the front page were all of royalty. The Sultan was obviously pleased to be in such good company. The second page contained a picture of a John Burns. No, Harris explained, John Burns was not a noble. Hafid quickly turned the page and Harris realized what he must do: the policemen, bank managers and secretaries whose pictures decorated subsequent pages were ennobled. Even the advertisements did not present insurmountable problems: the children in Fry's Cocoa were given titles, as was the Tatcho woman in décolletage. However, disaster lurked on the back page: the monkey in Monkey Brand Soap in evening dress sitting on the front of a locomotive. Swallowing hard,

Harris made him a duke. "You are very clever," Hafid said warmly. "You shall go to King Edward with a letter from me, and also to the Emperor of Germany," and so on through the crowned heads of Europe.

The viziers were not only ignorant, but venal. For this they were not entirely to blame. The concept of placing civil servants on a regular salary was entirely alien to Morocco. As in medieval and Renaissance Europe, officials expected to do well out of their offices. Walter Harris complained that "official life is a mass of bribery and corruption" which reached down to the lowest servant. To obtain an interview with a minister required a "long pocket and much patience." "An interview can be delayed by the meanest slave who will tell you that 'my master is asleep' or 'in the bath,' " until he is bribed. The Sultan's palace was permeated with an atmosphere of extortion. Visitors were swarmed over by servants who, both numerous and unpaid, shouted "Fabor! Fabor!" until tipped. If the visitor ran out of money, they were quite prepared to accompany him to his house to collect their due.

Transacting serious business in these conditions was virtually impossible, and intentionally so. Most Moroccan ministers, St.-Aulaire complained, believed that the best way to conserve their offices was simply not to exercise them. When he and the German minister, Count von Tattenbach, called on the grand vizier Si Feddoul Gharnit in 1905, they were ushered into a beautiful courtyard with marble floors, surrounded by Moorish arches covered with delicate arabesques in the center of which stood a fountain. While Europeans thought it bad form to allow conversation to languish, Moroccans sat for hours in silence sipping sweet mint tea, eating from baskets of fruit and pastries, listening to the splash of water in the fountain and breathing the air made sweet with the odor of roses and orange blossoms. When, at last, the two Europeans began to speak of political topics, the grand vizier delivered a lengthy monologue on the sexual superiority of black women over their white sisters. He then turned to the German's interpreter and said: "Tell your bachadour that his bachadoura will not be bored tonight," confessing that he had put amber, considered an aphrodisiac, into the tea. The interpreter, knowing that to translate such a suggestion would be disrespectful, remained silent. Tattenbach insisted: "Translate! I thought I heard His Excellency the Grand Vizier speak of Madame von Tattenbach." After a moment's reflection, the interpreter replied: "He asks you how she is and sends his compliments." Tattenbach thanked him profusely.

The influence of interpreters was not always so beneficial, however. Sir

John Drummond Hay, a gifted linguist with an excellent command of colloquial Arabic, was quite exceptional. Many other members of the diplomatic corps were at the mercy of their interpreters, most of whom were graduates of the Alliance Israélite, and some of whom had their own interests to pursue. Occasionally, the language barrier reduced official court presentations to the level of farce: diplomats, with great flourish and accompanying gestures, counted to one hundred, pausing at each tenth number for the interpreter to translate, more or less accurately, a prepared text. In more private *tête-à-têtes* between diplomats and officials, interpreters were not above slipping in a request for a house or a piece of land for themselves among the lengthy claims which the European had brought for settlement.

This then, was the makhzan which the French Foreign Office hoped to suborn by peaceful means. To men who knew anything about Morocco, the plans for reform proposed by Delcassé and St.-René Taillandier appeared to be a wild dream. How could one reform a country in which "self-interest is the only motive of the governing classes"? The British minister Arthur Nicolson agreed with Lyautey that the whole "rickety edifice" needed only the slightest push from outside to come tumbling down. Whichever method they favored, however, colonialists agreed that the Moors were so tired of their grinding system of government that they would welcome "any European invader." How little they knew the Moors.

CHAPTER III

THE COUNTRY

How little they knew the Moors, indeed! European powers proceeded with their plans for conquest confident that the people of Morocco would receive them with open arms. Tangiers, a dilapidated backwater on the southern shore of the Mediterranean, became one of the major focal points of European diplomacy between 1900 and the outbreak of war in 1914. But who were these people, what was this country, which Europe planned to win for civilization? Europeans woke up to discover that their governments were possibly prepared to go to war over a land about which they knew virtually nothing.

It struck more than one person as ironic that Morocco, the closest country in Africa to Europe, was the one about which Europeans possibly knew the least; when John Drummond Hay's school friend told him that Morocco was "a land in Africa inhabited by naked niggers," he was at least half correct. European knowledge of the country beyond Tangiers was scant, for Morocco was mapless. The natives had no need of maps. They simply followed the well-established trading routes. The absence of maps, however, became one of the greatest stumbling blocks to European penetration of Morocco: when eventually the French landed, they had no idea where they were going.

The reason for European ignorance of Morocco is not difficult to discover: the place was virtually inaccessible. This may seem a paradox, given its proximity to Europe. But unless one had a strong incentive to visit the country—and there was precious little there to attract either the capitalist or the casual tourist—the arguments against a trip into the interior were almost overwhelming. Morocco was a prisoner of its geography, an island bounded on two sides by the sea and by the Sahara to the south. She had no natural harbors and her few coastal towns were roadsteads rather than gateways to the interior. The wheel was unknown. So were roads. Travel followed rough tracks which were virtually impassable in winter. And there were the mountains, the great rib of the Atlas which curved through the country like a scythe. Peopled by fiercely independent and well-armed tribesmen, the mountains formed a very effective barrier against the penetration both of Europeans from the north and east and of the government from the west.

Geography was not the only barrier to European penetration. Travelers must also take into account the hostility of the population. Moroccans had no wish to meet Christians. This had nothing to do with religious prejudice, as Europeans often maintained, but stemmed from the legitimate fear that Christians had come to spy out the land. The result was that it was possible to travel alone in Morocco in the nineteenth century, but it required great tact, not a little courage, and, above all, careful planning.

The first requirement was a good cover story. Ali Bey, a Spaniard who visited Morocco in the early nineteenth century, reckoned that the more preposterous one's reason for visiting Morocco, the more likely the story was to be believed by the credulous inhabitants. The German traveler Gerhard Rohlfs, who toured the interior in 1861–62, let it be understood that he was under sentence of death in his native land for converting to Islam. Believing this, the Moors dropped their hostility and were positively helpful in suggesting how he might better adapt to their way of life: "It seems that I ought to have the word God often in my mouth; I should not say 'lead', for it was not *proper* to name the thing by which men were killed; I should say 'the light' which is just the opposite quality of lead. I must not stare at or speak to young women or girls." He soon learned that pacing up and down was thought "ungentlemanly" and that unconscious gestures could be open to misinterpretation: " 'Look at the infidel dog, how he has crossed his hands (I had sat down cross-legged and also crossed my hands). Certainly he is saying his sinful prayers.' I quickly uncrossed my hands and was admonished never to repeat such God-forgotten gestures in the company of believers." Any mention of Christians or Jews in a conversation must be followed immediately by a request for pardon.

Mealtime was always an ordeal for Europeans. Even in the best houses, Moroccans plunged their hands "half-washed or not washed at all" into a communal dish of couscous. The primary characteristic of a Moroccan meal, at least on the popular level, was the speed with which it was consumed. The leisurely or inexpert diner would be left behind by Moroccans, who, using only the fingers of the right hand, skillfully rolled the evasive grains of semolina into small balls or, grabbing one end of a slippery piece of mutton with a neighbor holding the other, tore it into large but manageable mouthfuls, taking care, however, always to leave something in the dish for the women and servants. "I sometimes let part of the mess fall on the ground, which gave them great offense and made them vent their anger in maledictions on the Christians." It was considered a great mark of distinction if the host dipped his dirty fingers into the dish and, selecting a piece of meat, popped it into his guest's mouth. Meals were accompanied by a symphony of belches, the Moors "merely saying by way of apology 'God forgive!' to which the others politely reply 'God be praised!' " A sip of water, the superficial washing of hands, and a muttered "Praise be to God" rounded off the dinner.

Surprisingly, Rohlfs discovered that language presented the least of his problems:

> The whole manner of living is so simple, the requirements are so few, the talk is so stereotyped and turns so nearly always on the same subjects, that, when one has mastered the construction of the Moorish mode of speech and has committed to memory the most necessary words, talking is easy. The great thing is always to have the words "Allah" and "Prophet" in one's mouth, to talk of Paradise and Hell, not to forget the devil, and devoutly murmur over the rosary as it slips through the fingers. Should it happen that one is doubtful about a sentence, or forget a word, and says instead of it "Allah is the greatest!" or "Mohammed is the favourite of Allah!" or "Allah confound the Christians!," no Moroccan would notice it even though the exclamation had no reference at all to what had preceded it, and would finish the sentence, or find the word wanted himself.

Nonetheless, a renegade's disguise and a modest command of Arabic did not constitute an infallible guarantee of safety. On at least two occasions Rohlfs passed within a whisker of extinction, near-victim of the suspicions, or the avarice, of the inhabitants. A French officer, Charles de Foucauld, circumvented the language problem by disguising himself as a Russian Jew, but the negative aspect of his disguise largely canceled out any advantages accrued from not being conversant with Arabic.

While these early travelers can be amusing about the Moroccans, they are seldom flattering. In the sixteenth century, Leo Africanus—an Arab traveler snatched by Christian pirates who himself subsequently converted to Christianity—had written of the inhabitants of Morocco that they were so greedily addicted unto their filthie lucre, that they never could attaine unto any kinde of civilitie or good behaviour.... Abounding exceedingly with choler, they speak alwaies with an angrie and lowd voice. Neither shall you walke in the day-time in any of their streetes, but you shall see commonly two or three of them together by the eares. By nature they are a vile and base people. ...

The early-nineteenth-century explorer René Caillé even suggested that, if the Islamic law requiring the amputation of thieves' hands were rigorously applied, Morocco would be a nation of one-handed men.

Most descriptions of Moorish character begin with a tirade and gradually subside into strings of unkind adjectives: "The Moors are children, vain children, obstinate through a shocking bigotry and ignorance scarcely credible," wrote Sir John Drummond Hay. Mendacious, thievish, envious, superstitious, gluttonous, indolent—"They combine, in short, all possible vices"—any politeness exhibited by a Moor seldom had its motive in goodwill. Moors told the truth and kept their word only if it was in their interest to do so: "Do you think that I am a dog of a Christian that I should be bound by my word?" the Sultan Moulai Ismael is alleged to have told a European diplomat. Nor could Europeans fail to be shocked by the overt homosexuality: "Sodomy is not a vice in Morocco, it is almost a virtue," wrote Jules Erckmann, a member of the French military mission in Fez. "They are so little embarrassed by it that they arrange a rendezvous in the middle of a cabinet meeting." Drunkenness, he observed, was the one vice which the Moors had yet to discover.

No aspect of Moorish depravity was more blatant for Europeans than their treatment of women. The unenlightened attitude of Islam toward women was partly to blame: "the temptress" was to be veiled and cloistered on earth, although, in the popular view at least, time in Paradise would be occupied principally in drinking and fornication. The backwardness of Moroccan society and the peculiar defects of the Moroccan character, however, meant that the woman's lot in Morocco was a particularly unhappy one. "Of the companionship in wedlock the Moor has no conception, and his ideas of love are those of lust," Budgett Meakin claimed. Uneducated, ignorant, held in "absolute subjection," women in Morocco were no more than a commodity: "I collect [concubines] as you Europeans collect pictures, to adorn my house," one toothless old caid told Cunninghame Graham. Moroccan men found it incomprehensible that European husbands were expected to remain content with one woman: "What do you do when she becomes old?"

Yet the status of women in Moroccan society was far less miserable than most European visitors were prepared to admit. Uneducated and ignorant they most certainly were, but they were not uniformly unhappy. Even Meakin cautioned that one must not suppose that Moorish women longed for the freedom of their European sisters. On the contrary, "they are full of sympathy for that poor, over-strained Nazarene woman, who is obliged to leave the shelter of her four walls and face the world unveiled, unprotected, unabashed."

The condition of Moroccan women varied greatly. Moroccan girls became adults at puberty. In the upper reaches of society, daughters were fattened on a diet of milk and sweet cakes and if considered sufficiently beautiful might be sent as a gift at the age of thirteen to adorn the harem of an influential caid or a vizier, or even the Sultan himself. In the harem, they were condemned to a life of comfortable though tedious confinement under the close supervision of eunuchs who bore aromatic names like Musk, Amber, Thyme, Essence of Roses, or Camphor. "They are mostly very young creatures with very full figures," Rohlfs, who gained access to the harem as a doctor, said of the Sultan's concubines: "Their dresses and ornaments, often rich and valuable, were covered with dirt, and some part of their clothes were generally torn." William Lempriere, an English military surgeon who was sent from Gibraltar to attend the Sultan in 1789, found the women of the harem "extremely ignorant, proud and vain of their persons, even to a degree of childishness. Among their many ridiculous questions they asked my interpreter if I could read and write; upon being answered in the affirmative, they expressed utmost surprise and admiration at the abilities of the Christians. There was not one among them who could do either." He was also baffled by their sense of propriety, so different from that of European women: they would pull up their dresses and show their thighs without shame, but refused absolutely to stick out their tongues for the doctor's examination. At last, after extensive negotiations, they agreed to cut a hole in a curtain and stick their tongues through this.

The life of a town woman was limited but far from intolerable. A Moorish house was not a woman's "prison," nor were its female occupants "slaves." They frequently went out, albeit heavily wrapped, to visit the tombs or their parents or to bathe in the *hammam*. At dusk, gaily dressed, heavily powdered and painted women weighted down with heavy jewelry climbed over the rooftops of Fez to visit their neighbors. They dressed to please other women rather than the men, whom they never saw. Meakin claimed that the absence of love marriages and the presence of several wives and concubines meant that "the strife and jealousies which disturb the peace of the household are continual." A concentration of competing women under one roof could hardly be conducive to domestic tranquillity. Even Sultan Moulai Hafid had to endure the reproaches of his household when they discovered that he was seeing other women—as if a man whose harem numbered over one hundred needed to look elsewhere for entertainment. But the expense of keeping the statutory four wives permitted by the Prophet, not to mention concubines, meant that the majority of Moroccan men remained monogamous.

Nor must one suppose that women were without influence. The Arab proverb "Ask your wife's advice and then do the opposite" is probably better seen as oblique testimony to the great influence of women in domestic matters, rather than as an indication of the low esteem in which they were held. The Sultan's women kept palace conspiracies well oiled and exerted all their charms to have their sons well placed. "Henpecked" husbands were not confined to Europe and, of course, the mother had the all-important task of selecting a wife for her son.

The Berber woman was the most influential: "There is no country in the world where men defer so much to the opinions and wishes of their wives" as in the Atlas, Rohlfs maintained. She was also the hardest-worked. It was not uncommon in the countryside to see a woman and a donkey yoked together to pull a crude wooden plow or two female legs staggering beneath a burden which would have taxed the strength of a European male. But this was the common lot of the peasant. In many respects, the Berber woman was far freer than her Arab sister. The hard hand of Islam lay much more lightly on the mountains, which meant that she went unveiled and, having met men, was much more likely to make a love match; Walter Harris was impressed with the "good-humoured and innocent chaff that passed between men and girls" in the Tafilalet in contrast to the rigid segregation of the towns.

The morality of Moroccan women was a subject about which European male observers had definite opinions, but upon which they offer disappointingly little evidence. Meakin spoke for them when he wrote: "It can hardly be going too far to say that no woman in Morocco is chaste who has it in her power to be otherwise." He claimed that women were married off at puberty and shut up for their own good. This is almost certainly unfair. Life in the warren of a Moroccan house with its extended family of half-brothers, uncles and cousins so lacked privacy that there was probably little about sexual habits that was likely to be hidden from a young girl, whether Arab or Berber. However, abduction of women occurred far more frequently than did seduction. Adultery was rare. Married women were cloistered, but they were also very insecure. Divorce was as simple as repeating the word three times in public, so that few women would risk an adventure that might jeopardize their house. Any affairs that were to be had in the cities, and they were precious few, were with the divorcees who had lost all hope of remarriage. If discovered, a clandestine assignation with a Berber girl could have fatal consequences for both lovers. The prostitutes and dancers of the *fonduks* or low inns were usually Berber girls who had dishonored themselves and their families. Travelers universally agreed that, in contrast to their attitude toward women, the Moors displayed a genuine affection for their children.

To be fair to Morocco's European critics, they were not blind to the fact that their own countries also contained a share of low characters and social hypocrisy. But European society saw itself in the light of its best elements. In Morocco, the ignorance and almost total lack of morality of the entire population meant that the "good" class of people had yet to emerge. Nor was it ever likely to emerge, according to Meakin, as long as young Moroccan males insisted upon "sowing their wild oats" with such reckless abandon that by their twentieth birthday they were "extinguished . . . incapable of anything." Progress in present conditions was impossible. Confronted with an invention, a process that offered a great improvement over Moorish methods, "unless above average, he would look at it as a cow looks at a new gate, without intelligence, realizing only the change, not the cause or effect."

Morocco held a fascination for Europeans because, away from the coast, it was an almost perfectly preserved medieval world. To strike out from Tangiers was to enter a time capsule—emperors, slaves, harems, fortified towns, filth, superstition, blood feuds and barbarism. In Morocco, Europeans saw a shadow of their own past. "I have seen England in the Middle Ages," crowed Cunninghame Graham on his return. "I have come back to it in the year of grace 1890." Fascinating, but also an affront to the age of progress.

European travelers to Morocco were certainly cheated, robbed and, on occasion, even murdered. But can Moroccans really have been so uniformly ignorant and evil as they are depicted? Three things must be noted about the unflattering picture of Moroccans painted by Europeans. In the first place,

Moroccan society, especially at its higher levels, was an insecure one. Men with wealth and influence had to act with caution, even with brutality, if they were to retain their power. Morocco certainly had no shortage of rogues in high places, and their example could be imitated lower down the social scale. Life was harsh, and kindness was a virtue that might seldom be practiced, least of all toward a *roumi.*

Secondly, many Europeans who found their way to Morocco hardly merited the consideration of the population. Morocco attracted many unscrupulous European adventurers, some of them in the pay of their governments, who did not hesitate to cheat unfortunate Moroccans or even to connive to have them condemned to one of the country's indescribably filthy jails, which was often tantamount to a death sentence. Other Europeans who traveled into the interior were quite obviously spies intent on preparing the takeover of Morocco by Europe. It is not at all surprising that Europeans met hostility. What is amazing, rather, is the numerous acts of charity they encountered: when he fell desperately ill in the Tafilalet in 1893, Walter Harris was nursed back to health by five of the Sultan's soldiers, while Gerhard Rohlfs was saved by a Muslim brother when he was left for dead by robbers in eastern Morocco, to name but two instances. For Moroccans, Europeans meant trouble, and the better elements of the population quite simply avoided them.

Lastly, some European writers quite intentionally exaggerated the less attractive qualities of Moroccans. Not a few overdramatized the dangers and hardships they had encountered with an eye to increasing the sales of their books. Others—the ardent colonialists—sought to convey a picture of a country so impoverished and a people so brutalized by an oppressive government that they must be rescued by the civilizing hand of Europe.

In any case, Europe's impression of Morocco was not uniformly black. Many were prepared to concede that all in the country was not an unchecked torrent of human depravity. If virtue existed there, it resided with the Berbers, who made up about 60 percent of Morocco's estimated five million people in 1900. Europeans found the highlanders more savage but superior to the lowland Arabs. Rude and primitive they were, but a healthy life lived out of doors produced a specimen far different from the indolent and cowardly town Moor. Even the marked homicidal tendencies of the Berber were socially conditioned and so possessed a logic that Europeans could comprehend. The most disconcerting thing about Arabs was that one never knew where one stood: life with them seemed one long journey down the corridors of deception. The Berbers, however, lived by a code, operated according to a set of rules that, though primitive, were at least predictable. "They are a most strong and vallient people, especially those which dwell upon the mountaines," Leo Africanus had written of the Berbers. "They keep their covenant most faithfully; insomuch that they had rather die than breake promise." But, he cautioned, "No nation in the world is so subject unto jealousie; for they will rather leese their lives, than put up any disgrace in behalfe of their women."

The Berber possessed a ticklish sense of honor which permitted few compromises. Bravery in battle was *de rigueur*, and a warrior suspected of slinking away in the face of the enemy was forced, if the village were in a tolerant mood, to wear a Jew's skullcap and eat only after the women were finished, until he redeemed his reputation. "Cattle and horse-stealing, with an occasional higher flight into the regions of the abduction of young girls, seem to be the staple industries of all pastoral countries, and nowhere but in western Texas are they taken very seriously," wrote Cunninghame Graham in defense of the Berber. But in Morocco, these things were taken very seriously indeed. Feuding was a way of life and disputes that arose over the theft of goats or the kidnapping of women could continue for generations. One tribal feud which lasted ten years and resulted in over forty deaths sprang from an argument over the killing of a visitor's dog. In this violent society, the passage from youth to manhood might be celebrated by a random murder: Meakin told of a boy who came to him for money to buy a gun. When asked why, he explained that he intended to kill his uncle. "They chaff me and call me boy because I have never killed a man."

Yet Berber honor was not directed entirely toward the destruction of human life. In the mountains, hospitality was the king of virtues, and once men had broken bread together, they were sworn to mutual defense. In this respect, the "vulgar, uncouthe, but faithful" Berber was infinitely superior to the treacherous Arab: "He will eat with a stranger and die to protect him afterwards." So sacred were the laws of hospitality in the hills that the safest way to travel there was to place oneself under the protection of the most notorious rogue in the district.

By 1900, travel to Fez had become more commonplace, but it was not an easy affair to organize. To travel alone was to court trouble as well as discomfort. A few primitive hotels run by Spaniards existed along the coast. Otherwise, hospitality might be found in the flea-infested douars of the seminomadic tribesmen or in the filthy cells of the *fonduks*—two-story caravanserai built around a central courtyard in which the animals were kept—found in the larger cities. Prudence, as well as comfort, required a more substantial organization. A caravan of ten to twenty men, plus an armed guard, was not thought extravagant, but neither was it cheap. "I have travelled in China and Japan, in Persia, Arabia and Abyssinia, and in many parts of North Africa, Turkey, in Asia and Syria, but 'old' Morocco was by far the most expensive to travel in," Walter Harris wrote.

A reliable guide was essential for any trip inland. The best one in Tangiers was known simply as "Rabbit," because of the peculiar shape of his ears and nose. If not actually touting for business on the quay, Rabbit could usually be found sipping cheap whiskey in the Soko: "How are you, old pal? How are you, old fellow? Want a guide? Colonel Pleydell and the American minister are my friends," comprised his usually raucous greeting, followed by a recitation of his distinguished acquaintances in Tangiers and Gibraltar and tidbits of local scandal, most of it unverifiable, which he shared promiscuously with his prospective employers. But "reliable" in Morocco was an adjective that could be applied only with caution. The traveler who left too many of the arrangements to his guide might arrive at his first campsite to find his tent hardly more than a large rag and camp furniture nonexistent. Prudence dictated that the journey begin in the afternoon and the first camp pitched not too far from town, as inevitably a few men and mounts needed to be changed and someone sent back with a long list of forgotten supplies.

The supply list was substantial. It was not always possible to live off the country, which produced little more than poultry and eggs. In lean times, the inhabitants might not part with their scarce produce at any price. Tea, coffee and candles could be bought in Tangiers; other provisions often had to be imported. "As I was going to travel with a lady, I indulged in a few luxuries, such as Brand's beef-tea, Korr's concentrated pea-soup (both of them excellent preparations), a few pots of marmalade and anchovy paste to counteract the taste of bad butter," wrote Captain Colville. "Also an extra revolver and a pair of derringers for my wife, a pocket filter, four enamelled iron plates and two cups of the same material and a small spirit lamp and saucepan." A medicine chest was essential: "Besides my own medicine chest, which contained castor-oil, laudanum, quinine and Sir John Oliffe's anti-cholera mixture, I took a plentiful supply of Seidlitz powders for the natives." Walter Harris also suggested that "a small bore rifle is advisable for great bustard."

European saddlery must not be forgotten. The Moroccan saddle was constructed of wood, shaped like a peaked roof with two exaggerated weathercocks at each end. "On the ridge are some curious lumps, which come exactly where lumps are least welcome to any person of Christian build." Even after taking the precaution of spreading a thick layer of blankets over the sharp ridge, Europeans found that after a few hours on muleback their legs had ceased to function. The poor quality of the leather also meant that the belly straps constantly gave way, sending the rider sprawling.

Lastly, there was one further addition to the traveler's baggage without which the best-prepared expeditions would dissolve into anarchy: a fairly extensive repertoire of curses. "Without it one can do nothing with the men; they simply do what they please and laugh at one." Only by expressing a hope that "his family may be scattered and his great-great-grandfather committed to the flames" could one goad a surly muleteer into action or bridle the greed of a shopkeeper who feared that these calamities might actually come to pass.

No aspect of Moorish culture was more universally admired by foreigners than the richness and variety of their curses. "The term 'elaborate' is the only one wherewith to describe a curse so carefully worded that, if executed, it would leave no hope of Paradise either for the unfortunate addressee or his ancestors for several generations," wrote Meakin. A cursing match usually began with a tug on the beard, a sign of contempt. The social anthropologist Edward Westermarck recorded one instance of what followed in 1926:

A: God damn your father, O naked one!
B: God damn your father, O lousy fellow!
A: O itchy fellow!
B: O leper!
A: O pimp!
B: O husband of a whore!
A: O one who has grown up in the market place! [i.e., feels no shame]
B: O boy prostitute!
A: O seller of charcoal!
B: O seller of sour milk!
A: May God give you fever!
B: May God give you fever without perspiration!

And so on until one lifted up his clothes to reveal his naked middle, a great sign of contempt that usually led to bloodshed.

If superficially the country behind Tangiers did not differ greatly from that of Spain across the straits—a veld of low hills baked to the consistency of sandpaper—one quickly sensed that this was Africa. Perhaps it was the absence of cultivation, of the furrows and vineyards which tamed the parched Spanish landscape. Even today, much of Morocco does not look lived in: the few native douars, one-room huts of clay and sticks surrounded by barriers of prickly pear (called Christian fig by the Moors), cling to the land rather than lord over it. The inhabitants, indeed all of life, appear to be there on short lease. And in 1900, the countryside was far more vacant than it is today. It bore eloquent testimony to the political instability of the country and the rapaciousness of its governors. The emptiness of the land stretched to the horizon and gave the countryside a vastness and a primitiveness that is distinctly African. On the left rose the mountains of the Rif, gray and forbidding, while one continued south along a primitive track, only occasionally pursued by ragged children who padded through the dust and scrub with outstretched hands.

In a well-organized caravan, an advance party left before first light while the bulk of the group followed on at a more leisurely pace. In this way, the traveler would find his noon camp prepared and lunch gently simmering over a fire. The same order was followed in the afternoon, the Europeans waiting out the midday heat, following on at about four o'clock, perhaps leaving the route to hunt, to find their camp prepared for them at sundown. In a normal day, a caravan might expect to travel twenty-five miles.

But nothing in Morocco was normal. If it rained, and in the winter and spring it poured, the tracks dissolved into quagmires. As bridges were few, a swollen river formed a barrier that might cause a week's delay. A few flat-bottomed, high-sided ferries existed at the major crossings, but just as the Moors had yet to see the advantages of the wheel, so they ignored the benefits of the ramp. Men slipped down the muddy bank, waded into the river and clambered over the side. Loading mules in this manner presented more intractable problems, and was accomplished only after much splashing and shouting.

The men also required watching. Mule driving was seldom counted among the more respectable occupations. In Morocco, those for hire in the Tangiers Soko commonly possessed two characteristics: they were usually incompetent and always thieves. They transformed campsites, especially in the morning, into scenes of unbelievable pandemonium—spilled loads, upended donkeys, overturned cooking pots, a discordant symphony of human and animal noises—so that departure appeared to be the result of divine intervention rather than organized effort. At night, they often made sleep impossible: "Packs of ravenous dogs barked incessantly, a pertinacious donkey made four separate determined attempts to enter my tent, a couple of amorous camels got their legs entangled in the guy-ropes, and the owners of these and other errant beasts ran yelling and cursing through the darkness," wrote British journalist Reginald Rankin. Nor was it prudent to leave the caravan too far behind. Captain Colville, exasperated by the slow pace of his men, forged ahead only to find that they failed to arrive, possibly victims of highwaymen, but more likely of their calculation that his mules and equipment would fetch far more on the open market than the muleteers were likely to earn in wages.

But porters were unlikely to defect until the final destination was almost within sight. *Mouna* was the reason. *Mouna*, or "the gift," was the hospitality owed by local caids to parties bearing letters of introduction from the Sultan, a vizier or a foreign consul. They were a form of travel insurance, easy enough to obtain, without which a journey into the interior was unwise. They obliged the caid to furnish guards at a designated campsite near the larger settlements and to provide food for the entire party.

This admirable custom was not without its inconveniences. The caid knew that he must answer to the Sultan for any harm that might come to his visitors. The local guards were left in no doubt as to what fate awaited them if they failed in their task. Therefore, both to ward off marauders and to keep themselves awake, they kept up such a terrible din—shouting, singing and firing—that sleep was quite impossible. This split opinion among Europeans in the camp between those who wanted rest and the remainder who, though exhausted, welcomed the security. St.-Aulaire, leader of the first faction, crawled from his tent to buy silence from the guards with a handful of duros. On returning to his camp bed, he found that his traveling companion, an engineer rather unnerved by the primitive nature of the country, was about to pay them to resume their reassuring noise.

Nor was the provision of food always a blessing. The quantity of *mouna* distributed depended upon the importance of the traveler. Colville discovered that, upon arrival in a town, his crew put it about that their employer was an intimate friend of the English Sultana. The news quickly spread to the casbah and his caravan was inundated with food. The result was predictable:

Unused to such largesse, his porters slowed the pace, deliberately delaying departures, stretching the normally eight-day journey between Tangiers and Fez into two weeks. Even by selling the substantial surplus back to the people who had provided it, enough was consumed to bring overextended digestive systems to the point of collapse. "One day my servant came to me with a mule driver and asked me to give him the drink that 'makes me go so', giving a spirited imitation of a man under the influence of Seidlitz Powder." Soon his thirteen men were all complaining. And no wonder, having consumed two sheep, two dozen chickens, one hundred eggs and three or four basins of couscous daily.

Accepting hospitality from a caid could be an expensive business. Not only did the guards and those who provided the *mouna* require tipping, but the caid himself expected a present. Few were content with a bauble, and instead demanded the traveler's prize shotgun, his watch, his field glasses, in short, things impossible to replace in Morocco. Medicines were also in great demand. Aphrodisiacs were especially favored: "He was a poor old man of nearly 90, with sunken eyes and toothless jaws," Colville said of one of his hosts who was no longer able to service his harem, "and I felt bound to tell him that I considered the case almost beyond the will of God . . . but I would do what I could for him."

Visitors had to be prepared for strange sights. Sir John Drummond Hay was stopped by a man holding a knife between his teeth making low bows in the middle of the track and muttering, "I place myself under the hem of your garment." "I thought the man was mad and was preparing to meet some act of fanaticism," when it was explained that he had killed a man and must be executed unless he could raise thirty pounds' blood money.

The visiting *roumi* also filled another function, one that was to expand with the conquest—that of short-circuiting an oppressive political system. The passage of an important European brought out the desperately impoverished peasants, who implored them to explain to the caid why they were unable to pay their taxes. Usually the request was accompanied with a ritual offering of milk. Drummond Hay complained that he was obliged to drink so many bowls of milk on his travels that it regularly spoiled his dinner. It also spoiled his clothes as, sitting on a nervous horse, much inevitably spilled down his front.

Occasionally, however, the demand for justice could take a more spectacular form, especially if the traveler were an ambassador: "One night, upon leaving my tent . . . I felt that my *babouches* [slippers] were drenched in a puddle of blood, the blood of a young calf who was bellowing pitifully," St.-Aulaire wrote.

> The sacrificer had cut off his legs in such a way that he was dying in front of me on his knees in a posture of supplication. By his side was a couple in tatters, but ennobled by their sorrow who, with wild gesticulations and strident cries from the woman, raucous from the man, spelled out, with pauses for translation, the drama of their son unjustly accused of murder and who was slowly rotting in the foul prisons of Fez.

Travelers to Fez had the choice of two routes; the easier of the two led down the coast, then across the rich plains of the Gharb through Meknes, the capital built by the tyrant Moulai Ismael in the seventeenth century to rival that of his contemporary Louis XIV. But by 1900, the vast palace, once the abattoir of Christian captives forced to build it, was only a shadow of its former glory, typical, said Harris, of the whole empire, "a ruin, a very grand ruin, held up merely by props, the jealousy of foreign countries and the now vanishing reputation of former power."

The more interesting route lay through Ouezzane. As the track climbed into the foothills of the Rif, one gradually passed into a landscape that was altogether different. The scorched plain was left behind and the air became imperceptibly cooler, not so much from the altitude as from the promise of shade offered by the olive trees which began to appear, first singly and then in groves. Soon one felt as if he had entered a country park—through fields, past streams, beneath hills clothed in the blue-green leaves of the olive trees, a scene so idyllic that it could almost have been laid out by some Moroccan Capability Brown.

In the midst of this garden lay Ouezzane, its square whitewashed houses climbing part way up the north side of the double-peaked mountain Bou-Hellol until they disappeared into a dark-green forest of olive trees, juniper and evergreen oaks. "Anything more romantic than the lovely scenery around the holy city of Uesan could hardly be imagined," wrote Rohlfs "—the thickly wooded hills in the vicinity of the town, with the jagged rocks of the Rif Mountains for background, the wonderful fertility of the earth."

If Ouezzane was one of the most beautiful towns in Morocco, it was also one of the most fascinating. Here, in a sanctuary separated from the town by walls and gates, lived the sharif of Ouezzane, whose holiness was only one degree below that of the Sultan himself. The sanctuary offered a vision of Islamic paradise, a vast garden surrounding a mosque where processions of pilgrims came for the sharif's blessing. Lodged in pavilions scattered through the gardens, they were fed and for three days allowed to wander through the trees, along the green-tiled verandas, contemplating the flowers, the arabesques which decorated walls and fountains and the splendid views over the mountains, until they moved on and a new batch of the faithful arrived to fill their places.

But this vision of paradise was imperfect. Rohlfs, who visited Ouezzane in 1861, found the sanctuary splendid but seedy, its gardens neglected and overgrown. As in most holy cities, sanctity rubbed shoulders with wickedness. In the cookshops and coffeehouses which lined the streets to the sanctuary were back rooms reserved for the town's numerous kef smokers, while wine and spirits could be bought with little difficulty.

Many Europeans considered the sharif of Ouezzane a sort of Islamic Pope. This was true neither in a canonical nor in a spiritual sense. Ouezzane was far more like Lourdes than Rome. The sharif was a purely Moroccan product revered for his *baraka*, or "blessing," bestowed upon him by Allah as a direct descendant of the Prophet. In fact, the sharif of Ouezzane stood near the summit of a whole network of "saints," all of them prepared upon request to explain the complicated lineage that tied them by blood to the Prophet. No village was without its resident saint, men who, according to Harris, managed to amass an average fortune by marketing an ersatz *baraka* to a gullible peasantry.

Harris chose to ignore the true function of the saints. In a society as riven as Morocco by tribal and personal feuding, the saints offered an important element of stability. They were above all adjudicators, neutral men from outside the clan or tribe qualified by virtue of their sanctity to settle disputes over inheritance or pasture rights, or even to negotiate an end to tribal feuds. As a saint's *baraka* was measured by his success rate, a clever and skillful diplomat clearly had inherited Allah's blessing in greater measure.

So revered was the sharif of Ouezzane's *baraka* in Morocco that his appearance anywhere touched off scenes of hysterical devotion. Only with great difficulty could the hundred or so guards keep back the crowds which fought to touch him, prod him with sticks, even to pelt him with stones in the hope that some of the *baraka* would rub off on the rock, which would be kept as an amulet. With such an adoring public, the sharif's progress through the country was necessarily slow, as Rohlfs recorded:

> Before sunrise . . . I was aroused by the firing of muskets and the horrible noise which does duty for music in Morocco, but this was only the introduction to the programme of the day. After a hasty breakfast, . . . we mounted our steeds and in the midst of gun-firing, the noise of the musicians and the lululu of the women, the procession started. But although we were within an hour's ride of the city, we did not get there till mid-day. Every now and then a fresh band of musicians with their abominable instruments would meet us, and we had to halt, or a company armed with guns arrived and gave the Grand Cherif a salvo, then formed into circles and jumping about like lunatics, fired their pieces into the ground, then threw them into the air to catch them cleverly again. Then a party of horsemen would bear down upon us at full gallop, fire their guns almost under our noses, then rapidly divide and turn off to the right and left of us.

They had to run the gauntlet of the horrible Isawa, the self-mutilating religious fanatics, drunken, convulsed and bleeding, before the sanctuary was finally reached.

Those who expected to find a wild-eyed mullah, the custodian of Islam, were in for a surprise. Rohlfs described Sharif Sidi Mohammed as a tall but corpulent man of thirty-one whose dark complexion and thick features revealed his Negro blood (his mother was black). His dress was extraordinary: in the place of flowing robes, Sidi Mohammed wore a French military tunic with gold epaulettes, red trousers, and a red skullcap with a gold tassel which touched his shoulder. A fine gold sword dangled from his waist. A revolver suspended from a red silk cord and stuck into the gold sash that swathed his middle betrayed his fear of assassination, which later grew into an obsession. This fear was not without some foundation: At one point, a Berber tribe, the Beni M'gild, planned to kill him in the belief that by thus arranging to have the tomb of Morocco's most revered saint on their land, the tribe would be greatly blessed. His two bodyguards, one of whom was an apostate Jew on the run from the law, were similarly dressed in parodies of French military costume.

The Ouezzane family had been endowed with more than *baraka*: they had also inherited a strain of insanity. But their peculiar behavior did nothing to diminish the reverence in which they were held by the faithful; on the contrary, it enhanced their holiness. Travelers frequently noted the respect with which madmen were held in Morocco, the reason being that while the bodies of the insane lingered on earth, their spirits were believed already to be in Paradise. But the aberrations of the holy family could sometimes take a disturbing form.

The sharif's eldest son and heir to his *baraka*, Moulai el Arbi, became addicted to kef and could be seen charging endlessly over the countryside pursued by a posse of his concubines, whose main task was to see that he returned safely home. Moulai Thami, the sharif's third son, regularly shot passers-by from his window. But he was above punishment, and even above restraint; the only measure taken was to station a soldier at the end of the street to give warning. As some, however, believed that death at the hands of a Ouezzane guaranteed immediate admission into Paradise, the butchery continued.

The sharif himself displayed a degree of eccentricity that bordered on madness. He expressed a great admiration for things European: one of his boasts, which he regularly made at mealtimes, was that, on his visit to France, he had eaten with a fork. This admission inevitably provoked curses of disapproval from his followers. He scattered models of steamships, trains and other paraphernalia of progress around the gardens of the sanctuary for the edification of visitors. Despite his exalted position in Islam, he openly scorned the hundreds of pilgrims who kept him rich with their gifts: "What fools these people are to give me money," he snickered at Rohlfs as a crowd of notables laid offerings at his feet. But he was not without a sense of humor. One of his favorite jokes, when the crush of the faithful was becoming too much for his guards to control, was to point to a traveling companion, preferably a European in Moorish dress, and cry, "There is the sharif!" The "dog of a Christian" was immediately buried in a scrum of old women and strongly smelling children while the sharif stood by laughing, "Hope you like it." Victims of the joke experienced the full force of the Arab saying "as hungry as a pilgrim's flea."

Sidi Mohammed's passion for things European inevitably drew him into the competition among the powers for influence in Morocco. The English-woman Emily Keene had come to Morocco as governess to the Greek-American Perdicaris family, who lived in some splendor in their villa Aidonia ("the Place of the Nightingales") near Tangiers. The sharif, who—unlike the rest of the Moroccan establishment—enjoyed visiting Tangiers, asked for her hand in 1873. In later years, Emily Keene told visitors to her home in Tangiers that hers had been a love match, that only a romantic impulse could have induced her to spend her life in an uncivilized and alien land. The truth was somewhat different. Negotiations over the marriage contract were long and difficult. Miss Keene wrested from the sharif a promise never to marry again, upon penalty of a large indemnity. When the sharif did finally take a second wife, a thirteen-year-old girl, Emily Keene was able to live very well off her caution money until her death in 1941.

The marriage was not a success. Within a few weeks of taking up residence in Ouezzane, Emily was writing frantic letters to her father, a prison governor, to rescue her. A life sentence in Broadmoor was preferable to the monotonous confinement of the harem. For her, marriage had never been more than a speculative venture, a means to power and wealth. The French proved willing to ally their ambition to hers. Together they conspired to depose the Sultan and replace him with the sharif of Ouezzane. In 1884, the sharif was made a French protected person and given an annual honorarium of forty thousand francs. But he lacked the strength of character to cope with the visions of his would-be manipulators. Visits to Algeria laid on by the French were transformed into vast drinking bouts—Emily explained to the perplexed captain of the French frigate assigned to take them to Algiers that her husband's inordinate consumption of champagne was necessary to combat seasickness—while the sharif's increasing tendency to bestow his *baraka* on members of the opposite sex, sometimes collectively, became an embarrassment. Both Emily and France quietly made other arrangements.

CHAPTER IV

FEZ

The best thing about the Ouezzane route was that one approached Fez from the north. Following the valley east from Meknes, the traveler could see the great walls of Fez from miles away, a blur on the horizon gradually assuming their imposing shape as one drew nearer. From the north, the city was invisible. In 1903, the track snaked through a land which was broken, brown and uncultivated, beneath huge outcroppings of rock, past cactus plants and giant geraniums. Fragments of aqueducts, almost hidden in ivy and flowers, and the appearance of more tracks—which wove in and out like railway lines approaching Paddington Station—were the only indications that a city of 100,000 was near. One rounded the long rocky crest of the 2,600-foot mountain of Zalagh and suddenly, below, lay Fez.

Moroccans sometimes called Fez "the Citadel" or "the Fortress." If one viewed it from above, the name seemed apt. Fez appeared to be a city under siege, closed in on itself, its gray mass surrounded by high, brown ramparts. There were none of the gentle gradations of human settlement which characterized towns in less turbulent lands—no farms and villages, only a few gardens which briefly followed the river as it flowed southwest. Beyond the walls, life appeared abruptly to cease. For Madame St.-René Taillandier, Fez had the appearance of a monastery, "a mysterious altar raised in an immense landscape to an unknown cult," its uniform grayness broken only by the green tiles which decorated the minarets and other splashes of color provided by orange, pomegranate and palm trees. Others, noting its high walls and windowless houses, compared it to a cemetery.

In 1903, Fez had been in existence for over a thousand years. Fez Djedid, the new town which contained the royal palace and the mellah, had in the thirteenth century been grafted on to the old medina (the Arab quarter), Fez el Bali, founded four hundred years earlier. Many loathed the town on sight. The austere charm of Fez seen from a distance began to diminish as one approached the gates, riding slowly past mounds of putrefying animal carcasses. One then plunged into a maze of narrow streets and cul-de-sacs of such complexity that, without a guide, a European almost might never reemerge. Colville described the shock:

> First knocked nearly off one's legs by a passing camel, then picked up on the other side by a blow from a donkey's pannier, one fights one's way along, here jammed into a corner with a hideous old hag, who hastily covers her face lest the infidel should behold her charms; then carried forward with the crowd, who are eager to kiss the garment of the great man who is ambling by on his mule; at one moment side by side with a respectable merchant, the next jostling with a grinning idiot, stark naked, a mass of vermin, sores and filth, who is quite likely as not to tear one to pieces with his teeth, while the crowd looks on and approves. Side by side by one are dirty, barefoot Jews, obsequious and cringing; strange, half savage creatures from' the mountains; good humoured looking negro slaves; and beggars maimed, halt and blind, scarcely less repulsive in appearance than the idiot saints. Suddenly one stumbles, and, picking oneself up, amidst a perfect cloud of flies, discovers the half putrid carcase of a donkey has caused the fall. . . .

Fez, while fascinating, was not exactly a tourist's paradise. Attempts by enterprising British and American travel agents to organize package tours toward the turn of the century had foundered on the sheer primitiveness of the place. Fonduks provided the only accommodation for visitors, but they were so squalid that the first act upon occupying one of the cells was to clean out the filth left by the previous occupants. Unless one carried letters to people influential enough to secure a house in the medina, in which case the unfortunate occupant was literally thrown into the street, Europeans were forced to stay in the mellah, the Jewish quarter.

The vexatious conditions in which Jews were forced to live were readily apparent in Fez: they were forbidden to go on horseback, and required to walk barefoot through the filthy alleys of the medina, and to remove the dead animals that lay in the streets. "Always clad in black or dark-coloured cloaks, with hideous black skull-caps or white-spotted blue kerchiefs on their heads, they are conspicuous everywhere," wrote Budgett Meakin. "They address the Moors with a villainous, cringing look which makes the son of Ishmael savage, for he knows it is only feigned. In return, they are treated like dogs, and a cordial hatred exists on both sides." "May God let you finish out your miserable life" was the normal greeting that Jews could expect from Moslems.

Most Europeans regarded the Fez mellah with horror: a walled and gated quarter in the shadow of the Sultan's palace into which Fez's eight thousand Jews were crowded. For Jews, however, it was a haven of safety. The mellah was under a Jewish caid, and Moslems seldom entered within its walls: "In the *mellah*, the Jew is at home." In contrast to the squalid state of the streets outside, the interiors of the houses were spotless and well maintained. There, one found the women dressed in brilliantly colored skirts and small velvet waistcoats embroidered in gold, their heads covered with silk scarves, preparing dinner over a fire in the central courtyard: boiled mutton, chicken, tripe, liver, spicy soup, fruit, either fresh or in vinegar, all washed down with *mahia*, a strong, clear alcohol made in the mellah. In poorer homes, the meal would be a more modest affair of boiled vegetables and hard-boiled eggs.

Europeans might be made welcome here—Jews, after all, were known to favor a European takeover of Morocco—but they were never comfortable. The nauseating and all-permeating stench of offal and *mahia*, the raucous disputes among the women which were suspended only during times of prayer, were unpleasant. But it was above all the sense of suffocation, the sheer lack of air in this ghetto whose only open space was a cemetery, that drove many Europeans into the medina.

After the crumbling appearance of the town, the luxuriousness of the houses of Fez came as something of a surprise. A blind entrance led into a courtyard which might, if the house were a wealthy one, contain a fountain, arabesques and Moorish arches. The rooms that radiated off the courtyard were furnished, often voluptuously, with low divans, oriental rugs and low brass tables. Cool in summer, these houses were penetrated by a damp cold in winter that the small charcoal braziers which did duty for heaters never managed to warm. Nor was the filth of the streets ever very far away. Fez was plagued by rats "of a most repulsive variety—large, fierce and naked, with pink feet," which invaded the cleanest of houses, crawled over beds and strolled with brazen fearlessness through gardens.

Houses also contained a contingent of servants, some of whom were surly and slothful, all of whom were incompetent, as Ellis Ashmead-Bartlett discovered:

Nothing is more remarkable than the number of persons who attach themselves to your household in Morocco, and whom it is impossible to shake off. New faces appear daily, and if you inquire the why and the wherefore of their presence, you are generally informed by one of your servants that the stranger is a friend or a relative of his who has merely looked in to pay him a friendly call. But in a day or two you find the friend or the relative still present, and doing odd jobs about the house in order to justify his inclusion in the heavy repasts at your expense, which are such a prominent feature of a servant's life in Morocco.

The house became a virtual prison. To go outside the city walls alone was to invite attack, while a stroll through the streets was fraught with difficulties. At night, one was required to carry a lantern. Packs of dogs, many of them rabid, also roamed the town after dark. The streets were so filthy that the poor often walked barefoot in order to save their *babouches*, the yellow Moroccan slippers. Occasionally, when the accumulation of filth and carrion became intolerable, a general cleaning was ordered. This consisted of opening the sluice gates in the upper quarters so that a torrent of water swept the medina. As prior warning was never given, a general panic inevitably ensued: the small, boxlike shops were flooded, merchandise was ruined, and human beings and animals alike stampeded for drier ground. Even the roof terraces were off limits: when Lawrence Harris climbed to his roof to enjoy the splendid views over the city, he was shot at from a neighboring house, a reminder that the terraces were reserved for the women.

Although (as noted earlier), Morocco did not have a capital as Europeans understood the term, Fez was in one sense very much its capital: it was the only true city in the country. Marrakech, by contrast, was called "the father of villages" because it was little more than an agglomeration of rural dwellings huddled behind high walls. Fez was an Arab town, proud and permanent. Its famous university and its *ulama*, or corps of religious doctors whose opinions were frequently sought in matters of state, made Fez a center of Islamic learning and Arab culture in what was essentially a Berber and, in many respects, only a superficially Moslem land. Its rival to the south was more like a Berber camp, transient, colorful, exuberant, a sprawling country market set in the middle of a palm-fringed plain.

Even a superficial acquaintance with Fez made one aware that, within its population, a capital-city mentality had taken firm hold: "The men of Fez are much superior to other people of Morocco, and more refined," European visitors were regularly told by Fassis, as the inhabitants were called. The city produced a distinct type: usually corpulent men with sallow complexions who moved with a slow, heavy walk, reserved in manner, slightly nervous and, above all, very pious. The city seemed in a constant communion with the supernatural: the mosques were full, God figured in every expression and men cultivated postures of melancholy piety. Or hypocrisy: after the French conquest, the Arab version of *Tartuffe*, Molière's play about a pious fraud, could not be staged in Fez because it was considered too close to the bone.

Proud of their culture but ignorant of the world beyond their walls, Fassis despised Christians, Algerians and other Moroccans, in that order. Walter Harris disliked these haughty townsfolk and claimed that the rest of Morocco shared his view: "Given up to every vice, they go about the streets covering their hands for fear of sunburn, muttering their prayers, talking of their importance and bravery, yet frightened by a spider or a mouse. The women of any of the other cities could defeat the men of Fez."

Fez's self-important posture was of more than passing interest, however. It had important political overtones. As much as the rest of the country may have chafed under Fassi arrogance and hauteur, it was to Fez that they looked for guidance in the important political questions of the day. It would have been unthinkable for Moroccans to acclaim a sultan who had not won the approval of the *ulama* of Fez. In much the same way as Paris determined the political fortunes of France, Fez became a weathercock whose gyrations must be carefully observed.

Fez—claustrophobic, squalid, proud—was also, at the turn of the century, still essentially a medieval city long after others in the Orient had succumbed to Western influence. Its artisans were organized into guilds and each trade occupied its own streets. Street criers called out the news. Fez assailed the senses. Walter Harris complained that the town smelled of "incense and dead cats," but there were a hundred variations in between: the sweet smell of cedarwood in the street of the woodworkers, the sharp odors of the spice market, the deplorable stench of the tanneries by the river. On the Bou Djeloud, the open space which separated Fez el Bali from Fez Djedid, circus actors performed and storytellers repeated tales from *Arabian Nights* or sang ballads of the great feats of the Arabs, which the crowd knew by heart, often joining in the refrain. One raconteur known as Father Driss, an illiterate slippermaker, became so famous that the Sultan Abd el-Aziz wanted to put out his eyes so that he could tell his stories in the royal harem. Fassis amused themselves with evenings spent in conversation, cards or chess, or by taking walks outside the walls often accompanied by a music box or a singing canary in a cage.

The slave market attracted no end of attention from European visitors. Held in the wool market at dusk, its continued existence was deplored by visitors from abroad as proof of Morocco's inability to conform to civilized standards of behavior. But the show in the wool market was subdued, businesslike. To Europeans brought up on tales by Harriet Beecher Stowe to expect terrible scenes of mothers and children tearfully separated on the auctioneer's block, the spectacle was pathetic rather than dramatic: "A middle-aged man, led slowly round by the salesman who is describing his 'points' and noting bids," opened the parade, wrote Budgett Meakin.

> He has first-class muscles, although he is somewhat thin. He is made to lift a weight to prove his strength. His thighs are patted, and his lips are turned to show the gums, which at merrier moments would have been visible without such a performance. With a shame-faced, hang-dog air he trudges round, wondering what will be his lot, though a sad one it is already. At last he is knocked down for so many score of dollars, and after a good deal of further bargaining he changes hands.
>
> The next brought forward are three little girls—a "job lot", maybe ten, 13 and 16 years of age—two of them evidently sisters. They are declared to be already proficient in Arabic, and ready for anything. Their muscles are felt, their mouths examined, and their bodies scrutinized in general, while the little one begins to cry, and the others look as though they would like to keep her company. Round and round again they are marched, but the bids do not rise high enough to effect a sale, and they are locked up again for a future occasion.

And on it went, a dreary procession of old black women far past their prime or young girls who were ugly, their faces ravaged by smallpox, or in some other way deformed.

By 1900, the great days of Moroccan slavery were over. The slave caravans, which in the seventeenth century had transported blacks through the terrible middle passage of sand between Fez and Timbuctu to fill the ranks of Moulai Ismael's elite black guard or to swell the numbers of his harem, were a distant memory. The reason was economic: slavery existed in

Morocco, but Morocco was not a slave society. Its economy in no way depended on slave labor as, for instance, the economies of many countries in the Americas had done. Agricultural slavery hardly existed. Blacks were no longer needed as soldiers. Concubines for the rich and powerful could be had for nothing from fathers eager to send their daughters as gifts. A trickle of Berber girls taken in hill raids were sold from door to door for fear that they might be recognized in the slave market and reclaimed. But these raids were not carried out by organized gangs of slavers, as in the Sudan. Slavery was of a more benign domestic variety. A woman would fetch up to fifty pounds because she was always useful about the house. Male slaves, however, were worse than useless: they were dangerous. "The Arabs do not need blacks to fight for them and what else can men do? So most grown-up slaves are given their liberty, for they cannot come into the house." Slave markets in coastal towns ceased to exist in the nineteenth century. That of Fez shut its doors in 1905, while the French closed down the miserable remnant of the Marrakech market in 1912.

The peculiar pattern of slavery in Morocco had curious consequences for the status of blacks. Color prejudice remained strong in Moroccan society. But blacks occupied both extremes of the social hierarchy: they could be found working as domestic menials or lounging in the higher realms of officialdom by virtue of the fact that their mothers had been introduced into great houses as concubines. As law determined that the favorite son inherited, not necessarily the eldest, many rose to high positions through their mothers' influence. The black ancestry of the sultans themselves was obvious to many visitors.

The slave market was not the only relic of the past to catch the visitor's eye. If he walked to the point where old and new Fez met, he would almost certainly see a crowd gathered around a man lying face down on a mat, his robes pulled up around his neck and shoulders to reveal his naked back and buttocks. A *tibib* sat cross-legged amid the clutter of his profession—a basket of charcoal, a pair of goatskin bellows, a dozen iron rods each about two feet long with curious knobs and hooks, poked out of a metal pot in which a fire burned—intently studying a folio of papers which contained only one sentence endlessly repeated: "There is no God but God and Mohammed is his Prophet." When the irons glowed red, the doctor extracted them from the fire. The crowd remained silent, concentrated, the beads passing through their fingers at a quickening rate as, with great delibera- tion, the doctor applied the hot irons to various parts of the patient's back and loins. The irons sang as they touched the skin, sending out an odor of burning flesh. The man gritted his teeth, beads of perspiration appeared on his forehead, but he stifled his cries. The operation over, the crowd relaxed. They praised God and Mohammed as the patient lay recovering at their feet.

A visit to the surgery of a Moroccan physician was almost always a painful experience. Fire, lunar caustic and blistering fluids applied directly to the place of pain were the treatments prescribed for most ills. When Gerhard Rohlfs, a failed medical student, offered some internal medicine for ophthalmia, the patient assured him that "I am ill in the eyes, not in the stomach." European doctors, who were the only Christians welcomed in Morocco, found it positively dangerous to apply modern remedies. Internal medicine was to be avoided, for, should the patient die, the doctor might be accused of administering poison. On the other hand, if the remedy was successful, then the patient would attribute his cure to Mohammed: "It is therefore best to practice in the way that is usual in the country—by fire and amulets." Rohlfs found that he was often obliged to drink half of the prescription himself before the patient would agree to swallow it. In the hands of Moroccans, modern medicine could often be dangerous. Sultan Abd el-Aziz filched a bottle of chloroform belonging to his English court physician and proceeded to put his entire harem to sleep. He then chloroformed one of the palace lions.

Medicine in Morocco was a mixture of pain and superstition. Verses from the Koran scribbled on cheap paper and worn around the neck offered the safest remedy. But any writings would do: Walter Harris, noticing an infected sore on the leg of one of his employees, gave him his visiting card and told him to take it to the European doctor in Tangiers. The next day, the leg was still swathed in the same filthy bandage: "I applied the card to the sore," the old man told Harris, unwrapping the cloth to reveal it. Otherwise, chemists in the marketplace offered a full range of dried animals and skins of moth-eaten birds as antidotes to illness.

Certainly the strangest sight offered to any visitor to Fez in 1903 was that of the royal palace. It was always possible to know when the court was in town. The streets of Fez Djedid, rather quiet otherwise, suddenly ignited with animation—noisy, gaudily dressed Berbers, part of the mobile town of twenty-five thousand merchants, porters, scribes and prostitutes that followed the makhzan in its ramblings through Morocco, filled the cafés and eating houses and generally scandalized the dour Fassis, who kept to the medina. In 1903, however, the Fassis were far more scandalized by what was going on within the palace walls than by the Berber carnival without. Over the year just past, their sense of scandal had deepened into outrage.

The first thing one noticed upon entering the grounds of the royal palace in 1903 was the number of empty packing crates that littered the gardens. Some of these had been arranged in such a way as to become supports for an obstacle course of ramps and bridges. Suddenly, from around the corner of a building, shot a young man in a voluminous white jellaba, looking like a vessel in full sail, pedaling a bicycle at great speed toward one of the makeshift obstacles. The bicycle climbed the ramp, leveled briefly as it crossed the bridge and descended rapidly down the far side to disappear behind a hedge.

The first vision of the Sultan Abd el-Aziz might well be a fleeting one, for he was often to be found astride a bicycle. (His advisers had originally provided a woman's bicycle, thinking it more suitable because of his robes. But when he learned that it was designed for the weaker sex, he immediately exchanged it for a man's conveyance.) Despite the handicap of his dress, he led the field. The second competitor most likely to appear was another Moroccan, a handsome man of about thirty. Mehdi el Menebbhi, the vizier for war, perspired lightly as he pedaled to catch up with his sultan. After a suitable interval, Dr. Verdon, the English court physician, or his brother Allan would pedal into view, sitting rigidly erect in their jackets, stiff collars and boaters. Next would come Gabriel Veyre, the court photographer, or Walter Harris if he were in town, as he often was. Lastly appeared a man of about sixty, bearded, round, obviously a European but wearing a tarboosh and turban, a white shirt and embroidered red waistcoat, Turkish balloon trousers and high black riding boots, a visibly reluctant but resigned participant in this two-wheeled steeplechase. This was Sir Harry Maclean, commander in chief of the Moroccan army.

Abd el-Aziz was an able sportsman: he excelled at bicycle polo, was a deft hand at tennis, football and gymnastics and adored billiards. His passion for these amusements was such that it was only with difficulty that his advisers could persuade him to put in a ritual appearance at Friday prayers. Under Veyre's guidance, he had become a competent photographer. He spent hours photographing his harem or sitting in comic poses, the results of which could be purchased from Jewish hawkers in the medina.

The Sultan's infatuation with European bric-a-brac became an obsession. His childhood interest in mechanical toys had been transferred to the bicycle. When Veyre introduced him to the gasoline-powered tricycle,

> he was drunk with joy. For an entire afternoon, he played with this new toy, speeding, turning, manoeuvring in every direction over the courtyard. When night fell, he was still not satiated with his new amusement. He ordered 30 black slaves to hold lanterns, candles, along his mad racetrack until the moment that, worn out, weak, he had to retire to his apartments to dream of his engine. The next day, master of his machine, he mounted it, rifle in hand, and, standing on the pedals, juggling his arm, he simulated a fantasia

—a Moroccan specialty executed on horseback and involving a pretended calvary charge, complete with rifle fire.

Other follies followed: cars, a miniature train which never ran for lack of rails, a grand piano, a barrel organ, theatrical uniforms, a hansom cab, a case of corsets, an elevator for a one-story palace, a camera of gold and silver with jeweled buttons, a printing press, saddlery from Mexico, ladies' underwear, trees from South America or Asia that were never planted, or, if planted, never watered, carved ivory figures, "an infinity of all that was grotesque, useless and in bad taste," complained Walter Harris. But Aziz stood before each newly arrived packing crate like a child at Christmas: "There was nothing he liked better than to watch a beautiful unwrapping. One had only to see with what enraptured eyes he followed the operation."

Moroccans began to suspect that their young Sultan was being played false by the Europeans who crowded into the court. They were not wrong. Almost everyone was on the take: Maclean sold him arms, Veyre procured his bicycles and automobiles, everyone was extracting a commission on something. Catalogues for the latest European fashions arrived. Aziz dressed his harem as if for a stroll on the Champs-Elysées and packed as many who would fit into his Louis XVI carriage. Around the gardens they turned, silk robes, wigs, large hats and boas, an absurd masquerade. Then Aziz took the reins. Maclean climbed up beside him, an English tourist stepped aboard and Veyre recorded the scene with his camera. Within days, the picture could be purchased in the medina. The "era of the traveling salesman" had begun, and with it the influx of adventurers who now turned up at the palace gates and left with their books full of orders for useless gadgetry. Moroccans were outraged. The Sultan, a direct descendant of the Prophet, was their spiritual leader as well as the King. "Imagine," wrote St.-Aulaire,

> the indignant stupefaction of the College of Cardinals and the Catholic world if the Pope threw away the Church offerings on frivolous distractions, in scandalous spectacles, introduced cabaret dancers and singers into the Vatican, chose his close friends from among Moslems and Buddhists, practiced sports while hoisting up his vestments, and you would have only a vague idea of the perturbation caused by the extravagances of the Sultan.

The Sultan's antisocial behavior was merely a symptom of deeper changes that Moroccans found far more disturbing. The situation was not unlike that of Russia under Peter the Great. After sustaining the Spanish defeat of 1860, Morocco was divided politically into two camps: one made up of those who believed in isolation and tradition as the best defense against encroachment from Western Europe, and the other which argued that a reformed, and consequently strengthened, government would be better placed to maintain the country's independence. Abd el-Aziz's ascendancy acknowledged the victory of the latter group, the reformers, led by Menebbhi and Si Feddoul Gharnit, the grand vizier. Aziz was full of good intentions: he drained the marshes around Fez and improved the water supply, cleaned up Morocco's stinking prisons and cut their population by half, removed the restrictions on the export of grain and fruit, and abolished the diplomatic ceremony which European envoys found so damaging to their national self-esteem. He and his ministers collaborated closely with such foreigners as the British minister, Sir Arthur Nicolson, to rationalize the tax structure, put Moroccan civil servants on a regular salary and transform the army into something resembling a military force.

But, as Nicolson had predicted, these reforms went contrary to the vested interests of too many people. The powerful *ulama* resisted anything tainted with Christendom; the religious brotherhoods or *zaouia*, like their monastic counterparts in Europe, defended their lands and privileges; the merchants, caids, soldiers and customs officials were reluctant to replace the bribes and extortion by which they lived with a government salary. There was a general disinclination for change in the population at large.

Nonetheless, the reformers forged ahead: why consult people who were opposed to progress? Besides, Menebbhi, Gharnit and other makhzan officials were growing rich on the bribes handed over by Europeans eager for access to the Sultan or keen to launch public works programs. Some found this distasteful, but corruption had a rich and venerable history in Morocco. What was more serious, however, was that within the short space of four years, the reform program and the extravagance of the court had combined with bad harvests to drain away the substantial treasury that Aziz had inherited in 1900 and push the country to the brink of bankruptcy. Like Louis XVI in 1789, Abd el-Aziz was to discover that financial mismanagement brought political disaster in its wake. In 1901, he placed his head in the noose by accepting a loan of 7.5 million francs from the Banque de Paris et des Pays-Bas. Other loans were to follow.

The comic aspects of this period were provided as much by the extraordinary jealousy and mistrust demonstrated by French diplomats toward the Englishmen who surrounded Aziz as by the antics of the young Sultan. The presence of Maclean, Harris, Verdon and Nicolson, not to mention the small brigade of English grooms, gardeners, electricians, plumbers, bicycle repairmen and so forth, offered ample evidence, the Quai d'Orsay felt certain, of a Whitehall conspiracy to take over Morocco. Nothing could have been further from the truth. Traditionally, Britain had stood as Morocco's guarantor of independence against the encroachments of Spain and France. But by 1903, London was beginning to think it preferable to entrust Morocco to the safe custody of France. The reason for this was simple: Britain needed a friend. The Boer War of 1899–1902 had demonstrated how painfully alone Britain was in Europe. "Splendid Isolation" and "Imperial Destiny" had perhaps offered adequate political guidelines in the 1880s and 1890s. But Admiral Alfred von Tirpitz's 1898 Naval Armaments Bill announced that Germany intended to challenge Britain's domination of the seas. The "Blue Water" theory of national defense began to give way to a realization that soon the British navy might prove inadequate. The South African war had stretched her fleet over several thousand miles of ocean. Next time the Germans might be able to gain a local superiority long enough to land their colossal, and very efficient, army on England's shores.

Since the early 1880s, when France began seriously to expand into Africa, her quarrels with Britain had been colonial ones. At Fashoda in 1898, Kitchener and Marchand stared down the barrels of each other's rifles while their governments decided who was to control the Nile; that was the last of a series of confrontations in Africa which had brought the two countries to the very edge of war. Britain clearly had to patch up her quarrel with her old

Gallic rival. Morocco would serve as the ticket to friendship between Britain and France, carrying them, arm in arm, into the firestorm of the Marne.

All this was in the future, however. As usual, Delcassé and his minions in the Quai d'Orsay were the last to sense the subtle shift of view that was already taking place in Whitehall. Instead of seeing Aziz's courtiers for what they really were—second-rate soldiers from unfashionable regiments or mediocre doctors without a hope of a lucrative practice at home, men of the sort who frequently congregated at the courts of despots whose thrones were too insecure to entrust important office to their own subjects—the presence of these Englishmen was construed as a plot that must be headed off by all means. There is something charmingly naïve about the message brought by carrier pigeon to the French legation in Tangiers from the Toulousian Dr. Jaffary, sent to Fez to offer competition to Dr. Verdon: "I have just administered suppositories to two of His Majesty's black concubines," the message declared triumphantly. "It is a great victory for peaceful penetration."

Infinitely more tragic was the fate of the racehorse, a winner of several sweepstakes at Auteuil, that was purchased at great expense from the Quai d'Orsay's secret funds and taken by cavalry colonel de St.-Julien in 1902 as a gift to the Sultan. The fine lines and delicate disposition of the thoroughbred were not appreciated by the Moroccans, who judged their horses, like their women, by weight alone. To Aziz, it simply appeared to be an underfed beast. After several weeks without exercise, the horse became unmanageable, and the Sultan ordered his stable lads to kill it with their knives.

The legitimacy of Abd el-Aziz's sultanate had never been universally accepted in Morocco. From the very beginning of his reign, he was not a popular choice to succeed Moulai Hassan, but rather one forced upon Morocco by his father's chamberlain, a cunning black named Ahamed Ben Mussa, and called Ba Ahmed. Moulai Hassan had been a warrior sultan. In 1894, he had led an expedition over the Atlas into the Tafilalet to exact tribute from a portion of his empire which had long resisted his government. His goal was to demonstrate to Europe, and especially to France, that the trans-Atlas regions were not the *bled el-siba*, a no-man's-land which the Sultan claimed but could not control. It proved a futile gesture. His army was unable to occupy the territory, and struggled back over the mountains in deepening snows. Moulai Hassan was already a sick man. The retreat was his death march.

To this half-starved and frozen *harka* stranded in the backland, loss of the Sultan meant disaster. Without his *baraka* and the threat of reprisals from the makhzan, the tribes would certainly have emerged from their douars and casbahs deep in the mountains to destroy the army. So when Ba Ahmed realized that his master was dead, he called the servants together and swore them to secrecy. Their fear must have been overpowering, for they kept their vow. For seven days it was business as usual: the servants walked beside the closed litter carrying the Sultan's body. Each evening his tent was pitched; Ba Ahmed entered with his papers to be signed while his servants carried in food and removed empty dishes. When the stench of the decomposing body became too great to shield the secret from the rest of the caravan any longer, Ba Ahmed announced that Moulai Hassan's choice had fallen on his son, Abd el-Aziz.

Ba Ahmed's motives in maintaining secrecy went beyond those of mere self-preservation. He sought to control the state itself. On the occasion of a sultan's death, his numerous sons traditionally staked their rival claims to the throne, rallied support among the tribes and launched a civil war which could last for years. In 1894, however, the disorder was particularly widespread. Most of the tribes had expected Moulai Mohammed, the Sultan's eldest son, to succeed to his father's throne. The fact that Moulai Mohammed was mad strengthened rather than diminished his popularity by increasing their reverence for him and their faith in his sanctity. Ba Ahmed had other plans, and put them into effect: Moulai Mohammed was locked away in the rambling palace at Meknes while Abd el-Aziz, then a boy of only thirteen or fourteen, became the figurehead behind whom Ba Ahmed ruled Morocco. And he ruled it with an iron hand. He sowed discord among the tribes, treated his enemies with great severity, tortured his opponents and left them to rot in fetid prisons. Ba Ahmed's six years as de facto sultan simply accelerated the movement of the population toward the coast and increased the popularity of the protection system. By brute force Ba Ahmed prevailed.

By far the most damaging effect of Ba Ahmed's regency for the independence of Morocco was that no steps were taken to prepare the young Abd el-Aziz for the responsibilities which must one day be his. Sir Arthur Nicolson, who visited the court at Marrakech in 1896, found "the Sultan amusing himself with his picture books and mechanical toys, while the Grand Vizir sits on the floor in front of him working with his secretaries." When Ba Ahmed was swept away by the cholera epidemic of 1900, Abd el-Aziz was thrust, at the age of nineteen or twenty, into a role for which he had not the slightest preparation.

The English war correspondent Reginald Rankin, who met Aziz in 1907, described him as

> a big, powerful man. . . . His face is broad and fleshy; the nose thick, the chin receding, the mouth good-humoured, smiling often to disclose enormously white teeth. His beard is very thick, and does little to hide the weakness of his profile. The eyes are his distinctive feature. They are extraordinarily intelligent, piercing and vivacious. . . . His hands are as well shaped as a woman's, and he has a nervous tic of biting his lower lip.

This was the man who was to lead Morocco in what was to be one of the most difficult and troubled periods of her difficult and troubled history. He was intelligent, but his education had been limited to the narrow rote learning of koranic verse. Like many Moroccans, he had no idea of the complexity of the world in which he lived or of the powerful forces which struggled for supremacy in it: the head of the French military mission reported in 1902 that Aziz believed the Transvaal to be in Europe and was quite unaware of the relative power and importance of the individual European states. But he was curious, sometimes disarmingly so: Veyre admitted that he was at a loss to reply when Aziz asked him, "What is the function of the Eiffel Tower?" He was kind, but spoiled. Walter Harris complained that he always cheated at cricket and would simply confiscate the bridge hand of another player if his was no good. He wanted to be a good and effective ruler, but his ideas of how to go about the business of government were distorted by the company he kept. His youth and lack of experience meant that he fell easy prey to adventurers who encouraged his tendency to play truant from the ceremonies and religious occasions that formed such a vital part of his office. Moroccans, he seemed to believe, could be won over by elaborate fireworks displays. But these garish events simply confirmed them in their view that his *baraka* had deserted him, and, in whispers, they called him "the Nazarene." At the same time, his antics strengthened the contempt and lack of compassion for him among the very men whom he befriended and relied upon. "It was a quaint proceeding," Nicolson wrote of his 1902 interview with Aziz.

He received me in a small wooden shed built up against the wall of the palace. There was only a billiard table in it and a few kitchen chairs. Outside, a white table, a packing case or two, a cage with a young leopard, and a rubbish heap within ten yards. Nothing could have been more squalid. His majesty was most affable, but I fear he is of very weak character. The way he clung to my hand and coat-tails and pleaded tearfuly for advice was pathetic. In short, I was disappointed in him.

Abd el-Aziz was a weak man. It is unlikely, however, that a stronger sultan could have rescued Morocco from the fate that stalked her. But it was the Europeans who surrounded him, flattered him, lived off him while at the same time mocking him, who, in the end, made it impossible for him to rule.

CHAPTER V

TAGHIT

It must be a joke. But Captain Susbielle was not laughing. "Not possible . . . never capable . . . hate each other . . . taught them a lesson in June." The first reports which trickled into Taghit in early July 1903 were dismissed: those Arab bureau boys never got it right; not real soldiers, just linguists turned loose in the desert. (In 1903, social anthropology was not yet a recognized branch of war studies.) Pay an Arab money for a story and he'll make it a good one. But still the stories came—a *harka* of eight thousand rifles! The French had never faced that many in seventy years of Algerian fighting.

And then, nothing.

The mid-August heat at Taghit was oppressive. Here in the no-man's-land that was the Algeria-Morocco frontier, only the date palms which threaded the narrow gorge of the Zousfana, far below, offered shade and humidity. But on the spur overlooking the river, the sun seemed as if it would bake the mud walls of the French post almost to powder.

Lieutenant Pointurier walked across the parade ground to collect his orders. "Parade ground" was a misnomer: his *mokhaznis*, as the native policemen were called, never "paraded," they just milled about, talked, loosed a shot into the air, into the ground, occasionally even into each other. For the moment, however, they squatted along the wall in a narrow strip of shade, swathed in dusty cloth, squinting at him from beneath long, brown fingers. "Nothing for three days," Susbielle told Pointurier. "Take thirty *mokhaznis* . . . pick up some legionnaires at El Morra . . . ride toward Béchar." Béchar was Morocco.

Moulai Amar ould Moulai Mostafa el Hannasi disliked the French. He hated Algerians. What is more, they had made him angry. The bombardment of the oasis of Figuig in May, followed by a sweep through the territory of the Doui-Menia around Béchar, had been designed by the French as a muscle-flexing exercise to persuade tribesmen to stay out of Algeria, to remain on the Moroccan side of the invisible border. Its effect had been just the reverse. On August 8, eight thousand members of the southeastern Moroccan tribes—the Oulad Djerir, the Doui-Menia, the Ait-Atta—crowded into Béchar. The meeting was quite unprecedented. For as long as anyone could remember, each of these tribes had stolen sheep, toppled date palms and kidnapped women belonging to the others. That they were now prepared to suspend their blood feuds, if only temporarily, and unite under Moulai Amar bore testimony not only to his extraordinary powers of leadership, but also to a collective fear of the French that superseded deep and long-held hatreds. The only absent chief was Bou-Amana, the man who for years had earned a good living by attacking settlements in Algeria. He explained that he was busy helping the pretender Bou Hamara keep the Sultan of Morocco's troops out of Taza to the north, and sent his blessing.

Moulai Amar laid a watch across all routes leading to the frontier. It was not necessary. Most informers, seeing the storm that was about to break over the French, simply melted into the resistance movement. Consequently, Captain Susbielle was clueless at the very moment that the Moroccans came to choose a target. For several days the tribal chiefs sat beneath the palm trees and talked, hour upon hour of discussion broken only for prayers and the ritual drinking of sweet mint tea. The men of the Oulad Djerir wanted to attack Ben-Aireg and then push on to Figuig. The *chaamba*, the notorious Arab raiders of the northern Sahara, favored concentrating efforts on the vulnerable convoys that linked the French posts along the Zousfana. But in the end, Moulai Amar prevailed.

Early on the morning of August 15, 1903, Lieutenant Pointurier's reconnaissance filed down the slopes of the mountain range called Djebel Béchar and slipped into the small oasis of Djenien. Crossing the hills at night was not the easiest of operations, and the men had been kept awake only by the stumbling of the mules and by the wretched discomfort of Arab saddles. Ahead, about an hour's slow ride across a rock-strewn plain, lay Béchar itself. As dawn broke, they could see the splash of green against the low khaki rises. Pointurier ordered his *mokhaznis* to ride on. The legionnaires would remain in reserve. If his Algerians had to run, the legion could provide a temporary defense at Djenien. This was a standard tactic in the desert, devised for pursuing sheep thieves. But what if several hundred tribesmen followed hard on the heels of the retreating *mokhaznis*? Pointurier's position was far from enviable. Most of the white troops immediately fell on the ground and went to sleep. How strange that Germans and Algerians were fighting Moroccans in the name of France. But this thought probably never occurred to Pointurier.

After what seemed only minutes, a *mokhazni* galloped into the oasis. The *harka*, a big one, had left Béchar two days ago. Its destination? Taghit!

Captain Susbielle cursed the military engineers: the architect of Taghit deserved a court-martial. Taghit was one of the frontier posts that linked the territorial command at Ain Sefra in the north with Beni Abbès to the south. For some 120 miles these posts followed the broad valley of the Zousfana—broad except at Taghit, where for seven miles the river slices a gorge two hundred yards wide between the stark mountains of the Beni Goumi and the Grand Erg, a Siberia of sand which stretches several hundred miles southeast into Africa. The *ksar* of Taghit lorded it over the gorge at a point where it narrows into a defile barely fifty yards across: a picturesque agglomeration of mud buildings several stories high, poised on the lip of a spur that dominated the palm groves beneath. The *ksar* occupied an excellent military position. The French post did not; it was, in fact, virtually indefensible.

Its defects were readily apparent, especially to men who expected at any moment to be attacked by a force more than eight times their number. The engineers had constructed a pentagon *behind* the *ksar* so that the valley and the slopes leading up to the spur were in dead space, that is, invisible from the walls. Furthermore, the redoubt was dominated on two sides by higher ground: its interior could be swept clean from the bluff opposite or from the top of a sand dune barely three hundred yards away. Lastly, the wells were some distance from the fortifications. Fighting in the Sahara in August was thirsty work. In a protracted siege, water became more precious than bullets. The only solution was to defend the fortress from outside.

To be fair to the engineers, no one could have foreseen that a situation of this seriousness would arise. Taghit had been designed as a glorified police station, a center of operations against bands from the Tafilalet which regularly raided Algerian villages and farms. The walled enclosure was an animal park and a supply depot, not a fortress. The bluff across the river had been crowned by a small masonry fortification. Into this, Susbielle crammed as many men and as much ammunition as could fit into the confined space; it would be impossible to reinforce them once the battle began. The dunes offered more intractable problems. The engineers had originally planned to build a blockhouse at the highest point. But sand makes poor foundations.

Susbielle sent a detachment up the hill and told them to hold out for as long as possible.

The garrison, like the redoubt, had not been designed with siege warfare in mind. Nineteenth-century officers were great believers in exploiting the "natural" fighting qualities of native soldiers. The majority of the 450 troops at Taghit were Algerians—*mokhaznis* and regular Armée d'Afrique detachments of tirailleurs and mounted spahis—lean, muscular men whose military advantage lay with their ability to move with extraordinary rapidity over impossible terrain to fall on the camps of unsuspecting intruders. They enjoyed nothing more than killing Moroccans, but on their own terms, out of the blue, with surprise and numbers on their side. Defending a piece of ground against a superior force was not their style; the ragged square, ammunition running low, the colonel cries "Make every shot count, boys," and, one by one, they fall? How ridiculous!

The weight of defense must fall on the European troops. At Taghit in August 1903, this meant a detachment of the African Light Infantry, the *Bats d'Af*. They were more a social experiment than a military unit. In 1830, the year the invasion of Algeria began, French politicians of vision had realized the obvious advantages offered by North Africa as a dumping ground for social undesirables. The army was given the job of organizing the deportations. The *Bats d'Af* were originally conscripted from the ranks of troublesome left-wing revolutionaries with which Paris was rife in 1830. By 1903, the *Bats d'Af* still contained a fair sprinkling of men who did not see eye to eye with the government, but the recruitment net had spread to include juvenile delinquents, petty criminals and other apprentices to the underworlds of Paris, Lyons and Marseilles who answered collectively to the improbable nickname of *les joyeux*, bestowed on them because of their constant complaining. Mutinous and troublesome in quiet times, fighting was what they did best.

What was one to do about the natives, the inhabitants of the palm groves of Beni Goumi along the river? They were Doui-Menia like many of the oncoming Moroccan *harka*. Until now, they had seemed to accept the French presence at Taghit, but then they had had little choice. If things began to go badly for the garrison . . . Susbielle called in their caids: "Take your people inside the *ksars* at Taghit and Barrebi [two and a half miles to the south]." He then did a bold thing: he gave them four hundred rifles. Susbielle waited.

A *harka* is not an army. It resembles an amoeba, being both shapeless and self-sufficient. Moulai Amar's *harka* moved south from Béchar in a series of spasms. Its marching order was haphazard: proud men on camels and small Arab ponies clutching single-shot Remingtons were followed on foot by their less fortunate comrades with antique muzzle-loaders, their stocks emblazoned with inscriptions in Arabic exhorting their owners to throw back the infidel. Women led donkeys and camels laden with household equipment. Barefoot children dashed about keeping tiny flocks of goats together with well-directed stones. Everywhere there was dust, and a cacophony of human and animal noises.

Early on the morning of August 17, 1903, the *harka* descended the dry bed of the Wadi Hadhannas as it loops to join the Zousfana about six miles south of Taghit. As they moved up the funnel of the gorge, the Moroccans could just make out the high mud walls and square turrets of the Baghti *ksar* through the palm trees. With a whoop, the more impetuous rushed toward it. It was empty, but it made a good fire.

By eight o'clock, the *harka* was strung out like a snake, its tail still in the Wadi Hadhannas and its fangs about to close on the *ksar* at Barrebi. The first rush by the vanguard of the *harka* was easily beaten back by the inhabitants. Susbielle sent Lieutenant Charles de Ganay, an Arab bureau officer, with his eighty *mokhaznis* to harass the attackers. They dashed back and forth, shouting, firing, doing little damage. But by slowly giving ground, they drew the *harka* away from Barrebi and up the narrow valley toward Taghit, where Adjutant Gabaig had stretched his tirailleurs in a thin line across the valley floor.

It was a typical Moroccan attack: a forward rush, fire on the run, rein up, retreat, reload, charge again. There was no control, no direction. Had the tirailleurs been better shots, had they had a machine gun, they could have caused great carnage. But they withdrew, slowly forced backward up the hill by the sheer weight of several thousand warriors pressing forward. Upon reaching the plateau, the tirailleurs formed a line which continued the controlled retreat toward the walls of the redoubt, firing at the attackers, who were becoming more and more numerous. Then Susbielle produced his trump card: two 80-millimeter cannon. These were small and light, about the size of a modern mortar, which allowed them to be carried easily on muleback. When set on their wooden wheels, they were only about knee-high. By the standards of Verdun in 1916, they were not particularly impressive. But the Moroccans were impressed; a few bangs and the forward elements of the *harka* tumbled back down the hill into the valley.

Morale in the French camp that night was not high. The first attack had been repulsed: two tirailleurs were dead and three wounded, including Adjutant Gabaig, who died the next day. But eight thousand Moroccans were camped in the valley below. The odds appeared impossible, and improved only marginally at dawn with the arrival of Lieutenant Pointurier and his legionnaires, who had marched the thirty-eight-and-a-half miles from El Morra in one night.

The next day, the eighteenth, witnessed a slogging match. Susbielle deployed his *joyeux* across the valley 1,300 yards south of the redoubt. Hidden behind rocks and trees, they held off the repeated attacks of horsemen who threw their emaciated ponies across the stony ground to within inches of the French rifles, stood up in their stirrups, the reins in the left hand and the butt of the rifle tucked under their arm, fired and withdrew. The *mokhaznis*, spahis and cannon kept the French flanks from being turned. A little ground was lost and three men killed, but by 3:30 in the afternoon, the day's fighting was over. More serious was the surrender of the *ksar* at Barrebi: surrounded by their cousins, with the French contained up the valley, the *ksar* dwellers defected to the attackers. If the same thing happened at Taghit, the results for the defenders might be disastrous. Susbielle installed a section of tirailleurs in the Taghit *ksar* to lend backbone.

For two days the strategy followed by the Moroccans had been brave rather than brilliant. It was becoming apparent even to the most confirmed believers in oriental fatalism that a new plan must be devised. A *mokhazni*, one of those constantly roaming the fringes of the Moroccan camp, brought Susbielle the news in the dead of night: a number of the *harka*'s more prominent chiefs had shifted their tents into the dunes a mile and a quarter southeast of the French position. At three-thirty in the morning, Captain Guibert, one hundred tirailleurs, a section of legionnaires and some *mokhaznis* crept out of the redoubt into the dunes. They had gone about 200 yards when they collided head-on with several hundred Moroccans coming from the opposite direction.

For a brief moment, ever so brief, in the half-light of dawn, the two groups stared at each other, half in surprise, half in embarrassment. The French fired first. The combination of good discipline and magazine-fed Lebels gave them an enormous advantage. A number of Moroccans fell.

Others tried to escape, but were prevented from doing so by the tightly packed scrum behind. It was like shooting fish in a barrel. Gradually, however, the Moroccan mass flattened out as those in the rear sought a way forward. Guibert, realizing that his flanks might be turned, withdrew almost casually toward the redoubt. The cannon kept the Moroccans in the dunes and off the plateau. It was breakfast time.

Prevented by the artillery from attacking the fort from the dunes, most of the *harka* slid into the valley to attack again from the south. Four hundred Oulad Djerir and Chaamba remained behind and rushed the French detachment at the top of the dune, drove them off it with little difficulty, and poured fire into the French perimeter. This caused momentary confusion inside the redoubt as tirailleurs, legionnaires and *joyeux* rushed about in the slow drizzle of lead finding shelter for the animals. Fire was returned, briskly at first, gradually subsiding into a slow sniping match.

The *harka* crawled up the sides of the spur from the valley. This time their objective was the *ksar*, bristling like a hedgehog with rifles. Again and again they swarmed up the steep incline, bent forward against the slope, only to break against the walls, caught in a deadly cross fire from the fort on the bluff opposite and the *ksar* above. All day it continued in a merciless heat, fanatical, futile, wasteful. Bravery, even Moroccan bravery, had its limits. At 8:30 that evening the Moroccans withdrew to their camp, leaving the slope littered with nearly two hundred bodies. French losses: one killed, five wounded.

No eyewitness accounts exist to tell us what now occurred in the Arab tents. But one can picture the scene: "Moulai Amar does not have the *baraka*." This alliance, like all alliances, was fragile. "God has permitted the cursed Nazarenes to take possession of the country of our forefathers." "God has punished the Moslems for our sins and wickedness." All day they talked. The French watched, but did not attack. Islam teaches that everything is written, but beneath the writing, fundamental economic interests began to assert themselves. For the Doui-Menia, Taghit's near neighbors, failure to dislodge the French conjured up nightmare visions of felled date palms, guarded waterholes and *razzias* (raids) by French-led Algerians. Those from further afield, the Ait-Atta and Arabs from the Tafilalet, were discouraged but not demoralized, quite prepared to continue the fight on someone else's territory. The Chaamba and Oulad Djerir were disgusted: "No wonder Bou-Amana declined to join the *harka*. The French are the richest tribe in the desert. Their convoys are an inexhaustible source of booty, especially rifles. Not old rifles, but modern repeating ones. And these sheep tenders and *ksar* dwellers must waste time attacking a French post. What fools!"

It is also probable that they all agreed on one thing: they had not been defeated. "It cannot be called a *baroud* [a true battle]," they said. "They never give us the opportunity for a fair fight, to see who are the braver warriors, French or Moslems. Our cavalry charges. They do not come out to meet us. They mow us down. Even those who charge right up to the mass of French soldiers, they slaughter them. Our men attack, they stay behind their walls and fire. Allah, how many bullets they have! This is no test of courage. There is no chance for a fair fight. It is pointless to remain." The difference in firepower between the two sides was readily apparent to the Moroccans. The implications of the French methods of warfare, however, would take them far, far longer to digest.

As they talked, the indications that they had missed their opportunity to overwhelm Taghit became more apparent. Forty horsemen, *mokhaznis* from Beni Abbès, galloped unscathed through the shouts, shots and confusion of the Moroccan tents toward Taghit. Scouts brought news that a large French column was approaching from the north, two days' ride from Taghit. At dawn on August 21, the Moroccans decamped. Susbielle watched them go, too exhausted to pursue.

"The spahi is the lord of the *bled*, the convoy driver is the serf." Lieutenant Selchauhausen of the Second Regiment of the Foreign Legion had for several days observed the two extremes of the Armée d'Afrique's social hierarchy. The differences were especially apparent about this time each morning, 9:30, when the heat went from merely stifling to quite unbearable. The convoy drivers, the scrapings of the Oran docks or old tirailleurs, almost all over sixty, barefoot, dressed in tattered pieces of uniform, appeared to be on the verge of sunstroke. They would surely have deserted if, in this arid waste between El Morra and Taghit, there had been any place to desert to. Only legionnaires were foolish enough, or desperate enough, to strike out into the desert. The spahis seemed immune to the heat. Trotting about on their small ponies, erect, alert, their turbans and scarlet burnouses impeccable despite the clouds of dust. They did not disdain the convoy drivers. They simply did not notice them.

The spahis had been officially constituted in 1842, although Algerian cavalry had been used earlier. Colonel Marey-Monge, father of the spahis, had originally intended his troops to be recruited from among sons of Arab noblemen. But while these never came forward in large numbers, the requirement that every recruit furnish his own mount kept the regiment from sinking into the proletariat, as was the case with the tirailleurs. No Arab with pretensions to social status would fight on foot, so that infantry service with the Christians remained a not altogether honorable calling in Arab eyes. The spahis' uniforms, which dated from the 1840s, were more elegant than practical, which was one reason why they seldom fought as a unit but did service as messengers and convoy escorts.

There was nothing remarkable about El Moungar as a convoy halt; no trees, no water, only sardine tins and excrement marked the spot. (Sardines were to the Armée d'Afrique what bully beef was to the British army.) When you left El Morra at 2 a.m., you arrived at El Moungar at 9:30. It was that simple. To the left a number of low dunes announced the fringe of the Grand Erg. To the right, the valley of the Zousfana dotted with low scrub leveled away to the foot of the Djebel Béchar, barely visible through the haze of heat. "Put out the sentries!" The 115 white-clad legionnaires of the escort formed a line, stacked rifles and opened their tins of sardines. The combination of fish and heat produced an odor of staggering unpleasantness. The several hundred mules and camels stood in a disorderly queue as their drivers squatted in shadows thrown by their bodies, chewing leathery dates and brushing away persistent insects. It was too hot to talk. It was too hot even to gamble.

September 2, 1903: The siege of Taghit had been lifted barely a week before, but no one was particularly worried, nor particularly vigilant. The *harka* had dispersed. It was assumed that the large supply convoy which had been delayed by the troubles could now travel south in safety. The first echelon—convoys had always to divide into echelons to prevent crowding at the waterholes—had passed without incident two days before. That is why everyone was surprised when shots were fired from the dunes. Lieutenant Selchauhausen joined the stampede of legionnaires toward the stacks of rifles. Then came a terrific crash from behind. Selchauhausen looked toward the plain. He saw no one, just puffs of smoke. It was the last thing he ever saw.

The legionnaires, or rather those still standing, hesitated, then charged. But there was nothing to charge. The captain and the sergeant major fell. Dragging their dead and wounded, the survivors made for the shelter of the dunes, through a melee of frightened animals, shed loads, panicked mule drivers and general pandemonium.

When Susbielle arrived at El Moungar from Taghit at 5:30 in the afternoon at the head of a squadron of spahis, command had devolved to a corporal. The twenty legionnaires still unwounded picked over the fallen animals looking for canteens of water. Most of the convoy drivers had disappeared. The Chaamba and Oulad Djerir had evaporated, taking with them the two hundred camels and their loads. Thirty-eight legionnaires lay dead and forty-seven wounded. No Moroccan bodies were found.

CHAPTER VI

THE CALL

Colonel Hubert Lyautey's first impressions of Ain Sefra were not favorable. "Terrible country," he wrote to his sister in early October 1903. "Nothing green, just stones and bare mountains." "But," he added, "the colors and the sky are superb and that counts for something." Barely a week before, boarding the steamer at Marseilles for Algiers, he had been happy, almost deliriously so. But that elation had gradually drained away. The empty desolation of the countryside was not entirely to blame.

Lyautey always enjoyed taking the ship to leave France. This time he had been at home for less than two years, but he felt that he had more than earned his release. The fact that his departure had been the result of an incredible stroke of luck, of a chance meeting at a Paris dinner party given for Charles Jonnart, the newly appointed governor general of Algeria, heightened his pleasure. The normal complacency of the French political world—consumed by its own domestic quarrels and largely indifferent to what went on beyond the shores of France—had been rattled by the attack at Taghit and the disaster at El Moungar. The nationalist press had not failed to capitalize on the military setback in the desert to embarrass the left-wing government of Emile Combes. The effect had only been short-lived, however. It had been relatively easy for Combes to give in to pressure by Jonnart and the colonialists in the Chamber of Deputies for a more aggressive policy in the South Oranais, the Algerian military district which included the Zousfana. Jonnart's choice for military commander at Ain Sefra had fallen on Colonel Lyautey. Combes had posed no objections. He wanted only to return to his priest-baiting. For his part, Lyautey felt like a prisoner prematurely paroled for good behavior. What he could not know at this stage, however, was that this call was the beginning of an association with Morocco that would last almost until his death. Lyautey was to become both Morocco's conqueror and, in colonial terms, her creator.

His feelings for France were complicated, even contradictory. He was, of course, fiercely proud to be French. He had dedicated his life to the service of his country. He believed, rather he wanted to believe, in the innate genius of the land. But France was in decline, in a desperate slide toward mediocrity. The Third Republic, this blasted republic whose politicians divided the country with their factious quarrels, whose careers had been constructed by pandering to the lowest instincts of Frenchmen—jealousy, greed, lack of vision and the desire for a comfortable, risk-free existence—was to blame. Since 1899, when the Radicals had been catapulted to power by the Dreyfus affair, political life had become quite intolerable. Best stay out of France, which was precisely what he was doing.

Lyautey may have expounded these views to his fellow passengers, but probably did not, for he was essentially an optimist. He was certainly no bore. And he was happy, rising early to pace the nearly deserted decks, watch the sky light up and the dark Mediterranean slide past. He sat down to breakfast in excellent spirits at an hour in the morning when his dining companions—in this case Monseigneur Oury, the Bishop of Algiers, and Prince Nam-Nghi, the deposed Emperor of Annam—were not normally suitable for general exhibition.

The other passengers probably did not recognize Lyautey, for he was not yet famous. To them he was just another soldier on his way to an Algerian posting, a forty-nine-year-old colonel growing gray in harness. But he seemed much more alert, more talkative, more gregarious than one might expect a man to be whose career, until now, had been rather mediocre. In fact, what struck people on first meeting Lyautey was his sheer nervous energy. He was lively rather than handsome: his heavy black mustache was yellowed by tobacco and his curious flat-top haircut accentuated a face that was too long and ears that were too large. But when he spoke—out of the corner of his mouth like a cavalryman used to shouting orders on parade, in short, sharp sentences—his steel-blue eyes became magnetic and his slight frame trembled. The range of his knowledge was catholic: he could discuss literature with the same facility as military tactics. Clearly, Lyautey was a unique beast in the military zoo.

People who knew him better, or were more observant, might notice other, more disturbing, traits. Beneath his apparent good humor, he took life very seriously. His urbane exterior barely camouflaged an outlook that was sad, even bitter, an enthusiasm for life tempered by the realization that it had brought him few rewards. As his subordinates soon learned, Lyautey was a man poised on an emotional knife edge, whose charm was liable in an instant to snap into fury. Lyautey did not meet people, he collided with them. The result might be great affection or lasting animosity. But even his enemies—and he would soon acquire some very powerful ones—were prepared to admit that this nervous, impulsive, even violent man was capable in a crisis of decisions of great lucidity.

Secretly, Lyautey might concede that entering the army had been a great mistake. But a military career seemed at the time to be a natural choice for a man of his background and education. He was born in Nancy, the son of an engineer who held a series of senior provincial posts in the civil service, and who had married into the local aristocracy. But the army threaded the fabric of his childhood. His grandfather, a veteran of Wagram, and his two uncles were generals. Lorraine, patriotic Lorraine, played host to many large garrison towns. It was as normal for young men from the east to join the army as it was for Bretons to become fishermen and priests. But Hubert Lyautey had not seemed destined for the army. Indeed, he had not seemed destined to survive childhood. In 1856, when he was only eighteen months old, he had been taken to his great-grandmother's house on Nancy's elegant Place Stanislas, there to watch the military review held to celebrate the baptism of Napoleon III's son, the Prince Imperial. His nurse placed him on an upper-floor windowsill. He fell, ricocheting off a cuirassier before hitting the ground. This saved his life, but he was twelve years old before he was freed from the beds, crutches and various plaster and metal casts which circumscribed his childhood. Consequently, he was left with a legacy of poor health which the cold, damp climate of northern France did little to alleviate. No wonder his spirits rose markedly when brought into contact with sun and heat.

This experience may help explain the often baffling dualism of Lyautey's character. Once freed from his constraints, he demonstrated an insatiable appetite for physical activity, for movement, for action. His body was not something he took for granted. He was proud of it. He moved it gracefully and dressed it well. In short, Lyautey was vain. But at the same time he retained from his years of confinement a taste for reading and reflection, and an imagination fed by his grandfather's stories of the Napoleonic Wars. Here was a man of great simplicity, modesty and kindness who could, at times, become prickly and arrogant.

Algiers in 1903 was still very much a colonial town. One could have no doubt that this was the southern shore of the Mediterranean, but over seventy years of occupation by the French had softened the hard edge of Africa.

Algiers was a picturesque collection of white villas smothered in purple bougainvillaea, of narrow, twisting streets, of palm trees and eucalyptus beside a bay of dazzling blue. In the gentle warmth of late September, with the air fragrant with carob, Algiers must have been delicious. But Lyautey was far too preoccupied to wax enthusiastic over his surroundings. General Maurice Bailloud met him at the quai and took him to the governor general's residence for dinner and a day of meetings and conferences, which left Lyautey only the briefest of moments to visit "my dear casbah," which he had last seen as a young lieutenant more than twenty years before.

The problem of the South Oranais was very simple, Lyautey explained to his new superior. To translate it into staff college language, it was "absurd" that the lines of communication ran along the frontier rather than perpendicular to it. The large supply convoys that circulated between Ain Sefra and Beni Abbès were unable to defend themselves against raiders out of Morocco at dozens of points. He had told Jonnart all this before, but the obvious could not be too often repeated.

The solution? Occupy Béchar. This would put posts like Taghit and El Morra well behind French lines. Béchar could then be transformed into a "zone" of operations from which the Doui-Menia can be brought to heel with a combination of military and "economic" action. Tie in the tribes to Algeria by trade, open markets, subsidize the imports so that eastern Morocco will be linked to Oran rather than to Fez. When the trans-Atlas caravans wither, when the Doui-Menia realize that their interests lie with the French rather than with the resistance, they will become the "mattress" between us and the Tafilalet, that network of palm oases which nestles beneath the arid anti-Atlas, an Arab island in a Berber sea and a center of opposition to the French in southeast Morocco. This was the method that General Joseph Gallieni had perfected in Tonkin and Madagascar. All it required was cooperation, cash and a reorganization of the frontier forces into light, mobile units ready at a moment's notice to pursue raiders into Morocco.

The problem was far more complicated in point of fact than Lyautey was prepared—publicly—to admit. Béchar lay within the territory claimed by the Sultan of Morocco. The fact that the Sultan could not garrison Béchar, nor collect taxes there, nor administer justice, did nothing to diminish the validity of his title in the eyes of the makhzan. The answer to this apparent paradox lay in the dual role of the Sultan as both temporal and spiritual leader. The people of eastern Morocco recognized him as their caliph, but at the same time refused to accept his government.

For Lyautey, as for most men brought up on western notions of polity, the Sultan's pretensions were sheer burlesque. States were defined by lines on a map, an area over which a government exercised its authority. Lithuania might as well claim Tierra del Fuego. What Lyautey could not ignore, however, was that, for the moment, the governments of Europe found it convenient to accept the Sultan's claims. The dividing line between Algeria and Morocco ended abruptly at Teniet Sassi, barely seventy miles inland from the coast. South of this point the frontier remained undefined, permeable, lawless. Nevertheless, the Quai d'Orsay, under its powerful chief, Théophile Delcassé, remained sensitive—oversensitive, Lyautey believed—to diplomatic opinion, and insisted on caution.

Lyautey, however, was not a man to be paralyzed by his ability to see both sides of a question. In Algiers he was asked for a soldier's opinion, so he gave Jonnart a soldier's answer, or rather a colonial soldier's answer: Occupy Béchar, changing its name to Colomb "to spare diplomatic susceptibilities." Everyone will assume that Colomb is in Algeria (the Quai d'Orsay's notions of the geography of the South Oranais were hazy, not to say nonexistent). Jonnart thought this a good plan.

General Fernand O'Connor, commander of the Oran division and Lyautey's immediate superior, was less happy to see him. Lyautey wrote to General Gallieni that O'Connor was "visibly hostile." He attributed this to jealousy and a difference in method. Certainly, O'Connor could not have been pleased that another man had been called in by Jonnart to pick up the pieces of Taghit and El Moungar. His displeasure grew during the next few days as Lyautey outlined his plans for pacifying the South Oranais. But Lyautey was being less than honest: the reasons for his cool, not to say frigid, reception at Oran ran far deeper than jealousy or arcane disputes over military tactics.

Since he had entered St.-Cyr in 1873, Lyautey had struggled to come to terms with his profession. A military career had been far from his mind when he left the lycée at Nancy for the Jesuit-run School of the Immaculate Conception on Paris's rue des Postes only a year earlier. He had decided to follow his father to the prestigious Ecole Polytechnique and then, perhaps, a political career, in retrospect a curious ambition for a man who despised the political arts. But Father Stanislas du Lac, the school's influential director, deflected Lyautey toward St.-Cyr; the Jesuits were eager to get their pupils into the army. The Ecole Polytechnique required two more grueling years of preparation. Besides, the glitter of the uniform appealed. Lyautey succumbed.

From the day that Lyautey entered the crumbling buildings on the southern outskirts of Paris that housed France's military academy, he knew that he had made a mistake. On the surface, there was much to appeal to the idealistic youth. "Part barracks, part college, part seminary," St.-Cyr as it then existed—it was senselessly flattened by the American Army Air Corps in 1944 and subsequently rebuilt at Coëtquidan in Brittany—oozed tradition. Originally founded in 1686 as a convent school, its ancient corridors were covered with marble plaques bearing the names of men who had died for France in almost every corner of the globe. Each year's class adopted the name of a great French victory—Austerlitz, Jena, Wagram.

Lyautey, however, found the atmosphere uncongenial. By 1873, a new spirit of determination was being kindled in France following her humiliating defeat in the Franco-Prussian War of 1870–71. The army was to be reorganized and expanded. Reforming generals like Louis Trochu and Jules Lewal, in a series of widely read books and articles, had sketched the blueprint for what was to be, in effect, a revolution in France's military organization. Patriotic conscripts would replace the long-serving regulars of Louis-Napoléon's legions. The French army would become more than a military force, it would be a "school of the nation," tearing young men away from their provincial roots and infusing them with a spirit of patriotism and a sense of belonging to a national community. This would require a new type of officer, more intelligent, better educated than had been the case in what was already being referred to as the "old" army. Henceforth, the officer would be a teacher as well as a leader. It was a role that Lyautey longed to play.

At St.-Cyr, however, things went on much as before. Where was the spirit of sacrifice, the enthusiasm for reform, the all-pervasive patriotism, of which everyone talked? The Left charged that this resistance to the winds of change sprang from the fact that St.-Cyr was an unreformed royalist fraternity whose members opposed the military reforms championed by Léon Gambetta and his republicans. This was an exaggeration. The corps of cadets was at the time dedicated to nothing more sinister than perpetuating its distinctive forms of juvenile delinquency.

St.-Cyr cadets had always been noted for their high spirits. However, a combination of strict and often senseless discipline and monotonous, outdated instruction was sufficient to push them to mutiny. In 1836, eight cadets had seized the school's powder magazine and withstood a siege of several hours before they were forced to surrender. This incident prompted the passage of a law which permitted the army to court-martial a cadet and force him to serve five years in the ranks as a private, a severe penalty indeed in an age when barracks conditions were primitive and soldiers recruited from among those too poor to buy a substitute. Four years later, the full rigor of the law fell upon forty cadets—almost one-third of the school's population—following a riot at the college. Nor did the political upheavals of 1848 leave St.-Cyr untouched: seventy cadets were broken to the ranks in that year.

By the time Lyautey arrived at St.-Cyr, such spectacular gestures were a thing of the past. But a spirit of sullen insolence persisted. Discipline in the classroom was fragile. Civilian instructors especially bore the brunt of disorders, which frequently forced them to abandon their lessons. When an extra measure of drill was ordered as a punishment, cadets replied with a "silent drill," going through the motions but refusing to stamp their feet and slap their weapons as regulations required. First-year cadets were mercilessly harassed by their seniors: endless kit inspections, physical exercises, hazing, six uniform changes a day, which included the ritualistic changing of gloves—white for class or visits, yellow for riding, blue (cotton) for exercises. Lyautey was even forced to polish the soles of his boots.

Sunday, blessed Sunday, offered the only break in this "ceaseless round of disaster, punishment and chivying." The cadets, drawn up under a leaden sky in their plumed shakos, blue uniforms with red epaulettes and swords, were inspected and then jostled into the train for Paris. Once at the Gare des Invalides, they dispersed, the fortunate ones to spend an uneventful but comfortable day with family or friends, the rest condemned to wander somewhat self-consciously from café to café.

The scene at the Gare Montparnasse around eleven o'clock on Sunday evening could be quite spectacular. Hundreds of cadets, their uniforms askew, wandered back in small groups, clutching each other for support, singing, shouting or noisily being sick in a corner. Here, a cadet is boasting to a handful of attentive listeners about his visit to a well-known brothel; companies often organized lotteries, the prize being a purse large enough to pay for an evening with a fashionable Parisian demimondaine. There, a swordfight which began on the quai is adjourned to the train as the carriages groan into motion; the college commandant regularly received bills from the railway company for damage caused by sword thrusts to upholstered parts of the carriages. As the train rattled through the Bellevue station, the passengers shouted their traditional hurrahs for a certain Madame Dubois, who, under the Second Empire, had allegedly showered her favors on several generations of cadets.

For a man who was later to enjoy a reputation as a wit and raconteur, Lyautey appears to have been a singularly humorless youth. He was far too worried about his faith, his country, his destiny, to be amused by the "childish" antics of his classmates, much less to join in them. For Lyautey, St.-Cyr remained a "barbaric country," and the only memories he carried away were of dull courses, rote learning, petty regulations, tedious hours of drill led by semiliterate sergeants, schoolboy pranks and bullying, a French version of *Tom Brown's School Days*. That was St.-Cyr in the 1870s, and Lyautey loathed it.

He loathed it, but he finished high enough on his class list to win a coveted place at the staff college. When, in 1875, Lyautey reported to this prestigious address on the rue de Grenelle in Paris, he immediately recognized another unreformed institution. Discipline was, of course, less strict; he was a sublieutenant now. But classes at St.-Cyr had been monuments to the pedagogical art by comparison to the memorization of endless tables of organization which passed for instruction at the staff college. "Boredom," he wrote in his journal, "follows me everywhere." He realized too late what they were trying to make of him—a clerk.

The French army in the Third Republic was not the place for a man as churned by ambition as Lyautey. As the century progressed toward its close, the once-powerful desire for revenge spawned by the 1870 war faded. Gradually, painlessly, France made the psychological adjustment to the amputation of Alsace and part of Lorraine by Prussia as the price of peace. The Third Republic, in which scandals, venality and spinelessness characterized the political system, bumped along like a circus act, entertaining but unworthy of a great nation. In a peacetime army, there is nothing to do—drill, file reports, take stock. Bureaucracy is elevated into the imperium of martial virtues. Promotion slows to a snail's pace. For twenty years Lyautey knew "the anguish of destiny passing me by."

Then, suddenly, in 1894, everything changed. Lyautey was ordered to Hanoi. It was not a promotion; it was a punishment. What had he done to deserve exile?

Lyautey's transfer has been blamed on a controversial article, "The Social Role of the Officer," which he had written in 1891 for the prestigious *Revue des Deux Mondes*. But this was not the sole or even principal reason for his being sent abroad. The simple truth was that Lyautey and the French army were not compatible.

In 1887 he had been named to command a squadron of cavalry at

St.-Germain, a fashionable garrison on the Seine just west of Paris, and in the intervening years his irrepressible urge for self-advertisement had brought him to the notice of his superiors. Since 1873, France had had an army raised by universal conscription. But barracks conditions for the citizen soldiers remained essentially those of the prewar professional army. This, as far as Lyautey was concerned, was a national scandal, and he intended to draw attention to it.

Lyautey was not a man of great originality, but rather one of passions and enthusiasms. He could see that garrison life at St.-Germain was one of exquisite tediousness. How better to relieve the boredom than to revive a movement begun by a Social Catholic named Albert de Mun in the 1870s but which had since sputtered out. While most soldiers were condemned to wander the streets in the evenings, Lyautey saw to it that his troopers had a club, administered by their own committee, with tables, notepaper, books and a billiard table. They also had a refectory, still quite rare in an army where soldiers often ate sitting on their beds, four men to a pot, while the corporal counted cadence to ensure that spoons were not dipped out of turn.

Of course, Lyautey had not invented libraries, game rooms and refectories for soldiers. On the contrary, they were to be found in more than one regiment. Their absence elsewhere was as much the fault of the government, which refused to provide the funds, as of the officers who took little trouble to organize off-hours activities for their men. Perhaps they realized, as Lyautey may not have, that their soldiers simply preferred the café to a game room where the adjutant could always pinch them for some unpleasant duty. In any case, having organized his model squadron, Lyautey brought all his friends to see it—and what friends! Soon after his arrival at St.-Germain, Lyautey had been introduced by an old family acquaintance into a circle of writers led by Eugène Melchior de Vogüé. It included such young lights as Marcel Proust, Henri de Régnier and Ernest Lavisse. Lyautey seemed an incongruous figure at their gatherings and dinners: a soldier who trod the rarefied heights of the Parisian literary world, a staunch royalist in a den of equally dedicated republicans, a devout Catholic in a ghetto of secular thought. He was well enough read to hold his own in discussion, and utterly charming, which reconciled his hostesses to the presence of a soldier in their salons. But if his literacy and charm were his calling cards, his antimilitarism was the open door. Lyautey, so traditional and conservative in many ways, was, as far as his own profession was concerned, a heretic. A soldier who held such views must be encouraged, and he was: his friends visited his experimental squadron and brought their political acquaintances with them, not conservatives like Albert de Mun, but ambitious left-wing republican politicians like Jules Charles-Roux and Paul Deschannel. The results were quite predictable: Lyautey became known as the "socialist captain," a sobriquet hardly calculated to endear him to his superiors.

The high command might have ignored Lyautey, but "The Social Role of the Officer" made that quite impossible. De Vogüé encouraged Lyautey to put his views into print. When, in 1891, his article appeared in the *Revue des Deux Mondes*, it could only be a matter of time before the army took its revenge.

"The Social Role of the Officer" restated the reformist goals of the 1870s. Like Albert de Mun, Lyautey argued that the forces had a social as well as a military function. The army which had risen phoenixlike from the ashes of defeat in 1870 had nominally been refounded as a school of patriotism and national unity whose task it was to heal the nation's social divisions. But these goals had been sacrificed to the professional values of the officer corps. "The officer does not know his men, he is not interested in them," Lyautey wrote. "The best officers aim for the War College, a staff assignment, that is, a life of office work, a clerk's job, which each year siphons off a greater part of the army's elite. Increasingly, troop command . . . is seen as temporary, an irksome task. . . ." The morale of the mass of regimental officers had been sapped by the spectacle of the lion's share of promotion and decorations going to an elite of deskbound staff men. Men without a future were men without motivation, buried in the trivia of garrison life and unknown to the soldiers whom they might one day lead into battle. Low morale meant poor preparation and a lack of cohesion, so important for a fighting unit.

What Lyautey said was that the French army had failed to adapt to national service. What he meant was that the officer had abandoned the conscript to the not too tender mercies of sergeants and corporals, by and large uneducated and ignorant men for whom the army offered an alternative to a life of rural poverty. It was they who, with the connivance of an aloof officer corps, gave national service a bad name, who transformed a patriotic duty into a nightmare of injustice, brutality and neglect, who alienated French youth and who were blowing hard on the embers of antimilitarism, which, if they burst into flame, might one day compromise the security of the fatherland.

This summed up Lyautey's attitude to military life as it was lived in

France: an absurd routine where the things of least consequence—the shine on a floor or the alignment of a pair of boots—were held to be items of Himalayan importance. Lyautey believed that the problem stemmed in part from the social recruitment of the officer corps. His colleagues were not aristocrats, whatever the army's critics on the left might claim (would that they were!). On the contrary, they were desperately middle class: cautious, myopic and poor. The army was too much like school, its officers frozen in attitudes of adolescence, "of schoolboy and master like those of all subordinates with senior officers in France."

"The Social Role of the Officer" firmly established Lyautey as one of the French army's renegade officers, as Pétain and de Gaulle were later to be. Disgrace, however, was not immediate. In 1893, Lyautey was promoted to major and given a plum assignment as chief of staff of the Seventh Cavalry Division at Meaux, near Paris. In August 1894, however, the blow fell. In the midst of maneuvers in Brie, a telegram directed Lyautey to report to Tonkin. He suddenly learned that the chief of the general staff, General Le Mouton de Boisdeffre, acting on complaints from Lyautey's superiors, had ordered a "change of air."

He might have resisted the order by invoking, among other things, the fragile state of his health. But he did not. To Madame de Guerle, the wife of a family friend and his patron in Paris, he wrote that he had tired of the dilettantism of the Paris salons and the grinding monotony of garrison life: "You know how highly I value action," he wrote to her. However, another, more important reason probably influenced his decision to leave France: Louise Baignières.

Louise was the sister of Lyautey's friend, the artist Paul Baignières. Intelligent, emotional, eleven years Lyautey's junior, she fell immediately and irrevocably in love with him. "It is time you married," his friends told him. "Louise is a good match," Madame de Guerle insisted. Louise's parents expected Major Lyautey to declare his intentions. Pressure mounted. When Hanoi beckoned, Lyautey bolted. Why? "I felt everything was absurd," he wrote to her. He shrank in horror from marriage, which, he claimed, destroyed any true intimacy. He proposed that their friendship remain platonic, which it did. They continued to correspond until his death.

All this had happened almost ten years before. Since then, Lyautey had been part of France's other army, the colonial army, whose great doings were regarded with a total lack of interest, not to say disdain, by metropolitan officers. He had helped General Gallieni to free Tonkin from the bands of Chinese pirates that terrorized the north. When Gallieni was dispatched to subdue the rebellious Hovas in Madagascar, he took Lyautey as his chief lieutenant, placed one-third of the island under his command and gave him a free hand to quell the rebellion led by Rabezavana, a former royal governor. This had proved a turning point in Lyautey's life, if not in his career. At last, he had found an outlet for his nearly boundless energy and a man upon whom he could fix his adulation: Gallieni replaced Albert de Mun, the hero of his youth.

But there was another reason why Lyautey was exiled abroad, why, ten years later, General O'Connor protested formally when he heard that Lyautey was to take command at Ain Sefra: He was a homosexual. He made no attempt to disguise it. It was well known in later years that he kept one or two catamites on his large staff, which was more like a court than a military entourage. But Lyautey never took his homosexual affairs seriously. He was too much the professional. If he favored young sublieutenants in bed, he promoted them strictly on the basis of their military merits.

Yet Lyautey could not wear his homosexuality comfortably. In France, homosexuality was condemned both by the Church and by moralists. Nor did it count among those peccadilloes that French society—often so radical in its politics but so conformist in its social attitudes—was prepared to tolerate, like keeping a mistress. Male brothels in Paris offered a whole range of pleasures, from beatings to sticking pins into rats. While there is certainly no evidence that Lyautey ever resorted to one of these establishments (as did, for instance, Proust), they did serve to deepen the association in the public mind between homosexuality and perversion. At best, homosexuality was regarded as an incurable illness. Later, in the interwar years, André Gide attempted to change the image of homosexuality from one of deviation to that of "Greek love." But this was almost a half-century away. In the 1890s, European homosexuals, outcasts in their own lands, might find more tolerance, and a more accessible selection of young boys, in North Africa.

It was Lyautey's attitudes, rather than his career, that seem to have been most deeply affected by his homosexuality. His sexual preferences certainly offended most of his brother officers, which is one of the reasons why he sought the company of writers, artists and left-of-center politicians with whom he shared relatively few political views. It also helps to explain why, after 1894, he was so enthusiastic about colonial service. Unlike British

colonial society, which did its best to impose a straitjacket of social conformity on its members, the French Empire collected misfits and restive characters, those who were impatient with the norms and values of the homeland.
It is perhaps ironic that this deeply conservative and even snobbish man felt
far more at home in this world of rebels and social castoffs than in that of the
provincial aristocrats and soldiers into which he had been born and educated. Lyautey was a romantic, a man of protest in constant revolt against
the mediocrity of life and the restraints of society. His homosexuality confirmed him in his attitudes, for it condemned him to be a perpetual outcast, a
man on the margins of many worlds but belonging to none. In a real sense,
this was also his strength: part of his originality sprang from the fact that he
stood personally on both sides of so many frontiers.

Lyautey's appointment to Ain Sefra was the beginning of his involvement,
indeed his immersion, in Morocco. It was to last twenty-three years. At
forty-nine years of age, his apprenticeship was finally over. He was no longer
someone's subordinate, he was no longer commanded. He was now the
master and he reveled in it: the trembling subalterns, the adulation he
believed he saw on the faces of the legionnaires jostling to tell him that they
had served with him at Mirken, Ke Toung or some other steamy Indochinese
outpost, the religious silence observed by everyone during his afternoon
siestas "of the sort that one finds only in countries where there are still
chiefs."

This was his chance and he was determined that no one, least of all
General O'Connor, would impede him, even if it meant breaking the rules.
Jonnart smoothed his path: Ain Sefra was declared an autonomous military
region. Lyautey became Jonnart's proconsul in the desert with the right to
correspond directly with the governor general, to command the artillery,
engineers and transportation troops in his subdivision, which, for some
extraordinary reason, were under O'Connor's control, and to launch operations without first obtaining Oran's consent. He was also allocated private
funds, supplemented by donations from colonialists at home, always useful
for bribing chiefs or obtaining information. (The arrangement left O'Connor
apoplectic with rage, but he was soon recalled to France.)

Eight years under Gallieni had transformed Lyautey into a true "colonial." From the moment he boarded the boat for Hanoi, he felt as if a great
weight had been lifted from his shoulders. How far away Paris seemed—
the dinners at Durand's, the evenings spent in the Café de Paris discussing the
latest play, the endless hours worrying about the cut of one's trousers or

the color of one's shoes. It was all too absurd! Moving from the minutiae and the parochial concerns of garrison life in France to the giant tasks of empire-building was like stepping from a small room into the open air: "What a pity not to have come here ten years earlier," he wrote to his sister from Tonkin. The atmosphere of bureaucratic caution, the fear of putting a foot wrong, the tediously slow climb up the promotion ladder which ruled in the metropolitan army, had no place abroad. His new colleagues were men with fire in their bellies. More, they were gamblers, men playing double-or-nothing with their lives and even, more daringly, with their careers. "I have assumed an enormous responsibility," Lyautey wrote to Gallieni, a month after taking command at Ain Sefra, "and I am condemned to succeed or break my neck."

When, in 1902, he had been recalled from Madagascar to command the Fourteenth Hussars at Alençon, he felt poleaxed. His active service abroad was dismissed as a few "nigger bullets" by his new commander, a man who had never heard a shot fired in anger. What's more, he was cautioned to "lie low." For this was the France of the Dreyfus affair, of Radical Prime Minister Emile Combes and his war minister, General Louis André, the "Red Donkey" who had vowed to eliminate from the army any officer who was not staunchly republican. And a republican Lyautey was not. Already, Masonic lodges in garrison towns were collecting information on the political and religious opinions of officers and their wives, information that was carefully catalogued in the War Ministry by General Percin, André's chief of staff. Lyautey contemplated retirement, but he was not a rich man; the bleak prospect of a fifth-floor coldwater flat kept him on the army payroll. For the moment he must rest content with his "prison" of narrow paved streets and squat gray houses, the endless emerald hedgerows and monotonous drizzle of the Basse Normandie. He maintained an uncharacteristic silence and concentrated on the "little things, the straps of spurs, rifle belts and so on. . . ." Then came the incredible stroke of luck.

Or so it seemed. For Lyautey's call to Algeria was more than a stroke of luck. The truth of the matter was that for the past few years he had been carefully groomed for the task. Gallieni had recognized in Lyautey an able public-relations man who would help gain support in France for colonial expansion. When the future hero of the taxis of the Marne returned to Paris in 1899 to secure funds for the development of Madagascar, he had brought Lyautey with him. Together they canvassed the ministries and salons, knocked on the doors of influential politicians, men such as Eugène Etienne, the deputy for Oran and leader of the powerful colonial group in the Chamber of Deputies. Gallieni would soon outlive his usefulness in the colonies and Lyautey would be his successor for the colonialists' next objective— Morocco.

To understand why Lyautey, a still relatively obscure colonel of cavalry, was selected to spearhead the French takeover of Morocco, one must first understand the nature of colonialism in France. This has been obscured by none other than Lenin, who claimed that colonialism represented the highest stage of capitalism, the search of a burgeoning, expansionist Europe for markets and raw materials. But for France, colonialism was never a jamboree of national muscle-flexing. Rather, it was a minority movement. It had to be, for colonial expansion was unpopular in France: businessmen saw Africa as a bad investment, and few emigrants could be scraped together to people the vast acres of conquered land. French expansion overseas was the work of a few patriotic men—a handful of soldiers, politicians and intellectuals—who believed that the acquisition of a colonial empire was the only way for France to regain the prestige lost in the defeat of 1870. Theirs was a minority view. Many patriots, such as Clemenceau, argued that by expanding abroad France was directing her strength away from the vital European theater. Why pick a quarrel with England over some inconsequential piece of property? Germany, *voilà l'ennemi!* The vast majority of Frenchmen, moreover, were completely indifferent to colonial conquests. Thus, no great economic forces pushed France into Africa and Indochina, only the ambitions of a group of colonial officers. Colonialism in France became like a very powerful car with quite inadequate brakes.

All this meant that Lyautey's appointment had not been a fluke. He was the choice of Gallieni and Etienne of Oran. General André, the Red Donkey, posed no problems. Although he detested Lyautey's political views, the evangelical fervor of his first years as war minister had mellowed. He had set his sights on a senate seat (which he was never to get), and this newly acquired political ambition had forced him to trade in the parliamentary marketplace rather than bully and steal. Etienne's "colonial group" counted 102 deputies in 1903. Etienne, therefore, could have what he wanted—damn the objections of such as General O'Connor.

Jonnart had been persuaded in an altogether more spectacular manner.

Seen from a distance, the oasis of Figuig appeared inviting: a green carpet of palm trees which straddles the Zousfana for four miles at a point where a flat, dusty plain meets the 2,200-foot massif of Beni Smir. Looking at a map, one would think that Figuig was a town. But it is not. It is more like a suburb. The oasis is studded with mud *ksar* whose high towers and crenellated walls stand guard over lush gardens watered by an intricate network of irrigation channels. But at the turn of the twentieth century its tranquillity was deceptive. Like most trans-Atlas oases, Figuig was in a perpetual state of civil war. It is no accident that a *ksar* resembles a fortress. Feuding over crops or water rights was a way of life and a ksarian's home was, quite literally, his castle.

When, in 1900, the French installed a camp at Beni Ounif, a few miles east of Figuig, the feuding was occasionally suspended long enough for the inhabitants to mount attacks on the French convoys that lumbered down the Zousfana. It proved a profitable pastime: by April 1903, the French had lost fifty men to raiders out of Figuig, not to mention the numerous animals and supplies that disappeared beneath the date palms. Etienne protested vigorously to the government on several occasions, but received little satisfaction. Paris, fearful that any action on Moroccan territory would evoke a testy response from Britain, Germany and Spain, dithered, complained to the makhzan and kept O'Connor firmly on the leash. The makhzan, for its part, sent a "garrison" to control Figuig: a miserable collection of old men and boys who were soon terrorized by the inhabitants into parting with their rifles. By the summer of 1902, most of them had melted back across the Atlas.

This was the situation when the new governor general arrived at Beni Ounif on his inspection of the frontier. On May 31, 1903, General O'Connor led Jonnart to a point about six hundred yards from the *ksar* of Zenaga, which stood on the extreme southwest salient of the oasis. If the general believed this to be a safe vantage point from which to view Figuig, he was mistaken. As the official party turned to ride away, they were fired upon from the *ksar*. The legionnaires of the escort returned the fire, but were reluctant to charge into the oasis, whose walls and gardens might become a death trap for so small a number. Besides, Paris had forbidden O'Connor to enter Morocco. The assailants for their part refused to be drawn into an open contest with the French, contenting themselves with badly aimed shots from the safety of their garden walls. When, after an hour of this, the legionnaires began to withdraw toward Beni Ounif, an estimated five to six hundred Moroccans fell howling on their heels. The combat that followed was described by one newspaper as "almost hand to hand." The French limped into Beni Ounif four hours later with one dead and several wounded. Etienne declared that Jonnart's escape had been "miraculous." The reaction on the right was easy to predict: the "Figuig ambush" was a humiliation; the army must retaliate. "At last we have decided to act," the right-wing *Petit Journal* declared prematurely. The alternative, it maintained, was apocalyptic: "Now we must finish this once and for all, or resign ourselves to the loss of our North African empire."

When, a few weeks after the "Figuig ambush," Jonnart was introduced to Lyautey at a dinner party given by Jules Charles-Roux, the ex-deputy for Marseilles, he knew that he had found his man. Lyautey's views on the tactics to be employed in the South Oranais, the "Gallieni method" as he called it, were of course interesting. Jonnart was on the lookout for a skilled bandit catcher. But the basic problem was greater still. Algeria would never be secure until Morocco fell under French control. France had practiced the politics of hesitation and timidity in the desert, which had simply served to embolden the Moroccans. Even when on June 8 General O'Connor had returned with a 75-millimeter cannon to punish Figuig (a minaret and a few buildings were collapsed as the inhabitants scurried like rats over the plain, dragging whatever could be hastily packed on the backs of mules and camels), Foreign Minister Delcassé protested that the makhzan and not France should discipline the troublesome oasis. Figuig remained unoccupied. The embarrassing reverses at Taghit and El Moungar made some kind of action urgent. Yet given the political situation in Europe and the balance of forces within the French government itself, a balance not favorable to the colonialists, the new commander must be energetic but discreet. Lyautey was a confirmed colonial, eager to extend French control into Morocco yet subtle enough to realize what was at stake. He also had important contacts in the political and literary worlds which might prove useful. Jonnart would undertake his education, teach him how to handle obtrusive ministers and parry objections from meddlesome diplomats in the Quai d'Orsay obsessed with their absurd policy of "peaceful penetration."

From his rather functional but comfortable headquarters at Ain Sefra, Lyautey could look out past the last scrawny poplars, the ubiquitous hallmarks of French occupation, toward "the vast monotony of the high plateau." The South Oranais did not offer an invasion route into Morocco.

Oudjda farther north would provide that. Lyautey's task for the time being was to pacify the south, to nibble away at Moroccan territory so that when Oudjda was occupied, his southern flank would be protected. He contemplated the future: Morocco would not be conquered, he wrote to his friend Max Leclerc, it would be . . . how should he put it . . . "digested."

CHAPTER VII

THE ROGUI

The news of the killing in Fez probably reached the Sultan's European guests as they sat in the palace gardens. It was October, perhaps the best month in Morocco, when the heat of the summer has worn off but the winter rains have not yet begun. The sun shines, the sky is a deep blue, and the temperature is perfect for tennis. But they no longer felt like tennis. This news was too serious. The Sultan must do something, they told each other; "outrageous . . . can't be allowed to get away with it . . . make it a test case." When Abd el-Aziz brought his bicycle to a momentary halt, they told him, respectfully but firmly, what was expected of him.

It is so easy to become lost in Fez. Today, there are no end of boys who press their services as guides on the unwilling visitor, follow at a distance despite his curt refusal and confident waving of the *Guide Bleu*, waiting for the moment, and it inevitably comes, when the confused and disorientated traveler turns to him and asks to be led back to the Bou Djeloud. In 1902, however, the boys whom the traveler encountered crowded around to chant, spit and perhaps throw stones.

When he set out on his walk, David Cooper, a young English missionary on a visit in Fez, must have tried as so many do to remember turnings, landmarks, to keep his sense of direction. But walking in Fez is an ordeal. An extreme sense of unease brought on by the noise, filth and claustrophobia has constantly to be controlled. Gradually, imperceptibly, the senses are anesthetized. Soon, one ceases to count turnings, to remember a fountain or a piece of latticework, but shuffles along with the general movement. This is probably why David Cooper did not notice the wooden beam suspended from the end of two lengths of heavy iron chain about ten feet above the street, which announced the entrance to the precincts of the Mosque of Moulai Idris, the most sacred shrine in Morocco.

Or perhaps he saw it and did not realize its significance. What next occurred is not difficult to imagine. First came the angry shouts; it took an instant to realize that they were directed at him. He was confused. Better not stop. He took a few more steps forward. The crowd swelled around him:

ghostly figures, agitated, their bronzed faces distorted in outrage. A stone struck his shoulder. A second thumped painfully into his back. He turned to flee, but where? His mind could only take in fragments of what was happening around him—eyes, fists, mouths full of jagged teeth. Then, a tribesman in a coarse brown jellaba stepped from the crowd. He seemed calmer than the rest as he walked toward the Englishman at bay. It was the calmness of determination. The crowd seemed to freeze as they realized what was about to happen. He placed the barrel of his rifle on Cooper's chest and pulled the trigger.

The killing of an unknown Protestant missionary in the streets of Fez by a religious fanatic may be regarded as an odd incident upon which to decide the fate of a regime. But that is what it did. The Europeans at the palace were upset by the news of Cooper's death. That was quite understandable. Of course, it probably never occurred to most of them that their own presence in the Sultan's entourage was to a degree responsible for the anti-European mood beginning to grip the city. For them, it was a clear-cut case of murder. Christians were no longer safe on the streets. It was perfectly intolerable. For Moroccans, however, the story which emerged of Cooper's death was not clear-cut at all.

Murder was common enough in Morocco. But it was not committed casually. In the hills especially, murder was a ritual. Elaborate rules set out not only the conditions in which it might be permissible, but also determined the manner in which it was to be punished. One could kill in revenge. But one must never kill a guest with whom one had broken bread. Poor Jews were fair game; rich Jews were likely to fall under the protection of a caid or other influential person. And, of course, murder was justified in the name of religion. Cooper, an infidel, had defiled the shrine of Moulai Idris. The Fassis would probably have bombarded poor Cooper with stones and left it at that. But tribesmen lived by the gun.

If only Abd el-Aziz had been less inexperienced, or had received better advice, he might have been able to handle this delicate situation more adroitly. To his European friends, the medina was a closed book. He should have handed them a body, any body, and told them that justice had been done. It would not have been the first time, nor the last, that a makhzan official had satisfied a European claim with the corpse of an alleged offender. What made the Sultan's position even more difficult was that the murderer refused to leave the mosque, and the Mosque of Moulai Idris was a sanctuary that no sultan with a sense of self-preservation would dare violate.

Lengthy consultations ensued, and it was finally agreed that the tribesman would leave the mosque to present his case before the Sultan. When he was led into the vaultlike hall of the palace in which the hearing was to take place, he was accompanied by the chief *muqaddam*, or administrator, of Moulai Idris, and wore around his neck a school slate, a holy relic purporting to have been the property of the Saint, upon which were written verses from the Koran. Both circumstances served to indicate that, although no longer within the precincts of the shrine, he fell nonetheless under its protection.

The Sultan sat on a chair. Around him, cross-legged on the floor, sat his *majlis*, or council. The tribesman fell on the floor before Abd el-Aziz and began to kiss his feet. Aziz signaled to two servants to lift the man up. As they did so, Aziz took the sacred slate from the tribesman's neck and kissed it. The defendant then began to state his case in a high-pitched wail. It was a simple defense—the Christian had defiled the sanctuary—but he added a clinching argument: "Moulai Idris himself told me to kill him!" This made the Sultan angry: "Well, then," he shouted, "I too! Moulai Idris has just told me to kill you! Withdraw!" The tribesman was dragged into the courtyard and—as the Sultan, Walter Harris, Hastings, a representative of the British Minister, the *majlis* and the *muqaddam* looked on—was executed. The Sultan ordered that two hundred duros—about $200, or £40—be given to the shrine, and left.

Two hundred duros! With this, Abd el-Aziz hoped to compensate the *muqaddam* for the violation of the most revered sanctuary in Morocco, compensate the *ulama* for this direct challenge to the supremacy of Islam and thus to their position in the state, compensate the nation for what they saw as the just killing of an infidel who had violated the sacred shrine. It was more than tactless; it was a sacrilege. For this error, Abd el-Aziz would pay dearly. Already the whispers were running through the medina: "This is not a son of Moulai Hassan who leads us, but the son of Maclean. He is an English soldier." Aziz had played into his enemy's hands.

One has only to look at a map to appreciate Taza's strategic importance. The gap to which the town gives its name offers the only corridor through the chain of mountains which otherwise stretches unbroken from Tétouan on the Mediterranean to Agadir on the Atlantic. The floor of the valley is only a mile or two wide. To the north and south the mountains rise gradually in a series of treeless ridges. To the east, the funnel opens out onto a dry steppe, with Algeria beyond.

Taza itself is beautifully situated, as Ali Bey discovered in the early nineteenth century: "It is surrounded by ancient walls, and the minaret of the mosque rises out of them like an obelisk. The rock is at some places very steep, and covered with fine orchards; its lower part is surrounded with gardens; at one side with a falling river, and the other with several brooks forming cascades. A half-decayed bridge increases the interest of the picture."

Before the days when the steamer offered a more comfortable, rapid and less expensive way to reach Mecca, the track—which snaked east from Fez over low baked hills before it joined the Wadi Inaouane and followed it to Taza—swarmed with pilgrims. Taza's position beside the main highway that tied Morocco to the rest of North Africa had made it one of the country's most prosperous towns, and rumors of its wealth lingered into the twentieth century. But they were only rumors. The enormous flocks of goats and cattle, the tents which covered the valley floor in front of the town which Ali Bey had seen a century earlier, were a distant memory. Taza lay like a town marooned, bypassed by trade which now flowed directly from Europe into Morocco's ports. The town itself was dilapidated and many of its houses abandoned.

The Cooper affair was to lead directly to a revival of Taza's strategic fortunes, if not of its economic ones. Until news of the Sultan's blunder reached Taza, the career of Djilali ben Driss, or Bou Hamara, "the man with the she-ass," as he called himself, had been a modest one. Born near Ouezzane, he had joined the *tolba mohendisin*, the corps of engineers set up by Moulai Hassan to modernize the country. His literacy and ambition had taken him into the secretariat of the Khalifa of Fez. While in this important position, however, he demonstrated a talent for forgery which landed him in jail. When he was finally released on the ascension of Abd el-Aziz, he left Morocco to tour Algeria and Tunisia, there to acquire skills as a mimic and magician with which he hoped to launch himself in the "saint business." He returned to Morocco in 1902 and began to lay the foundations for his *zaouia* among the gullible Ghiata tribesmen, Berbers whose mud douars crowned the ridges to the south of Taza. His tricks were as dishonest as they were simple: One of his followers would be sent to a house to ask for mint for tea. If this request was refused, the house "mysteriously" caught fire in the night.

Quite naturally, the flames were attributed to the intervention of Allah and proved the sanctity of Bou Hamara.

But it was the Cooper affair that transformed Bou Hamara from a minor magician into a pretender to the throne of Morocco. Bou Hamara toured the *jemaa*, or tribal councils, to announce, after swearing them to strict secrecy, that he was in reality Moulai Mohammed, the son of Moulai Hassan, whom they had all thought dead. Ba Ahmed had locked him away at Meknes, Bou Hamara told the wide-eyed Ghiatas. He showed them the traces of the shackles, real enough, which still marked his wrists and ankles. His diseased left eye was also offered as proof of his identity, as Moulai Mohammed was known to have possessed but one good eye. On the death of Ba Ahmed, his story went, el Menebbhi had convinced Abd el-Aziz that Moulai Mohammed was at the head of a coordinated plot to overthrow him with the aid of an uprising in the Sus. Upon receiving the order to execute his prisoner, the Pasha of Meknes instead gave him two hundred napoleons and told him to flee. An unfortunate substitute was found to occupy his grave. Now, with the help of his astonished listeners, he was ready to reclaim the throne which had fallen into the hands of infidels and false Moslems. As proof of his support as well as of his identity, he produced letters written by tribal chiefs in the South to Moulai Mohammed promising to march with him to Fez. The tribesmen—unable to read, much less detect an obvious forgery—accepted his evidence. News of the Cooper affair added weight to his argument by casting further doubt on the legitimacy of Abd el-Aziz. It transformed his small following into a mass, if localized, movement with its capital at Taza.

Bou Hamara was to plague the makhzan for the next seven years. The French journalist Jean du Taillis, who visited Bou Hamara at his camp in the Rif in 1905, found "a man in the prime of life [he was forty-one], swarthy, but with regular features and a face pleasantly framed by a short, black beard. The overall effect of his face is friendly and very noble." His pretensions to the sultanate had led him to create a rival makhzan in form, if not in power: he sat on a wooden chair, his feet propped on a leather cushion beneath a tent open on three sides and lined with red-and-green cloth. Several men squatted before him on a large carpet while around him stood several hundred soldiers splendidly dressed in European-style blue-and-red uniforms with gold braid on the collars and sleeves, and armed with an assorted, but modern, collection of rifles. Blue silk flags flapped everywhere, eight drummers and twelve trumpeters kept up a constant noise, and a bronze cannon fired at suitable intervals "for reasons of ceremony." Each time it thundered, this counterfeit makhzan would immediately prostrate themselves crying: *"Allah i barek amar Sidi!"* ("God bless the life of our Lord!").

Du Taillis also noted several indications that Bou Hamara was not a man to be trifled with: a wall near the camp was decorated with at least fifty human heads, trophies from a recent *razzia* against tribes who refused to recognize his authority. He was also invited to witness the fate of a deserter, Achmet, a man of about thirty, who was dressed in two thick woollen jellabas soaked in petrol and, with a match, transformed into "a horrible brazier."

The pretender, calling himself the Rogui (meaning "The Pretender"), lived in a style which the impoverished Ghiatas, who formed the mainstay of his support, could not possibly have subsidized. His soldiers were much better dressed and armed than the ragamuffins who made up Abd el-Aziz's army. For the answer to the source of his wealth, one needed to look no further than his chief adviser, a Parisian adventurer named Gabriel Delbrel. Through Delbrel, Bou Hamara received subsidies from Oran businessmen eager to finance the chaos which they believed would hasten the French occupation of Morocco. Spanish businessmen also provided funds in hopes of securing access to the minerals in the area of the Rif which Bou Hamara controlled. In the long run, the Pretender's association with the "Nazarenes," the same crime with which he charged Abd el-Aziz, would seriously under-cut his support and lead to his downfall. But that was in the future. For the moment, he concentrated on solidifying his base in the mountains by forcing tribe after tribe to submit and, drawing upon his talents as a forger, adding new verses to the Koran which proved that a Mahdi would arise in Taza to "radiate the ardent fire" throughout Morocco. The *ulama* of Fez examined these verses and rejected them as sheer invention. But Bou Hamara was writing for the popular market.

Fez could hardly tolerate a pretender sixty miles from its doorstep. In October 1902, Abd el-Aziz dispatched letters to the chiefs of the Hayainas, close neighbors and old enemies of the Ghiatas, asking them to smash Bou Hamara. History does not record what happened when the two tribes met. Probably after desultory fighting, a "baroud of honor" fought to save face, the Hayainas, or several factions of them, threw in their lot with the Pretender. Whatever occurred that day, it was plain that Bou Hamara would have to be dealt with by the army. An expedition was prepared to march against Taza.

To Europeans, the power of Bou Hamara must have seemed modest indeed when compared to the forces available to Abd el-Aziz. Apart from a small palace guard, the Sultan could call upon the *jaysh*, a militia of Arab tribes settled strategically over the country who performed military service in lieu of taxes. Each tribe supplied a *sha*, a cavalry unit of five hundred men subdivided into companies of one hundred commanded by caids *al-mia*, roughly the equivalent of a captain, seconded by *muqaddams* (sergeants). However, while the *jaysh* were more or less adequate to police Morocco west of the Atlas, they had proved impotent against the French at Isly in 1844. After their complete collapse against the Spaniards in 1860, Moulai Hassan decided that he must have an infantry on the European model. Caids were called upon to assemble levies of recruits who were then organized into *tabors*, or battalions. Foreign officers, mainly English, were hired to train these *askar* in the rudiments of drill while selected Moroccans were dispersed among the various military schools of Europe to acquire a knowledge of modern warfare. In this way, Moulai Hassan was able to build up a force of 21,500 regular infantry. He also made a start on a modern artillery corps by purchasing cannon abroad. An Italian officer was hired to organize an arsenal at Fez.

By the standards of Moroccan warfare, an organized force of 21,500 men trained and equipped by Europeans should have been formidable. In practice, it was a shambles. To fill out the ranks of his *askar*, Abd el-Aziz ordered his caids each to supply a quota of recruits. These caids immediately called in the richest men and informed them that they were conscripted. They, of course, purchased their release. The caids would then proceed down the list of citizens in the order of their wealth until they arrived at those too poor to buy their way out. The only consolation that remained for these unfortunates was the knowledge that they would have ample opportunities to desert. Each caid then informed the makhzan that he was sending 500 men and claimed his bounty for each, when the true number was closer to 150, of whom 100 would desert before they reached the battlefield.

Men recruited in this way made poor soldiers. Captain Jules Erckmann of the French military mission complained that he was given only old men and boys to train, some of whom were actually blind. They were extremely reluctant to wear boots or to sight their rifles, preferring to fire from the hip. Desertion was rife: Caid Maclean reckoned on between thirty and forty desertions daily, more at harvest time. The only thing regular about an *askari*'s pay was its failure to arrive. Soldiers begged in the streets or, organized into armed gangs, operated as highwaymen. Discipline was nonexistent. Reginald Rankin described a military review that he witnessed in 1907:

> The Minister for War and the Army Council were squatted in a semi-circle in the middle of a grassy plain. Near them a brass band emitted the most heart-rending noises. Between the legs and the music stands of the bandsmen a madman, stark naked, was turning somersaults; on our approach, someone huddled him into a sort of yellow dressing-gown, in which he continued somersaulting. Past the War Minister the troops marched in fours, their brown legs twinkling merrily out of step, some with their rusty muskets at the trail, some at the slope, the privates conversing cheerfully together, the officers roaring unregarded orders. Up and down the column ran vendors of sweets, also soldiers, but without their arms, and Sergeant Balding (late of the 13th Hussars) sat by on his grey barb trying to look serious. The *mehalla* had nearly gone by, but the War Minister was still unsatiated; the head of the column, close on the city gate, was ordered to wheel round and repeat the performance. Whether from a desire to gratify the Minister as soon as possible, or in order to get back quicker to lunch I cannot say, but the leading tatterdemalions set such a slashing pace that soon the column was moving at a run, and round it came, hustling and jostling, until it caught up its tail, and then round again, like the millers in the toy, and round and round, until, I suppose, the delighted War Minister had performed the unrivalled feat of reviewing twenty thousand men with only four thousand on the ground.

The Moroccan army might have been forgiven its lack of presence on parade had this been compensated for by exemplary courage in battle. But displays of individual bravery were not the style of the *askar*. A *mehalla*, as a makhzan military expedition was called, resembled an army of late medieval Europe, half regular, half feudal levies. To keep this army in the field, Abd el-Aziz had to resort to loans from European bankers. War, therefore, must be made to pay for itself through pillage. For the Sultan, a *mehalla* became an Internal Revenue force sent to collect taxes in areas where his caids had no authority. For the soldiers, pillage substituted for pay, which was permanently in arrears. But as there were no rich cities to be sacked and little of value to be taken from the poor douars of the dissidents—except possibly sheep, which were a nuisance to herd and which were usually sold off at prices far below their market value—prisoners provided the most substantial booty. Sometimes hundreds of prisoners could be seen chained together by the neck, the living forced to support the weight of the dead and dying, trudging in the wake of the *mehalla*. Those who commanded no ransom were butchered and decapitated, their heads salted (a task which traditionally fell to Jews), and hung on the city gates while the crowd stood about making jokes about the "grimaces on the face of the enemy." Captured women were hawked from tent to tent on campaign, and if they found buyers at all, it was usually among the makhzan officials who accompanied these expeditions.

A *mehalla*'s methods of warfare also resembled those of medieval Europe, minus the chivalry. Deploying over a broad front, the army lumbered forward, sometimes covering only a few miles a day, "a barbarous mass . . . more to be feared by the peaceful peasants than by the enemy." By "eating up" the countryside like locusts, a *mehalla* sought to intimidate dissident tribesmen into submission without the bother of battle. When Lyautey first saw Abd el-Aziz's army in 1907, he thought it indistinguishable from a crowd traveling to the souq, an orderless mob of soldiers accompanied by their wives and children, merchants dashing among them selling bread, meat, fish, onions and spices, caids followed by their closely veiled harems riding on mules, flanked by eunuchs on horses, countless numbers of sheep and goats, while the rear was brought up by a cavalry of tribal levies or men who volunteered in the hope of loot, "all going fast or slow as they pleased."

A *mehalla* fought in this manner from necessity rather than from choice, for it was disadvantaged in many ways. It was incapable of maneuver. Its officers were as feckless and venal as its soldiers were cowardly. Their ignorance of the military arts made it impossible to institute a coordinated strategy. Those sent to train in Europe were seldom rewarded with responsible commands on their return. The *mehalla*'s armaments were usually inferior to those of the tribes it was meant to subdue. Moulai Hassan's great arms-buying spree had presented the nations of Europe with a God-sent dumping ground for their surplus obsolete weapons, whereas the tribes could purchase the latest contraband repeaters. His artillery park counted almost eighty guns, no two of which were alike. The steady flow of Spanish renegades who once had manned the Sultan's artillery had dried up. Abd el-Aziz was one of the few men in Morocco able to fire a modern gun. On the road to Marrakech, Aziz once challenged Menebbhi to a competition with a Creusot 75, deliberately placing the aim off center so that the war minister would miss the target, a large outcropping of rock, virtually at point-blank range: "What's this," Aziz cried, laughing. "You are my war minister and you don't know how to shoot!"

To describe in conventional military terms the campaign of the *mehalla* sent by Abd el-Aziz against Bou Hamara would be misleading. The Sultan refused to take Bou Hamara seriously: even after the Hayaina, the tribe upon which he counted for support, had defected to the Pretender, Abd el-Aziz was more concerned with the refusal of the Beni M'tir, a tribe occupying the hills southwest of Fez, to pay tribute than with the antics of the magician at Taza. He sent his brother, Moulai el-Kebir, at the head of 2,500 men to deal with Bou Hamara. Although it was a contemptuously small expedition under the circumstances, it met with some initial success. The *mehalla* crawled east from Fez to the Wadi Innaouen and Hayaina country. There, in a "battle" that lasted from November 5 to 8, it brought the Hayaina back into the sharifian camp and won from them a promise to march with the *mehalla* to Taza. It was a prudent step. Every good makhzan commander took the trouble to surround his sluglike army with a shell of tribesmen who could absorb the shock of any real fighting that might need to be done. Together, they moved very slowly toward Taza, stopping frequently, subsisting at the expense of the tribes through whose territory they passed. Then, the predictable happened. On December 6, as the *mehalla* camped within sight of Taza, the Hayaina fell upon their allies. The sharifian camp was thoroughly pillaged, and the *mehalla* so disorganized that it returned to Fez far faster than it had come.

The news of this reverse before Taza was brought to the Sultan on December 9 as he returned to Fez from his expedition against the Beni M'tir. Abd el-Aziz, angered by Bou Hamara's adoption of the parasol, the symbol of sharifian authority, displayed uncharacteristic energy in dealing with what he now recognized as a serious threat. Money flowed out of the treasury to buy support among the tribes near Taza. *Jaysh* levies arrived from the Haouz province in the south to add strength to a new expedition, twenty thousand strong, under the personal command of the minister of war, el Menebbhi.

The choice of el Menebbhi as commander in chief was a popular one among the Europeans. Young—he was barely thirty—and good-humored, he frequently organized hunting parties or fireworks displays in their honor. He was also remarkably handsome, or so thought the normally restrained Madame St.-René: "more handsome than ever on his horse, in his white veils, with his oblique eyes and his seductive smile which one could compare with the marvelous smile of the serpent under the apple tree." A cousin of el Glaoui, the Atlas lord whose power was waxing in Marrakech, el Menebbhi had served as the chamberlain Ba Ahmed's private secretary.

On the death of Ba Ahmed in 1900, el Menebbhi, aided perhaps by the fact that he and the young Sultan were almost the same age, was able to gain the confidence of Abd el-Aziz. In this way, he became briefly the most powerful man in the makhzan. He conspired to have the grand vizier el Moktar stripped of his wealth and exiled to Meknes, and his place taken by Si Feddoul Gharnit. Abd el-Aziz sent el Menebbhi on a mission to France in the summer of 1901. This absence almost ended his career, for his enemies prevailed upon the Sultan to replace him as minister of war. But he was able to outmaneuver them: he returned secretly to Morocco, gained entrance to the palace at night and threw himself at the feet of the Sultan, who promptly reinstated him. Although Europeans counted el Menebbhi among the makhzan's infinitesimal number of competent officials, his energies so far had gone into intriguing against his enemies. Now, the war minister's martial abilities would be tested.

The plan, if that is what it was, called for the *mehalla* to march toward Taza in five separate columns, each with its own commander. Menebbhi remained for the moment in Fez. But his absence proved disastrous. Already morale in the *mehalla* was not high, this being largely a consequence of the Sultan's diminished prestige. Since the Cooper affair, the troops' enemies had redoubled their taunts: "You are no longer true Moslems because you fight with the aid of Christians," and tagged them with the pejorative epithet of "Oulad C'ronel" in honor of "Colonel" Maclean. For this reason, Abd el-Aziz kept the army's European officers at court and forbade them to campaign with the men whom they had trained. Madani el Glaoui's tribal levies from the south were also showing a marked reluctance to fight for a compromised Sultan. Inevitably, the makhzan commanders, in the absence of el Menebbhi, began to quarrel among themselves.

Bou Hamara knew how to exploit his advantages. His men would be fighting for their lives: "We are not here to carry out a fantasia," he told them. Messengers each morning brought him letters of support from distant tribes, which he had written himself the night before, thus increasing the illusion of strength. He also recognized the advantages of attacking "chickens without a cock," especially at mealtime when the sentryless makhzan camp was preoccupied with filling its bellies. When, on the evening of December 22, 1902, his Ghiatas and Hayainas attacked, the *mehalla* dissolved into chaos. The *askar* began to fire on Glaoui's men from the Haouz, seize their horses and ride for Fez, leaving everything—sheep, weapons, a trunk full of duros, even the women—to the attackers.

As the remnants of the *mehalla* straggled into Fez, the city was on the verge of panic, expecting at any moment to see the advance elements of Bou Hamara's force appear on the horizon. Fassis began to lay in provisions to withstand a prolonged siege. Desperate to shore up his tottering throne, Abd el-Aziz resorted to the extraordinary step of transferring his brother Moulai Mohammed from Meknes, where he had in fact been imprisoned for eight years, to Fez for display at the Mosque of Moulai Idris as visible proof that the Rogui was an impostor. The Europeans completely lost their heads. St.-René Taillandier reversed his hitherto anti-Algerian stance and wired Delcassé to order a French attack on Bou Hamara's rear at Oudjda. The French and British foreign ministers hurriedly conferred and decided that they must limit their actions to protecting their nationals. The British stood by at Gibraltar and the French at Oran for orders to evacuate their citizens through Tangiers. For a week they waited with bated breath.

On January 4, 1903, news arrived that Bou Hamara had retired to Taza. Why had he not pressed his advantage? Most likely, he realized that his claims to the throne would never survive the scrutiny of the *ulama* of Fez. Without their blessing, no one could hope to rule Morocco. Better to remain with his illiterate Ghiatas than to venture among the sophisticated Fassis, who would quickly see through his masquerade.

Bou Hamara's retreat gave the makhzan a desperately needed breathing space. Menebbhi reorganized his *mehalla* while Abd el-Aziz purchased a following among the tribes near Fez. On January 29, it was Bou Hamara's turn to be taken by surprise, at his camp on the Wadi Innaouen. Menebbhi recaptured the cannon he had lost in December, but the Rogui himself eluded him. The state of the weather, as well as the state of his soldiers' morale, forced Menebbhi to spend the next month campaigning close to Fez. In early March, the *mehalla* returned to Fez with fifty prisoners and as many heads, which were hung on the Bab Mahrouq, but whether these belonged to the enemy or had been taken in frustration from a pacific douar was never established.

In the spring, the makhzan renewed preparations to retake Taza. With a seven-and-a-half-million-franc loan from Spain and Britain, Abd el-Aziz began in April to distribute arms among the Zemour, imprudently, for many deserted to their hills between Fez and Rabat as soon as they collected their

rifles. Under French pressure, the Sultan consented to allow Algerian Lieutenant Ben Sedira Abd Er Rahman, a member of the French military mission,
to accompany the *mehalla*. He was given a jellaba and quick lesson in the
use of a 75-millimeter cannon, and set out with the six-thousand-man expedition in May. The presence of artillery improved the *mehalla*'s firepower, if
not its speed. In early July, as it camped beneath the walls of Taza, Bou
Hamara made one last attempt to defend his capital. Three antiquated
cannon boomed from the town walls, a signal for a night ambush. The
makhzan camp was surrounded by a circle of fire. Seventy men were killed
and over a hundred wounded. Only their unfamiliarity with the country and
the distance from Fez kept the *askar* from deserting. Menebbhi was firm,
ordering fires and lights extinguished as a hail of lead fell into the camp. The
caids Glaoui and Goundafi kept a close watch on the tribal levies, who had
the disconcerting habit of switching sides at such critical moments. Order
was maintained and, as daylight came, the fire slackened and gradually died
away. The Rogui's men melted back into the Atlas.

Ben Sedira's seventy-five opened the gates of Taza on July 7. The next
two days witnessed an orgy of rape and destruction which Menebbhi proved
powerless to stop. The town's Jews fled for sanctuary to the Spanish enclave
at Melilla—all who could escape, that is, for many of their women, joined
together by cords, were put up for sale in the marketplace.

The makhzan was ecstatic, believing that the capture of Taza had put
paid to the career of Bou Hamara. But the Sultan's optimism proved premature. When Abd el-Aziz attempted to make a triumphal entry into the town,
he was turned back by hostile tribesmen. The sad truth was that the conquering
mehalla had become imprisoned there. The besiegers were now besieged, as
the Ghiatas closed like a noose around Taza. Menebbhi returned to Fez,
leaving Madani Glaoui in command. The situation of the makzhan troops
became increasingly difficult, and all contact with Fez was soon lost. This
left but one option: With the aid of Ben Sedira's seventy-five, Glaoui was
able to make a fighting retreat east to Oudjda.

Over the next few years, through a series of alliances and wars, the
Rogui was to extend his control over much of the northeast from the Sebou
to the Moulouya. It was a tenuous grip, however, and more than once Bou
Hamara came close to defeat and assassination. Nor was he able, despite a
prolonged siege, to capture Oudjda. Nonetheless, his successful defiance of
the makhzan seriously weakened Abd el-Aziz. The Sultan's prestige was
dashed and his treasury bankrupted by the ruinous campaign. This would

give the French extra leverage when dealing with the makhzan. Menebbhi was the first casualty. His failure brought out his enemies, forcing him to slip away on a pilgrimage to Mecca to escape murder. He subsequently retired to Tangiers to live as a British protected person. And in the wake of his—and his Sultan's—defeat, more trouble was inevitable. Bou Hamara's irredentist example was soon emulated by another, even more ruthless bandit caid—Raisuni.

CHAPTER VIII

EL RAISUNI

Mountains dominated Morocco's politics the way they dominate her geography. The mountain tribes belonged by tradition and by temperament to the *bled el-siba*, the "land of dissidence," but this seldom troubled the tranquillity of the plain. Independent, suspicious, Balkanized into thousands of villages and valleys, mountain people rarely united long enough to challenge the power of the Sultan in the western lowlands—that is, until 1903. Bou Hamara's successful defiance of the Sultan was an open invitation for every tribe seriously to reconsider its relationship with the makhzan: "When the head no longer commands, the arms and legs go where they please." Spasms of disorder—robbery, pillage, the destruction of crops—grew throughout the country in the summer and autumn. "The makhzan is as weak as a child," was the opinion echoed in every market and tribal council. "It has cannons, but Bou Hamara still dictates his law in Taza. Why don't we do as he?" And they did.

Abd el-Aziz's attempts to reform the makhzan with European advice contributed in no small way to that disorder. The young Sultan was caught in an impossible dilemma: To strengthen his grip on his increasingly restive country, he must reform and modernize his government and army. Yet, as the Shah of Iran was to discover three-quarters of a century later, his reliance on Europeans to this end aroused the hostility of his people and encouraged the very disorder he was struggling to control. The foreigners counseled him to be progressive and humane. But in the political climate of Morocco at the turn of the century, this otherwise laudable policy was to prove disastrous. Ba Ahmed had filled Morocco's prisons with his political enemies, with those of his friends and of his friends' friends. The brutality of his "government of fishes" had quite rightly sickened and outraged Europeans. Out of a belief in progress, in civilization and the perfectibility of man, they encouraged Abd el-Aziz to rule through justice and kindness. The young Sultan had made a good start by emptying his jails and embarking upon other "progressive" reforms. Yet this leniency was badly understood in a country where traditionally one man's liberty meant his enemy's destitution and enslavement. Kindness was the luxury of the weak, generosity a defect to be exploited. Even so, it was sheer bad luck that the Sultan opened the prison doors in 1903 to free a man whose cunning, ruthlessness and talent for survival were to make Bou Hamara appear clumsily amateurish by comparison.

Sherif Moulai Ahmed Ben Mohammed el Raisuni has left us an extremely interesting, if extremely biased, self-portrait in a series of remarkable interviews which he gave to the British writer Rosita Forbes in 1923, two years before his death. In them, he constructs an image of a patriot and defender of the weak, a Robin Hood of the Rif. But even in his own testament he can do little to mask his extraordinary savagery. This was the man who made the Rif a center of revolt which was to nettle Abd el-Aziz until his downfall in 1908.

Like all successful Moroccan politicians, Raisuni combined villainy with sainthood. He was born around 1870 into a well-known upper-class family at Tétouan, where the Rif descends to meet the Mediterranean at a point not far from Tangiers. He could trace his ancestry to Moulai Idris, Morocco's patron saint, and a mosque in Tétouan which served as a family mausoleum, and venerated place of pilgrimage, bore testimony to his lineage.

Raisuni's father probably intended for him to become a religious lawyer, perhaps even a member of the *ulama* of Tétouan, for he gave him what was by Moroccan standards an excellent education in religion and law. It soon became apparent, however, that Raisuni was not cut out for the life of a respectable town Moor. According to his own account, the break came on the day a mountain woman stumbled past his house, her clothes torn and arms covered with blood, shrieking that her husband had been murdered by bandits. The young man avenged the husband's death and in the process discovered a vocation for the more active life of the hills.

Over the next few years, Raisuni acquired a reputation for cunning and audacity as he gradually established one of the most successful protection rackets hitherto seen in the Rif. A combination of respect for his holy blood, his herculean strength and his phenomenal bravery kept his followers in line. Raisuni's bravery was demonstrated on several occasions, perhaps never more spectacularly than once in the midst of a skirmish when, in full view of the enemy, he dismounted, spread his rug, removed his slippers and began to pray as bullets kicked up the dust around him. His servant fell dead, splattering Raisuni's babouches with blood. His prayers completed, Raisuni replaced his stained slippers, rolled up his carpet, mounted his horse as another servant holding his stirrup dropped, and resumed the fight.

His very success bore the seeds of his first temporary eclipse. His plunderings around Tangiers especially annoyed the diplomatic community, which, as usual, sought any excuse to bring pressure to bear on the makhzan. He proved too elusive for the makhzan troops sent to capture him; indeed, Raisuni was invariably tipped off well before an operation by *askar* who had little stomach for a fight. In exasperation, Ba Ahmed told the caid of Tangiers, Sidi Abderrahman, that it must be Raisuni's head or his.

In the event, Raisuni proved astonishingly easy to capture. The bait offered was a simple rifle, albeit a very shiny and modern one. "You do not know what a gun is to an Arab; it is his son and his master," Raisuni later said in justification. "Note how lovingly he holds it across his knee, even at the council, or when he is eating. Without it, he does not feel himself a man." Raisuni was invited to Tangiers to see it by Sidi Abderrahman himself. It would be his, Raisuni was told, in exchange for a few hostages. Perhaps it was a deal worth risking one's neck for—lives, after all, were cheap in Morocco, new rifles were expensive. On the appointed evening, he duly rode through the streets with his men to the very entrance of the caid's house. Before dismounting, however, he demanded bread and was given it. This should have made him safe from treachery, for now he fell under the laws of hospitality, which Sidi Abderrahman would be obliged to honor; however, it did not save him. Indeed, the story of Raisuni's life seems to bear testimony to the fact that these "sacred" laws of hospitality were more often honored in the breach. Raisuni dismounted and entered the caid's house while his men waited outside. Hardly had he sat down before the feast that had been prepared for him when Abderrahman's *mokhaznis* pounced and bound him hand and foot. Outside, Raisuni's men scattered when told that their chief was dead.

Raisuni spent the next few years in the prison of Mogador, far away from his native Rif. Conditions there were indescribable: vermin, rats and filth were the prisoners' constant companions. At one point in midsummer, he remained chained for three days to a corpse which his jailers refused to remove, fearing that the prison governor would claim that he had escaped. Given this appalling experience, one might think that later, when himself a caid, Raisuni would have treated his own prisoners with more consideration. But his regime at Asilah was marked by the same casual cruelty, as he admitted:

It was a small place, not much bigger than this tent, so it looked crowded, for there were nearly 100 prisoners there. To make room half of them had been fastened to the same chain, and one or two were perhaps dead, for the gaolers are always careless, and perchance there was no smith to break open the irons. It was very dark and nothing could be seen clearly. The eyes of the men were like green lamps. Do you know when you look into a hole and, unexpectedly, you see twin points of light, and it is a face watching you? So the prisoners watched without moving. Some of them almost naked and shivering. Others were so thin that their bones tore the rags which were on them. Truly, the will of Allah is strange. The pleasure of crime is momentary and its punishment eternal.

After spending four or five years in prison (he was very vague about time), Raisuni was freed. His release has been attributed to the intervention of high makhzan officials, including Menebbhi and Sidi Mohammed Torres, the Sultan's representative in Tangiers. It is more probable that he gained his liberty as part of Abd el-Aziz's general prison clean-out. However, Raisuni's release proved to be a horrible mistake. He returned to Tangiers and, upon discovering that his property had been confiscated, once again took up the only trade he knew, that of a brigand.

In 1903, barely thirty years old, Raisuni entered into the most spectacular phase of his career. Walter Harris, who was briefly Raisuni's reluctant guest in that year, described him as

tall, remarkably handsome, with the whitest of skins, a short, dark beard and moustache, black eyes with a profile Greek rather than Semitic, and eyebrows that formed a straight line across his forehead. . . . His manner was quiet, his voice soft and low, his expression particularly sad. He smiled sometimes, but seldom, and even though I knew him better later on, I never saw him laugh. With his followers, he was cold and haughty, and they treated him with all the respect due to his birth.

One of Raisuni's first acts upon reentering public life was to come to the aid of his sister, whose husband was planning to take a second wife. Raisuni resolved this family quarrel by the simple expedient of invading the wedding feast and slaughtering the bride and her mother. He then sought to avenge himself on those who had betrayed him five years earlier. Their families were not spared. From his stronghold at Zinat, a rambling building, half fort, half house, which stood on a rocky promontory about twelve miles from Tangiers, Raisuni conducted a reign of terror. Kidnapping became his bread and butter, with a lucrative sideline in pillaging the caravans that traveled from Tangiers into the interior.

His resemblance to Bou Hamara had by now become too obvious for the Sultan to ignore. Early in 1903, the caids Sidi Abderrahman and Abd el-Malek led a *mehalla* against him. This was routed. Sidi Abderrahman escaped disguised as a slave, someone for whom no ransom would be paid. Abd el-Malek, however, was less fortunate. When the sharif of Ouezzane appealed to Raisuni to spare the caid's life, Raisuni released him—after having him blinded.

A second expedition was sent to reduce Zinat, this time successfully. Raisuni, of course, had ample time to escape the ponderous advance of Maclean's *mehalla*. However, he made off with a valuable prize—none other than Walter Harris, who had ridden out from Tangiers to observe the attack on Zinat. To describe Harris as specifically Raisuni's prisoner is perhaps an oversimplification; he was, rather, a shared prize. Raisuni's defiance of the makhzan had made him a sort of local resistance leader. The advance of the *mehalla* to the fringes of the Rif swelled the number of tribes in Raisuni's camp, each of whom attempted to impose their special conditions for Harris's release. The situation became so confused that Sir Arthur Nicolson, the British minister in Tangiers who took the negotiations in hand, hardly knew with whom to deal. Nor was his task eased by the attitude of the Sultan's representative: "Mohammed Torres behaved like an old brute," Nicolson recorded in his diary. "Said that Harris was in the hands of the Lord. I said he was not, but in the hands of a devil. . . . I must say I *boil* to have to humiliate myself and negotiate with these miserable brigands within three hours of Gibraltar."

Harris resolved the problem of divided authority by eliciting a list of the captives whose release from Tangiers' prison was demanded by the tribes in return for his own. This list, fifty-six names in all, was sent to Nicolson. When the tribesmen, angered by the British minister's statement that the list was too long, threatened to kill their captive, Harris had a ready reply for them:

You have kindly given me a list of all your relations who are in Moorish prisons. This list is in Tangiers. You will have the satisfaction of killing me, but remember this—on 56 consecutive days one of your sons or brothers or nephews will be executed, one each morning; and more, their bodies will be burnt and the ashes scattered to the wind. You will see the smoke from here.

To believers in corporal resurrection, this prospect was simply too horrible to contemplate. Harris was duly released.

Harris put a brave face on his captivity—thirty-six hours without food, a few fleas and a forced encounter with the horribly mutilated body of an unfortunate *askari*: "This is what you will look like in a few days." In fact, Nicolson found the normally ebullient Harris "thin and rather subdued" on his return. This did not prevent him from trumpeting in print that he had outwitted the "slow thinking Moor." The sense of triumph was premature, however. One Moor in any case had observed with interest the sense of crisis with which the kidnapping of Harris had infected Tangiers. The message was clear: the diplomats would not allow their more prominent citizens to be abducted without bringing intolerable pressure to bear on the makhzan. Raisuni decided to play for higher stakes.

Tangiers had for some time become a haven for wealthy European exiles drawn by the climate, the presence of a substantial diplomatic community which added elegance to what would otherwise have been a shabby North African backwater, and by the town's cheapness and exoticism. If Walter Harris was the doyen of this exile community, Ion Perdicaris was its most wealthy member. He lived in some splendor in his villa, Aidonia, on the shore just west of Tangiers: a comfortable white house with green shutters and a terrace from which one could look across the garden ("groves of myrtle, roses and arbutus falling to the sea") to Spain beyond. A small man with a closely cropped white beard, about sixty years of age, Perdicaris had been born in America to a Greek father and an American mother, while his wife (nicknamed "Queen Victoria" by French diplomats), his daughter-in-law and stepson, Cromwell Oliver Varley—all of whom lived at Aidonia in idle retirement, painting, hunting and riding—were British. A few grandchildren, some tame pheasants, a female crane and a menagerie of monkeys completed the list of residents.

On the evening of May 18, 1904, almost a year after Harris's release, the family had just finished dinner. The adults were having coffee on the wisteria-draped terrace when a commotion was heard behind the house. Shots were fired. The two men in dinner jackets rushed to investigate. After more clamor, the noise ceased. Mrs. Perdicaris and Mrs. Varley eyed each other with half-puzzled, half-anxious expressions. Slowly, they rose and cautiously approached the servants' quarters. There they found the servants bound and gagged. Tall men in brown jellabas menacingly armed with Martini rifles stood guard as Perdicaris and Varley, their hands bound behind their backs, were hoisted facing backward upon mules. Mrs. Varley rushed toward her husband only to be knocked to the ground by a rifle butt. Mrs. Perdicaris screamed. The two men, swaying precariously upon their mules, were led off beneath the cork trees toward the hills. Mrs. Varley rushed into the house to telephone Sir Arthur.

Raisuni wasted little time making his demands known: Sidi Abderrahman was to be dismissed and replaced as caid of Tangiers by Raisuni himself. The makhzan was to withdraw its *mehalla* from "his" territory. It was to imprison certain of Raisuni's enemies and release his friends. A number of villages would now pay their taxes to Raisuni directly. Finally, he demanded a ransom of 350,000 pesetas (about $70,000) for the freedom of Perdicaris and Varley. As he had no confidence in the Sultan, it was the British minister and the American consul who must guarantee that these conditions would be met. Raisuni warned ominously that his patience could not stand protracted negotiations.

Raisuni's demands were, of course, quite preposterous. Or were they? News of the kidnappings had thrown the Tangiers diplomatic community into an outsized funk. Europeans felt that they were no longer safe in their beds. Nicolson and the American consul, Samuel R. Gummere—perhaps believing that they might become Raisuni's next victims—both wired home for support. And what support! The Americans sent six heavy cruisers, which were soon joined by the British battleship *The Prince of Wales*. Moroccans were intrigued by this massive display of firepower anchored off their shores. Raisuni, however, was unimpressed: "Since when have the sharks come out of the sea to eat the mountain wolf?"

The invasion of Tangiers by American sailors had its amusing side. In the second half of the nineteenth century, many European aristocrats had sought to restore the flagging financial fortunes of their families through marriage to American money. Any European who could scrape up the title of count or marquis sought out an American heiress. Consequently, the embassies of Europe were stuffed with men of "good families" who had married wealthy American wives. The results for the rigid pecking order of pre-1914 diplomatic communities were sometimes catastrophic. American money acted as a great leveler. In Tangiers, the wealthy American wives of second and third secretaries denied themselves few luxuries—the most elaborate clothes, sedan chairs, houses full of Jewish servants—so much so that the Moors took them, and not the wives of their husbands' superiors, to be the "bachadouras," a mistake the American women were in no hurry to correct.

The arrival of the American ships in late May 1904 served to stimulate these pretensions even further. The young American officers, many of them educated at Harvard or Princeton, shook somnolent Tangiers, however momentarily, out of its social lethargy. They were feted and shown the town by American hostesses eager to cash in on this concrete manifestation of American power and prestige. And that prestige was in the ascendant. Already, the Moors had heard that a country called the United States had defeated the Spaniards in a place called Cuba. Here, at last, were the conquerors of the conquerors of the Moors. In Tangiers, at least, this was potent medicine. The Moors could even be heard attempting to get their tongues around the name of "Roosevelt."

In Washington, however, President Roosevelt was feeling distinctly uncomfortable. The Perdicaris affair had given him the opportunity to exercise the sort of blustering gunboat diplomacy at which he excelled. His order "Perdicaris alive or Raisuli dead" made striking headlines, and ones that would silence mutterings in his own party about "that damn cowboy." But just as the President had settled back to savor the crisis which was bound to win him the nomination of the Republican convention due to meet in Chicago on June 21, the State Department received a most unsettling letter. Mr. A. H. Slocomb, a cotton broker from Fayetteville, North Carolina, wrote to say that he had met Mr. Perdicaris in Athens in the winter of 1863. The purpose of Perdicaris' visit, Mr. Slocomb continued, had been to obtain Greek citizenship and so to protect property he had inherited through his mother, a native of South Carolina, from confiscation by the Confederate government. A hurried search of the Athens records revealed that Perdicaris was indeed a Greek subject and had therefore forfeited his American nationality. Roosevelt, staggered by this news, had no choice but to brazen out the crisis and pray that Perdicaris' true nationality would remain a secret, which it did until 1933.

In Fez, news of the arrival of the *roumi* off Tangiers transformed the town into a powder keg. The twenty or so Europeans in Fez secreted jellabas and made arrangements to hide themselves in the houses of friendly Algerians:

if the Americans and the British stormed ashore, it would surely be the signal for their massacre. At the palace, pressure was brought to bear on the Sultan to meet Raisuni's demands. The foreigners entrusted negotiations to St.-Aulaire, one of the Quai d'Orsay's young prodigies. His was not an easy task, and he needed to draw upon all of the subtle tricks instilled by a Jesuit education to carry his points. The makhzan was naturally reluctant to cave in to Raisuni's extravagant demands for the sake of a couple of hostages. "Not without humor," the Sultan and his viziers reminded St.-Aulaire that in pleading the case of Raisuni he rather undermined his thesis that France sought a more "civilized" and orderly Morocco. What St.-Aulaire proposed would be "an enormous victory for anarchy and a reversal of all principles." The Moroccans were right, of course, but they nonetheless acceded.

Negotiations with Raisuni proved more intractable. Perdicaris and Varley were well treated—allowed to write to their wives, receive food parcels and do a certain amount of supervised hunting. But the first caid sent by the makhzan to treat for the hostages' release was an enemy of Raisuni; he was turned over to some villagers, who slit his throat. After this incident, it became more difficult to find negotiators. Finally, the sharif of Ouezzane agreed to act as intermediary and on June 25 he brought Perdicaris and Varley, "much improved in health," into Tangiers. The Americans and British sailed away. Perdicaris promptly sold Aidonia and moved his family to Tunbridge Wells.

The crisis was over. But who had benefited? Raisuni obviously: he saw his old enemy Sidi Abderrahman removed, and promptly stepped into his job as caid of Tangiers. He also pocketed a ransom of seventy thousand dollars. The French had also profited: St.-René Taillandier had played upon Nicolson's sense of insecurity to convince him to allow the French military mission to organize the Tangiers police. This, together with the monopoly on loans to the Moroccan government with the customs receipts as surety, which was negotiated in 1904, was reckoned by St.-Aulaire to provide the touchstones of the protectorate. Roosevelt got his presidential nomination by acclamation and a letter of profound apology from Perdicaris.

Some people like to see Raisuni as a Moroccan patriot, a precursor of Abd el-Krim, the man who raised the Rif against the French and Spanish between 1921 and 1925. Perhaps, but his actions certainly brought the protectorate nearer. The kidnapping of Perdicaris and Varley combined with the antics of Bou Hamara near Taza to convince opinion in Europe and America that Morocco was fast becoming ungovernable. Raisuni's actions strengthened the hand of men like Lyautey, who argued that the sooner Morocco was conquered the safer Algeria, and the more secure world peace, would be. It is possible that Raisuni simply planned his *tour de force* for short-term gain without weighing the long-term consequences. This, however, is unlikely. Raisuni was savage, but he was also extremely astute. It would be a mistake to assume, as did contemporary European diplomats, that because Morocco was primitive and undercivilized by European standards her leaders were unintelligent. While many displayed a startling ignorance of the world beyond their shores, they were calculating and so much masters of the art of subtle maneuver as to place their European opposite numbers in the shade. It is more probable that Raisuni realized that the European absorption of Morocco was in the cards and sought to profit by it. The Anglo-French Entente, which was common knowledge by April 1904, provided that Britain would henceforth defer to France on Moroccan questions. And it was Raisuni who, as caid of much of northwestern Morocco in 1911, invited the Spanish to occupy his territory, preferring the presence of a weak and inefficient Spain to a strong France. But that is another, and much longer story.

The makhzan, under irresistible European and American pressure, had caved in to Raisuni's blackmail. It was perhaps only fair, then, that the Tangiers diplomatic community was forced to live with the consequences of their action. For Raisuni was now caid of Tangiers and life there certainly became more interesting. It was traditional for caids to dispense justice at the city gate. Raisuni did so on the Grand Soko, within full view of the French legation. The spectacle for those used to the hushed and self-conscious dignity of European courts of law was a bizarre one: the caid reclining on a divan—"Lying," said Walter Harris, "in both senses of the word"—listened as both parties to the dispute shouted out their cases simultaneously. One must not suppose that this led to confusion; no case was ever decided on its own merits, but rather on the size of the bribe paid beforehand. Therefore, the man with the deeper pocket invariably won. The unsuccessful litigant was immediately seized and led away screaming to be flogged, or worse, on the Soko. The French diplomats were well placed to witness this spectacle several times weekly. Even by closing the windows, they could not escape the screams which gradually subsided into pathetic moans as the whip bit deeper. It tried even the stoutest European stomach, the more so because they had bad consciences. But there was worse: Raisuni revived amputations and the more refined tortures which had been abandoned as too barbaric. Soon, the view from the legation was improved by the heads of Raisuni's enemies which now began to appear above the city gate. Raisuni himself could not understand why the Europeans complained:

> I had brought security and peace to the country, but they feared a little blood spilt in the market place or a few heads stuck on the wall. . . . Men complained that I was severe, but I was never unjust. It is sometimes wise to spend the lives of a few in order to buy the safety of many. The Arab has a short memory. He forgets his own troubles in a few days and other people's at once. You think if you imprison a man, it will stop others committing his crime. I tell you, the reason for a man's absence is never remembered, but the presence of his head on a gatepost is a constant reminder!

Despite Raisuni's claims to have brought order to Tangiers, Europeans did not feel secure. Raisuni's Rif tribesmen, draped in their brown jellabas and armed to the teeth, swaggered through the town picking quarrels or entering European shops to "requisition" a rifle, a bolt of cloth, a teapot or whatever struck their fancy. Raisuni's casual disregard of international treaties meant that the protected persons of European embassies felt the lash like everyone else. Europeans were outraged. They were also intimidated. Raisuni began to pay social visits on the diplomats in his official capacity as caid, and even barged uninvited into their bridge parties. Europeans seldom returned his calls, however, for fear that they might be detained too long. The threat of kidnapping loomed over all of his dealings with the diplomatic community. When once he intimated that this was how he might resolve one of his disputes with St.-Aulaire, the French landed a party of sailors to guard their legation.

The dénouement began on May 27, 1906. On that day, around six o'clock in the afternoon, a young Frenchman named Charbonnier was riding his horse on the beach south of town near Harris' villa when he was approached by a group of Andjeras tribesmen, supporters of Raisuni. What happened next was never established, but St.-René assured the Quai d'Orsay that Charbonnier's "mild and kind nature absolutely excludes the possibility that there was on his part a provocation or an imprudence." Charbonnier was later found on the beach dead from a bullet wound in the back of the head.

This was the moment for which St.-René, indeed the entire diplomatic community, had been waiting. The situation in Tangiers had been tense since the signing of the Anglo-French Entente of 1904. With the Algeciras Conference of January 1906, called to resolve the dispute between France and Germany over Morocco's future, this tension had increased to the boiling point. The Moroccans realized that the *roumi* had now settled virtually all of their differences and were poised for a takeover of their country. A recession in these years aggravated the deteriorating political climate. Famine and disease spread. Peasants fled the countryside into the already overcrowded port cities. Nor were tensions diminished by Europeans who began to buy up large tracts of land near harbor towns. It is against this background that the murders and violence of 1906–07 must be placed.

St.-René immediately saw that Charbonnier's murder could be made to serve two purposes: first, to ruin Raisuni and, second, to force Abd el-Aziz, who was dragging his feet, to sign the Algeciras Agreement. The French minister immediately went to see Mohammed Torres and demanded a reparation payment and, touchingly, "the erection of a small commemorative monument at the spot where the crime was committed." When Torres began his by-now-familiar delaying tactics, St.-René conjured up the battleships *Kléber* and *Jeanne d'Arc* to add substance to his argument. The second goal—to convince the Sultan to sign the Algeciras Agreement—perhaps as the result of the extra pressure brought to bear by the Charbonnier affair, was achieved on June 18. Only on July 4, when St.-René—backed by an admiral and seven other naval officers, not to mention the two battleships swinging at anchor in the bay—paid Torres a visit, did the old gentleman hand over a check, agree to find the culprits and build the monument.

The European giveth, the European taketh away—in December, the caid of Tangiers learned that a *mehalla* was on its way to arrest him. St.-René's argument that the Sultan must restore order—the opposite of the one used by his colleague St.-Aulaire two years before—had produced results. Raisuni scurried to the safety of Zinat as the *mehalla* plodded behind on his heels. Walter Harris witnessed the subsequent Battle of Zinat:

> Clear in the still air a bugle rang out in the camp. They must have heard it away at Zinat, for suddenly from the summit of the rocks above Raisuni's fortress a long thin column of white smoke arose, then another and another, and then from peak to peak, as far as the eye could reach, the fires were answered. The mountaineers were signalling to one another that the great battle was imminent. Down in the camp below us the infantry were "falling in" and the cavalrymen mounting their horses,

and it was only a few minutes later when amongst the beating of drums and the blowing of bugles, the neighing of horses and the fluttering of coloured banners and flags, the Shereefian troops marched out on to the plain. A hoarse shout arose from every throat, "Ah! salih en-Nebi, Rasoul Allah!" an invocation to the Prophet, repeated again and again, and answered by a far-away and fainter cry of the same words from the fortress and rocks of Zinat.

Once all the troops are out on the plain they are drawn up in formation for the attack. On the right were the artillery, two field-guns, and a couple of Maxims, carried by mules. Near them, amidst a panoply of banners, rode the Commander-in-Chief and his staff, a group of a hundred or so persons well mounted and gaily dressed, with their bright saddles of every shade of coloured cloth and silk adding to a scene already brilliantly picturesque. In the centre were some 800 infantry with a strong support of tribal cavalry, while on the left a somewhat smaller force formed the flank. The contingent of loyal mountaineers in their short black cloaks could be seen already scaling some low hills away on the extreme right. Then slowly the whole army advances.

It was a moment of thrilling excitement. From the rocky hill where I had taken up my point of vantage the whole scene was passing at my very feet. On my left the fortress and rocks; on my right the slowly advancing forces—the left flank within a hundred yards or so of where I stood. At Zinat there was not a sign of life, though with my glasses I could see the glint of rifle-barrels in the embrasures of the house, and now and then amongst the precipices and rocks above it. The troops are within 1,200 yards now, and in the open, but still advancing slowly, for the most part in close formation, and offering even at that range—a long one for the Moors, who are proverbial bad shots—an excellent target. The sunlit air is so still that every little sound rises unbroken from the plain below: a word of command here, a bugle-call there. Then suddenly the firing opens from Zinat—the quick nervous spitting of the Mauser rifles,—rendered the more impressive from the fact that nothing can be seen, for there is not a single man there who does not use smokeless powder. A few Askaris are seen to fall, killed or wounded, and the advance ceases. The whole army replies, firing at an impossible range into a solid fort and still more solid precipice with rifles that have only reached Morocco after they have long been discarded as useless in Europe, and with powder that issues, evil-looking and evil-smelling, from the barrels of their weapons. After all, it made little difference where they fired, for few or none had ever handled a rifle before, and there was nothing to shoot at. Meanwhile, the cavalry galloped to and fro in every direction, except to advance, waving flags and firing their rifles, apparently at the green plover that swept over in flocks, disturbed by the unusual racket.

Inane impotent warfare, carried on by undisciplined and uncourageous men, whose uniforms alone bespoke them as soldiers.

A curl of thin yellow smoke, widening as it ascended, rises from the rocks far above the house—the first shell fired by the artillery, followed by another and another, which, although aimed at the house itself, fall in widely different directions, more than one nearer the Maghzen troops than the enemy. During the entire action of this Saturday, although the range was only about 1000 meters [1,100 yards], the house was only struck twice, and even the explosion of these two shells did not force the defenders to abandon the flat roof and windows, though they cannot have failed to be effective. Meanwhile the troops on the left, under the cover of the rocks, had entered and burned a village out of Raisuni's line of fire, and were returning toward the camp laden with loot, under the impression that their duty for the day was over. Nor did any one attempt to persuade them to re-enter the fight, and I watched them disappear, staggering under huge mattresses, chests of painted wood—the dowry of every Moorish bride,—and a thousand other household articles. For a background—the burning village, the flames of which rose lurid and roaring into the still air, to pass away in great rolls of heavy white smoke.

. . . [At two o'clock] another attempt was made to advance. The whole line pushed forward, but 700 or 800 yards from Zinat they broke, and—well, if they did not exactly run, they certainly returned very quickly. It was at this moment that two picturesque incidents occurred. From Raisuni's house emerged a woman, who, crossing the open ground under a heavy fire, mounted upon a rock and thence cursed the troops. She threw back her thick "haik," and, tearing her hair, waved her arms towards heaven, but the firing drowned her voice. Then slowly and majestically she drew her veil around her and retired. A few seconds later eight men, no doubt encouraged by her bravery, rushed into the open grounds, shouting and jeering at the retiring forces, and firing the while with their Mausers. It was then that the Commander-in-Chief fell wounded in the neck. A mule was brought, and, supported by his retinue, he was hurriedly taken back to the camp. By this time the army had used up all their shells and nearly all their cartridges. Even a reserve force, hidden in a river-bed a mile in the rear, had been firing at that range at the mountain ever since the morning, to the imminent danger of their advancing comrades.

The army was now retiring in good order, followed by Raisuni's eight men, who every now and then sped a parting shot at them. The battle of Zinat was over. The great effort of the Maghzen had failed, and the stronghold and village, except for a few holes made by the shells, stood as placid and peaceful in appearance as it had been in the morning. The great Shereefian army had proved itself to be—like everything else in Morocco, except perhaps Raisuni himself, a gigantic bluff.

The battle was not quite over. The following day the *mehalla* returned, this time with a valuable reinforcement—Lieutenant Ben Sedira. With two shells he did more damage than the many shots fired the previous day. The *askar* approached hesitantly until, realizing that Raisuni had abandoned his fortress in the night, they gave a whoop and charged. The army dissolved into a mob. From a safe distance, Raisuni watched them staggering beneath carpets, mattresses, boxes, vases of artificial flowers, sacks of flour and grain, even a canary in a cage: "At last the troops charged, but they were very doubtful, each man wishing to keep behind his neighbour," Raisuni remembered. "I do not know how soon they discovered that the village was empty, but then their courage was great. Shouting to each other triumphantly, they attacked the furniture we left behind, and in a minute the whole army turned into porters. If we had walked in among them they would have paid no attention to us."

Raisuni was again out of a job. He still had one bolt left in his quiver, however. This time his victim was none other than Sir Harry Maclean, commander in chief of the Sultan's army.

Ensconced in the hills above Tangiers, Raisuni had remained a nuisance. In the spring of 1907, Maclean was sent to treat with him, armed with a pardon from Abd el-Aziz and a promise that he would be reinstated as caid of Tangiers. At the same time, the Sultan had written a second letter to his war minister explaining that he hoped to trick Raisuni into entering Tangiers, where he could be seized. Through an incredible but all too typical blunder, the palace scribes had mixed up the letters, so that Maclean handed

Raisuni the letter intended for the war minister. The unsuspecting Maclean was enticed away from his camp and made Raisuni's prisoner.

Raisuni chose to believe Maclean's claims of innocence, and for a few weeks they became good friends: they hunted together and Raisuni even sent to Tétouan for a set of bagpipes, which the Scot loved to play, "those curious pipes like cushions full of air which his people play. They make more noise than music, and even the blacks cannot sing against them." Raisuni demanded twenty-five thousand pounds from Britain and the status of a British protected person in exchange for Maclean. Negotiations dragged on. Finally Raisuni, growing impatient, told Maclean to write a letter "that will move them." The Scot refused, so Raisuni told him that he would write it "before you sleep." For the next two days, drummers kept up a constant din outside Maclean's tent. When this failed to produce the letter, Raisuni added cymbals. "Truly, I disliked it myself, so I went away to avoid it." Another day still failed to move the by now red-eyed Maclean, so Raisuni handed the task to a "master of noise . . . all men in the house held their ears and ran." At the end of five days without sleep, Maclean gave in. The English government made Raisuni a protected person and the bandit chief settled for a ten-thousand-pound down payment. The sharif of Ouezzane once again traveled to the mountains to take the hostage back to Tangiers.

Raisuni's role in Moroccan history was not yet finished; his most important contributions were yet to occur. But he had already effectively served the purpose of the Europeans, by demonstrating that Morocco had become virtually ungovernable. This anarchy must not be allowed to continue unchecked. It was grist for Lyautey's propaganda mill, and he ground it for all it was worth.

CHAPTER IX

THE LYAUTEY METHOD

Lieutenants Rousseau and Husson seemed perfectly at home in their surroundings. A wisp of blond hair just visible beneath the hood of the burnous, a pair of blue eyes and the fact that, for the moment at least, they were speaking French, was all that distinguished them from the seventy Arabs who squatted beside their horses, reins in hand, looking on as the two young Frenchmen conferred over what was obviously the remains of someone else's meal. Around them the hammada, the stony desert of the Guir, stretched away in all directions, yellow, empty, silent.

They could only shake their heads in disbelief. For twenty-six hours they had tracked el Aroussi—they knew it was el Aroussi, for he had obligingly dropped off the two kidnapped shepherd boys at Kenadza to tell them so—covered 100 miles of difficult terrain, stopping only briefly between midnight and first light when the trail had been obscured by darkness, and still they had not caught him, despite his handicap of twenty-four stolen camels. Now, to drive home his contempt for his pursuers, el Aroussi let them know that he had stopped for a leisurely dinner.

In the heat of the chase, the French force had already broken the bounds of prudence by venturing unsupported onto the hammada. This time Colomb-Béchar had decided to make an example out of the raiders. The fact that el Aroussi was the culprit—the man who last year had killed four dispatch riders between Taghit and Colomb-Béchar—had steeled French determination. It would be a feather in the caps of the two young native-affairs lieutenants if they could overtake him before reinforcements arrived, but that was now quite impossible. Another fifty waterless miles of rock and desolation lay between them and the Tafilalet. Most of the *goumiers* were Algerians from Géryville. You could always tell the Algerians, for they spent far too much time on horseback, unlike the men of the plateaus and desert, who walked at the heads of their mounts. But there was also a fair sprinkling of Doui-Menia and Oulad Djerir, members of el Aroussi's own tribe, whose loyalty might shift dangerously in a fire fight. Desert fighting required specialists, and among them el Aroussi was a master. Even in this vacant land, as smooth as an egg for as far as one could see, an ambush was always to be feared. It was one of the raiders' preferred tactics: draw the pursuing *goums* onto the hammada, the bare plateau which separates the valley of the Guir from the oasis of the Tafilalet, and, while their attentions were concentrated on the horizon, strike them from behind. The two lieutenants suddenly felt very vulnerable: Better play this one by the book. They retraced their steps for twenty miles to the waterhole at Tiberbatine.

The "book" in this case had been written by General Lyautey. When, at 8:30 on the morning of October 29, 1906, an Arab had rushed into Lieutenant Colonel Pierron's headquarters at Colomb-Béchar to report (if his shouts and wild gesticulations qualify as a report) the theft of his camels from their pasture about eighteen miles northeast of Colomb-Béchar, Pierron had immediately scrambled his *goumiers*. Within 45 minutes, Lieutenant Rousseau and his fifty Saharians had set out with three days' rations. By slicing across the possible escape routes, they had picked up el Aroussi's trail six miles west of Colomb-Béchar in barely an hour. A *goumier* carried the news back to base, and Lieutenant Husson led his twenty Saharians to the spot where Rousseau waited. Together they followed the trail, which led, as expected, toward the Tafilalet.

This was phase one of Lieutenant Colonel Pierron's *contre-djich* (counter-raid). A *contre-djich* was not the sort of action that staff officers in France discussed, debated and dissected in their ponderously academic *Kriegsspiele*. Nor did it ever provide the theme for a field day at the enormous training camp at Châlons-sur-Marne in eastern France. It was a desert set-piece, and bore all the hallmarks of the man who had laid down the order of battle— Lyautey.

Phase two: Captain Descoins arrives at Tiberbatine with his seventy-eight spahis on the evening of October 31. Most of the spahis, like the *goumiers*, were recruited from around Géryville—lean, brown, parrot-faced men whose uniform was more picturesque than practical: a turban, a long, flowing cape which might be white, blue or red, high riding boots, baggy white trousers and a red girdle so long that relieving oneself required five minutes and a friend to help put every piece back in place. Their European officers and NCOs tried to instruct them in the rudiments of military life as practiced north of the Mediterranean, but with patchy results: Lyautey complained that his spahis maneuvered "worse than a territorial squadron in France," but he was able to do very little about the Armée d'Afrique's obsession with turning perfectly good Arab fighting men into a North African version of hussars, beyond lightening the load they were required to carry on campaign.

Phase three: The arrival of the legionnaires. At five o'clock on the afternoon of November 2 they walked into the camp, weighted down under their full packs and enormous blue overcoats, and followed by 161 camels upon whose humps crates of supplies and ammunition swayed precariously. Under Lyautey, the legion's lot had not been a happy one. He had little time for them; they were forever selling their rifles and deserting. He also accused the German recruits of supplying newspapers across the Rhine with reports of his secret encroachments into Morocco. But, more important, he thought them better at road-building than desert warfare: "Not only can they not reconnoiter," he wrote, "they can hardly protect themselves," and dismissed them as ambush bait.

Captain Doury, commander of the Saharian company of irregular troops at Colomb-Béchar, accompanied the legionnaires. Lyautey considered an Arabic-speaking native-affairs officer with a good knowledge of local tribes essential to the success of a desert expedition, and Doury was such. He served as interpreter, guide, intelligence officer and insurance policy against cases of mistaken identity. The native-affairs officer also acted as a brake on the tendency of combat officers to dispense justice in a somewhat indiscriminate manner. His job was not to prevent mayhem, but simply to see that retribution was doled out as evenhandedly as possible. The hardened desert warriors who commanded legionnaires, spahis or tirailleurs saw him as a bloodless intellectual with an irritating tendency to draw subtle distinctions in a population that, as far as they could tell, was uniformly hostile.

The French army, or at least part of it, prided itself on its ability to "go native." The expedition that set out from Tiberbatine at seven o'clock on the morning of November 3 was barely distinguishable from the bandits whom they pursued, in more ways than one. The Saharians, spahis and clutch of native foot, recruited by Captain Doury mainly from applicants waiting for a vacancy to occur in the mounted Saharians, walked where they liked, chatted like magpies or played their flutes. The legion, the poor legion, stayed behind with the camels at Tiberbatine. By four o'clock in the afternoon, they had reached the western edge of the hammada. Captain Descoins called a halt. Several hundred feet beneath them, bathed in the late afternoon sun, the stony, honey-colored ground stretched away to the Tafilalet.

As Captain Descoins waited for night to fall, it might have occurred to him that what he was about to do was sheer folly. The land between

Colomb-Béchar and the Tafilalet was well known to the nomads, but not to the French. He had no maps and had to rely for his direction on native hearsay, folklore. If he became lost, his expedition would surely perish. This was not quite the desert, but water was scarce. First the horses would falter, and then the men, one by one, until the *contre-djich* was reduced to a few bleached bones. Nor could he have much confidence in the Saharians. They were marvelous raiders, but poorly disciplined and mercurial. If attacked by a stronger force, they might easily lose what little cohesion they possessed and disintegrate into a *sauve qui peut*. His raid would become a mad dash, perhaps a hopeless one, back to the legion's lines at Tiberbatine. His only strength was in surprise. The Tafilalet would not be expecting him.

As night fell, Lieutenant Rousseau led his Saharians on foot down the western face of the hammada, carefully marking the route of descent for those who were to follow. Sergeant Aissa of the spahis pushed forward with a few men to locate the well at Talghemt, eleven miles to the west. Only at midnight, when Descoins learned that the well was guarded by his spahis did he lead his men off the hammada toward Talghemt. There they waited.

At 6:30 on the morning of November 4, three Saharians galloped into Talghemt, shouting their news before the well-lathered horses were even reined to a halt. With the infallible tracking skills of their race, they had picked up el Aroussi's trail. "To your horses." The tension of the night march, the hours of tedious waiting, vanished in a surge of adrenaline. Descoins shouted for his irregular foot to hold Talghemt. With his mounted troops—sixty Saharians, twenty spahis and a handful of French officers—he followed, silently this time, the old tracks and dried camel droppings for over twelve miles. By some extraordinary luck, they had passed through almost twenty-five miles of not entirely uninhabited country without having been detected. The outriders gave a sign. There, in the middle of a narrow plain, was a douar: a random scattering of flat, black tents stuffed with cushions, carpets and cooking pots, the meager household possessions of a people who shuttled with their sheep between the plain and the palm oasis.

Military reports can lie. Lyautey's report of the Tafilalet raid almost certainly does. According to him, Lieutenants Bonamy and Rousseau threw themselves at the flocks of sheep that nibbled the sparse vegetation on the plain around the douar, ignoring the shouts of their owners, while Captains Descoins and Doury "interrogated" the women, the only ones left in the tents, who confirmed that el Aroussi had indeed spent several nights there on his return from his Algerian raid.

But the scene at the douar was probably a much less sedate affair than Lyautey was prepared to admit. In the South Oranais, truth more often than not made for bad public relations. The Saharians were notoriously difficult to control. Once the scent of the *razzia* was in their nostrils, they reverted to type. This was why they had joined.

When did the nomads first realize they were being attacked? Was it the barking of the large troop of dogs which guarded every douar that made the women look up, or did they hear the firing and shouting of the raiders as they swept toward the camp? It was a scene which Algeria had witnessed hundreds of times since 1830 and which would soon become a common enough occurrence in Morocco, one of rape and devastation. The French officers did not intervene—perhaps el Aroussi had stayed in the douar, perhaps he had not. What did it matter? The important thing was that the Tafilalet be made to feel the hard hand of revenge. This douar would do penance for all the unpunished raids into Algeria, for all the raiders who had slipped through their fingers like phantoms, for their inability to occupy Morocco itself.

The most difficult phase of the operation was now to begin. The camels and sheep had to be driven through a country which was now alerted to the presence of the raiders from Algeria, over the hammada to Colomb-Béchar. (Lyautey makes no mention of the women, but one may safely assume that if they were young and plump they were included in the booty.) Soldiers, especially soldiers on the run, make bad shepherds: many of the forty camels and several hundred sheep wandered off while the rest were being stampeded ahead. But the soldiers were too busy to notice. On foot, on horseback, the nomads began to arrive to take up positions on the ridges and behind the rocks which flanked the French retreat. The race was now on. Descoins must make it back to the hammada before enough men emerged from this baked and dusty waste to block his path home. He dispatched the spahis at the gallop. They collected the detachment left behind at Talghemt and climbed the steep western face of the hammada on foot to occupy the saddle over which their retreat would take them.

Meanwhile, the Saharians plodded ahead under a light sprinkle of lead, the mass of them riding more slowly than they would have liked behind the bleating, panicked beasts. Occasionally, they dismounted and, led by their officers, cleared their pursuers from a ridge with a classic foot charge. By nightfall, everyone had reached the summit of the hammada. There was no time to rest. Their pursuers left behind in the plain below, the French-led force made rapid progress over the plateau. At one o'clock in the morning they dropped off a captured shepherd boy with a message for the Ait Khebbash explaining that the raid was a reprisal for their complicity with el Aroussi. (It was a nice touch—el Aroussi had done the same thing.) By eight o'clock on the morning of November 5, they were safe with the legion at Tiberbatine, not a man, not a horse, missing.

Lyautey was jubilant. The *contre-djich* had been a "model operation," a combination of daring and prudence which had been crowned with success, although he admitted that he had been "truly anxious" as he awaited news. It simply proved what he had been saying all along about the value of native troops. The native foot especially had accomplished a "tour de force" by marching a hundred and twenty-five miles in forty-nine hours. French prestige was restored, troop morale high, and France's enemies confounded. The Tafilalet was no longer an inviolate sanctuary, a brigand's nest placed out of bounds by international agreement. This *razzia* firmly established the principle of "collective responsibility." Lyautey was quite clear on that point. Now the Ait Khebbash and others living west of the hammada would think twice before supporting raids into the Guir.

The Tafilalet raid was more than a tactical success. It announced the victory of a system—the Lyautey system. In his three years at Ain Sefra, Lyautey had revolutionized tactics on the Moroccan frontier, remodeled an army grown fat and lethargic and put it back on the offensive. When Lyautey had reported to Ain Sefra, a fresh brigadier, in 1903, the army which he took over was like a dazed prizefighter capable only of absorbing punishment handed out by its lighter, more aggressive opponent, not of anticipating or countering it. The problem was not one of numbers. He had plenty of soldiers, even perhaps too many—over eight thousand. But they were trained to the "Germanic" standards slavishly aped by the French army since 1870: drilled, disciplined and weighted down with all the impedimenta required for a winter campaign on the Rhine. It was a ponderous force which rationalized its inability to move by occupying the oases along 250 miles of the Zousfana to deny them to the enemy. But the raids continued; enough wells remained unoccupied to slake the thirst of raiders who slipped out of Figuig or Béchar, through the "barrier" formed by the French posts along the Zousfana, to strike at targets deep in Algeria or, even better, at the supply convoys that kept the posts alive. The French army looked on, dumb and inert, as the Moroccans killed its men and stripped it of its supplies.

The army at Ain Sefra did not need a commander of tactical genius, a new Napoleon whose *coup d'oeil* would sway the military balance in some classic battle. This was not the style of the "war of the flea" where fighting was done in miniature, in penny-packet actions led by lieutenants and captains. The army at Ain Sefra needed a manager, a man who would sharpen the punch and rebuild the confidence of a force which, for too long, had been on the receiving end. Lyautey's job was to get his troops back into the ring.

In 1903, Lyautey had sold Jonnart a package that combined political, economic and military action. It was a brilliant piece of salesmanship pitched to the sensibilities of politicians and journalists. The pacification would be carried out essentially by economic means. The Moroccans would be lured into the market at Beni Ounif (later shifted to Colomb-Béchar when the railroad reached it) by cheap goods. There, French native-affairs officers would be able to make important contacts, gather intelligence and bribe the right people. At the same time, Moroccans would be brought face to face with the glaring contrasts between the stability and peace offered by the French regime and the anarchy of life on the plateaus. They would be seduced into following their own interests. As always, a few dissidents would continue the old way of life. But for these latter, Lyautey had a surprise—the Saharians.

The idea of a camel corps for desert fighting was as old as Bonaparte's 1799 invasion of Egypt. It had been revived by the French in 1842. But a camel requires extremely delicate handling. The experience simply confirmed the Arab view that Frenchmen and camels could never be friends, and it was quietly abandoned in 1845. However, by the 1890s, the occupation of southern Algeria had taken the Armée d'Afrique to the very fringes of the Sahara. There, the French army faced a new enemy—the Tuareg—the tall, willowy nomads of the desert. Mules were no longer adequate for fighting over what must be the world's most inhospitable terrain. The French army must adapt to the camel or give up any idea of dominating the desert.

The task fell to Captain, later General, Henri Laperrine, a small bearded man who, from the day he took command of the Saharian spahis and tirailleurs in 1898 until the Sahara finally claimed him in 1920, was the French army's acknowledged expert on desert warfare. It took a very special kind of officer to command a Saharian unit. Mastering the languages and the art of camel riding were the easiest requirements. The men had to be treated with as much tact as the animals they rode. One had to be sensitive to the subtle hierarchies, both tribal and racial, which determined social relationships in the desert: Arabs would not serve with Tuaregs and no one would serve with blacks or slaves. One also had to be prepared to put up with insolence and lack of respect. For this was the desert, where every man who carried a rifle was a lord. The Saharians were not a military unit as any European understood the term; there were no salutes, no parades, no discipline even. Some called them a militia, but even this is an inadequate comparison. The Saharians were a tribe, created by the officer who was their patriarch. If the trooper was not happy, he simply took the two camels he had brought with him upon joining, and departed. It was a system adapted to the desert. It was the only one that worked there.

When Lyautey came to Ain Sefra, he found the Saharians the "ideal cavalry" for the type of war he had to wage. (In fact, they were not cavalry at all, but mounted infantry who were meant to do their fighting dismounted.) They were able to endure the physical hardships imposed by the desert, the extremes of temperature, the thirst and, above all, the solitude of the great wastes which Europeans found unbearably oppressive, *le cafard*, which so often cracked the morale of legionnaires. The Saharians ate next to nothing—a few grains of wheat, some dried dates, lamb fat and salt—which meant that they needed no complicated supply organization. Their bravery was beyond question. They also possessed a sense of direction that left Europeans openmouthed with disbelief. They were able, quite literally, to smell their way through the desert by sniffing handfuls of soil.

Since they had spearheaded the French occupation of the Touat oasis in 1899, the Saharians had languished, used unimaginatively by Oran as convoy escorts along the Zousfana. Lyautey now gave Laperrine his head: in 1903 three companies of Saharians were created at Gourara, Touat and Tidikelt. The following year, a fourth company was created at Beni Abbès and a fifth, this one horse mounted, at Colomb-Béchar. It was fatal to sit still in the South Oranais. The Moroccans, like rats, would nibble a sedentary army to death. The French had to move to stay alive. And Lyautey kept his Saharians on the move, constantly swirling over the desert for ten days at a time at up to 250 miles from their bases. Unlike the *mokhaznis*, who were little more than bodyguards and messengers for native-affairs officers, they were stiffened by French NCOs, who gave them extra cohesion as fighting units.

This then was Lyautey's plan for pacifying the South Oranais. The French army no longer occupied points on the map, it occupied "zones." Nor was it simply an army. Under Lyautey's program of political and economic, as well as military, pacification, it had been transformed into an "organization on the march."

Lyautey not only set up an organization, he also breathed fire into the men who ran it. He would sweep out of the hills into the camps of unsuspecting commanders at the head of his enormous staff, his *zaouia* they called it, after the Moslem religious brotherhoods. If he had been given advance warning of the visit, officially or unofficially, the wise commander took the trouble to arrange a proper reception—a guard of honor, a fantasia, a simple but elaborately served meal—for the brigadier loved ceremony, especially when it was organized for his benefit. His touch was definitely Napoleonic—lots of smiles, ear-tweaking and familiar banter. But one had to judge his mood carefully. General Georges Catroux told a story of his first meeting with Lyautey in 1908 which illustrated the man's volatility. When Catroux, then a fresh subaltern in the legion, gave one of the stock replies to Lyautey's greeting—"In great shape, General, and happy to be marching at last!"—he provoked a hurricane of abuse: "Who said anything about marching! No one is marching! Get that idea out of your head! There are not any operations and there aren't going to be any! I don't want any fighting. . . . We're going to occupy Oudjda and that's all, without fighting. . . . I don't need your bayonets, I need men armed with picks and shovels. I need a road built between Oudjda and Marnia. That's what you are going to do. Your legionnaires are good diggers."

Lyautey disliked big operations. They were far too likely to attract attention from an often hostile press. He also disliked the hardened warriors who led them, men whose sole concern was their own reputations, a promotion or a Legion of Honor, although he knew how to use these men. Small-unit operations carefully prepared by native-affairs officers offered a more subtle and intelligent way of making war, and one which appealed to his sensibilities. There was no place at Ain Sefra for officers with a "metropolitan" mentality, for whom the passive routine of regimental life had become an opiate. His officers were expected to show initiative: build roads, dig wells, vaccinate the population against disease, keep their troops constantly on patrol so that the debilitating *cafard* would not set in, "show force so you will not have to use it," not wait for directions from headquarters. Here, fifty years before they became the standard techniques of counterinsurgency warfare in Algeria and Vietnam, Lyautey applied a "hearts-and-minds" strategy in the South Oranais.

None of this made Lyautey a popular commander. But even his worst enemies had to admit that the man had style. At Ain Sefra he lived like the provincial aristocrat he was, down to the family silver, which he had imported from Lorraine. European visitors were treated to Schubert lieder sung by German legionnaires or drawn into a discussion of the latest books published in Paris, about which he knew far more than they. But in the desert, his beloved desert, he was a prince. Nothing would have passed an inspection carried out by the book: His uniform was hidden beneath a huge burnous of royal purple, bordered in gold and decorated with the silver stars of rank. The "Saber, regulation cavalry" had been replaced by the one his grand-father had carried through Europe almost a century earlier. His campaign kit had also belonged to his grandfather and contained a silver cup engraved with the names of "Moskova, Lützen, Bautzen." His saddle holsters were covered in tiger skin, a souvenir of Tonkin. But the *pièce de résistance* was his tent: "as big as an apartment, lined with cloth and silk," he said of it, the ground covered with thick oriental carpets, the ceiling with scarlet cloth. Outside a huge spahi, the largest he could find, stood guard beneath his pennant which spanked the wind.

This was the commander of the South Oranais: authoritarian, egotistical, a force of nature rather than a personality. Even his style smacked of theatrics, a show put on for his influential visitors from Paris, who arrived skeptical anticolonialists and departed after several days of the Lyautey treatment—happy natives under enlightened and civilized administrators—enchanted. The man seemed to live on a stage: the palm trees, the white-domed mosques, the robed Arabs at prayer, "the muted sound of flutes and tambourines," the mountains, this "vast fairyland," simply provided the mise-en-scène for his great desert spectacular.

Lyautey's public mask is very difficult to penetrate. His numerous letters, which were obviously written to be quoted and passed from hand to hand, give only the most fleeting of glimpses into the inner man. As his ego was vast and in constant need of refreshment, Lyautey surrounded himself with more than his fair share of sycophants, careerists and impressionable men quite overawed by his formidable personality. The need to keep this court occupied and entertained meant that Lyautey was constantly performing, constantly onstage. This left little scope for genuine relationships, especially among his entourage, which, one suspects, he secretly despised. Lyautey was a rebel and could only muster a genuine sympathy for another of his sort.

One such person was Isabelle Eberhardt. To people familiar only with

Lyautey's public face, this friendship, which was established in 1904, seemed incongruous. Few who have written of Lyautey mention it, perhaps because they are unable to explain it. But it reveals far more of Lyautey's character than do his letters. The incongruous aspect of the relationship between Lyautey and Eberhardt sprang from their wildly different social positions: he an aristocratic soldier with important political and social connections, she a Russian Jew in a particularly advanced state of social rejection. But he was as fascinated by her as she was passionately attracted to him. Sex was at best latent in the affair, if it existed at all. The attraction lay in their shared similarities of character. She was a "rebel," Lyautey wrote. They both were, but her rebellion was complete. She had drifted through Europe, finally arriving in Marseilles, where she had worked as a docker. From Marseilles, it was but a short step to Algiers. She had been conquered by North Africa. She converted to Islam and married a sergeant of spahis, whom she soon abandoned to wander in the inhospitable South Oranais. She dressed as a man, called herself Si Mahmoud and often slept rough.

Lyautey had stumbled over her one night as she slept outside his tent wrapped in a burnous (his *zaouia*, fearing that she was a spy, had kept her at a distance). Their friendship lasted only for a few months, but by all indications it was an ardent one, a private rather than a clandestine relationship. Everyone knew that she came to his headquarters late at night to talk, often until dawn. It was certainly one of the few true friendships of his life. "We understood each other, the poor Mahmoud and I," Lyautey wrote after her death. What he meant was that she had helped him to understand himself. He was fascinated by her freedom, freedom from the "prejudices . . . clichés . . . the lawyers, corporals and the mandarins of all sorts" which tied him to the social order. But he could not imitate it.

On October 21, 1904, Ain Sefra was torn to pieces by a flood which destroyed Si Mahmoud's house. When news of her death was brought to Lyautey, he asked if her diary had been recovered. His soldiers were sent to search for it. For several days, under his close supervision, they cut trenches through the mud and silt until at least part of the diary was found (and later published). Her death had been a blessing: "I feared that she would be condemned to a life of madness and constant deception," he wrote. "Poor Mahmoud." Her death was a blessing for him too. How silly at this late stage to flirt with alternatives. There were none. He no longer needed an analyst, only a confessor.

Perhaps the most admired aspect of Mahmoud's freedom for Lyautey was her freedom from the anguish of failure. Failure haunted him. The problem was not the Moroccans. It was the "dissidents"—Lyautey's term for anyone who opposed him—in the Quai d'Orsay and their chief, Delcassé. The only way to secure the frontier, and ultimately shelter Algeria from an Islamic *jihad*, was to "digest" Morocco. Béchar had been his first bite. But Ras-el-Ain, his second mouthful, proved almost too large to swallow.

The occupation of Ras-el-Ain began quietly enough. In early June 1904, Lyautey traveled to Oran to organize the expedition: three infantry companies, three squadrons of spahis, an artillery section and a swarm of several hundred *goumiers* under the command of Major Henrys, his chief of staff. The reason for the occupation, he said, was that Bou-Amana was active in the north. Perhaps he believed it. But the old chief had not fired a shot in anger at the French since he had led the great *jihad* of 1881, for the simple reason that the French had subsidized his retirement. Bou-Amana was not willing to jeopardize his yearly stipend for the sake of a few rifles. Henrys proceeded to take Ras-el-Ain without a shot fired, except, that is, by the Algerian sentries, who fired at almost anything. ("It amuses and distracts them," Lyautey said.) Lyautey visited the place himself a few days later and declared it a "marvelous spot"—five casbahs, a few trees, "superb waters—I bathed and swam," a "delicious" week of night rides, sleeping wrapped in his burnous, all under a full desert moon. And, of course, the final Lyautey touch: Ras-el-Ain was "diplomatically" rebaptized Berguent so that Paris would not be aware that another few square miles of Morocco had been "digested."

In private, Lyautey gloated over this triumph. The French army had jumped sixty miles farther forward. He had organized it discreetly, with "the prudence of a snake." But his optimism was premature. By mid-July, he began to suspect that echoes of the expedition had reached Paris. The first indication that his secret might have leaked out occurred during a banquet for the Moroccan Committee.

Large meals had become the distinguishing feature of colonialist meetings, so much so that the colonial party was referred to as *le parti où on dîne*. On this occasion, Eugène Etienne spoke at some length about Lyautey and his role in the South Oranais. The newspapers gave Etienne's speech front-page treatment. Lyautey was flattered, but worried. He reminded Etienne that it was a particularly delicate time, that it was not "discreet" to focus the attention of the press on Berguent, that such statements could excite jealousy. He was correct. The press began a campaign critical of military penetration on the Algerian-Moroccan border. The Sultan complained to Tangiers, which complained to Delcassé, who complained to the government. Lyautey's secrecy was blown: on July 31, the "fatal telegram" arrived ordering him out of Ras-el-Ain—the Berguent trick had not worked this time—and back to Algeria.

What to do? Any other officer would have heaved a sigh and followed orders. Not Lyautey. He had already announced that he was marked out for great success or complete ignominy. Playing safe was for metropolitan officers.

He was stunned by the telegram. Jonnart had told him that everything had been "arranged" concerning Berguent. He contacted Algiers only to be told that Jonnart had left on a yachting holiday in the Mediterranean and had "cut the wire." The important thing was to "gain time" until he could arrange to have the order rescinded or at least modified.

The War Ministry was the first to feel the full force of his fury. It was "surrender," he told war minister General Louis André, a "second Fashoda." The native population at Berguent wanted the French to remain: staring down so many rifle barrels, it was unlikely that they would have said anything else. Lyautey was a disciplined soldier. But there was a higher discipline—to one's country, and to the people under one's protection. To leave now would be to abandon them to reprisals too horrible to contemplate. Then, he placed his neck firmly in the noose: if Paris insisted upon the evacuation of Ras-el-Ain, then Paris could have his resignation.

He would resign. This is what he told Etienne, Jonnart and everyone else he knew in long screeds which poured out of Ain Sefra. It was a bold gamble. What if they called his bluff? It was, he said, "the only chance, the last chance, to make them think again." The next days were "the most anxious hours of my life."

On August 7, the verdict was wired from Paris: "Withdraw," it read—his heart stopped—but "when the situation permits" and "by stages." His carefully spun network of friends, which stretched from Algiers to the Palais Bourbon, had protected him. This was not a victory, but it offered a "breathing space," time to canvass, to change a few minds. Meanwhile, he threw Tangiers a scrap by sending a platoon of French Zouaves back to Algeria.

Chez Maxim's is not a temple of *haute cuisine*, a place where Frenchmen go to dine in religious silence. The food is quite decent, but one goes there to meet friends or to transact business in highly agreeable surroundings, not to stretch the taste buds. By the turn of the century, Chez Maxim's had become something of a colonialist haunt. That is where Lyautey went to meet Jonnart and Etienne when he arrived in Paris on September 14 for what was to be the confrontation between the colonialists and their adversaries in the Quai d'Orsay. Through a haze of cigar smoke, they discussed their strategy. Then they strolled across the Place de la Concorde, over the bridge to the left bank and Delcassé's ornate rooms in the Foreign Office with a view over a quiet stretch of the Seine.

For three days they talked. Lyautey was nervous, and strained to keep his self-control. His views on "peaceful penetration" were already on record: it was impossible to take over by peaceful means a country where virtually everyone was armed and prepared to resist, just as it was absurd to treat with a Sultan whose authority was not recognized in a major portion of his territory. But he did not belabor his point. The object of the talks was to find a compromise. Lyautey proposed an ingenious one: His French Zouaves at Ras-el-Ain would be replaced by Algerian tirailleurs. These would be joined by a contingent of the Sultan's troops under an officer from the French military mission. When the situation was stabilized, the remainder of the French troops would withdraw, leaving a mixed force commanded by French officers but nominally under the Sultan's authority. Etienne and Jonnart thought this an excellent plan. Delcassé and St.-René Taillandier rejected it out of hand. They were not interested in compromise, only in "withdrawal." That, Lyautey told them, was "impossible."

It appeared to be a standoff, "block against block," with no one willing to budge, until the colonialists received help from a totally unexpected source: Prime Minister Emile Combes and General André. Unexpected, first because neither man was a colonialist; and second, because there was little love lost between the conservative Lyautey and his Radical bosses. But the Radicals were eager to ax Delcassé, a moderate republican whom they had inherited from preceding governments. Delcassé defied the laws of parliamentary instability: governments came and went with dizzying frequency, but Delcassé remained, like Banquo's ghost, a moderate at a Radical banquet. He criticized their priest-baiting, their doctrinaire and petty vendetta against army officers and conservatives, and they wanted him out of the government. Lyautey would become the vehicle to undermine his prestige.

Lyautey won. He remained at Ras-el-Ain. The Sultan sent a contingent of *askar*: a hundred old men and boys unwillingly conscripted in Tangiers. But the joke was on Delcassé. They were only expert at stealing, not at fighting, "wretched players recruited for a gala evening in a poor provincial theater," Lyautey called them. Within a month, forty of them had deserted to the French, complaining that they were starving. Clearly, the French occupation of Ras-el-Ain would continue indefinitely. In November, Etienne again sang Lyautey's praises, this time in the Chamber of Deputies. Delcassé, St.-René Taillandier and "peaceful penetration" were on the way out. In the end, however, it was not Combes who showed them the door, but a far more powerful, unexpected and sinister figure: Kaiser Wilhelm II.

CHAPTER X

1905: THE COUP DE TANGER

"My Emperor is coming to see me!" The diplomatic colleagues of Baron Richard von Kuhlmann, the German minister in Tangiers, were quite obviously less pleased than he was by this news. The French had suspected that something was in the air: for some days, Moroccans had spat at them in the streets or thrown them looks full of malice. "The 'Sultan el Brouze' [King of Prussia] is coming to the rescue of Abd el-Aziz. He has thousands of soldiers as close to the French capital as Oran is to Fez!" Had Morocco at last found a savior?

On the morning of March 31, 1905, the German Emperor did indeed come to see his minister in Tangiers. But Wilhelm II appeared a decidedly reluctant actor on the world stage as he stood, pale and nervous, on the bridge of the German liner *Hamburg* in a force 8 gale. Like many military men, he looked incongruously ordinary out of uniform, even though his suit was well tailored. His heavy mustache, hung on a face almost completely devoid of charm, made him appear more like a policeman than the "Emperor of the Atlantic." He could clearly see the reception committee that waited for him on the shore: the Sultan's uncle, Abd el-Malek, led the makhzan delegation, their pristine white jellabas billowing in the spring gale. Next to them, the European diplomats in full uniform held tightly to their white-plumed bicorns, all except Kuhlmann, that is, who wore the glistening spiked helmet of a captain of Uhlans. Caid Maclean stood at the head of a guard of honor of more or less uniformly dressed *askar*. However, the French had taken special pains to demonstrate to the Kaiser that he was visiting "their" Tangiers: the *Hamburg* was bracketed by two French cruisers, the *Du Chayla* and the *Linois*. On shore, a picket of French marines formed a hedge while French residents of Tangiers, with the encouragement of their legation, had decorated the streets in the national blue, white and red.

For some hours, the Kaiser debated whether or not the state of the sea permitted a landing. This indecision proved too much for the shivering diplomats. The patience of the Belgian consul was the first to crack under the pelting rain: he led what became a precipitate retreat of his colleagues toward the German legation, where a reception had been prepared. Abd el-Malek and the Moroccans remained loyally at their posts. Finally, at about 11:30 in the morning, Wilhelm decided to attempt a landing. Dressed in a field uniform—silver helmet with chin strap, polished black boots, red gloves, his revolver hanging on a cord around his neck and his saber dangling at his side—he was lowered into the whaler, rowed toward the shore and carried the last few yards through the water by two large German sailors. When he topped the wooden steps onto the quay, he appeared haggard and not quite composed. Perhaps it was a touch of seasickness. More likely, he was unnerved by the enormity of the gesture he was about to make. Abd el-Malek bowed deeply. Wilhelm said a few words to him in an inaudible voice. No one, including Abd el-Malek, who spoke no German, had understood what the Emperor had said. Only on the following day, when Kuhlmann released a stylized version to the press, did everyone realize that his words had been of immense importance.

The Kaiser was hoisted onto a horse and, his semiparalyzed arm hanging limply by his side, was led through the streets followed by a cortège of generals, admirals and aides-de-camp. It must have looked as if the cast of a Wagnerian opera had wandered by mistake onto a stage set for *Aïda*. Slowly, through the cheering crowds, they made their way toward the Grand Soko, where they were met by a scene that bordered on pandemonium. In fact, it was nothing more than a warm Moroccan welcome: groups of Rif tribesmen in their traditional warrior dance shouted, pitched their rifles into the air, caught and fired them in one deft movement. Others beat drums and sang, while the women shrieked ululations of welcome from the rooftops. The noisy, pulsating mob appeared to the Germans, already aware of Tangiers' bad reputation for disorder, to be a riot. The Kaiser looked even paler than before. His horse, despite the fact that its head was held by two men, was rapidly becoming unmanageable. One of the Emperor's lieutenants rushed to French captain Fournier, one of the instructors of the newly created Moroccan police force, and told him to disperse the crowd. The captain merely shrugged his shoulders. The task was certainly beyond his slender powers.

The Kaiser dismounted and entered the German legation. There he met the diplomats who had deserted their posts by the shore, uttered a few homilies about "respecting the interests of German commerce," made his excuses, returned to the *Hamburg* and sailed away. The Moroccans were very disappointed, as they had arranged an afternoon of gunpowder play followed by a great feast in the casbah. The next day, perhaps appropriately April 1, Kuhlmann announced that the Kaiser's visit had been meant to underline Germany's commitment to Morocco's continued independence. France, Britain, the world, were staggered.

Why this amazing statement? The story behind the Kaiser's declaration has its origins on the other side of Africa. In 1896, a handful of French marine officers, hardened veterans of the tough campaigns in the Western Sudan, and around two hundred handpicked Senegalese riflemen under the command of Colonel Jean Baptiste Marchand set off from the mouth of the Congo River on what was to be an epic trek across Africa. Two years and three thousand miles later, they heaved up on the Nile at a place called Fashoda, a small collection of mud buildings several hundred miles upriver from Khartoum. With as much ceremony as they could muster, they broke out the dress white uniforms which they had brought for this occasion and planted their tricolored flag.

The Fashoda expedition had been the brainchild of the colonialists led by Delcassé and Etienne. These men had never forgiven the British their "perfidious" occupation of Egypt in July 1882, and since that time had sought some way to pressure them into concessions there. The presence of a French garrison in the Egyptian hinterland would force London to come to terms with France's "historic claims" on the Nile. The Chamber of Deputies which had been elected in August–September 1893 was a particularly unstable one, even for the Third Republic. With five governments over the next four years, all of them too preoccupied with their own survival to worry overmuch about the machinations of the colonial lobby in Africa, Delcassé and Etienne were given virtually a free hand to launch Marchand across Africa.

Between the time Marchand disappeared up the Congo River until he emerged at Fashoda, things had changed in France. In June 1898, Delcassé became foreign minister in the cabinet of Henri Brisson, a post which he was to hold for the next seven years. He was no longer the irresponsible protagonist of colonial expansion, but the master diplomat charged with guiding his country through the treacherous waters of European diplomacy. The perspective from the Quai d'Orsay was entirely different from that in the choked, crowded back streets of the Left Bank, where the colonial ministry was housed. The massive continent south of the Mediterranean began to recede in importance, to be replaced by new concerns which were to obsess him over the next few years—France's place in Europe.

A similar, although slightly different, evolution had occurred among Etienne and his colonialists, one that eventually was to bring them into conflict with Delcassé. While committed "Africans," their spiritual base was Algeria. Algeria was the linchpin of the French colonial empire, its crown jewel, in much the same way that India formed the centerpiece of the British Empire. French colonialists placed colonial problems in an Algerian perspective. Tunisia had been absorbed in 1881, thereby guaranteeing the safety of Algeria's eastern borders. In the west, however, Morocco remained, turbulent and unstable, "a fireship on the flank of Algeria." Thus, by diverse routes, Delcassé and Etienne had reached the same conclusion, namely, that it was unwise to tweak the lion's tail. Delcassé needed Britain's friendship to counterbalance German influence in Europe. Etienne also wanted to avoid antagonizing London, which stood as the principal guarantor of Moroccan independence. Perhaps London and Paris might work a deal: France would drop her claims in Egypt in return for a free hand in Morocco.

Buried in the bush, Marchand was unaware of the subtle change of view which was taking place in Paris. He was also unaware of the events taking place in Egypt. Since the Gordon fiasco of 1885, the British had abandoned the Sudan to the depredations of the Mahdi and his successors. A decade later, however, calls to avenge Gordon's death increased as news of the horrible brutalities of the Mahdists in Sudan reached Europe. In the scramble for African lands, the empty Sudan acted as a vacuum which drew the competing colonial powers. The French, it was well known in London and Brussels, had designs on the Sudan as part of an east–west imperial axis stretching from St.-Louis du Sénégal to the Red Sea. The Italians were attempting, with little success, to stake a claim in Ethiopia. On top of it all was the old fear that a resurgence of Mahdist energy might once again threaten the Suez canal. All of these fears and ambitions were brought to a head in 1895 when the Conservatives under Lord Salisbury ousted the Liberals in the general election. The British colonial office fell to the bellicose colonialist Joseph Chamberlain, who had no intention of allowing France a foothold on the Nile.

In 1896, Chamberlain had ordered Kitchener to begin a slow southward march toward Khartoum. On September 1, 1898, the English general arrived at Omdurman, across the Nile from Khartoum, with a force of over twenty thousand men, gunboats mounting a hundred guns and a vast supply convoy of camels and horses. On the next morning at dawn, in the shadow of the great dome of the Mahdi's tomb, fifty thousand Sudanese tribesmen in a line four miles long attacked the British. They were massacred. Within a short two hours, over ten thousand bodies lay in piles over the desert. At about 11:30, Kitchener, surveying the battlefield from horseback, announced that the enemy had been given "a good dusting." The Sudan was now British— almost. After a brief and emotional ceremony in the grounds of the palace where Gordon had been slain eleven years before, Kitchener was handed a sealed envelope with urgent orders from England: these told him to proceed up the Nile in all haste to dislodge a French force at Fashoda.

What the French thought they might achieve with the occupation of Fashoda has never been entirely clear. Fashoda itself was a dreadful place, desolate and malarial. It never seems to have occurred to any of these men bivouacked in clouds of mosquitoes under a fiercely humid sun to question why it was important to occupy it. From Paris, the Marchand expedition was seen at its simplest as part of the great African land grab: the Sudan is vacant, so we shall occupy it. Small expeditions of this sort operating not too far from their bases had been the bread and butter of African expansion in the Western Sudan. But to march a force of fewer than two hundred men across the breadth of Africa to establish a remote post on the Upper Nile was preposterous. Two things could happen to it: either the Mahdists would wipe out Marchand's force or the British would. Omdurman meant that the task fell to Kitchener.

When London first learned toward the end of 1896 that a French force had left Brazzaville for the Sudan, they assumed that it must number at least six hundred men. Nothing smaller could hope to establish a viable post and provide for its own defense. When Kitchener heard that the French were, in fact, but a mere handful, he detached two battalions of Sudanese, a hundred Cameron Highlanders, a battery of artillery and four Maxim guns from his substantial army and sailed up the river in five steamers toward Fashoda. As he approached the French camp on September 18, he sent a messenger ahead with an invitation to Marchand to dine aboard his flagship on the following day. The meeting passed off well. Kitchener, dressed in his Egyptian uniform and red fez, had arrived in Fashoda under an Egyptian flag so as not to affront French sensibilities. A fluent French speaker, the normally severe general proved the very soul of affability, congratulating Marchand on his splendid march, adding only that he must protest the Frenchman's presence at Fashoda. The French chief replied with equal courtesy that he intended to defend himself if attacked and, in the meantime, he must await orders from Paris. They agreed to let their respective governments sort out matters. The two men and their officers then settled down to a friendly round of visits before Kitchener established a small Egyptian camp next to that of the French and sailed back to Khartoum. Before he left, however, he handed Marchand a stack of French newspapers, explaining that he was sure that his French friends might want to catch up on news from home. This proved one of the most brilliant psychological ploys of Kitchener's career. The Frenchmen threw themselves eagerly on the newspapers (which had been carefully selected by Kitchener), only to learn that for the past eighteen months France and her army had been torn apart by the Dreyfus affair; and they wept.

The Fashoda crisis was eventually resolved, but not without acrimony. The press of the two countries swapped vituperative insults. Prussia, after all, was a relatively recent enemy; Franco-British animosity had a long and venerable history. The British government stood firm. The French, who were already beginning to have doubts about the wisdom of the Marchand expedition even before it arrived at Fashoda, eventually gave way. On December 11, 1898, the French struck their colors at Fashoda and marched out toward the Red Sea, preferring not to take the easier route through British territory to Cairo. The British garrison at Fashoda inherited their vegetable garden and their substantial stocks of wine and champagne. In March 1899, Lord Salisbury and Paul Cambon, the French ambassador to the Court of St. James's, signed an agreement which recognized British interests in the Nile valley. This paved the way for the signing on April 8, 1904, of the Franco-British Entente whereby Britain agreed to support French aims in Morocco. Bou Hamara and Raisuni had done much to convince the British that the country needed a firm hand. The Entente was followed on October 30, 1904, by a Franco-Spanish treaty providing for respective spheres of influence in Morocco.

The French had, at last, achieved their desire: a free hand in Morocco. They had neglected one thing, however, and that was Germany. This was to prove to be an almost fatal oversight. Berlin was in a peculiar mood. Mutterings about *Weltpolitik* and Germany's need for "a place in the sun" betrayed the feeling of profound insecurity in the German political elite. The Chancellor, Prince von Bülow, complained that the older, established powers of Europe refused to recognize "our dignity and our recently acquired authority as a world power." Most of this was for home consumption. The Kaiser and his entourage felt that many in Germany resented the unification of the country under conservative Prussia in 1871. They were also alarmed at the rise of the German Socialist party, the SPD, which gained votes with each election. Bismarck had attempted to buy off the workers with social legislation. By the 1890s, reactionary, nearly feudal Germany had the most advanced social legislation in Europe, far ahead of that of left-leaning France. But this tactic had failed to buy off working-class discontent: support for the SPD continued to increase. So the government played the chauvinist card: the naval laws of 1898 and 1900 sought to create a navy that would be the visible manifestation of German greatness. Britain would tremble. France, indeed virtually every other continental power, was already scared stiff of Germany's massive army.

News of the Entente reached Berlin in a rather garbled form. The Germans suspected that it was a military alliance, another link in the chain of encirclement which already included the Franco-Russian Alliance of 1893, when in fact it was no more than a straight colonial trade-off, Morocco for Egypt. If Germany supported Moroccan independence, von Bülow calculated, Britain would back off from her alliance with France. France, then, would be isolated as her only other ally, Russia, was engaged in a catastrophic war with Japan. The Moroccan question was simply a means to this end. A neat plan, but it contained at least one fallacy: it assumed that Britain would desert her new ally. This was unlikely. The Fashoda crisis followed closely by the Boer War of 1899–1902 had demonstrated all too painfully how friendless Britain was in the world. The German naval laws, which were a direct challenge to British mastery of the seas, drove this point forcefully home. By 1904, Britain had found her friend in Europe. She intended to stick by her. The Tangiers crisis of 1905 was the first step in transforming the colonial Entente of 1904 into the European military alliance of 1914.

On April 18, 1904, barely ten days after the signing of the Entente, St.-Aulaire, first secretary of the French legation at Tangiers, set out for Fez to negotiate a loan of 62 million francs by a French consortium led by the Banque de Paris et des Pays-Bas. A Delcassé man and partisan of "peaceful penetration," he hoped to convince the Sultan to give up vital rights to customs receipts as surety for the loan. It would prove a delicate task, so delicate in fact that no more senior diplomat would risk his career by attempting it. Nor was his mission made easier by the Entente, the news of which was greeted with much bitterness in Morocco: everywhere he was told "England has sold Morocco to France." In Fez, St.-Aulaire was housed in splendid discomfort and left to cool his heels. Finally, on May 14, Abd el-Aziz consented to an interview. The French diplomat found the Sultan sitting on a Louis XV chair in the palace gardens, a pale, trembling figure wearing white gloves which were far too long for him. St.-Aulaire had almost to shout to make himself heard above the roar of the caged lions. But after a relatively long talk, the Sultan agreed to allow the loan negotiations to proceed. By May 23, St.-Aulaire had sewn up his financial package: the makhzan agreed to negotiate only with French banks and to allow French customs officers to take 60 percent of Moroccan customs receipts.

The French were ecstatic. "Peaceful penetration" appeared to have gotten off to a roaring start. Then suddenly, unpredictably, Germany decided to replace Britain as the champion of Moroccan independence. In January 1905, von Bülow wired to the Sultan German support for his resistance to French demands. The visit of the Kaiser to Tangiers on March 31 was calculated to underline in a particularly dramatic fashion the strength of that support. No wonder the Kaiser was so nervous and even half reluctant to disembark at Tangiers. He realized that his action was a colossal gamble. To bolster his resolve, von Bülow had placed the Kaiser before a *fait accompli* by announcing the visit to the press and then persuading the Kaiser that it would be undignified, even humiliating, to withdraw.

The Emperor's visit to Tangiers was an ill-considered act, typical of the blustering, erratic nature of German diplomacy in the decade before 1914. Spain was told that she must abandon her October 1904 agreement with France, which had partitioned Morocco into spheres of influence. The French Prime Minister, Maurice Rouvier, was informed in no uncertain terms by Berlin that his foreign minister must go: "So long as Monsieur Delcassé remains in office, there is no possibility of an improvement in Franco-German relations." It was an offensive display of bullying. Rouvier contemplated war, but his chief of staff quickly dissuaded him; the Dreyfus affair had wrecked the army. The best officers were resigning and morale was low. In terms of numbers and firepower, the French could not match German strength. Her only ally, Russia, was paralyzed in Siberia by Japan.

Humiliated, Rouvier decided to negotiate. He offered von Bülow territorial compensation elsewhere in Africa, but having posed as the champion of Moroccan independence, however dishonestly, von Bülow could not now abandon his new protégé. The Moroccans, believing at last that they had found in Germany a true protector to replace defaulting Britain, proposed an international conference. Berlin agreed to this proposal. Among the signatories of the 1880 Madrid Convention on Morocco who would be invited to take part, France, von Bülow calculated, would find little comfort.

The Triple Alliance would guarantee the support of Austria-Hungary and Italy. The United States, together with the small nations of Europe, would rally to von Bülow's policy of the "open door." Spain, sensing France's isolation, would fall into the German camp, while Britain's support of France would be purely "platonic."

The conference opened in Algeciras on January 16, 1906. Even the choice of the Spanish town was a defeat for the Germans and their Moroccan allies. These had favored Tangiers, but the wisdom of gathering some of Europe's most prominent diplomats in a town where Raisuni held sway was so questionable that even the Germans had to give way. The diplomats, their wives, journalists, concession hunters and other hangers-on crowded into the Reina Cristina Hotel, a "low-storied, bow-windowed structure under Scottish management" which looked across the bay to the "crouching mass of Gibraltar." For the next three months, they haggled over points so arcane that no layman might divine that the very power structure of Europe hung in the balance. They talked Morocco, but their thoughts were only of Europe.

The Germans were led by Herr Joseph von Radowitz, a man whose charm possessed a distinct hint of menace, and the blustering Count von Tattenbach—"the worst type of German I have ever met," wrote the British representative, Sir Arthur Nicolson. Their objective was to prevent the French from gaining a predominant position in Morocco. The French, on the other hand, sought to establish their influence in Morocco through the port police and the creation of a state bank. In Monsieur Paul Révoil, a small man with a waxed mustache, they had an eloquent and supple advocate. A lawyer by training and a diplomat by profession, his experience as French minister in Tangiers and ex-governor general of Algeria put him in a position to speak with authority on the Moroccan question.

Révoil played an open hand, courting the smaller powers—Holland, Portugal, Belgium, Sweden—and charming the vacuous American representative, Henry White. The Germans, in contrast, frittered away their initial advantage by giving each delegation a different account of their motives and plans. Gradually, imperceptibly, the sympathy of the conference shifted toward France. The anarchy into which Morocco appeared to be plunged was the clinching argument for a firm attitude toward Morocco. That the French were largely responsible for this state of anarchy was not understood by the delegates. The American, White, allowed himself to be convinced by Révoil that only French officers and Algerian NCOs were capable of organizing an effective Moroccan police force. The Italians also fell into line. The smaller powers went along with the majority. Germany held what a poker player would call a busted flush. By giving a little on the question of the state bank, the French won a complete victory. For Berlin, Algeciras had been a fiasco.

Worse than a fiasco, it had been a disaster. Germany's world position was worse after the Tangiers crisis than before. She had tried to isolate France under cover of the Moroccan question and failed. France and Britain had drawn closer together: staff talks between the two armies were authorized in January 1906. In the words of French diplomat André Tardieu: "The *entente* passed from a static to a dynamic state."

In Morocco, France was now firmly established. With Spain, she had divided police duties in port cities. The Moroccan state bank was dominated by the Banque de Paris et des Pays-Bas. What was more, the removal of Delcassé (at German insistence) now freed Lyautey and the colonialists from the restraining hand of the Quai d'Orsay. "Peaceful penetration" had lost its staunchest advocate.

The victory of France was also a defeat for the Sultan Abd el-Aziz. German claims to protect Islamic independence had been exposed as so much hollow rhetoric. With the increase in the number of foreigners in Morocco, the Sultan began to lose control of his country. Attacks on Europeans increased, like that on Charbonnier in Tangiers in 1906. The French had produced the anarchy. Only the French could suppress it.

CHAPTER XI

CASABLANCA

The outcome of the Algeciras Conference proved to be the last straw for the woe-laden Sultan Abd el-Aziz. His ally Germany had let him down badly. Before the ink was dry on the Act of Algeciras, the French had reinstalled the military mission in Fez which had been dismissed by the Sultan, their customs officers had settled into Moroccan ports, and French and Spanish officers took the Moroccan police in hand in coastal towns. Everywhere they looked, Moroccans saw an influx of Europeans, and they were not pleased. European travelers found that the once-friendly population was now decidedly hostile. Attacks on Europeans increased, and were duly noted by consular officials: Albert Charbonnier was murdered in Tangiers in 1906; in the same year a French tourist was set upon when he tried to photograph some Moroccans and would have been beaten to death had he not been rescued by a passing *mokhazni*; an official of the Compagnie Marocaine was beaten and left for dead on the road between Marrakech and Safi. What a naïve man Delcassé had been. "Peaceful penetration" proved to be nothing more than "methodical provocation."

Delcassé's miscalculations could be turned to good advantage by the colonialists who prepared, now that the Quai d'Orsay had been neutered, for more spectacular advances into Morocco. All they needed was an excuse, and the ex-foreign minister had kindly provided them with one. One of Delcassé's pet projects had been the establishment of medical dispensaries in Moroccan towns. What could offer more convincing proof of France's benevolent intentions in North Africa? In fact, in the volatile political climate of Morocco following Algeciras, the arrival of Dr. Mauchamp at Marrakech, the first of these French doctors to venture away from the coastal towns, offered another provocation. Medicine as practiced in Morocco required great tact. If traditional Moroccan doctors relied upon lunar caustic, hot irons and spells, it was with good reason. The goal of Mauchamp's mission was obvious to many in Marrakech: he had been sent by the *roumi* to treat men hostile to a French takeover of Morocco, and two years later they would suddenly and mysteriously die. "Only in Morocco are such fables believed," wrote the French minister Eugène Regnault, who had replaced St.-René Taillandier in 1906, in his report on the Mauchamp affair.

Perhaps Emile Mauchamp did not realize how much the atmosphere had deteriorated in the spring of 1907. He had just returned from his annual leave in France with a geologist friend, Dr. Louis Gentil. The day before, March 18, the two men had erected a pole and some cabling on the roof of Mauchamp's house so that Gentil could carry out a triangulation survey. When he opened his surgery at 10:30 on the morning of March 19, he was met by the *muqaddam* of the neighborhood. The people, the *muqaddam* explained to Mauchamp's interpreter, Mohammed, were upset by the equipment on the roof. It was, they said, a telegraph system through which Mauchamp could communicate with the French on the coast. Mauchamp's impatient, slightly imperious manner had not made him popular in Marrakech. Perhaps this showed through as he explained to the *muqaddam* that it was simply a pole, but if the *muqaddam* wanted it removed, he would do so.

Mauchamp left his surgery with Mohammed to walk the two hundred yards to his house. He was destined not to arrive. A crowd blocked his path. Mauchamp explained through his interpreter that he was about to remove the offending equipment. It was no use. Mohammed was put to flight and sought refuge in a nearby house. Mauchamp was less lucky. The crowd made his escape impossible. A man stepped forward and slashed him with his knife. Wounded, Mauchamp lurched down a side street followed closely by the mob. It was unlikely that he would have gone far even if this alley had not ended in a blank wall. The men jostled each other to stab him. Then they sacked his house. When, two hours later, the *mokhaznis* of the pasha of Marrakech arrived, Mauchamp's body had been stripped and a cord tied around his feet (it was to be dragged to some clear ground several hundred yards away and burned). By early afternoon, Mauchamp's books, his tennis racket and other articles pillaged in his house were for sale in the market.

Mauchamp's murder produced the predictable sense of outrage in Paris. Many accused the pasha of Marrakech, Moulai Hafid, and his *éminence grise*, a Syrian Jew named Judah Holzmann who the French claimed (quite wrongly) was a German physician, of orchestrating his murder. This is impossible to substantiate. What is certain, however, is that Mauchamp's death served Lyautey's ends. Quietly, effortlessly, on March 29, 1907, he marched his troops into Oudjda on the northeast frontier. Algeria had taken yet another bite out of Morocco. Lyautey wrote to his friend A. E. M. de

Vogüé that he awaited only a massacre to put his "snowball method" into action. The metaphor was perhaps inappropriate for a Moroccan summer, but his wish was granted.

Casablanca is not a particularly beautiful town. Today it sprawls along several miles of flat, uninteresting coastline, the industrial and commercial heart of Morocco. In the late nineteenth century, the coastline around Casablanca was not only flat and uninteresting but empty as well. Perhaps this was the attraction of Casablanca for the Europeans who transformed the small casbah of Dar el Beida into a modern city—its emptiness and the richness of its largely underdeveloped hinterland, the Chaouia. At Rabat, el Jadida, Safi or Essaouira, they would have had to contend with an entrenched population. At Dar el Beida, they could begin virtually from scratch. Life there was also phenomenally cheap by European standards. A large house could be rented for fifty francs (two pounds or ten dollars) a month; a servant cost ten francs per month; a donkey could be bought for ten francs and a horse for fifty. Food cost a pittance. The Chaouia contained plentiful game. Casablanca might not be paradise, but for many Europeans it offered a standard of living far superior to what they might expect at home.

The substantial influx of Europeans around the turn of the century placed Casablanca, like Tangiers, in a special category among Moroccan towns. As the small casbah was swamped by new arrivals, both Europeans and immigrants from the interior, Casablanca could no longer maintain the traditional structures of Moroccan town life. There were no *ulama*, nor was there a stable class of native merchants as in Fez. A caid and a small garrison were the only visible signs of makhzan authority. Casablanca was a haven of the uprooted: brash fortune hunters from Europe, Algeria or the Levant eager to pick over the meager bones of Moroccan commerce for their own profit, local merchants on the make, poor peasants forced out of the interior by famine or disorder who formed an unhappy and potentially volatile proletariat around the fringes of the city. On the surface, Casablanca appeared in 1907 to be Morocco's city of the future: commercial houses were well established, protégés numbered almost ten thousand and the recently established Compagnie Marocaine had begun work on a jetty for the harbor. Once that was completed, Casablanca's commerce would take off. But beneath this façade of optimism, it was a deeply unhappy city.

Like London or Paris in the eighteenth century, Casablanca in 1907 offered a few of its inhabitants the prospect of rich rewards and threatened the great majority of them with bitter disappointment. Tension between the towns and the pastoral tribes in the countryside was traditional in Morocco. In the Chaouia behind Casablanca, this tension reached dangerous proportions. The large European population meant that the protégé system was more developed in Casablanca than elsewhere in Morocco. It was also more abused. Many families in the hinterland had brothers, uncles or cousins locked away in the Casablanca prison for defaulting on debts to Europeans or to their protégés. Casablanca was seen as a cancerous tumor whose growth threatened their traditional way of life and their religion.

The beginning of the harbor work in 1907, and the arrival of the French customs officers in July of that year, strengthened this view. The country people claimed that the French were even collecting revenues at the shrines of Moslem saints. On July 28, 1907, a deputation of tribesmen representing eleven Chaouia tribes marched into the caïd's residence. They told the weak and ineffectual Sidi Bou Bekr Ben Bouzid that he must dismiss the French customs men and stop work on the harbor. But it was the steam engine that especially infuriated them. The Compagnie Marocaine had constructed a narrow-gauge railway to carry stones from the quarry to the jetty and in the process had driven it close to a Moorish cemetery. Each day this diabolical machine steamed back and forth blowing its whistle—a whistle being a sign of derision in Morocco—an insult to both the living and the dead. Bouzid told them to return the next day for an answer. In the absence of the French consul, he asked an English merchant what he should do. "Close the gates and man the walls," was the answer, but Bouzid did nothing.

The French had been contemplating a landing on the Atlantic coast of Morocco for some time. In the war archives at Vincennes is a War Ministry memo, dated August 27, 1905, which argues strongly that the two methods tried to bring pressure upon the makhzan—naval demonstrations and the occupation of territory on the Algerian frontier—had so far failed to produce results. Only by landing troops on the Atlantic shore could the Sultan be made to bend to French will. All one needed was the massacre so ardently wished for by Lyautey to set the "snowball" rolling.

Over the next two days, Europeans in Casablanca began to notice that the normally deferential Moroccans were beginning to show signs of insolence. Europeans were pointed at and insulted in the streets. This sort of thing might happen in Fez or Marrakech, but it was virtually unknown in "European" Casablanca. On the morning of July 30, rumors flew among the

Europeans that a Portuguese had been attacked. But the spark which ignited the revolt was provided by the engine. A band of 150 Moroccans, apparently infuriated by the whistle, attacked the engine at one o'clock in the afternoon of July 30 as it passed close to the Moorish cemetery. By placing stones on the rails, they brought it to a halt. The engine driver, a Frenchman named Rata, jumped from his cab and fled toward the town, but he was caught and beaten to death. The mob then ran toward the quarry, where they attacked the European workmen. In all, nine Europeans died. Their bodies were exposed on the rocks, pelted with stones and mutilated.

In the town itself, the European consuls attempted to prod Ben Bouzid into action. *Mokhaznis* must be sent to rescue the remaining workers in the quarry and to bring the Europeans in from the outlying farms. Bouzid left the consuls to organize the rescue parties with the ill-armed, ill-paid and unreliable soldiers of the garrison. As these parties were about to set out, the soldiers pointed out that they had no cartridges for their rifles. Bouzid explained that the bullets remained locked in the customs sheds, as the soldiers would only sell them. There was a further delay while the cartridges were recovered and distributed. By late afternoon, both the Europeans on the farms and those at the quarry who had escaped the massacre by hiding among the rocks had been brought into the town.

One of the Sultan's uncles, Moulai el-Amin, now took charge. Ben Bouzid was dismissed. Then, in a cunning maneuver to defuse the volatile situation in the town, Moulai el-Amin announced that a meeting of the tribesmen would be held outside the walls to discuss the massacre of the Europeans. Once the tribesmen had left the town for the appointed meeting place, Moulai el-Amin closed the gates. Through his forceful action, order was restored. Casablanca remained quiet for the next four days. Europeans could walk through the streets unmolested. It appeared that the crisis had passed. It had not. The massacre of the Europeans was just the pretext for which the French had been waiting.

At four o'clock on the morning of July 31, St.-Aulaire was awakened by his Algerian servant. Downstairs in the French legation in Tangiers waited the captain of the steamer *Arménie* with an urgent message from the French consul in Casablanca. St.-Aulaire, still in his pajamas, was told of the massacre of the nine Europeans. It was what he half-wished to hear. St.-Aulaire merely had to set in motion a prearranged plan without awaiting orders from Paris which, "if they did not exclude action, would certainly undermine its effects by delaying it."

Only one French naval vessel, the *Galilée*, stood off Tangiers. Before 6 a.m. the ship's captain, Commandant Olivier, was facing St.-Aulaire: "You understand as I do how important it is for France to arrive there first and, if possible, alone to protect the life and property of foreigners," the First Secretary explained. The caid was to be told in no uncertain terms that he would pay with his head if one more Frenchman died. "Don't hesitate to bombard if it is necessary to protect the foreigners."

St.-Aulaire then began to take the steps which would transform the Casablanca flare-up into a full-blown international incident. First, he wired Paris to announce the revolt and to recommend the immediate dispatch of an expeditionary corps to rescue the endangered Europeans. Second, he called in the legation's interpreter, Si Kaddour Benghabrit, an Algerian in the service of the Quai d'Orsay. Benghabrit appeared, his round face and small goatee framed in turban and robes. His presence in the Tangiers legation gave France an enormous advantage over her rivals in Morocco. Not only did he speak colloquial Arabic, which few European diplomats since Sir John Drummond Hay had bothered to master, but he was also extremely well informed on makhzan politics. St.-Aulaire rated Benghabrit among the best diplomats he had encountered in a career that stretched over almost a half-century. He was certainly the best in Morocco. For that reason, St.-Aulaire assigned to him the most delicate task: before evening, he was to bring a letter written by the Sultan's representative, Mohammed Torres, expressing regret for the incidents in Casablanca and inviting the French urgently to take all necessary action to prevent an even greater catastrophe. This was simultaneously an avowal of the makhzan's inability to control Casablanca and the blank check St.-Aulaire required in case Germany or Spain complained that French intervention contravened the Algeciras Agreement.

St.-Aulaire's last touch, however, was a real stroke of genius. German protests, he knew, would pale beside those from left-wing French deputies led by the brilliant socialist Jean Jaurès. The French left was not, strictly speaking, anticolonialist. What they objected to was the brutal military nature of French colonial expansion. Visions of Jean Jaurès standing before the deputies in the plush semicircle of the Palais Bourbon pouring out condemnation of the French invasion of Casablanca in his rich southwestern accent caused St.-Aulaire many sleepless nights. That is why he organized the "Society of French Workers" in Tangiers. For the moment, it consisted of a president, a table and two chairs, all paid for out of the Quai d'Orsay's secret funds. As the nine victims of the Casablanca massacre were all "proletarian" (although only four were French), the president of the Society of French Workers signed a telegram dictated by St.-Aulaire which subsequently appeared in the Quai d'Orsay's *Livre Jaune* on the crisis. It called on the government of the French Republic to avenge the murdered workers and to protect those still living in the name of "workers' solidarity." "That," the president said with satisfaction, "should stop Jaurès' gob."

St.-Aulaire then set about feeding rumors to the press that German agents were behind the massacres. This was a tactic which had been used during the Mauchamp crisis and had prevented a German protest over the occupation of Oudjda. The German minister was away from Tangiers and his first secretary, the docile Baron von Langwerth, dared not protest a legitimate rescue bid for fear of bringing the ire of Tangiers' Europeans down upon his head.

French records and official histories are vague about what happened over the next few days, but even they hint that the military may have exceeded their orders. For a fuller version of events, one must turn to unofficial sources, according to which the *Galilée* arrived off Casablanca on August 1 at eight o'clock in the morning. Commandant Olivier met the French consul, Monsieur Neuville, to be told that calm had been restored and that his sailors were to remain on board ship. The news produced an extraordinary reaction among the officers and sailors of the *Galilée*. They had steamed into Casablanca expecting action. First they were disappointed, then annoyed, and finally enraged. They remonstrated with their commander: Had not nine Europeans been killed? Should not their deaths be avenged? These Moroccans must be taught a lesson. Olivier remained firm: the *Galilée* must await the expected reinforcements before taking any action that might unleash the fury of the Moslems upon the European residents. But his reasoned argument fell on deaf ears. The temper of his crew bordered on the mutinous.

For four days, the *Galilée* rolled at anchor on the Atlantic swells, her guns loaded and their muzzles pointed toward the low, dirty silhouette of Casablanca. On the afternoon of August 4, Monsieur Maigret, French vice-consul in Gibraltar, arrived aboard the *Galilée* to finalize plans with Olivier for the arrival of the reinforcements, expected at any moment. As he stepped aboard, the disappointed expectations of the crew, brought to the boil by four days of tedious confinement and oppressive heat, exploded in the face of the hapless vice-consul. The officers crowded around him as he attempted to make for Olivier's cabin, demanding that a landing party be sent ashore. "But the town is quiet," Maigret told them; a landing party might only upset that calm. It was a dialogue of the deaf. The time for reasonable talk had long since vanished. Murders, the sailors insisted, must be avenged. By refusing to do so, Maigret had "trampled on the flag of France."

Maigret arrived in Olivier's cabin in a state of extreme agitation. It is perhaps difficult today to imagine why a silly accusation thrown out in the heat of the moment by excitable subalterns produced such an exaggerated reaction in a man whose profession was synonymous with calm and imperturbability. But Maigret lost his head, completely. It is perhaps useful to remember that the decade or so before the Great War was the high renaissance of the nation-state. Growing national tensions blew hard on the embers of chauvinism. Nowhere were the effects of international rivalry more apparent than in the men who represented their nations abroad— diplomats and soldiers. One must be aware of the tense state of mind and distorted visions of these men to explain what happened on the following day.

Maigret left the *Galilée* amid the hisses and catcalls of her crew, determined, he told Olivier, to demand that Moulai el-Amin hand over the murderers, or else. When he arrived at the French consulate, however, the Sultan's uncle had already begun to anticipate French demands by offering to allow the French to take over the town's defenses. Moulai el-Amin was no fool. He realized that French reinforcements were due at any moment, and that then anything might happen; better to hand over the town while it was still quiet. In that way, both his and his nephew's responsibility would be minimized. When Maigret signaled the contents of Amin's letter to the *Galilée*, the crew exploded with joy. The landing was scheduled for five o'clock on the morning of August 5. By then, it was mistakenly believed, the larger *Du·Chayla* would have arrived off Casablanca.

What happened over the next few hours would belong to the realm of pathetic farce were the consequences not so tragic. In the French consulate, the refugees kept a vigil all night, expecting to be able to see the approaching French ships from the roof. At one point they broke into frantic cheers when they believed that they had seen the white foam of a large number of ships. The excitement lasted for some time. But there were no ships. At least, not until 5 a.m. when they could clearly observe three boats crowded with armed sailors push away from the *Galilée*. They were astounded that such a small party was going to attempt a landing.

The harbor gate was open when Ensign Ballande jumped ashore at the head of his sailors. The three Moroccan soldiers guarding the gate were not sure what to do. They had received no orders, they had been told nothing of a landing. Behind them, the town was just beginning to wake up. The streets were filling with women and children on their way to the fountains for water. The soldiers hesitated, then began to close the heavy wooden gates. Ensign Ballande rushed forward, shoved his arm between the gates and forced them open with his shoulders. His sailors rushed after him. In the confusion, the rifle of one of the Moroccans discharged. This was enough to unleash all the bottled-up energies and frustrations of the sailors: in a nearly crazed state, they charged up the narrow streets toward the consulate only 250 yards away, shooting, bayonetting, bludgeoning anyone who fell across their path, mostly women and children. Some Moors returned their fire, but in a desultory fashion. A real bloodbath was only narrowly averted at the consulate when the interpreter persuaded the sixty Moroccan guards. to vanish before the sailors opened fire on them too.

As the sailors tumbled into the grounds of the consulate, the Europeans who had sought refuge there shoved aside the piano, beds, tables and settees with which they had barricaded the building. Embraces were exchanged in a general euphoria of congratulation: the brave sailors of the *Galilée* had broken the siege of the consulate. Or so they thought. Almost immediately, the prearranged signal for the bombardment to begin was hoisted on the roof of the consulate. Loud cheers went up on the *Galilée*. As the heavy naval shells began to slam into the fragile masonry buildings, Casablanca erupted. The gates were thrown open and the Arabs flooded into the town to begin an orgy of pillage. Nor were they deterred by the shelling. On the contrary: "It is true that the great guns destroy houses, ruin mosques, perhaps kill a few people, but what does it matter?" they said. "Directly the guns begin to shoot, we have our opportunity to loot with but small risk to ourselves." By evening, the sound of the bombardment had drawn in others from farther afield. The real siege of Casablanca's Europeans was about to begin.

The French consulate, bristling with ironmongery and virtually the only building which the guns of the *Galilée* were sure to spare, was safe enough. Its defenders confined their efforts to sniping at looters and to an occasional sortie to a nearby European grocery shop to do some looting of their own:

the Moors, fearing that European tinned goods contained pork, left the grocery shops untouched. Others, however, paid dearly for the impetuous actions of the *Galilée*. The rioters made for the mellah. Many Jews were murdered and their daughters led away. For some months after the Casablanca incident, poor Jews could be seen wandering in the Chaouia starving and nearly naked. Those who could afford it bought back their women, "the young girls for three loaves of sugar, the older women for less, according to their ugliness." Some of the wealthier Moors also found that their harems had been depleted.

Nor were isolated Europeans spared. Many fled to the safety of the consulates. "But we caught some in their houses," Lawrence Harris was told by an Arab.

Ha! Those houses were beautiful. We of the country had never seen such wonderful things. We were afraid of them. Surely they must have been from the evil spirits. So we smashed and tore down all we saw. At one house, an Espagnol Nazerani shot at us from his window. Allah! Allah! he shot well. Hassan of Dukella and Hamet his brother rushed to the door, but when we picked them up after they had fallen, both had been shot exactly between the eyes. Wahli-Wahli, he could shoot, that Nazerani. Many fell before we smashed the door, but we only found his woman. We wrecked and burnt and sang. We searched for many hours for that Nazerani but found him not. Moussa, the one-eyed, found some wine, and the accursed drink of the Nazerani turned true Mussulmans into fiends. I took none of it, but I watched as they shrieked and danced round the blazing heap of goods in the courtyard. For hours they danced when suddenly, Moussa fell over a board and a corner and disappeared down a hole. We laughed and looked down, and, by Allah, we saw the Espagnol and Moussa struggling. That Nazerani had been in the hole all the time while they danced over him. We got them both up at last; Moussa was dead, his throat had been torn out. Before they killed the Nazerani they took him to a room and showed him that which was his wife. Ay, the sight was not good. He bared his teeth and his eyes grew big and although he had no knife, many good Mussulmans knew pain before he fell with knife wounds that covered his body.

By the late afternoon of the fifth, the Europeans, reinforced by French and Spanish marines off the *Du Chayla* and a Spanish gunboat, had begun to establish a defense perimeter around the European consulates. By the seventh, the combination of constant bombardment and indiscriminate shooting of anything that moved by French and Spanish marines had reduced the twenty-five thousand people of Casablanca to a mere handful of terrified citizens cowering in the bombed-out shells of their houses. The streets were a rubbish heap of cadavers, "enormous, blown up with gas, their sex stiff in a monstrous erection."

The real slaughter, however, had only begun. On August 7, the long-awaited reinforcements finally arrived—two thousand Senegalese tirailleurs and foreign legionnaires.

It was standard French policy to call out only colonial troops abroad. To dispatch regiments from France to snuff out a colonial brushfire would have raised howls of protest that the frontier defenses against Germany had been denuded to salvage the valuables of a few capitalists. It would also have meant flooding Morocco with French conscripts. Colonial soldiers, all professionals, argued that short-service Frenchmen could not bear up to the rigors of an African campaign. Their real fear, however, was that conscripts would take their complaints to deputies, as they did in France. Soon the colonies would be crawling with politicians and parliamentary committees of inquiry. This was certainly not a problem posed by the Senegalese and legionnaires.

The Senegalese tirailleurs had first been founded in the 1850s by General Louis Faidherbe, the governor general of Senegal. They were expanded during the 1880s, when, led by tough marine officers, the tirailleurs spearheaded the conquest of the Western Sudan, the western bulge of Africa south of the Sahara which became French West Africa. The Senegalese certainly made up one of the most colorful units in the French army—tall, good-humored blacks, dressed in short blue jackets, balloon trousers and a red fez, either barefoot or wearing sandals. In camp, they were accompanied by their "free wives," often women they had acquired on campaign as part of the spoils of war. In Casablanca in 1907, the blacks behaved decently. Not so the legion.

The foreign legion formed the best-known unit in the French army, perhaps in the world. It was certainly the most romantic. Examined closely, however, most of the romance appeared tarnished. Paris in 1831, the year the legion was founded, abounded with foreigners—soldiers of the disbanded Swiss Guards of the Bourbons and others who had been attracted by the political disturbances of July 1830. As with the *bataillons d'Afrique*, the government of Louis Philippe sought to use the legion to empty Paris of troublemakers.

The essentially political origins of the legion help to explain its rather checkered military record. In its early days, companies were grouped by nationality. But after the legion was virtually annihilated in Spain during the Carlist wars of the 1830s, it was reorganized into polyglot companies. As French, the language of command, was only imperfectly understood by many of these soldiers, the legion acquired a reputation for being rather sluggish in maneuver. Occasionally, an energetic and imaginative commander such as Colonel François-Oscar de Négrier would organize elite mounted companies capable of covering up to thirty miles a day over the roughest terrain. But the main task of the legion was to provide convoy escorts, labor companies and sedentary garrisons.

As a rule, foreign mercenaries make poor soldiers, and those who served in the legion were no exception. Men who enlisted after a drinking spree, on an impulse, or to escape the law or some personal problem had reason to repent of their action at leisure. Desertion, therefore, became the running sore of the legion. So did indiscipline.

Several things kept the legion from disintegrating altogether. First, each' company contained a nucleus of dedicated soldiers, many of them French professionals who were officially allowed to join after 1881. Second, the romantic reputation of the legion, its exotic garrisons and the accelerated promotion offered for colonial service meant that the legion received the pick of St.-Cyr cadets and the best men promoted through the ranks, which assured it of a solid corps of officers. Last, the legion was sent to serve in such remote areas of the globe that cohesion was often imposed by the alien nature of the country, the hostility of the population, or the simple fact that there was no place to desert to.

When they reached Casablanca on August 7, 1907, the legionnaires reverted to type. Groups of them searched the houses, stripping and shooting any man they found alive, Jew or Arab, and looting what there remained to loot, as one Arab remembered:

In a deserted house I hid myself and watched from a window. From time to time, troops of soldiers would come down the street killing everybody and everything. Wahli-Wahli! it was worse than before. From a house opposite, an old fool of a Jehudi heard the tramp of French soldiers coming along. He thrust his head out of the window and cried,

"Vivent les Français." He thought they had come to save him from us; but the answer to his welcome was a bullet through his head. For days I hid in that house, hungry and afraid, with the body of the old Jew hanging out of the window opposite for my only company.

Discipline virtually broke down in the legion, and by August 11 several of them had been court-martialed, and entire companies shipped back to Algeria. The ships' guns began to find the range of the outlying villages where many of the refugees from the slaughter were hiding, driving them further afield.

By August 18, order reigned in Casablanca. Bands of Jews press-ganged by legionnaires labored for two days under a sweltering sun to sweep the streets clean of bodies and other debris. The caid Ben Bouzid was forced to follow the sweepers. Then he was taken aboard a French ship to exile in Algeria. As the Arabs began to drift back to what remained of their homes, they were first made to pass through the military commander's office, where Arabic-speaking French officers—sometimes armed with riding crops, which they were prepared to use at the first sign of insolence—put them through an inquisition. When the examination was completed and the Moor sufficiently humiliated, his name was entered into a book and he was allowed to go home.

The French had now achieved their foothold on the Atlantic coast. This, the anonymous author of the War Ministry memo of August 27, 1905, had predicted, would strike the makhzan both "morally and materially." He was correct, but in a way he had not foreseen. On August 16 in Marrakech, Moulai Hafid, the brother of Abd el-Aziz, was proclaimed Sultan. Morocco now dissolved into civil war.

CHAPTER XII

THE CHAOUIA CAMPAIGN

The handling of the Casablanca disorders by the French had been both cynical and barbarous, and there was worse to follow. But the events of August 1907 must be placed in perspective. Colonial warfare was a savage business and the soldiers who fought it possessed compassion in short measure. Nor could Europeans and Jews who fell victim to Arab looters expect quarter. One of the most damning charges one can lay at the feet of the French is that by their brutal actions, they spread the aura of a national struggle over a sordid scene.

Nor would it be correct to conclude that such masters of deceit as St.-Aulaire and Lyautey were without scruple. They earnestly believed that the acquisition of Morocco was vital to French interests. They also believed that colonization would benefit Morocco. Despite their veneer of hardened realism, most of these colonialists were incorrigible romantics. Lyautey in particular had been seduced by the savage beauty of Morocco, the natural courtesy and hospitality of the Moroccans, the grand solitude of the mountains and the mystery of the towns. At the same time, he and others were genuinely appalled by the injustice, the corruption and cruelty, the profound misery which survived in the midst of exquisite civility. And, at their best, these colonialists were remarkably free of racism: Moroccans were not inferior, merely different. Under French tutelage—or, more precisely, under *their* guidance—Moroccans could be freed from the intolerable brutality of their rulers. It would be wrong to see men like St.-Aulaire and Lyautey as exploiters, even if exploitation was the end result of the protectorate. If their class of colonialist had one defect, and it was an enormous one, it was to believe that they could avoid the mistakes made elsewhere by French colonial regimes, especially in Algeria. A moment's reflection should have told them otherwise.

These colonialists never really understood the society which they sought to suborn. This was only natural. They were not Moroccan specialists. On the contrary, it was a point of pride with them that they were colonial generalists. It is probably just as well that they profoundly misjudged the effects of their actions on Morocco itself, for their ignorance ultimately proved to be their strength. They set themselves the long-range goal of Moroccan conquest. In dealing with other interested European nations, as well as with their own politicians, they often showed themselves brilliant opportunists in attaining that goal. But Morocco for them remained a closed book. When attempting to analyze the effects their policies were likely to have on the country, they fell back on the clichés and prejudices, the formulas which, while flexible in theory, in practice proved rigid and unworkable. For this reason, the conquest of Morocco lurched from crisis to crisis, for the French action consistently provoked what was for them an unexpected response. Time and again they followed the wrong policy or backed the wrong man. Time and again they were forced to fall back upon superior firepower to extricate themselves from a political mess of their own making.

The Casablanca operation is a case in point. Its goal was to bring pressure to bear on Abd el-Aziz. What it did, however, was to crystallize a revolution which temporarily pinned the French on the beaches and eventually brought about the overthrow of the very man whom they had worked so long to bring under their influence.

The revolution came out of Marrakech and was the product of a profound political transformation brought about by European intervention in the country. The lords of the Atlas were a new factor in the politics of the south. Fifteen years before Casablanca erupted, the High Atlas to the south and east of Marrakech, whose peaks watch majestically over the town, contained no "lords," only petty barons. These men earned their living by extorting money from the merchants who traveled the passes which link Marrakech to the Tafilalet and the Sus. They were little more than small family businesses which operated out of the mud casbahs dotted along the caravan routes. In true mountain tradition, each family hated its neighbor, and blood feuds periodically reduced the population by a few score. But the invulnerability of the casbah meant that no family could extinguish its rivals and extend its power.

In the 1890s, however, this situation was transformed almost overnight. The reason was simple: modern arms. In the autumn of 1893, Sultan Moulai Hassan, already a dying man, struggled with his *mehalla* through the snows of the High Atlas on his return from the Tafilalet. As he approached the rambling, crenellated casbah of Telouet, he was invited to rest there by the caid, Madani el Glaoui. There was little indication that this twenty-seven-year-old man would one day be one of the most powerful figures in Morocco. He was certainly not handsome: thin, swarthy with irregular, yellow teeth; he nevertheless possessed in full measure the graceful charm of his race. His was a welcome invitation, and the Sultan remained at Telouet for several days to recover his strength. As he left, he presented Madani el Glaoui with a remarkable gift—a Krupp 77-millimeter cannon.

The Sultan's gift changed the history of the High Atlas. In a stroke, every casbah in the Atlas had been rendered obsolete. Madani el Glaoui wasted little time in putting his new weapon to use. By placing the cannon 300 meters from a casbah, just out of musket range, he could pour thirty shells into its outer walls in a matter of minutes. His mountain men would then surge through the gap blown in the masonry and butcher most of the inhabitants. After distributing the captured women among his followers and sending a few heads back to decorate the battlements of Telouet, he would hitch his 77 to his camel or to a mule and bounce it down the pass to the next casbah.

The emergence of a powerful baron in the south did not pass unnoticed elsewhere in Morocco. A man like Madani el Glaoui was a useful ally for Moulai Hassan's chamberlain, Ba Ahmed, in his struggle to rule Morocco with the boy Sultan Abd el-Aziz. The eventual triumph of Ba Ahmed in the bitter civil war that ravaged the country on the death of Moulai Hassan also proved a victory for Madani. But he was not the only man to profit. By 1900, the High Atlas had effectively been divided among three men—Madani el Glaoui, Abd el Malek Mtouggi ("a schemer without peer"), and Tayeb el Goundafi—all of whom had been supplied with modern chassepots and Martini rifles by Ba Ahmed, supplemented by what they could purchase from gunrunners at Essaouira. What is more, these mountain men had extended their power into the plains—Glaoui toward the Tafilalet, Goundafi into the Sus, and Mtouggi into the plain of Marrakech.

The three men emerged almost overnight as the power brokers of Moroccan politics. They fed upon the unrest and disorder which now became virtually permanent with the increased European presence in the country. In this tumult of shifting personal and tribal loyalties, defections and rebellions, the "lords of the Atlas" offered armed support—for a fee. Like the *condottieri* of Renaissance Italy, these Berber outsiders had moved with great force into the world of Arab politics.

If the Europeans in Casablanca were aware of these developments in the south, they gave no indication of it. Marrakech had become a place of intrigue, centering upon the parvenu Atlas lords in their garish new town palaces. Europeans ignored Marrakech. For them it was hardly more than an overgrown, if picturesque, Berber village. Fez was the "capital" of Morocco, the inner citadel of the makhzan. It was there that the fate of the country would be decided. Therefore, they remained blissfully ignorant of the great events taking place in the south.

Of these three mountain chieftains, Madani el Glaoui was the most remarkable. The other two were accomplished players on their provincial stage, but neither was a conspirator of international class. They were content to rule their mountain kingdoms from their dank, rambling casbahs, descending occasionally on Marrakech to pick up tidbits of makhzan gossip and to keep the pots of conspiracy well on the boil. But only in the High Atlas, surrounded by their turbaned and well-armed retainers, their court jesters, troops of slaves and concubines, were these complicated but essentially unsophisticated men truly at home. However, Madani's visions, like his ambitions, ran beyond those of the ordinary feudal baron. He alone realized that the fate of Morocco was to be decided in Europe. He had European newspapers and parliamentary debates translated to keep abreast of the forces at work beyond Morocco's shores. Like Raisuni, he was determined, when the Europeans came, to do well out of them.

Why did Madani's ambitions become fixed on the Sultan's half-brother Moulai Hafid, the pasha of Marrakech? Perhaps patriotism played its part. He had certainly lost faith in the ability of Abd el-Aziz to crush his own domestic enemies or to modernize the country. But he no doubt realized that the young Sultan was doomed, that his growing unpopularity with his own people would eventually bring about his downfall. From that moment, Madani began to make his own arrangements. He was not content to await events. Disorder grew by the month. Why must he wait to make a deal with some pretender thrown up in the north? He would produce his own Sultan, organize his alliances, arrange his finances and march him to Fez at the head of a triumphant *harka*. His choice fell upon Moulai Hafid.

It was not a bad choice. Moulai Hafid was the fourth son of Moulai Hassan. Only in his mid-thirties, he was already recognized as a scholar of some repute in Moslem law and theology. He had also written a book of poems. Nor was he ignorant of the world beyond Morocco, although his knowledge of it was gleaned largely from reading out-of-date Egyptian newspapers. His appreciation of the complex forces at work in Europe was therefore hazy and distorted. All Europeans who had met him, and he had been very hospitable to many in Marrakech, agreed that he was extremely handsome: his face was intelligent, with a high forehead and dark, almond-shaped eyes framed in a close-cropped black beard and mustache. His hands and feet were beautifully kept. But his bulk suggested the corpulence of inactivity rather than physical strength.

Despite his attributes, Moulai Hafid did not have the makings of a ruler. His temperament was essentially that of a scholar, introverted and aloof. He also possessed a nervous disposition which became more pronounced as the strains of politics began to press in upon him. Lawrence Harris, who met Hafid in 1909, remarked that his intelligent face was marred by "a fearful and suspicious look" and that his hands trembled visibly. Three years later, French general Henri Gouraud thought that Hafid appeared "unbalanced." Madani el Glaoui, however, was only interested in producing a malleable Sultan, not a worthy one. Glaoui knew his man: Moulai Hafid was a scholar, but he was also self-indulgent and consumed by greed. He longed to possess power, women, wealth. All these things were promised by Madani. Hafid need only do as he was told.

How long Hafid and Madani el Glaoui had been preparing their con-spiracy is not known. But by 1906, rumors that something was afoot had reached the ears of Abd el-Aziz. Twice, in 1906 and 1907, Aziz tried to depose his half-brother as pasha of Marrakech, but without success. Hafid was cocooned in the protective custody of the Glaoui. But his options were now closed, even if Hafid did not immediately appear to have recognized this fact. In August, when the Chaouia exploded, Madani decided that the time had come to thrust his man forward.

Madani and Hafid met under cover of a hunt to discuss their plans. At the feast which followed the slaughter of sixty-two gazelles, as the Berber girls swayed and sang in their shrill nasal tones, Madani whispered to his guest that the "hour of destiny" was at hand. Hafid demurred. His position was a dèlicate one. El Glaoui wanted to play the role of king-maker, but could he count upon his rivals, el Mtouggi and el Goundafi? And what of the *roumi*? How could he expect to unseat his brother, who was backed by a powerful French army? The sorry truth was that Hafid did not have the stomach for a *coup d'état*.

Madani settled the issue by a *coup de théâtre*. On August 16, he summoned all the southern notables including the *ulama* to the rambling Dar al Makhzan in Marrakech. There, in the presence of Moulai Hafid, a Marrakech Jew named Joshua Corcos who was Madani's financial adviser read in a voice quivering with emotion appeals from the tribes in the Chaouia begging Moulai Hafid to offer himself as leader to throw back the infidel. Perhaps these letters really had come from the Chaouia tribes. The silence of the assembly, however, indicated that the notables were not altogether convinced. *Lèse majesté* was a dangerous business. Each man began to weigh his personal position, calculating the certain risks against the possible gains. A wrong move now could prove fatal. The tension in the hall must have been terrible, each man knowing that his life, and the lives of his family, hung on a simple yes or no.

Everyone shifted nervously. The caids said that the approval of a sultan was the responsibility of the *ulama*, the religious lawyers. Not surprisingly, the *ulama* defended the opposing thesis that the decision lay with the caids. After two hours of inconclusive discussion, Madani broke the deadlock by shouting: "May God prolong the life of Moulai Hafid, our Sultan!" On cue, his men who had packed the courtyard outside the window echoed, "Long live our lord!" Stunned but subdued, the caids filed one by one to sign the declaration recognizing Moulai Hafid as Sultan. There was only one dissenter, Moulai Moustaffa, brother-in-law of both the Sultan and the pretender, who argued that the act was both treasonable and blasphemous. Madani flew into a rage. Three of his men placed the points of their daggers on Moulai Moustaffa's chest, but before they could thrust, Moustaffa threw his arms around Hafid. At that moment, the muezzin called the hour of prayer. As the assembly trooped off toward the Berrina mosque, Madani, the new grand vizier of the rebel court, raised the parasol, the symbol of sharifian authority, over his new Sultan.

The effects of Madani's actions were soon apparent to both Aziz and the French. The treason quickly spread to Safi and El Jadida. In the south, only Essaouira, an overwhelmingly Jewish town, remained loyal to Aziz. Europeans began quietly to evacuate Fez and Marrakech. On September 12, the Sultan transferred his makhzan from Fez to Rabat just to the north of the Chaouia. On September 26, a Hafidist *harka* pitched camp at Settat, fifteen miles from Casablanca. The French had calmed Casablanca, but the Chaouia was in an uproar.

In Casablanca, the French busied themselves fortifying their beachhead. The commander, General Antoine Drude, soon established a defense perimeter which consisted of an interlocking series of narrow slit trenches and incorporated garden walls and ruins of houses. Behind the trenches stood small, triangular two-man tents, the open end facing outward so that the defenders could slither straight from their bedrolls in case of attack. And there were several. On August 18, Algerian spahis and French chasseurs patrolling the perimeter skirmished with mounted Arabs. The gunfire drew in other Moroccans from farther afield until gradually an attack developed on a section of the line held by tirailleurs. The French line erupted with rifle fire as the excitable Algerians sought to match their coreligionists in sheer volume of noise. But when the French brought their 75s into line, backed by naval gunfire from the ships in the harbor, the Moroccans evaporated.

The 75 was a marvelous little toy and one perfectly suited to a country like the Chaouia. As cannon go, it was extremely light and could be managed together with its ammunition caisson by four horses or, at a pinch, two mules or camels. Its mobility was matched by its rapid rate of fire, making it superior to its German rival, the Krupp 77. It could lob shells up to six miles, although in the days before the Great War and the perfection of aerial observation, it seldom fired over two-and-a-half miles. Its disadvantage lay in its straight trajectory; an enemy taking refuge behind hills or forests was safe from its shells. But there were few of either around Casablanca.

A pattern of combat was soon established: each day after breakfast, the French would send out a patrol composed of two reduced companies of legionnaires of about 150 men each and a squadron of spahis, preceded by a small swarm of *goumiers* imported from the South Oranais. For two hours they would tramp in a square formation over the low, empty hills. Suddenly, a clutch of Moroccan horsemen would surge up seemingly from the earth itself, ride hard at the French, fire, turn, reload, charge again into the teeth of the crackling French square. The legionnaires lay on the ground, the more experienced loading their Lebels one bullet at a time to avoid jammed magazines. The officers remained standing, nonchalantly, behind the lines of prone soldiers. To take cover was considered bad form for an officer, even though the legionnaires little appreciated the increased volume of bullets that sang overhead each time an officer walked past.

For some minutes this aimless skirmishing would continue, the French firing volleys with no apparent effect at the dispersed and constantly moving horsemen or in answer to puffs of smoke on a neighboring hill as the Moroccans fired their black-powder cartridges. The *goumiers* rushed about firing at anything or, when no obvious target was visible, at the sky. They continually rushed across the legionnaires' line of fire and raised so much dust that soon the enemy was barely visible. Under the covering fire of the artillery, the French square would withdraw toward the safety of their own lines, carrying the wounded on iron-framed stretchers lashed to the backs of mules or donkeys to the dressing station at Casablanca.

On September 12, Drude decided to break the Moroccan siege of Casablanca with an attack on their principal camp at Taddert, eight miles distant. At dawn, two thousand men, mainly tirailleurs and legionnaires, screened by three hundred cavalry, set out across the undulating plain. From the beginning, they had to face the Moroccan horsemen swarming on their flanks, but the range of French weapons kept them at a safe distance. Finally, they topped the last ridge. Beneath them lay the Moroccan camp.

This was Drude's chance to achieve a decisive victory over his elusive foe. Already on the far side of the camp, a mass of men, horses and mules laden with household goods were streaming away toward a gap in the low hills. In the camp itself, the white-robed horsemen who had been occupied in harassing the French rushed among the tents hastily collecting their most important possessions. All Drude had to do now was to throw his cavalry across the *harka*'s line of retreat while his well-drilled infantry charged into the camp from the west. It was a chance too good to miss. But Drude opted for the textbook over the imagination. Cavalry was to be used to protect the flanks of infantry, not in unsupported attacks. The staff college was quite clear on that. The fact that the enemy was in utter disarray and incapable of resisting a cavalry charge did not persuade Drude to depart from the rules. Nor was the infantry to attack until the position had been softened by artillery. Drude behaved as if Taddert were held by entrenched Prussians rather than Moroccans in a panic. He halted his line while the 75s pounded the tents for a full half hour. His cavalry protected his infantry's flanks from an enemy whose obvious desire was to flee eastwards with all possible speed. When the tirailleurs finally charged the by now nearly deserted camp, they dissolved into a mob of looters. Their officers had to beat them back into line with the flats of their swords.

Drude had bungled what was to prove his last opportunity to inflict a crushing blow on his enemy. Paris ordered him to remain henceforth within his defense perimeter at Casablanca. The Prime Minister, Georges Clemenceau, had agreed to send troops only to protect Europeans, not to launch a conquest of the Chaouia. Casablanca for the next few months was to become an internment camp. The Moroccans, so recently on the verge of defeat, were now emboldened: "The French are like fish," they said, "they cannot leave the sea."

Clemenceau's decision may also have been motivated by the news that

Abd el-Aziz planned to leave Fez for Rabat. The Prime Minister had decreed that the French must not become entangled in the brewing clash for the throne between the two half-brothers. On the very day that Drude's attachment to the plodding tactics of the *école de guerre* had cost him a victory, Abd el-Aziz's *mehalla* left Fez for the coast. It was a not unimpressive collection of about seven thousand people who set out with the Sultan on September 12, but the signs of demoralization were already apparent. When the bloated army crawled into Rabat several days later, almost half its original number were missing. Many of the soldiers, unpaid for months and enticed by the prospect of loot, drifted off to join the rebels in the Chaouia. Of those who remained with their Sultan, many were reduced to begging in the streets of Rabat or to selling their rifles. With the Hafidist *mehalla* of three thousand now ensconced at Settat, three armies faced each other in the Chaouia.

For the moment, however, no one moved. The French remained confined within their breastworks by ministerial decree. For the Sultan and his challenger, one of the main problems was finance. Aziz was able to pry a trifling sum out of the French by pawning the crown jewels. They, in return, decorated the Sultan with the Legion of Honor. It was an unfortunate choice of decoration, and a clear indication of the Sultan's unpopularity that his subjects now whispered that it was a symbol of Christian baptism—not a surprising conclusion to draw as Abd el-Aziz now appeared in public with the white cross of the Legion pinned to his jellaba. But much beyond token support, the French government was unwilling to go.

Moulai Hafid, too, had his financial problems. Above all, however, he was only too well aware that Marrakech was a rickety power base from which to launch an invasion of the Chaouia. Not everyone had enjoyed being stampeded into his camp by Madani. He was also well aware, as most of his followers were not, that no sultan could rule Morocco without French support. The knowledge that he must eventually make peace with the French made him reluctant to attack them. But Hafid was already Madani's prisoner. He agreed to send a *harka* to Settat; its original three thousand swelled by December 1907 to ten thousand.

It was the enormous buildup of rebels at Settat which decided the French at last to come out and fight. The task was handed to General Albert d'Amade, who now replaced Drude. On the face of it, d'Amade seemed a good choice. He was not a "colonial," but his fluent command of English and his posting as French military attaché in London had taken him to South

Africa, where he had been the French observer attached to Lord Robert's staff during the Boer War. This should have familiarized him with the problems of dealing with an elusive, mounted foe. But he seemed to have learned little from the experience. Nor was d'Amade popular with his men: cold, aloof, humorless, his soldiers called him "d'Amade in England," a poor pun which referred as much to his character, which they believed to be typically British, as to his service with the British army.

D'Amade's problem was an interesting one. The Chaouia runs seventy miles from north to south, the flat plain along the coast rising by gradual stages to a plateau about 1,500 feet high from which the outlines of the Atlas are visible. Bare, covered in spring with a carpet of wild flowers, it was excellent country for cavalry. Unfortunately, the vast bulk of d'Amade's fourteen thousand troops were infantry—foreign legion, French Zouaves, Algerian and Senegalese tirailleurs. His cavalry was composed of French chasseurs (which were in fact mounted infantry, although seldom used as such), Algerian spahis and a cluster of *goumiers*.

How was d'Amade to solve this problem? One of the most frequent criticisms leveled at his predecessor, General Drude, had been that his patrols had been aimless affairs. D'Amade would set his army a goal: Settat. This was, after all, the headquarters of Moulai Hafid's *harka*. At daybreak on January 12, 1908, d'Amade left Casablanca at the head of 2,500 men. They made a colorful sight as they advanced through the knee-high yellow mustard grass—the chasseurs in their white kepis, blue tunics and red breeches; spahis in their white cloaks, red Zouave jackets and baggy blue Turkish trousers; tirailleurs in their red tarbush, baggy breeches and red cummerbund. The infantry traveled in two squares, the fighting square marching in front followed by the supply square. Around them churned the *goumiers* in their blue-and-white jellabas. On the first night, they reached Ber Rechid. The small settlement had been abandoned at the news of the approaching army. On the fourteenth, the column was joined by a battalion and a half of legionnaires and set out on a night march which, at dawn on January 15, placed them before Settat.

The French attack was a model of drill-book precision. The infantry formed in a long line, shoulder to shoulder, and advanced as one man, halted, knelt by sections, fired a volley, rose and advanced anew. In front of the Senegalese, a hot fire poured out of a douar of camel-hair tents which, had it been accurate, might have caused some casualties. Though bullets flew everywhere, no one on the French side was hit. Surprisingly, the Moors brought a field piece into line, an ancient weapon which they had liberated from the Sultan's arsenal at Marrakech. Its shells plowed into the clay soil without troubling to burst. D'Amade deployed his men to sweep up the isolated douars which dotted the hills around Settat. The chasseurs cut down about forty Arabs who attempted to escape from Settat. Otherwise, the Moors galloped out of French reach, howling, turning in their saddles to fire over the rumps of their horses, leaving the infantrymen, their bayonets fixed for the charge, looking a trifle foolish. Settat, no more than a collection of miserable hovels, proved to be occupied only by Jews, who approached the French force bowing and smiling to kiss the hems of the soldiers' uniforms. As d'Amade had been forbidden to occupy Settat, he withdrew immediately to Ber Rechid.

This was d'Amade's first disappointment, and there were to be many more. Clearly, the precepts of Napoleonic warfare which laid down that the goal of a campaign must be to occupy the enemy's cities did not apply in Morocco. Moroccans were pastoralists. To occupy their cities did not break their resistance in the same way that, say, the fall of Paris had traditionally undermined the will of France to oppose the invader; on the contrary, such occupation simply produced more guns for the rebellion. But how could one entrap this elusive Moroccan foe with a force composed mainly of infantry? D'Amade tried several methods. The first was an old Armée d'Afrique tactic—converging columns. On January 21, d'Amade left Casablanca with a force of two thousand men marching north along the coast toward Rabat. When he reached the casbah of Bou Znika, on the coast about fifteen miles south of Rabat, he swung about and struck off in a southeasterly direction away from the coast through the cork forest of Sehoul. The plan was to catch the Moroccans between columns converging from Bou Znika, Ber Rechid and Mediouna. This tactic may have worked for Bugeaud in Algeria seventy-five years earlier, but in the relatively flat country of the Chaouia, against mounted men, it failed. The Moroccan horsemen slipped through the French grasp like mercury. Worse, the plan almost led to disaster. As the column marched southward on a beautifully sunny, springlike day, they could hear the guns of Colonel Boutegourd's column. Marching northward from Mediouna, Boutegourd had been swarmed over by the Moroccans, who were only kept at bay by the lively firing of shrapnel shells from his 75s. Even d'Amade's arrival did not put an end to the attack, which only sputtered out at nightfall.

There were lessons to be learned from the battle of the Wadi M'Koun. Converging columns worked only if there was something to converge on, like a camp or a casbah, or if the enemy were on foot and unable to speed away. In the Chaouia, to divide one's force simply allowed the mobile Moroccans to concentrate on the weakest column. In addition, the movements of d'Amade's column had been betrayed by the captive balloon which dragged along behind it. In the days before airplane reconnaisance, the balloon permitted commanders to see what the enemy was doing on the other side of the hill. But this *cafard* (betrayer), as the soldiers called it, also served very effectively to warn the Moroccans of the approach of a French column. When they saw the balloon scrape across the horizon, especially in the flat country of the Chaouia, they fled.

Converging columns had not worked. Perhaps he would have better luck with economic warfare. This, after all, was how Kitchener had eventually ground down Boer opposition. D'Amade had witnessed the formation in South Africa of mounted infantry—lean, tanned Australians and New Zealanders—whose "drives" against the Boers in the vast expanse of the South African veld had netted far more cattle than human captives. But if commandos could not eat, they could not fight, a fact that even the great Boer commander de Wet had been forced eventually to recognize. The Moroccans might be taught a similar lesson.

On February 2, Colonel Boutegourd launched a small force of infantry and a squadron of chasseurs to seize a herd of cattle at Sidi el Mekki. A night march followed by a surprise attack at dawn drove off the guards. But before he could return to Ber Rechid with his booty, Boutegourd was assailed by five thousand horsemen. The French fell into a square and fired for dear life. They were saved thanks largely to their machine gun. But they had to fight their way back to camp dragging eleven dead and forty-one wounded, and without the cattle.

D'Amade was running out of ideas. He marched to Settat again. The Moors, who were very much in evidence, did not put up a serious fight. The danger came far more from grain silos—concealed pits three feet across and ten feet deep—which could prove fatal to horsemen. D'Amade set his batteries on a hill overlooking Settat and showered the town with melanite shells. When the French entered Settat, they found it occupied only by the pitiful remnants of the Jewish community, which had greeted them as liberators only a fortnight earlier and had suffered for it. There was hardly anything left to plunder. The *goumiers* were reduced to breaking up doors for firewood. The French packed the Jews onto ammunition wagons and marched back to Casablanca.

In mid-February, d'Amade revived his converging columns idea, essentially applying the same plan which had come to naught on the Wadi M'Koun. On the seventeenth, Colonel Taupin led his column southeast from Bou Znika to link up with columns under d'Amade and Colonel Brulard coming up from the south. Taupin marched through the forest of Sehoul and began to climb onto the plateau of M'Koun. At a place called Ain Rebbah, at a point where the track led through a narrow valley, he was ambushed. The Moors actually broke into Taupin's square before they were thrown back in hand-to-hand fighting, but only after the French had lost five officers and thirty-four men. Taupin was so bloodied that he abandoned his attempt to link up with Brulard and d'Amade and limped back to the coast. This allowed his adversaries to concentrate on Brulard as he marched over the flat plain north from Ber Rechid. When Brulard finally reached d'Amade's column, he had lost thirty men. D'Amade, at the head of the strongest of the three columns, had not heard a shot fired in anger all day.

These setbacks on February 17–18 caused a panic in Casablanca. Even in Paris there was disquiet: why could not a large French army defeat a semibarbarous people, many of whom were armed only with sticks or smooth-bore muskets? It was a question for which Clemenceau wished to have an answer. And the man who would give it to him was Lyautey.

Lyautey and Clemenceau would one day become great enemies. This is not surprising, for in many ways they were remarkably similar both in background and in character. Both were backwoods aristocrats, Lyautey from Lorraine in eastern France, Clemenceau from the traditionally royalist Vendée, a low flat region on the Atlantic coast just south of the point where the Loire River reaches the Bay of Biscay. Both men were highly strung, brilliant thoroughbreds, hugely ambitious and insufferable egotists. Two such explosive characters would inevitably find a subject about which to quarrel. As it was, the subject was provided for them—politics. Despite the similarity of background and the fierce patriotism which they shared, they stood, in 1908 at least, at opposite ends of the political spectrum. Lyautey wore his aristocratic lineage, and royalist sentiments, proudly. Clemenceau was a Radical, a Dreyfusard, a man who saw himself as the heir to the Jacobin traditions of the Great Revolution of 1789. But there was one more point of fundamental disagreement: Clemenceau was violently anticolonialist. This was the man who had sardonically described the French occupation of Tunisia in 1881 as Bismarck's most successful coup because it made Frenchmen forget the amputated provinces of Alsace-Lorraine and brought France into conflict with Italy. Since then, he had found no reason to alter his opinion. France pursued the silly will-o'-the-wisp of an African empire while Germany daily grew stronger on the continent of Europe.

But Clemenceau mentioned none of this when he summoned Lyautey from Oran, where he was now divisional commander, in mid-February 1908. He was the Prime Minister who had been saddled with Casablanca. Like many prime ministers before him, he discovered that, once launched, a colonial expedition was virtually impossible to recall. For this arch-anticolonialist, Morocco was a millstone around his neck. Every day the papers reported French "setbacks" in the Chaouia. In the Chamber, Jaurès bleated on about the barbarism of the French conquest. Clemenceau wanted a man who would settle the Chaouia affair once and for all. Lyautey, whose methods relied more on persuasion than on power, would, he hoped, extricate the government from its embarrassing situation.

Facing Lyautey in the Prime Minister's elegant Louis XV rooms in the Hôtel Matignon on that cold, wet February morning were the foreign minister Stephen Pichon, the war minister General Georges Picquart and the Tiger himself. Lyautey's blood must have boiled to see Picquart in the seat of power, for he was very much the creature of Clemenceau. As Lieutenant Colonel Picquart, he had attempted to expose the flimsiness of the evidence against Captain Dreyfus, first to his superiors and then to the vice-president of the Senate. This courageous act had earned for Picquart a transfer from the rue St.-Dominique to the wilder reaches of the Sahara and eventual dismissal from the army. However, the victorious Dreyfusards had honored him as one of the heroes of the "Dreyfus revolution." Picquart had been reinstated in the army and promoted (far above his abilities, even the left agreed) almost overnight from lieutenant colonel to major general. Clemenceau then named him to the army's top post, that of war minister, in October 1906.

Lyautey's views on the Dreyfus case were more perceptive than those of most of his military colleagues, and those of his political enemies on the left. He knew there had been no conspiracy. The "Dreyfus affair" had been a simple case of bureaucratic corruption in the general staff: blinkered, ambitious men eager to gain a quick conviction, to dig out the traitor like a rat from a hole, and subsequently refusing to admit that by acting in haste they had made a mistake. The real culprit in the affair, however, was Clemenceau. It was he who had led the witch hunt against the army. It was he who had organized the Dreyfusards, supplied their *mot d'ordre* and sent them into combat against the "enemies of the Revolution." It was he, the hater of soldiers, who rubbed salt in the army's wounds by elevating the mediocrity Picquart to the War Ministry.

This is what Lyautey felt about two of the men sitting before him. Perhaps it is all the more surprising that they came out with an extraordinary offer: Lyautey was to take over the Casablanca command. The bald head of the sixty-seven-year-old Clemenceau shone and his heavy white mustache wiggled vigorously as he explained—adopting the boyish manner which inevitably announced one of his rare attempts to be charming—that the number of troops would be swelled to a command befitting Lyautey's status.

It is perhaps also surprising that Lyautey rejected their proposition almost out of hand. Why? The reason was a simple one of loyalty, according to his biographer. D'Amade and Lyautey had been classmates at St.-Cyr. When they met, they still addressed each other with the familiar *tu* reserved for family and close friends. Lyautey boasted to St.-Aulaire that politicians attempted to treat soldiers as if they were the same egotistical breed of men as those who inhabited the committee rooms of the Palais Bourbon, ready to climb to success over the prostrate bodies of their colleagues. "It makes me laugh," he said.

But there was certainly more behind Lyautey's refusal than loyalty to an old comrade. Why should he be agreeable to Clemenceau, a man whom he detested, and to his creature Picquart? Let them sweat a bit. Besides, and more to the point, he saw the Chaouia expedition as a great mistake. The whole thing had been desperately mishandled. The French should have capitalized upon the Casablanca massacres immediately to proclaim the protectorate. By invading, they had simply raised the whole country against them, produced a second pretender at Marrakech to set beside the one already at Taza, and become bogged down militarily in the Chaouia.

Let me be given [he had written in early 1907 before the Casablanca revolt], "with the first incident or massacre, a free hand, the choice of means and men, and my own choice of time, and I undertake to bring pressure upon Fez in a definitive manner, painlessly, and *at small expense*. And I shall do this by making use of military and political means, of my intelligence services among the tribes, disintegrating them, making a friendly party ahead of me, making a snowball—in a word, putting into practice my formula of the "organization on the march."

It was certainly too late for all that now. With Clemenceau in command, it would never work in any case. For instance, the Prime Minister had strictly forbidden the occupation of Settat. Lyautey believed that Settat must become a base of operations if the Chaouia were to be pacified. By now, however, the region's geography was far too well known in Paris for the cunning commander of Oran to be able to get away with his trick of altering the names of towns.

So Lyautey did not want the job. Still, one cannot simply refuse the request of a prime minister, especially if that man is Clemenceau. The general proposed a compromise: he would undertake a fact-finding mission and report on d'Amade's conduct of operations. If he found d'Amade unequal to his task, Lyautey would agree to take command. But the fact-finding mission was merely a delaying tactic. Lyautey had no intention of reporting unfavorably on d'Amade. "I decided to cover him even before I saw him at work," he said to St.-Aulaire.

Lyautey arrived in Casablanca in March. By then, d'Amade had had occasion to take a few more bloody noses, such as that at R'Fakha. On February 29, as a French column marched north along the Wadi M'Koun, d'Amade ordered his chasseurs to hold the right flank on the far side of the river. The choice of the chasseurs for this task was, in theory, a sound one. The chasseurs had been founded in 1831 in Algeria for use primarily as mounted infantry. They carried cavalry sabers, but were also armed with carbines. If attacked, they were to dismount, form a firing line and await reinforcements. In practice, however, the chasseurs' special mentality made them prone to taking the tactical law into their own hands. Eager to downplay their status as glorified infantry and gain acceptance among the more prestigious mounted troops, they sought to match the cavalry in panache and offensive spirit.

So, when these troops came under fire from Moroccans hiding in the tall grass on a crest called R'Fakha, they charged, sabers in hand, to clear them out. Some of the Moroccans were hacked down by the French blades, but most simply lay down until the horses passed over them, then stood up to fire at the backs of the French cavalry. Colonel Luigné, seeing the confusion of his milling men who were being fired at by Moroccans on foot, decided to rally on the spot. Unfortunately, when the order was transmitted to the bugler, who was some distance away, he blew the rally call immediately. The chasseurs began to withdraw toward the bugler rather than rally on their colonel. As they did so, they collided with a second section of chasseurs who were thundering up the hill toward the battlefield. The confusion was extreme. As the French attempted to reorganize, they saw to their horror that their comrades, who lay wounded on the hill or who had been dehorsed, were being hacked to pieces by the Moroccans who were now swarming over the knoll. Another charge was therefore ordered to rescue the survivors of the first. The Moroccans made them work to recover what remained of their comrades, mainly headless torsos. Only the arrival of a company of tirailleurs who had waded across the river allowed the chasseurs to disengage—with twelve dead, twenty-five wounded and minus thirty horses. The Moroccans then, with surprising agility, shifted their attack against the main bulk of the column, where the steady firing of the legion backed by 75s repulsed them with ease. Colonel Luigné rode up to d'Amade, saluted him with his saber and said: "My General, you told me to hold the crest of R'Fakha. I held it."

R'Fakha had not reflected well on d'Amade's ability as a commander. He had left his cavalry unsupported by either artillery or infantry, thereby violating a fundamental tactical rule. Indeed, d'Amade was to inflict his mediocre abilities on the French army well into the Great War: he was relieved twice, once in 1914 and again in 1916, as commander of the French contingent in the Dardanelles. But in 1908, his mediocrity was obscured by three things: first, by Lyautey, who had decided in advance to "cover" him to spite Clemenceau. Second, his lack of tactical genius was compensated for in part by the extraordinary marching of his soldiers. Since Napoleonic times, the French had prided themselves on their ability to cover great distances on foot rapidly. The Armée d'Afrique, especially, kept this tradition alive. Before 1914, there were probably no soldiers on earth who could outmarch them. Last, d'Amade was aided by the tactical rigidity of his enemy.

The Moroccans made extraordinarily brave warriors. The French marveled as, time and time again, they rushed forward into the very mouths of the French guns. But they seldom altered their life-style to fit the demands of what was, for them, a major war. For the Moroccans in the Chaouia, battles began at 10 a.m. and ended around 5 p.m. Seldom, if ever, did they attack the French at night, when their frontal assaults might have brought some success. They insisted on fighting in broad daylight when they could be blasted from 600 yards. By getting an early start, the French were on occasion able to steal a march on their opponents.

February had not been a brilliantly successful month for d'Amade. March, however, would treat him better. His continuous marching in the country east of a line drawn from Bou Znika to Settat had forced the tribes opposing him to take refuge in the hilly country in the extreme east of the Chaouia, where the grass downs melt into a series of stony upland ridges, some of them rising to three thousand feet. It was in such country near the village of Abd el-Kerim that the French reached one of the Moroccan camps on the morning of March 8. The Moroccans appear to have been particularly casual about its defense. The French advance met only desultory resistance. When the soldiers, in line again, topped the last ridge, they saw the Moroccan tents stretched out before them on a small plateau surrounded by a barrier of prickly pear. By sighting two guns down a narrow ravine through which most of the Moors, including women and children, attempted their escape, d'Amade was able in half an hour to kill more Moroccans than he had in the preceding two months. The carnage sickened him, however, for he stopped the cannonade before the hemorrhage of refugees from the camp had subsided, an act of charity for which he was later criticized. The tirailleurs then pillaged the camp, performing impressive feats of bringing down chickens with well-aimed stones. Others drifted among the tents dispatching the wounded—"*Il n'est pas encore mort, le salaud, la charogne*" ("He isn't dead yet, the bastard, the carrion"), followed by the report of a chasseur's carbine. It was a very savage war.

Moroccan morale was now on the point of collapse. D'Amade, like so many other mediocre commanders, relied chiefly on attrition to grind down his enemy. The Moroccans had obliged him by attacking his unimaginative but invulnerable squares, and he had cut them down by the hundreds. Occasionally, the Moroccans caught out an isolated detachment and inflicted great harm, as at R'Fakha. But the French losses remained trifling, and it soon became apparent, even to the most fanatical Moor, that they were unbeatable. This was not the warfare the Moroccans were accustomed to. Traditionally, they relied upon noise—shrieking and the sound of firing— to carry the day. It was a way of making war among nervous, excitable people. Firepower was a concept as alien to them as atheism. What impressed the Moroccans most was the steady unperturbability of the French line: "By Allah! we rode at them as we did when we ate up the Dukella; but they moved not and before we could wheel round to ride away to reload our guns, we were right upon them. Yet they feared not, and only a few of us were left alive to gallop away. Never have I seen such fighting and understood it not."

The killing of prisoners and the mutilation of dead and wounded were long-established practices in Morocco, from which only those wealthy enough to command a ransom were exempt. Heads were prized as a trophy of victory, so much so that Moroccans often buried their badly wounded alive rather than leave them to the tender mercies of the enemy's women. Not surprisingly, what French soldiers feared most was being left wounded on the field of battle, as at R'Fakha. Nor did the French take prisoners. This is probably less horrifying than it at first appears. Certainly, during the Casablanca revolt and in its immediate aftermath, the French shot many captured Arabs out of hand. After watching a French patrol execute three Arabs armed only with knives lashed to the end of sticks, the English observer Ellis Ashmead-Bartlett complained of the lack of "sporting instinct" in his cross-channel neighbors.

Rumors of this brutal behavior soon reached Paris, and on September 17, 1907, War Minister Picquart wired General Drude that the shooting of prisoners was to cease. But this order, like so many others sent from Paris, was virtually ignored. There were also a few legionnaires who actually went man-hunting around Casablanca, killing Arabs, stripping them and selling their belongings. This could not have accounted for many deaths, but these bloodthirsty men certainly made an impression on the Moroccans, their activities inflated out of all proportion, no doubt, by constant retelling.

During the Chaouia campaign, the problem of prisoners resolved itself because the French seldom captured any. The Moroccans' horses carried them beyond the grasp of the slower French. The constant impression of those on the French side until the very final stages of the campaign was that modern firepower was less effective than had been thought because the battlefields were littered with so few casualties. This was certainly a false impression. French firepower usually kept the attackers at a great distance so that the French did not see, or find, Moroccan casualties. Also, the Moroccans probably carried most of their dead and wounded away. The French almost certainly dispatched any wounded they did find; French reports frequently mention measures taken to care for their own wounded, but nothing is said of enemy wounded.

It was the scorched-earth policy followed by d'Amade that, in the end, broke resistance in the Chaouia. In this, the *goumiers* proved particularly

A street in Fez

Sultan Moulai Hafid, on horseback amid a crowd of his retainers. Above, Colonel Emile Mangin, head of the French military mission in Fez, with Algerian Lieutenant Ben Sedira (left) and the Sultan (right)

Local recruits—askar—in Fez, 1911. Above, some members of the French military mission. Adjutant Pisani is in the foreground, holding a leather bag; Major Brémond is in the center, with the bespectacled Lieutenant le Glay to his left. At far right is Sergeant Koudai, later one of the Marrakech hostages

At top, French sailors and civilians on the roof of the consulate in Casablanca during the 1907 bombardment and riots. Below, French officers inspect the antiquated arsenal of the pretender Moulai Zayn at Meknes, in June 1911, after his surrender

Algerian tirailleurs man a defense line outside Casablanca in 1907 (top), while French troops make use of mule-borne litters to transport wounded (inset). Below, the fortified *ksar* at Taghit on the Zousfana

Near Taza in 1914, a French 65 mm. mountain gun goes into action (top). Below, rebels are marched off in chains, and are executed (bottom) as the French repress the mutinies in Fez, 1911

With an early reconnaissance aircraft flying overhead, a troop of mule-mounted cavalry moves forward near Taza

The junction of east and west, May 1914. General Hubert Lyautey is in the center, with General Baumgarten at right and General Gouraud at left

effective. They would return to camp, waving their swords and shouting as they shepherded their stolen goats, cattle and sheep between their horses. Life soon became quite impossible for the three hundred thousand or so inhabitants of the Chaouia as the *goumiers*, tirailleurs and legionnaires raided their flocks and pillaged and burned their douars. These tactics of attrition began to bring the tribes into submission. Those who wanted to continue the struggle came from far away, the Haouz and even the Tafilalet, men who were happy enough to fight on someone else's territory. These were dealt with by d'Amade on March 15.

The campaign had, until now, been conducted principally in the eastern Chaouia. On March 14, d'Amade redirected his forces toward the south. By interrogating villagers to the southwest of Ber Rechid at noon on the fifteenth, he learned that a large *harka* was located about twelve miles away. He ordered every man to drop his knapsack and each sixteenth man to remain behind to guard them. With this lightened force, he marched in the direction of the Moroccan camp. As usual, the Moroccans made no real effort to defend their camp: as the French approached, their horsemen swarmed on the hills but fell back rapidly. The French were soon in a footrace. The infantry, formed in a line almost two miles long with cavalry on each flank, trotted through a plantation of figs, jumped a few ditches and then came before an absolute sea of flat, camel-hair tents. The dimensions of the Moroccan camp seemed unbelievable, as did its panic. The foreign legionnaires and tirailleurs fixed bayonets and, with a yell, charged into the teeming encampment.

It is a measure of the nature of the fighting in the Chaouia that the rout of the camp of Bou Nouala was hailed as a great victory. Decisive it certainly was, but it was more like a pig-sticking than a battle. For weeks these soldiers had been kept marching backward and forward in search of an elusive foe. A soldier, especially an infantryman, bitterly resents any unnecessary expenditure of energy. Now, at last, they had caught the enemy in his lair. "Let me get a chance at the 'Bou Chaibs,'" the correspondent of the *Times*, Reginald Rankin, heard a grizzled legionnaire mutter as he trotted toward this sea of tents, "and I'll pay them out for this infernal foot race." Pay them out he did. The rifles of the French line rattled. The air vibrated with the coughing of the 75s. As each shell exploded over the camp, Moroccan women shrieked. White flags went up on many tents which had not been set alight by the exploding shells. But the French were not interested in giving quarter:

> The Arabs now threw away their arms and pretended they had taken no part in the fight. The French went forward; a group of men on the left crouched with some women beneath the shelter of a tangle of rocks. They expected quarter; the French drew nearer; and still they sat quietly on. But the Frenchmen's blood was up; they had been treacherously fired at under the cover of a white flag; with a shout their bayonets were levelled to the charge. The Arabs fled yelling in every direction. . . . The long blue line surged on; the sun sank behind a dark pall of violet clouds; the air was thick with the cries of dying men and the stench of burning tents.

Every man found alive was slaughtered. Women were left: some shrieked, others were simply too dazed to utter a cry. They simply rocked back and forth on their heels moaning before their smoldering belongings or the disemboweled bodies of their husbands. As the French marched away, the petty explosions of the small stocks of black powder kept in every tent mingled with the wailing of the women and the cries of the children.

The sacking of the camp of Bou Nouala virtually ended resistance in the Chaouia, although it produced howls of protest from Jaurès in the Chamber. D'Amade seized Settat for the third time. Lyautey told him to remain there, promising that he would smooth over the breach of orders with Clemenceau. This did not prove difficult. He caught the Prime Minister in a good mood, so that his cute little performance went down well: "The desk is the plateau of Settat. . . . The door is the access from the south. . . . If I get down on my knees behind the desk, I cannot see the roads. . . . But if I get onto the desk . . ." and he climbed from the floor onto Clemenceau's desk. The Prime Minister was probably far more influenced by Lyautey's rather juvenile humor, so close to his own, than by his strategic arguments. Or, perhaps, he simply did not care.

There was one final act to be played out in the drama of the Chaouia: that between the two brothers. Moulai Hafid might have triumphed quickly had he marched resolutely against his brother from the first. But that had been impossible. His supporters saw him as the champion of the *jihad*, the holy war, against the *roumi*. Aziz was a tool of the French. Why attack the puppet when the puppet master is within range? Moulai Hafid allowed his *mehalla* to break itself against the rock of the French squares until, chastened, they were prepared to return to a type of warfare which they better understood.

Since Abd el-Aziz had abandoned the north for Rabat in September 1907, the towns in the interior led by Fez and Meknes had wasted little time in declaring for Moulai Hafid. If the pretender could reach them, he might be able to extend and consolidate his power base beyond Marrakech and the Haouz. But how? The French blocked his path in the Chaouia. He must make a deal with Moha ou Hamou, leader of the powerful Zaian confederation, who controlled the lands between the Chaouia and the Middle Atlas. Moha ou Hamou agreed eventually to desert Abd el-Aziz. The bargain was sealed by the marriage of Moulai Hafid with Moha ou Hamou's daughter.

Only in May 1908, however, were negotiations completed. Moulai Hafid took a few hostages from the Haouz to guarantee good conduct in his rear, left one of Madani's brothers in charge in Marrakech, and marched through Zaian territory to Fez. His reception there was enthusiastic: women in their most colorful dresses, weighted down with heavy silver jewelry encrusted with rubies, emeralds and turquoise, crowded onto the rooftops. The cloud of red dust thrown up by Moulai Hafid's procession could be seen advancing closer. When, at last, Moulai Hafid emerged, resplendent in white robes, sitting on a cream horse beneath the large saucer of a parasol, the high-pitched ululations of the thirty thousand women rippled over the town.

With Hafid in the north, Abd el-Aziz decided to strike at his brother's base in Marrakech. He was encouraged by news that Madani's exactions in the south had turned Marrakech against him. El Mtouggi, jealous of Madani's power, would welcome the humbling of his powerful neighbor. The French, although officially neutral in the civil war, allowed Aziz free passage through the Chaouia. More, they allowed their military mission to accompany the Sultan's *mehalla*. On July 12, 1908, Abd el-Aziz set out from Rabat at the head of five thousand men, three 75s and two machine guns. They marched without haste, pausing to plunder Glaoui property along the way or to pick up contingents of tribesmen. On August 8, the *mehalla* crossed the Oum er Rbia, the river which divides the Chaouia from the Haouz. There was now virtually nothing to stop him from seizing Marrakech—except, that is, the low morale of his own *mehalla*. On the morning of August 19 after a night march, they sighted the enemy camp. The *mehalla* was strung out over three or four miles. Abd el-Aziz insisted that the 75s be brought into action, over the objections of the French instructors, who pointed out that the Hafidist camp was out of range. As predicted, the shells fell short. Aziz then ordered his tribal levies to attack. What happened next is obscure. The most coherent account of the "battle" claims that the horsemen swept toward the camp, a few shots were exchanged and they galloped back shouting that they had been defeated. This was all that the *mehalla* had waited to hear. The ill-disciplined *askar* fell to pillaging their own camp and shooting their own horsemen to steal their mounts. The groups of peasants who had followed the *mehalla* joined in. Bullets flew in all directions and the camp was in total confusion even though the enemy had yet to attack. Abd el-Aziz kept his head. He placed his harem on mules, gathered up what was left of his belongings, and retreated north with his makhzan and the military mission amidst a mob of beaten soldiers. At every farm and douar they were met by a fusillade. Occasionally, members of the *mehalla* attempted to assassinate the Europeans and were dissuaded only with great difficulty. Finally, the refugees reached the French camp at Settat and safety.

The French were now forced to concede that Aziz was a beaten man. They negotiated his abdication, gave him an annual pension of seven thousand pounds (thirty-five thousand dollars) and allowed him to retire to Tangiers. Moulai Hafid was now Sultan of Morocco.

CHAPTER XIII

THE BENI SNASSEN AND BOU DENIB

Lieutenant Georges Catroux of the foreign legion was normally quite happy to have visitors. Hospitality in the mess was a long-established tradition in these isolated posts on the Algerian-Moroccan frontier. Even artillery officers were welcomed. But Lyautey was quite a different matter. Catroux saw the commander of the Oran division riding toward him on that morning in early September 1908, erect, alert as if he were actually enjoying the heat and the dust. (In fact, he was. It eased his rheumatism.) In seconds he and his infernal *zaouia* would be crawling all over Bel-Riadha, an entire opera house of prima donnas—the son of General So-and-So, the nephew of Count Such-and-Such, all well dressed and well connected. Perhaps Lyautey would even have one of his fancy literary friends from Paris in tow. Then he really would feel obliged to put on a show. *"Alors, mon petit Catroux, comment ça va?"* The trouble was, one never knew how to answer. Catroux had learned that the hard way last year at Oudjda. He would have to feel his way cautiously.

And well he might, for Catroux's commander was in a foul mood. "When you drag along regular troops, seventy-fives, horses, you have to feed all that lot." Lyautey almost shouted at the officers crammed into the "mess," which was little more than a few packing crates nailed together with a board for a table. "You need shells, you need bases and men to guard them." This, then, was why Lyautey was angry with Catroux; he was in charge of guarding a supply base for General Alix's column, which had passed through the day before to relieve the garrison at Bou Denib. "That's no way to operate in this country!" The *zaouia* nodded its collective head in agreement. This was certainly not the first time they had heard this after-dinner speech. "If I had been in charge of this affair, I would have levied a thousand horsemen from the Hamyans, a thousand from the Trafis, and I would have launched a surprise *razzia* against the Ait-Bouchaouen, with the support of several light regular units. In short, a quick brutal strike back and forth and not a hammer to crush a fly." Catroux kept his mouth shut. It did him no good. A few days later, Lyautey delivered the same speech to General Alix, with the minor amendment that he was simply repeating the remarks he had heard spoken by that clever Lieutenant Catroux.

Lyautey was aggrieved at the way Alix had handled things at Bou Denib. There were three ways to pacify a country. You could plant forts in the middle of it and leave the dissidents alone. This was the method of the Spaniards and Italians. It was self-defeating, for the forts became prisons, the wardens captives, and the country could not be made profitable. Second, you could launch mobile columns, keep them constantly on the move burning crops and villages, not allowing dissidents to settle, until they made peace from sheer exhaustion. This is what d'Amade had done in the Chaouia. It worked, but it left bad blood. Or one could combine the two: establish a post and keep light, mobile groups moving around it. The post became a market where the locals were encouraged to trade, where they felt secure and where the French could gather intelligence. This was the Lyautey method. The question that the general failed to answer satisfactorily, however, was, did it work?

The answer to the question was: not very well. Of course, Lyautey was far too proud to admit to failure. Certainly his letters give no hint of doubt, full as they are of selective judgments and irony. Nor was his *zaouia* of flatterers likely to cross their commander with an honest criticism. The posts that Lyautey had established in eastern Morocco were hardly more than a few brick buildings built along two intersecting streets laid out by the military engineers. A handful of Spaniards settled them and earned their living by selling cheap alcohol to the troops. But these posts were little more than pens for soldiers, thousands of them, bored, drunken, restless, who had to be kept constantly occupied with reviews and inspections.

Nor did his program of "economic penetration" enjoy anything but an ephemeral success. The Moroccans came into his posts to sell their sheep, goats and dates at prices far higher than they would fetch in the Tafilalet or Fez. They were also happy to visit the army doctors whom Lyautey imported as part of his "hearts-and-minds" approach to conquest. But the marketplace never proved to be the "great agent of dissolution of the dissidents" which Lyautey had hoped. The Moroccans saw no contradiction between trading with the French one minute and plundering them the next. By drawing commerce away from the Tafilalet and Fez with his artificially inflated prices, he succeeded in alienating powerful interests there. In 1906, these people ordered a boycott of French markets. By July, trade in French posts had virtually dried up.

Nor were Moroccans offered many incentives to settle near to French posts. *Goumiers* and tirailleurs could behave with great arrogance, riding into a "friendly" douar to demand that a sheep or several chickens be prepared for their dinner. The French habit of requisitioning mules and camels for their interminable convoys was not very popular either. At worst, to settle near a French post could prove positively dangerous, for French justice tended to punish those closest at hand. When, for instance, robbers lifted three rifles from the camp of Major Théodore Pein on May 26, 1906, Pein led his men to a neighboring douar and took fifty camels as "security." Lyautey entirely approved of Pein's action: "Either the tribes will recover the rifles, or the robbers, or we shall keep the security." This was hardly the way to encourage confidence in the French occupation. It must come as no surprise, therefore, that by mid-1906 Lyautey's program of "economic penetration" lay in tatters. The Tangiers crisis of 1905 made a general rising in eastern Morocco appear as imminent as it had in the west. Lyautey was scared stiff. That the *harka* failed to organize, at least not in 1906, was due more to the turbulent nature of tribal relations, to their inability to find a holy man powerful enough to unite the feuding factions, than to any effective counteraction by Lyautey.

Lyautey's military reforms met with little more success than did his economic ones. He was the French army's most prestigious advocate of "going native," of lightening the load of his troops and increasing their mobility. "In Africa, one defends oneself by moving," he was fond of repeating. In many respects, this made sense. Laperrine's camel-mounted Saharians had been an interesting and, in many ways, a successful experiment, although they owed little to Lyautey. But they were designed to fight in the sand dunes of the Erg, not on the stony plateaus which separated Algeria from Morocco. Nor could Laperrine be persuaded to look west. He was far more an explorer than a soldier, entranced by the desert and essentially uninterested in the conquest of Morocco. In March 1906, he abandoned his post without permission to ride to Timbuctu and back. Lyautey was furious: "Experience proves, to my great regret, that my authority over Colonel Laperrine is insufficient to prevent such acts." It was, however, an impressive ride. It would have seemed churlish to discipline Laperrine, so Lyautey simply requested that he be transferred to the Sahara command.

This left the *goum* at Colomb-Béchar. Lyautey was forever singing their praises in public, but in private he was less enthusiastic. Native troops could prove excellent when incorporated into regular units of the colonial army or the Armée d'Afrique. Units of partisans, or *goumiers*, were much less effective, however. If closely supported by regular troops, they were adequate for *razzias*. In formal combat, they could prove a positive liability: they fired all their ammunition in five minutes and fled if pressed. The *goum* at Colomb-Béchar was less well armed and far less mobile than the bands of raiders it was set to catch. Moroccans, operating in small groups, continued to attack supply columns, which Lyautey reduced in size but could not live without, and to plunder herds in Algeria. Only on a very few occasions was the *goum* able to track the raiders down.

The problem was partly one of recruitment. Lyautey's original intention was to draw his *goumiers* from among the same pastoral tribesmen as those who raided into Algeria. However, these Moroccans did not come forward in any significant numbers. It may have been policy not to recruit too many of them in any case, as the French feared they might prove unreliable; men who for generations had made their living as poachers could not be turned overnight into trustworthy gamekeepers. Consequently, Lyautey was forced to find his *goumiers* mainly around Géryville. Several generations of peace had deprived these Algerians of their traditional warrior education, and without a strong cadre of French officers and NCOs, they proved inferior to Moroccans in natural fighting and tracking abilities.

Lyautey's claims that he would call on tribal levies to fight his battles in the South Oranais were no more than empty boasts. One of the fundamental myths of the conquest of Morocco is that the French simply used one tribe to conquer another by exploiting the traditional hostility which divided Morocco into warring factions—that Moroccans, therefore, not the French, ultimately provided the means for the French takeover. This is simply not true. As a method of conquest, it would have proved ineffective even if tried on the frontier. When it was attempted in the Sus in 1912–13, it proved a fiasco. Tribes did not "conquer" other tribes, they merely raided them. And once a mass resistance movement gathered, as at Taghit in 1903 and Bou Denib in 1908, no tribe would have dared swim against the tide to oppose it. Indeed, the great French fear was that the call for a *jihad* might elicit a response in Algeria. As a consequence, French officers were reluctant to arm men who might turn against them.

Another great weakness of the French on the frontier was the absence of a reliable intelligence network. A sound knowledge of the tribes, their divisions, and their principal leaders was considered the essential element in Lyautey's "organization on the march." The Intelligence Service was detailed to draw up studies of the tribes, set out spies and bribe those who might use their influence for France. As an academic organization drawing up ethnographic studies, it was a great success. As a spy service, it was largely a flop. Intelligence officers received a poor return on their money. Tribesmen gave them vague or fragmentary information, always holding back something to sell on the next market day. It was far more useful to have the *mokhaznis*, or native police, invite the informant to lunch, for he told them far more than he would reveal to the intelligence officer "in confidence." Lyautey also hoped to buy influence, to exploit divisions or excite controversies among his enemies by handing out bribes—"St. George's Cavalry," he called it. There was, of course, no shortage of Moroccans eager to take his money. But bribes handed out by French officers who had only a superficial knowledge of Moroccan society almost inevitably went to the wrong people, "small men who had no influence. They promised great things, but they had no power to carry them out."

Badly armed, less mobile than their enemy, inadequately informed, the French fell back upon the only option open to them—the *razzia*. If they could not punish the guilty, they would punish whom they could catch. The "Lyautey method" boiled down in practice to a series of reprisal raids for damage inflicted. The dreadful *razzia* was institutionalized and perpetuated. The "economic penetration," "zone of attraction," "native politics," "organization on the march," increasingly began to sound like so many hollow clichés. Sometimes, in a lucid moment, Lyautey would admit that "in this country, force alone imposes respect."

Why, then, does the myth still linger that the French relied far more upon persuasion than force to conquer Morocco? Essentially because "hearts and minds" was more a public-relations exercise than a workable military formula. As in all guerrilla wars, the problem for Lyautey was to deprive the determined handful of warriors of the support and sympathies of the noncombatant population. Lyautey's "economic penetration" sought to persuade this soft center that their interests lay with supporting the French. As we have seen, this proved too simplistic an approach and ultimately failed as a millitary theory. If Lyautey continued to retail "hearts and minds," it was for reasons connected far more with the political situation in France than with that in Morocco. Only by claiming that he was "civilizing" Morocco, that the Moroccans actually preferred the French presence to their normal state of anarchy, could he sell colonial expansion to a French public skeptical of its value. "Hearts and minds"—or "native politics," as Lyautey called it—tells us much about the nature of colonialism in France. In Britain, the imperial idea was a popular one. The British believed, rightly or wrongly, that in some way their bread was buttered by colonial expansion. British public opinion was prepared to tolerate draconian methods like the scorched-earth policies used by Kitchener in South Africa provided they brought results, however short-term. The French, without the economic motive, were at best ambivalent about the acres of scrub and desert which their soldiers insisted on bringing under the flag. The luxury goods which France produced found no ready market in Africa, while French investors were notoriously reluctant to sink their savings into the colonies. Therefore, French officers adopted the only role left open to them, that of the agents of civilization. Their novel methods of colonial warfare, which combined economic and military penetration, persuasion with force, were developed largely as a public-relations exercise to convince France itself that colonialism benefited the conquered.

To be fair to him, the breakup of Lyautey's "organization on the march" in 1906 was due to events beyond his control. The Tangiers crisis of 1905 excited passions east of the Atlas. The murder of Dr. Mauchamp in Marrakech in March 1907, followed by the occupation of Oudjda—"a filthy, dilapidated labyrinth; the main street is only one meter fifty wide. A cow can block it. People everywhere; you cannot move without stepping on a child"—brought the reaction to a head.

The massif of the Beni Snassen stretches like a great slug for forty-five miles along the plains of northeastern Morocco between the Wadi Kiss, which forms the border with Algeria, and the Moulouya. The rocky, scrub-covered hills rising at their highest point to 4,659 feet offered a refuge for the inhabitants, who, like most of the mountain populations of the north, were both poor and predatory. The French had discovered the defensive advantages offered by the Beni Snassen's redoubt once already in 1859, when they had been obliged to renounce a pursuit of Beni Snassen raiders into Algeria. That is why they should have been more cautious when it became apparent in the summer of 1907 that their occupation of Oudjda had provoked a certain effervescence throughout the east, and especially among the Beni Snassen tribesmen. But they threw caution to the winds. Lyautey reckoned that the Beni Snassen were awaiting the end of the harvest, then they would attack. He ordered his commanders to keep their soldiers on the move "to destroy the legend of the immobility of the Oudjda garrison" and to prevent the *cafard* from sapping morale. Inevitably, perhaps intentionally, on November 7, one of these patrols which was nosing around the base of the massif came under fire. Reinforcements were brought up with 75s, a few villages blasted and a fine of five thousand francs imposed on the cowed inhabitants. When the fine was not paid, Lyautey authorized operations. The war with the Beni Snassen had begun.

The declaration of hostilities was followed by a period of phony war as Lyautey ordered up troops from as far away as Tunisia. For one who was to complain in 1908 that General Alix was prepared to use "a hammer to kill a fly," Lyautey was going to use a sledgehammer: he was prepared to attack only when the weight of numbers was firmly on his side. As a campaign, it would prove very different from the one the French were fighting in the Chaouia. The Beni Snassen were not horsemen. They fought on foot, which strictly limited their mobility. They could not sweep around the French squares, cut off isolated groups and stragglers, and then slip away on their fast ponies. That is why when on November 23 a French column came upon a camp of two hundred tents near a small village at the foot of the massif, its inhabitants were content to fire on the invaders from behind the masonry walls of the gardens and paddocks while the remainder escaped into the mountains, driving their goats before them. The following day, however, a second French column of 250 tirailleurs and eighty chasseurs patrolling the Wadi Kiss was attacked by a *harka* of two thousand men. The French retreated in good order across the river into Algeria. The Beni Snassen prudently elected not to pursue. But in every camp and tribal *jemma* (council), men said that the Moroccans had inflicted a grave defeat on the French "faction." This brought in new recruits, particularly horsemen from the plains. On the twenty-seventh, the newly swollen *harka* crossed the Kiss to attack the small village of Bab-el-Assa, defended by a force of about 400 tirailleurs, spahis and *goumiers*. The partisans, in the excitement, shot off their ammunition quickly and fled, leaving the tirailleurs' flank exposed. The Moroccans now caught the tirailleurs in a cross-fire that subsided only at dusk, leaving twelve Algerians dead. The French claimed that they had killed eighty Moroccans, but it was impossible to tell.

On the twenty-ninth, however, the Moroccans pushed their luck too far. Dividing into two *harkas*, they attempted simultaneously to break up the French concentrations on the Kiss and to attack Port Say at the mouth of the river. The first *harka* of four thousand men was caught by 75s as they approached the French camp up a narrow ravine. They attempted to rally, some of the men plunging their hands into the entrails of their fallen comrades and smearing their faces with the blood as they charged the barking French guns. It was a slaughter. The Moroccans left three hundred dead as they retreated towards Morocco. Those who attacked Port Say made little progress against the garrison of Zouaves backed by the destroyer *Arc* standing off the coast. After its initial success, the Beni Snassen resistance now began to crumble. Apart from their already not inconsiderable losses, they were desperately short of ammunition; the French had observed men moving along the firing lines collecting the spent cartridges to be filled with black powder. With the market at Oudjda closed to them and Port Say blockaded, they had little opportunity to restock.

On November 30, a large French column arrived on the right bank of the Kiss. Only small commandos of the Beni Snassen were now in evidence. The bulk of the *harka* had withdrawn to Aghbal, an important market town on the slopes of the massif, where the men debated their next move. Colonel Branlière decided to encourage those who wished to disband. On December 5, he led a strong force to Aghbal which stopped within artillery range and began to bombard some of the outlying buildings. The Moroccans contented themselves with sporadic fire from the ridges around the town, but declined to attack. Branlière marched away. When he returned four days later, the Beni Snassen had vanished into their mountain, as they had half a century before.

The fragmentation of the *harka* presented Lyautey with a problem. To assault the mountain would involve serious risks. The Beni Snassen, fighting a guerrilla war on their home ground, each farm or local shrine transformed into a fortress, each defile or ravine concealing an ambush, could make life extremely unpleasant for the invaders. Nor could he afford to spare the troops for a long campaign of pacification, for unrest was already beginning to appear further south. Lyautey's solution to his difficulty was, it must be admitted, ingenious: if the mountain was the redoubt of the Beni Snassen, he would simply besiege it.

With his eight thousand soldiers, he welded a ring of posts joined by three strong columns around the massif. This prevented the Beni Snassen from restocking the ammunition, sugar, salt and candles which they relied upon.

It was economic warfare at its most basic, and the mountaineers soon began to feel the pinch. Only on the southern slopes of the mountain at

Ain-Sfa did one of the columns encounter resistance, which was quickly dispersed with a whiff of shrapnel. On December 17, most of the caids trooped into Oudjda to make peace. Lyautey splintered his three large columns into several smaller ones which now wove through the mountain from west to east. A few shots were fired, but the French were met almost everywhere in silence. One caid even invited Colonel Branlière and his staff to a feast of roast boar. When the colonel asked why the caid was not eating, the Arab replied: "Here, only dogs eat that meat." Only then did the colonel realize that he had been insulted. He jumped up in a rage and demanded that the caid pay for his insult with 1,000 goats and sheep. He received 1,100, although many wandered off when placed in the charge of their inexperienced legionnaire shepherds.

Lyautey set the *aman* (fine) for the Beni Snassen at 250,000 francs, payable in kind. Each caid then had the task of convincing the intelligence officers that his faction had not participated in the rebellion, or at least had been reluctant rebels, forced to fight by their powerful neighbors, all in an attempt to reduce their contribution to the general war reparations. From December 19, the caids and headmen filed into Mautimprey to bring their goats, sheep and donkeys and to surrender their weapons—mostly old Martinis and Remingtons, the more modern rifles having been left behind despite French threats to burn the house of any man found armed.

Lyautey had won a great victory. The rebellion had been crushed without too many lives lost, which won him the congratulations of his government. Paris welcomed Lyautey's quick and nearly bloodless campaign because it had saved it another embarrassing outburst from Jaurès. But the Lyautey "method" had not been much in evidence. The Beni Snassen gave in because they had been thoroughly blooded by the French, deprived of ammunition, and threatened by starvation. As their losses mounted, so their confidence drained away as the less committed tribesmen drifted back to their douars.

Lyautey had struck lucky a second time. By crushing the revolt of the Beni Snassen, Lyautey had added to his legend, a legend which had been born in 1903. Then, he had arrived in the South Oranais at the very moment when the defeat at Taghit had splintered another tribal coalition. Therefore, the application of "native politics" appeared to bring peace, when, in fact, it was the action of the troops at Taghit that had firmly clamped the lid on the revolt. Calm in the South Oranais had been maintained by the threat of the gun, not by the winning of "hearts and minds." Nor would the Lyautey method be able to cope with a rebellion that would make the Beni Snassen uprising appear a Sunday school picnic by comparison.

It cannot be pleasant to be awakened by a Moroccan armed with a large knife and obviously intent on mischief, and several French soldiers had just such an experience on the morning of April 17, 1908, at Menabba in eastern Morocco. The Moroccans had at last gotten in among them, howling, shooting, slashing the French tents with their curved knives and murdering, or attempting to murder, anyone still in occupation. The Moroccans had attacked the French camp at first light out of the *east*. A wave of several thousand, most of them stripped naked and well oiled to keep out the cold, had crept in the night to within fifty yards of the French camp without so much as dislodging a stone. The French knew that they were in the presence of a large *harka*. Four of their *goumiers* had been killed during a reconnaissance on the previous day. But the *harka* was camped to the *west* of the French bivouac. The bulk of the sentinels, therefore, had been told to keep an eye in that direction. It proved a fatally shortsighted order.

Nineteen soldiers were to die and another 101 would be wounded before breakfast. That more were not killed was due to two things: first, that the Frenchmen, so precipitously roused from their slumber, were as naked, or nearly so, as their attackers. In the confusion of the half-light, and without the telltale pair of trousers or jellaba, it became very difficult to distinguish friend from foe. It was like a riot in a nudist colony. Second, the Moroccans were suddenly struck with a case of gold fever. After sowing confusion, they began to help themselves from the rich pickings of French supplies—saddles, rifles, ammunition, not to mention the animals—which would make them substantial men of property overnight.

If it was the desire for loot that kept the quarrelsome members of this *harka* united, it also proved its undoing. The attackers now disintegrated into a mob. They began to rifle the supply train and dispute the spoils, even shooting each other in the process. This gave the French time to organize. For a full hour, several hundred Frenchmen, most of them in various humiliating stages of undress and shivering in the cool dawn air, collected rifles and ammunition for the counterattack. "The sands of the sirocco penetrate even the shell of an egg," the Arabs say. They had certainly penetrated the mechanism of the machine gun, which at this critical moment refused to fire. Finally, the French collected themselves sufficiently to launch their attack. It took three assaults before the legionnaires finally cleared the camp of marauders. The Moroccans made off toward the west, leaving the spahis without horses, the supply column without mules and almost a hundred men without rifles. Cartridges and tins of sardines had disappeared by the crateful. The French had been humiliated.

Moulai Lahsin, the extraordinary man who had led this *harka*, must have been pleased with his victory. It had not been easy to galvanize Moroccans into action against the French. For over a year he had traveled the arid highlands east of the Atlas from north to south preaching the *jihad* in *zaouias* and tribal councils: "The Moslem world is decaying. Its people are bad Moslems for they forget their duty to fight the *Nazarani*. Moslems must purify themselves in a holy struggle for the command of their land and the soul of its people. We must attack the French in their camp at Béchar." Some old men had refused to be convinced: "Moulai Lahsin is a sharif, a descendant of the Prophet and of holy blood, but he comes not from an old *zaouia*. He has founded his own at Douiret Sbaa—'the Lion's Den.' What proof is there that he has the *baraka*? What proof is there that he will not lead us into another slaughter, as at Taghit? The French faction has many rifles and much ammunition. We Moslems are poor. Our bravery is great. But what good is that against men who hide behind their walls like cowards? We are brave men and good Moslems, but we are not fools." Others refused to join an alliance with their enemies, even against the infidel. The struggle between the Sultans in the west also added a complicating factor. Moulai Lahsin was a Hafidist who carried letters from the pretender supporting his *jihad*. By the second week of April 1908, however, Moulai Lahsin had gathered four thousand rifles at the "Lion's Den" before he set out for Colomb-Béchar.

Moulai Lahsin was the victim of his own success. This *harka*, like every *harka*, combined the celestial with the carnal, the pursuit of salvation with the profit motive. The presence of a respected holy man with proven *baraka* was essential for the success of any enterprise of this scale, for it guaranteed Allah's blessing. And Allah's blessings had been great: guns, saddles, mules, more ammunition than the southeast had seen in a generation and, well, sardines. After Menabba, the *harka* had dissolved as its warriors carried their spoils back to their *ksars* and douars. That is why when Lyautey's successor in the South Oranais, General Vigny, led a punitive column west from Colomb-Béchar, he struck into thin air. The *harka* had vanished into the parched hills. Thereupon he marched his men to Douiret Sbaa. He was too late. Moulai Lahsin had vanished, but Vigny had the pleasure of blowing the "Lion's Den" off the face of the earth.

It was all very well eradicating Moulai Lahsin's *zaouia*, but that hardly avenged Menabba. Vigny had not long to wait, however. Moulai Lahsin's *baraka* was now very strong, and there was now no shortage of men eager to try their luck against the French. By early May, the intelligence service reported that a *harka* of six thousand men was forming at Bou Denib. On May 12, Vigny led a strong column from Bou Anane. At four o'clock on the morning of May 13, Vigny broke camp and by eight o'clock he had clashed with the *harka* at Beni Ouzien, about six miles east of Bou Denib. It developed into a colossal skirmish. The Moroccans who had horses rode backwards and forwards, occasionally approaching the French lines but in general keeping out of range of the 75s. Those on foot fired from behind the mud walls surrounding the palm oasis. Gradually, the weight of the French firepower began to make itself felt. About midday, both armies began to shift, fighting, toward Bou Denib.

Bou Denib is a typical settlement of the region. A wadi, in this case the Guir, slices through the desolate, caramel-colored plateau, forming a wide trench in which a few date palms and a *ksar* form the elements of human settlement. When, at about two o'clock in the afternoon, the French arrived at Bou Denib close on the heels of the retreating, but not yet disorganized, *harka*, they were in time to watch their enemy take up positions in the *ksar* north of the river and in the palm trees of the oasis. The French cavalry impetuously and without orders flung themselves at the palm grove. It was a spontaneous and an imprudent reaction, for once among the trees the momentum of the horses was stopped by the fallen trunks. The Moroccans were quick to take advantage of the confusion and the French took "considerable losses." As the cavalry filtered back to the French lines, Vigny decided that the *ksar* and the palm oasis were too heavily defended. The 75s had proved their worth against troops in the open, but shrapnel was harmlessly absorbed by the date palms. The melanite shells had hardly dented the walls of the *ksar*. Better finish the fighting tomorrow. Just as Vigny ordered a general withdrawal, however, one of his staff officers noticed the Moroccans streaming out of the palm trees and the *ksar* toward the west. The French executed a volte-face and occupied Bou Denib.

The *harka* again fragmented. Vigny must now pursue. A large faction had departed Bou Denib toward the northwest. It was obvious from the trail that it contained a large number of mules, horses and camels, all heavily laden, not to mention the women and children. At most, it could cover two and a half miles an hour over the stony ground. A mobile column was formed of spahis, mounted legionnaires and tirailleurs capable of traveling at least three and a half miles an hour. All they must do now is follow the well-marked track and they were bound eventually to overtake that portion of the *harka*. Unfortunately, a young staff officer recently arrived from the *école de guerre*—a *roumi*, as metropolitan officers were known in the Armée d'Afrique—suggested another plan: by taking a different and shorter route, the mobile column would be able to pass the *harka* and ambush it farther on. This plan was adopted. It was a foolish decision. Seventy-five years of experience fighting in North Africa combined with the knowledge that their maps were inaccurate should have served as a caution. If the *harka* had chosen the route they did, it was because it was the most practical, perhaps the only practical, track. After struggling for over thirty-five miles through the mountains, the mobile column ran out of water and was forced to return to base empty-handed.

The French estimated that they had killed between five hundred and six hundred Moroccans at Menabba and Bou Denib in April 1908, but there is no way of knowing. Whatever their losses, however, the Moroccans were not discouraged. The French incursion deep into Morocco together with Lyautey's decision to install a permanent garrison at Bou Denib stimulated resistance. Now the Tafilalet, which in April and May had held aloof from Moulai Lahsin's movement, held aloof no longer. The specter of the *roumi*, for so long a ghostlike presence in far-off Algeria, was now made flesh. Bou Denib is less than forty miles from the Tafilalet. The movement which in August brought an unprecedented twenty thousand people into the *ksar* at Tazzouguert, only twelve miles up the Guir from Bou Denib, had now far outgrown Moulai Lahsin. Tribes from the Middle Atlas, the Tafilalet, the Wadi Ziz and the high plateaus joined to form this *harka* of unprecedented size for what would prove the ultimate test of strength with the French in the east.

The Guir at Bou Denib cuts east-west through the palm grove. On the north bank stands the *ksar*, guarding the small plain of Djorf which stretches four miles to the foot of a chain of small mountains. Beyond these mountains stands Tazzouguert, where the *harka* massed in August. South of the Guir rises the hammada. On a spur of that plateau, the French constructed a small blockhouse. It was from this structure, with its sweeping view over the palm grove, the *ksar* and the plain of Djorf, that the French observed the *harka* on

August 29 as it seeped through the pass separating Tazzouguert from the plain and pitched its tents at the foot of the mountain about four miles from Bou Denib. From the blockhouse, it appeared like a large patch of snow on the simmering plain.

The French had gathered the mass of their several-hundred-man garrison around the heavily fortified *ksar*. Not surprisingly, the Moroccans who flowed out of their encampment on September 1 rode toward the blockhouse south of the wadi, held only by seventy-five men. It took them most of the morning to ride the few miles to the foot of the spur. But when by midday they had massed below the blockhouse, they made an impressive sight to the handful of men crammed into the square, two-story masonry building. Out of this mass rode a man in a white jellaba, up the spur to the blockhouse to deliver the *harka*'s challenge:

> To the chief of the French "faction" at Bou Denib. May beneficence be on those who follow the upright life, those who humble themselves before merciful God and seek justice. Know that, since your arrival in the Sahara, you have badly treated weak Muslims. You have gone from conquest to conquest. Your dark soul fools you by making you race to your destruction. You have made our country suffer intense harm, which tastes as galling to us as the bitter apple. The courageous and noble Moslem warriors approach you, armed for your destruction. If you are in force, come out from behind your walls for combat; you will judge which is nobler, the owl or the hawk.

The "owl" referred to Lieutenant Vary's comparatively insignificant garrison. If the French bothered to reply, there is no record of it. This is a pity. Now was the moment for a defiant gesture that would have gone down in the annals of the Armée d'Afrique. Perhaps Vary was too frightened to reply; probably he did not understand a word of the Moroccan challenge. In any case, it would have been foolhardy for Vary to have abandoned the fragile security of the blockhouse to face certain massacre outside. Therefore, at around 3:30 that afternoon, their challenge unanswered, the first wave of Moroccans came up the hill.

Lieutenant Vary's position was less hopeless than it might at first appear. It had hardly required a military genius to predict that the Moroccans would direct their initial attacks against the most vulnerable French position, at

Bou Denib. The lieutenant had taken the precaution of calibrating the artillery in the *ksar* to support the blockhouse. Thus, at 3:30, through an optic telegraph set up on the roof, he called on Major Fesch to open fire.

For the next eighteen hours, the French came under constant assault. Major Fesch kept the hillside swept with shrapnel, but on several occasions the attackers managed to break through the surrounding wire and crawl to the blockhouse itself. Through the optic telegraph, Vary was able to adjust the fire from the *ksar* to great effect. The most dangerous attack came at 10:30 that night, when a wave that Vary put at several thousand threatened to inundate the small fortress. Several Moroccans managed to scale the two-story wall and jump into the central courtyard before they were killed by grenades.

After this attack, the situation in the blockhouse appeared desperate. Eleven cases of ammunition had been used, leaving only three. Vary ordered his men to fire only when necessary. Most had not eaten since morning. The attackers had lost heart, however. By 2:30 in the morning, the only Moroccans left on the slopes beneath the blockhouse were those collecting their dead.

For the next three days, the *harka* remained in its camp to the southwest of Bou Denib. The wails of the women mourning their dead drifted over the tents. Otherwise, there was little activity. Nor did the Moroccans react on September 5 when an enormous relief column of four thousand men under General Alix arrived at Bou Denib. This proved another missed opportunity for the Moroccans, for Alix's march had been a difficult one: his men and animals had suffered horribly from lack of water and were so tired that they had not even bothered to form flank or rear guards. Also, General Alix was by temperament a cautious man. A show of force by the *harka*, the steady harassment of guerrilla attacks, might well have persuaded him to return to Colomb-Béchar. But guerrilla warfare was the way of the weak. A *harka* was meant to overawe the French with a colossal show of force. So the Moroccans waited on the plain of Djorf for their enemy to arrive.

On the seventh, Alix marched out of Bou Denib toward the Moroccan camp. Most of his legionnaires and tirailleurs were formed into a large square. Alix planned to make directly for the Tazzouguert pass, seal off the *harka*'s line of retreat, and then turn back to crush it in its camp. Confusion marked the battle from the very beginning. Alix did not set out until daylight, thereby forfeiting the surprise of a dawn attack. His massive square also proved cumbersome to direct. In the end, however, it did not matter. As soon as the Moroccans saw the advancing French, they rushed to the attack. They would be defeated at Djorf, as they had been defeated everywhere, by their own impetuous bravery.

The eventual outcome of the battle was not obvious to the French soldiers confronted with a vast sea of attackers; by seven o'clock, the Moroccan lines stretched for three miles and were well over a mile in depth. Captain Charles Kuntz, who had ridden into Bou Denib two days earlier with Alix, realized that the reports had not been exaggerated: "There are easily twenty thousand men there," he thought. This long line moved toward the French square, its flanks folding around the invaders like a primitive animal about to absorb its prey. Part of this singing, undulating line was soon hidden by the smoke from the black powder cartridges. Then the French batteries struck up their thunder. The tirailleurs and legionnaires looked on without firing a shot. The *harka* was eight hundred yards distant, still beyond effective rifle range. The Moroccans hesitated, but those in the rear pushed forward, preventing the front ranks from retiring. At 8:30, the Moroccan horsemen galloped toward the French lines. The machine guns began their deadly tattoo and, at four hundred yards, the rifles of the tirailleurs crackled. Even at this moment, the Algerians continued to wager: "You see that one in the red burnous? I'll knock him off in three bullets." A riderless horse pitched into the square. The line of infantry opened, releasing the *goumiers*, who leaped at the Moroccans like dogs on the scent, while a platoon of tirailleurs trotted behind to offer support. More cannon were shifted from the tranquil side of the square to the face under attack. Under this constant battering, the *harka* soon disintegrated into small packets of men, firing, shouting, dying. For almost a full hour the French square continued to spit lead until, at 9:30, as if obeying some invisible signal, the mass of Moroccans turned and fled. The scene before the French was so suddenly, unexpectedly and completely transformed that they stood motionless.

By the time Alix gave the order to pursue, the *harka* had split, half through the pass to Tazzouguert, the others departing toward the Tafilalet. The tirailleurs were furious: Alix's hesitation had given the Moroccans ample time to escape. They had left nothing in their camp worth pillaging— just a few fragments of blankets and tents, lots of bones, excrement and flies. The *harka* had not carried everything with them, however. In the Tazzouguert pass, the French found over a hundred bodies of wounded men who had crawled behind bushes or under rocks to die, bloated and fly-covered, many armed only with sticks and stones.

Bou Denib and Djorf had inflicted a great defeat on the Moroccans in the east and one from which they would not recover for some years. Individually, the Moroccans made excellent soldiers. But they lacked the armaments and the organization of the French. Had they adopted guerrilla warfare, they might have made the French invasion very difficult. But this was not their way: Brave men fought openly, offered their breasts to bullets. Victory won by stealth was dishonorable.

Bou Denib and Djorf broke up the last great tribal coalition. From now on, the French could devour the tribes piecemeal.

These battles were also defeats for Lyautey, for his "methods." This was why he had been so angry when he met Catroux on that morning in early September 1908. But he need not have worried. No one in Paris was aware that a great experiment had just collapsed in a heap. They did not have time to notice, for their attention had been drawn by events in the west.

CHAPTER XIV

A NEW SULTAN

"Patience is a great virtue," said Sidi Abdallah Fasi, assuming an air of mystery and waving his finger from side to side. That look and that gesture were by now familiar to the representatives of Germany, Spain and France who waited in the summer of 1909 to see Moulai Hafid. The vizier attempted to distract them. "Have you ever eaten pork?" The question was directed at the French representative, Si Kaddour Benghabrit. The young Algerian diplomat, dressed in a high turban and jellaba of transparent whiteness which showed a light-gray robe beneath, attempted to remain dignified while appearing affable. He devised an answer which he knew would please the vizier: "No, not to my knowledge; but I may have eaten it by mistake, for the Christians love to try to make us eat pig without our knowing." The French had been wise to send a Moslem to deal with the Sultan. It demonstrated that France was an Islamic as well as a Christian power. "It is a disgusting habit eating such an animal," Fasi replied. The conversation again trailed off. The representatives perspired lightly, listened to the buzzing of the flies, smoked another cigarette and waited.

Suddenly, the *mechouar* (courtyard) of the palace came alive. The band which had been lounging against the garden wall hurriedly collected its instruments and began to play "God Save the King" in the flat, discordant notes of Near Eastern music. The guard of honor under the direction of an Englishman quickly shouldered its assorted rifles, swords, bayonets and polo sticks and sprang more or less to attention. The European representatives rose, but more· slowly than they had done several weeks earlier. Behind them, other favor seekers jostled to salute the Sultan. In the center of the *mechouar*, clinging to the guns, three poor wretches began their plaintive chorus for their cases to be heard: "Allah m'Sidi! Allah m'Sidi!" Into this spasm of noise and confusion marched Moulai Hafid, looking neither left nor right, a handsome figure who towered over the jabbering guards who accompanied him. Behind, at a respectful distance, three women followed.

A typical morning at the palace in Fez had begun. The next several hours would be spent by the Sultan reclining on his yellow divan inside his portable summer house—a small glass-roofed structure on wheels which servants moved to follow the shade—and talking to his viziers or to his women. If the weather was pleasant, he would sit for hours on the palace wall enjoying the view over Fez, indulging in gossip, sipping sweet tea and eating cakes while the band continued its hideous parody of military music—"British Grenadiers," "Cock o' the North," the "Marseillaise"—until silenced by the Sultan. Occasionally, an agile figure dressed in rags would make a mad dash for the sanctuary of the guns. Palace attendants would set out in pursuit. If caught, the intruder was pummeled, kicked and ejected from the courtyard. If he succeeded in reaching the guns, cries of *"Ya Sidi!"* echoed above the din of "British Grenadiers." Thus, the Europeans thought, each day passed in irrelevant activity, pointless interviews, risqué stories and gossip. Time means nothing to a Moor. He was put on earth to waste it.

They were wrong. Moulai Hafid was not contemptuous of time. He had merely for the moment to use it slowly, deliberately. His political options, like those of his deposed brother, swung between two alternatives, neither of which was particularly attractive. His followers called on him to lead a *jihad* against the French. This, the Sultan knew, would be suicidal. Besides, where was he to get the money? His treasury was empty. He had searched the palace from top to bottom to find his brother's cache of gold. But there had been no gold, only empty packing crates, polo sticks, billiard balls, women's hats, a palace crammed with useless bric-a-brac for which Abd el-Aziz had paid a fortune. Hafid became ill when he surveyed the debris of his brother's reign. The French, of course, would lend him money, but only on conditions which his followers would not accept—the recognition of the Act of Algeciras and of all accords signed by Aziz, payment of the indemnities for the Casablanca bombardment and the reimbursement of the French for the expense of the Chaouia campaign. "If some Frenchmen are murdered in England, does France send soldiers to burn villages and destroy towns and then demand money from King Edward?" Moulai Hafid asked.

I can see what they want to do. They see I am helpless and depend upon the recognition of the powers and they impose terms that will cripple me. If I refuse the note, they have the excuse to fight and take the country from me. If I accept the note, I am entirely in their power. What is the good of a bankrupt sultan? Where am I to get the money? You know I have none. My soldiers are without pay and grumble. There is little money in the country and the tribes bring in very small sums. I am losing all patience and if things continue as they do—well, let them come and take my country and make an end to it all.

Beneath Moulai Hafid's display of oriental indolence, much was happening in Morocco. The Sultan was losing his grip. From the beginning he had been the creature of Madani el Glaoui, who now, as grand vizier, was in the process of increasing his wealth beyond anything Morocco had yet seen. To those who had welcomed the "Sultan of the *jihad*," Moulai Hafid increasingly seemed a prop behind which Madani could plunder the country. The Berber from the High Atlas seized the property of those who had supported Abd el-Aziz and demanded more money from the tribes. Signs of opposition grew; a deranged tribesman attempted to declare Moulai Mohammed sultan at Friday prayers. A plot by a group of tribesmen to assassinate Moulai Hafid was uncovered in October 1908. Hafid ordered a campaign of terror against his enemies. Those who opposed him were poisoned, beaten, imprisoned or murdered. To the legend of Hafid the religious fanatic was added that of Hafid the murderous tyrant.

In the end, the demands of finance triumphed over the appeal of the *jihad*, but the negotiations with the French were far from smooth. Both Germany and Spain recognized Moulai Hafid as the legitimate Sultan in September 1908. However, it was the French who, under the Algeciras agreement, controlled both 60 percent of the customs revenues and the Moroccan State Bank through which a loan must be negotiated. The only man who could break the stranglehold that France held on Morocco was Field Marshal Helmuth von Moltke, chief of the German general staff. In the autumn of 1908, it looked as if he might well have his chance. The pretext this time for war between France and Germany was, as it had been in 1905 and would be again in 1911, Morocco.

The 1908 war scare sprang from another "affair" provoked by the competition and professional rivalry between French and German representatives in Morocco. The presence of large numbers of Germans in the foreign legion had always galled German diplomats. They saw it as perfectly compatible with their duty discreetly to encourage their compatriots, and legionnaires of other nationalities, for that matter, to desert. The French had long known that the German diplomatic corps in Morocco had organized a "desertion agency" for legionnaires. It was a minor pinprick, however, and certainly not worth provoking a major diplomatic incident over.

But on the morning of September 25, 1908, the German consul in

Casablanca pushed the French too far. The French military headquarters learned that several suspected deserters were about to embark on a German ship standing off Casablanca. A junior officer was sent to investigate. He arrived at the quay in time to see six men—three Germans, a Swiss, an Austrian and a Russian—accompanied by an official of the German consulate and his *mokhazni*, being rowed away from the shore. The officer shouted. The Moroccan oarsmen took fright and abandoned the boat, which was now caught by the surf and capsized. The eight men were fished from the water by the French sentries and arrested. They protested that they had been given a *laissez-passer* by the German consul which the French had no right to ignore. The French released the consular official and his guard. The deserters, however, had enlisted under the French flag and therefore fell under French jurisdiction. Berlin objected and demanded an apology. Paris refused. Tension mounted.

This was just the sort of friction that colonial competition enhanced. In the event, both Berlin and Paris decided that the argument was not worth the candle. On November 24, 1908, they agreed to offer mutual excuses and refer the matter to the International Court at The Hague (where the French won the case). At this point, with the settlement of the "affair of the Casablanca deserters," Moulai Hafid had no choice but to make peace with the French. He needed money. He also was in desperate need of military assistance; Madani el Glaoui's exactions among the tribes had provoked discontent in the countryside which the Sultan's unpaid, rapacious *mehallas* proved unable to subdue.

On January 3, 1909, two days before Paris formally recognized Moulai Hafid's government, the French military mission arrived in Fez. Since France had prevailed upon Moulai Hassan, Hafid's father, to accept French military advisers (at the makhzan's expense), French soldiers had been a permanent feature of the sharifian court, advising the Sultan on military affairs, sending back reports to Tangiers and secretly mapping the country for a future invasion army. It proved a thankless and frustrating task. At court, French officers were treated as unwelcome guests, while the possibilities of their exercising any constructive influence over the makhzan's mutinous troops were negligible. They were tolerated in part because the Sultan had no choice, but also, and more importantly, because they provided artillerymen for his guns. The *mehalla* was such an inefficient fighting machine that victory often turned on a few well-directed shells from a 75. Since the French mission had accompanied Abd el-Aziz on his last march to Marrakech in

August 1908, however, it had been dissolved. Now, it was resurrected, under the command of Lieutenant Colonel Emile Mangin.

In the jellaba, which now became his working uniform, Emile Mangin was scarcely distinguishable from a Moor: dark, of medium height, he had shorn his head and shaved his beard down to the line of his jaw. Only the Belle Epoque twirl at the end of his mustache and his pince-nez betrayed him as a *roumi*. Mangin was called *Projecteur* by his colleagues, in part to honor the searchlight he had perfected, but also to distinguish him from Charles "Sénégal" Mangin, who would also play a significant role in the conquest of Morocco. The French minister in Tangiers, Eugène Regnault, had recommended Mangin to lead the military mission because of his experience as chief of the Tangiers police since 1906. Mangin's intelligence and experience in dealing with Moroccan policemen were thought to have prepared him to deal with the "indolence, the delays, the disabused skepticism which have so often annihilated the good intentions of the officers of our military mission."

Mangin certainly began sensibly enough: "With Moroccans always have a smile," he told the men of his mission. No harsh words, no draconian punishments, but tact and diplomacy would see the mission through to success: "The habit of obedience will come little by little." But the habit of obedience obstinately refused to come. The frustrations of the military mission grew, and with them demands that the sharifian army be absorbed into the Armée d'Afrique. This was at the root of the mutinies of 1912.

In the beginning, however, Mangin sought merely to put some starch into the *mehalla* so that Moulai Hafid could reestablish his badly shaken authority. Most of the Rif was in open revolt. Elsewhere, tribes moved in and out of the sharifian camp with each puff of the political wind. The soldiers of the mission were attached to the *mehallas* which were kept moving around Fez in the spring and summer of 1909 to put out the brushfire rebellions of the tribes. It proved an unpopular assignment with the French.

In April 1909, Moulai Hafid sent a force to punish the Beni M'tir, a tribe that occupied the highlands to the southwest of Fez, for having given refuge to one of his political enemies. Adjutant Pisani was placed in charge of the 75. With the first Berber attack, the *mehalla* broke and ran, leaving Pisani and three *askar* dangerously exposed. Pisani fired his gun until the shells were exhausted. Then, taking the breech-block, he mounted a horse and fled in pursuit of the retreating *mehalla*. Pisani's experience made the French soldiers understandably reluctant to follow the unreliable *mehallas* on campaign. But danger was only part of the reason: the indiscipline of the *askar* sickened them. The *askar* behaved like highwaymen, stealing, holding travelers for ransom, selling their arms and deserting. Prisoners were shown no mercy: their teeth were extracted and arms and legs amputated. The Sultan demanded heads as visible trophies of victory. Heads he received, but not always those of his enemies. Often poor peasants paid the price of *askar* cowardice and cruelty. "I am told that such acts are in conformity with the religious laws of the country, but I cannot forget that our presence has facilitated the capture of these prisoners," Mangin wrote. It was his first inkling that French intervention in Morocco, ostensibly to spread civilization, had merely made barbarism more efficient. Mangin begged his superiors to allow the mission to confine its activities to training; French presence in the *mehallas* "has given the population a fine idea of the value of our civilization." But this could not be allowed. The Sultan's unpopularity had caused Bou Hamara, the Rogui, to become active once again.

Since Bou Hamara had squeezed Abd el-Aziz's forces out of Taza in 1903, his fortunes had varied. This was inevitable. Only a man of extreme cunning and ruthlessness could remain powerful in the shifting tribal alliances of the Rif. Treachery as practiced there was an art form at least as sophisticated as in the Italy of the Renaissance. In the summer of 1904, for instance, one chief offered to submit to the Rogui. He invited Bou Hamara's caids to his camp to count his weapons, and the caids were received with great honor. After several days of festivities, three of the most important guests were taken to the *hammam*, where they were murdered by their host while they bathed. In 1905, Bou Hamara's *mehalla* had besieged Oudjda until beaten off by Lieutenant Ben Sedira's 75. The following year, the Rogui was wounded in the chest by a would-be assassin, which left his health permanently damaged. But he continued to fight, transferring his *makhzan*, complete with its cannon and parasol of authority, from place to place.

In the spring of 1909, he took advantage of Hafid's unpopularity and his preoccupation with the Beni M'tir to threaten the Sultan in his palace. In mid-April, the Rogui pitched his camp only nine miles from Fez. In a panic, Hafid ordered reinforcements from the Haouz, distributed money to his *ulama* and began to arm a city militia with the antiquated rifles in his arsenals. But, as in 1903, Bou Hamara declined to attack and moved away toward Taza. Perhaps his *baraka* was no longer strong enough to hold his coalition of tribes together. His followers had begun to criticize his frequent contacts with the *roumi*. In the beginning, Bou Hamara had been supported by Oran businessmen. Lately, he had turned to the Spanish. By selling mining rights to Spanish companies eager to exploit the mineral resources of the Rif, he had been able to finance his wars. But this did little for his reputation as a leader of the *jihad*. Feeling against Spain was running high in the Rif: in July, Spanish railway workers had been murdered near Melilla. The Spaniards made preparations to invade, while Rif tribesmen prepared to repel them in what promised to be a reenactment of the Chaouia.

> After serving France, [they said] the Rogui sold the mines to the Spaniards, as he sold them the casbah of Selouan. Now that Spain prepares to invade the Rif, the Rogui fights around Fez to prevent the Sultan's troops from helping us, and if Spain takes the Rif, the Rogui will help them conquer the territory around Ceuta and Tétouan. The Prophet orders us to fight Christians to the death, and the Rogui is also a Christian, although he calls himself a Moslem.

The grand vizier, Madani el Glaoui, and the French military mission had served to make Moulai Hafid unpopular. But Bou Hamara offered no real alternative to the simple and devout tribesmen looking for a powerful leader. They fell in and out of alliances, quarreled among themselves, fought neighboring tribes, while the threat of foreign invasion grew. Madani el Glaoui exploited these divisions as only he could, keeping the tribal coalitions against Moulai Hafid off balance, splitting them with bribes, gradually stripping away Bou Hamara's support until, by mid-July 1909, the Rogui was reduced to a mere brigade of a thousand men and two guns. It was against this reduced force that Moulai Hafid ordered his six-thousand-man *mehalla* into action.

Seen from a distance, this force must have appeared impressive as it moved like a swarm of voracious insects toward the territory of the Hiyana, Bou Hamara's main source of support, northeast of Fez. Upon closer inspection, however, it resembled an army of beggars, "a miserable horde hardly dressed," wrote Captain Maurice le Glay of the French mission. Only a thousand of them were armed and these had only five cartridges apiece. Its strength, as usual, lay with its 75s commanded by Ben Sedira and Pisani. As the *mehalla* moved northward, the Hiyana came forward to make their submission, no longer willing to fight for a discredited Rogui. The Berber women kissed the cannon, the visible symbol of the Sultan's power. Incredibly, Bou Hamara did not attempt to escape, but merely waited for the attack, which came on the morning of July 31. The *askar*, fortified with the knowledge that the enemy was weak, attacked with uncharacteristic vigor. Bou Hamara's men resisted well at first, but the sheer weight of numbers soon drove them northward. Ben Sedira urged the Sultan's commanders to pursue. But it was too late for that. The fragile cohesion of the *mehalla* had dissolved as it sacked Bou Hamara's camp. A thick cloud of smoke lingered over what remained of the Rogui's tents. The *mehalla* had suffered only twelve killed and eighteen wounded, most of them in the fighting over the spoils.

On August 9, tribesmen came into the makhzan camp to announce that the Rogui's troops were strung out along the Wadi Ouergha, about two hours to the north. On the following day at about two o'clock in the afternoon, the *mehalla* lumbered into contact with the Rogui's men. The battle that was fought over the next two days was no more than a series of disjointed skirmishes. Bou Hamara's etiolated army was caught at a great disadvantage. The *mehalla* was able to surround and devour them piecemeal. With the battle obviously going against Bou Hamara, his erstwhile allies, the Beni Ouriaghel, turned on him. His convoy guards fled, but only when night fell did the Rogui make off toward the northwest.

On August 15, the first of the trophies arrived in Fez: 160 prisoners, many chained together by the neck, the Rogui's throne, his parasol of office, rifles, banners, tents and his two cannon were paraded through the streets. On the following days came more prisoners, including twenty black girls from Bou Hamara's harem, and sacks full of heads to be displayed on the gates of Fez. Henri-François Gaillard, the French consul, attempted to search through the salted heads for that of a Frenchman who was rumored to be in the Rogui's entourage, but their state of putrefaction made the task too grisly to pursue. One group of sixty prisoners was made to parade through the streets each carrying the head of a fallen comrade. For the next three days, the 320 prisoners were publicly tortured in the *mechouar* or at the Bab Mahrouq under the placid gaze of Moulai Hafid. Mangin reported that most were beaten, although seven had their left legs amputated and twenty-four lost their right hand. Others, however, recounted still more horrible tortures, including the "salt torture," whereby four deep cuts were made in the palm of the hand into which the fingers were forced. The hand was then liberally salted, bound up with leather and left until it became a useless appendage.

For three days while these tortures were imposed, Fez was plunged into an atmosphere of medieval bacchanalia. Merchants circulated through the crowds selling pastries, bands played and women laughed derisively beneath their wrappers at the sufferings of the tortured and mutilated. In London and Paris, newspapers printed detailed accounts of the agonies of the mutilated men left to perish from gangrene or tetanus. As a result, Moulai Hafid received a flood of abusive mail from Europe wishing upon the Sultan the same sort of misery he was imposing upon Bou Hamara's rebels. One Englishman expressed a desire to enclose Moulai Hafid's head in a cage filled with famished rats. Hafid had these letters translated and found them hilariously funny. He was also not a little proud of his reputation for ferocity.

Nonetheless, his savage retribution did produce a joint protest from the diplomatic community. He completely rejected their calls for mercy: Bou Hamara's men were rebels. For seven years they had sown disorder and anarchy within the Empire. "The partisans of the Rogui have excited such anger that it is not within my power to prevent what is happening." Besides, the Sultan told the French consul Gaillard, this would serve as an example to others who might be tempted to defy sharifian authority. As if to show his contempt for European opinion, on September 25 he trotted the rebel survivors out of prison and those who still had a hand intact were made to undergo the salt torture. He also informed the powers that he would no longer deal with them directly but only through his representative in Tangiers. France, in retaliation, forbade her soldiers to accompany the *mehallas* on campaign.

One prisoner would excite far more compassion than the rest. Indeed, Hafid's treatment of Bou Hamara himself came to encapsulate for Europe the barbarism of the makhzan. The French were ticklish on the subject of Bou Hamara, for it was they who had made his capture possible. Mangin complained that he might have been taken earlier had the *mehalla* on August 10 not waited for the French-directed artillery before moving forward. But the French had been unable to exercise any control over the battle between the *mehalla* and the Rogui. The tribal horsemen attached to the Sultan's forces rushed about in all directions while the *askar* characteristically concentrated their attentions on loot. As a consequence, the pursuit was abandoned. Bou Hamara could easily have escaped. But he did not. Mangin blamed "the excessive temerity of the Rogui. . . . This man seems to play with danger," for his downfall. For the next two weeks, he remained within striking distance of the *mehalla*, attempting to conjure up support from the tribes. But without money he was powerless, for few would follow him out of patriotism or personal loyalty. On the morning of August 22, ten deserters from Bou Hamara's camp informed the *mehalla* that the Rogui and only fifty guards had sought refuge in a nearby *zaouia*.

The choice of the *zaouia* was an act of desperation, but as a final gamble it was not a bad one. Hafid's attitude toward the religious brotherhoods was not dissimilar to that of Henry VIII toward his monasteries: they provided a focus of local influence which could become local opposition, and served as a counterweight to central authority. They also siphoned off revenues which each monarch believed belonged more properly to the court. Some of Hafid's most intractable opponents were to be found in the *zaouias*, but their religious connections had not saved them from arrest and torture. Therefore, the Sultan's caids were unlikely to forfeit their lives simply to respect the sanctity of a holy refuge. However, the local tribesmen took a more traditional view of the inviolability of religious sanctuary. They now surrounded their shrine and made plain that they intended to defend it.

What happened next—indeed, the entire final episode of Bou Hamara's life—is a subject of some controversy. Mangin reported that the Rogui, realizing the odds against him, simply walked out and surrendered. Lieutenant Ben Sedira maintained that one courageous member of the *mehalla*, stripped to the waist, climbed over the wall and set fire to the *zaouia*. The horsemen then captured Bou Hamara hiding among the fleeing women. The most likely version is provided by Captain Maurice le Glay. Writing seventeen years after the event, le Glay claimed that, as usual, Ben Sedira and Pisani were called upon to break the deadlock between the tribesmen and the *mehalla*. The sight of the domed *zaouia* standing out on the plain "like a nose on the middle of a face" was simply too tempting a target for these artillerymen. The first shell exploded on the dome, spewing masonry over the defenders. The circle of tribesmen surrounding the *zaouia* broke and ran. Bou Hamara also rushed out but threw himself to the ground with the second shot. Almost immediately, he was seized by the nearest *askari*, stripped and beaten, until the caids arrived to rescue him.

Even at bay, Bou Hamara was defiant: "like a miserable thief" dressed only in trousers, his naked torso covered in dust and perspiration, he taunted his captors that they had needed the Christian and his guns to take him prisoner. He then looked at Pisani and said: "*Roumi*, if you want to do something useful, kill me." Bou Hamara was lashed to the 75, which had played such a vital role in his capture and which now became an altar of sacrifice. The *askar* began to bring the heads of Bou Hamara's men to the caids, who paid them five duros for each one. The heads were then balanced on the gun, on the barrel or on the wheels, some dropping to the ground around the feet of the Rogui amid the laughter and obscene taunts of the *askar*. All night they reveled while the caids remained locked in raucous debate about who should have the honor of bringing the Rogui in chains to Fez.

On August 24, public criers in Fez announced the arrival of the Rogui. For twenty-four hours the city had been *en fête*. Moulai Hafid had spent the preceding day distributing gifts to the leaders of the guilds and other notables and in supervising the construction of a platform thirteen feet high upon which the strong, low cage containing the prisoner would be displayed in the courtyard of the palace. Now, at five o'clock in the morning, the column was visible from the town walls as it approached from the north along the Ouezzane road. Moulai Hafid followed its progress from the terrace of the palace. Through his binoculars, he could distinguish, in the middle of 1,500 ragged *askar*, the Rogui as he was tossed from side to side in his small iron cage lashed to the back of a camel. The procession came through the Bab Bou Jat and pushed slowly through the immense crowds into the *mechouar*, where Moulai Hafid waited, flanked by his viziers. When Bou Hamara was, at last, set before the Sultan, Moulai Hafid asked him why he had led the rebellion. The Rogui refused to reply until he had been fed. He was brought two *tagines* of chicken and mutton, which he ate slowly. Then he demanded tea. At last, he replied: "I did as you did. You succeeded, I failed."

The prisoner's defiant answers belied his piteous state. Mistreatment at the hands of the *mehalla* combined with an attempt to take his own life had left him weak. Moulai Hafid wanted the Rogui preserved for the moment. For one thing, he believed that the pretender had money stashed in European banks which, through promises of kindness, he might convince him to relinquish. Also, his harsh treatment of Bou Hamara's followers had produced such outrage among Europeans that the Sultan, upon reflection, sought to redeem his reputation by a show of mercy. He ordered food and new clothes to be brought to the prisoner. But again he closed him in his small cage, where he squatted for the next few days, one of Fez's major tourist attractions. Moroccans filed past to insult him while European tourists came to gawk and take pictures.

For the next fortnight, Moulai Hafid cajoled, threatened and bribed his prisoner in an attempt to have him sign over the 18 million pesetas which he believed the Rogui had hidden in a Spanish bank. When Bou Hamara persistently denied that he had any money, the Sultan threatened him with instant death: "That does not trouble me," Bou Hamara replied calmly. "Everyone dies in his turn. But never forget that it is because of me that you are Sultan. I succeeded, after seven years of struggle, in shaking the throne of Abd el-Aziz and it is you who have profited." Hafid then resorted to humiliation: he dragged all of the Rogui's surviving followers out of prison and had them march in review past their ex-chief's cage while the band played "God Save the King" and other martial tunes. The prisoner foamed with rage in the hope, it was said, that the Sultan might make a quick end to his life. But Moulai Hafid toyed with Bou Hamara: on September 6, he announced that he had decided to spare his life, but had condemned him to perpetual imprisonment in his cage. Others reported that the Sultan and his court used the caged man for target practice, attempting to shoot as closely as they could without actually hitting him.

On the evening of September 12, Moulai Hafid received a request from the representatives of Britain, France and Spain for an audience. Forewarned that the Europeans intended to request Bou Hamara's release, he agreed to meet them outside of town at Dar Debibaigh. On the following day, the Sultan kept the three diplomats, dressed in morning clothes with starched winged collars, simmering in a bell tent under the scorching sun while he ate radishes and gossiped with his court in an adjacent tent. In the palace, a servant unlocked Bou Hamara's cage and told him: "The Sultan has ordered that you die, follow me." Bou Hamara was unable to walk, so he was carried to the menagerie and thrust into the lion cage. However, the well-fed animal only succeeded in mauling the Rogui's shoulder. One of the servants then killed him, some said with a shot to the head, others with a dagger. His body was then burned.

The capture and execution of Bou Hamara strengthened Moulai Hafid's position, but only briefly. The euphoria of victory soon wore thin. The Sultan was broke. Europe offered the only source of money. However, each step taken in the direction of Europe meant the loss of support in Morocco. In dire need of a loan, Hafid signed a new accord with France in March 1910 by which the French promised to evacuate Morocco as soon as the makhzan was capable of restoring order. This cleared the way for the negotiation of a new loan. On May 13, France offered the makhzan 90 million francs. In return, the French took over the remaining 40 percent of customs revenues that still went to Fez, as well as a host of local taxes. This gave France a financial stranglehold on the makhzan that was well nigh total. The Sultan was a beggar in his own country. The only course open to him was to extort more money from the tribes and from wealthy Moroccans. The tribes fought back. Many of his caids, however, were less fortunate.

In May 1910, Moulai Hafid arrested Ibn-Aissa, the caid of Meknes, and his family on the trumped-up charge that he was plotting a revolt. Few believed that these charges had any foundation. The caid's favorite, it was said, had her nipples crushed by Hafid's torturers in an attempt to make her give up her jewelry. The affair received such wide publicity in Europe that Hafid was forced to agree to allow doctors to visit the caid and his wife in prison. Ibn-Aissa did not complain, asking only for a new set of clothes. The two English women missionaries who examined his wife, however, found her shoulder was out of joint and her wrists badly marked by manacles. Pressure from Europe became so great that in August the Sultan released his prisoners.

The Aissa affair combined with hundreds of similar tragedies to strip Moulai Hafid of support. In June 1910, the French military mission reported that the Sultan was as unpopular as Abd el-Aziz had been in 1907. The country was rapidly becoming ungovernable. Only a strong infusion of French instructors and the complete remodeling of the *mehallas* could reverse this slide into anarchy and impose order on the increasingly rebellious tribes.

CHAPTER XV

THE FIRST SIEGE OF FEZ

Captain le Glay was quietly amazed. As a military formation it might not pass muster at the *école de guerre*—only 1,800 of the 2,600 troops were armed and the *askar* still trailed an enormous amount of personal baggage—but for a royal "army" to be formed into something resembling a square, with the supply convoy in the center and cavalry around the flanks, was evidence that in the five months since November 1910 the French military mission had performed a small miracle. The *askar* had even been persuaded to leave their women and slaves in Fez. Of the three arms, the cavalry was probably the most reliable. Under the old system, each *tabor* (battalion) contained a *mia* (company) of cavalry made up of the best troops. These had been whipped into remarkable form by two Englishmen who had been incorporated into the French military mission—William Redman, a civilian born on the coast at Mazagan who spoke both Arabic and Shilha like a native, and Thomas Bolding, an ex-sergeant of the Thirteenth Hussars. The artillery, commanded by le Glay, had made progress and the glimmer of an esprit de corps could be detected there by the perceptive. The *askar*, the infantry, gave the greatest cause for concern, for while the cavalry and artillery were commanded directly by Europeans, the *askar* still fell under their own caids.

For the better part of a week, the *mehalla* had marched west through the wild country along the south bank of the Sebou. Their mission was to tame the Cherarda, who had rebelled against Madani el Glaoui's tax collectors and severed communications between Fez and Tangiers. "Open the road," Mangin had ordered, but le Glay knew better. One had only to look at the loot that the cavalry periodically brought back to the square—mules, horses, camels and sheep—to realize that the French had become Madani's gendarmes. There could be little doubt that this was a commercial expedition. Madani el Glaoui had even placed his son, Sidi Mohammed, in command—"*le nègre de papa*," "daddy's little nigger," the French officers called him, both because of his Negro blood and because he served as his father's menial. Mangin and Sidi Mohammed had already quarreled over this question of looting. The war minister (for that is what Sidi Mohammed was) insisted that the appropriation of animals was a legitimate form of tax collection. "They belong to the Sultan," he shouted, and clinched the argument. Then the Sultan should take them away, thought le Glay, for the animals made a terrible racket at night, almost as much noise as the squeaking violins and high-pitched voices of the singers in Mohammed's tents.

The Frenchmen maintained the veneer of military discipline in the *mehalla* with difficulty. Captain Reynier, on loan from the Algerian *bureau Arabe*, attempted to coordinate the movements of the square from its center, but his commands—given in classical Arabic—merely produced confusion. The bugler, who could not understand orders issued in this purified tongue, usually blew the wrong calls. As a consequence, the square expanded and contracted like an accordion, or suddenly shot off in the wrong direction, so that Reynier eventually took over the bugle himself. Despite these problems, the *mehalla* made progress, but slowly. It stopped at frequent intervals as tribal emissaries arrived to do homage, ask to submit, talk, or simply spy out the strength of the amoeba-like force.

On March 3, 1911, four days after the *mehalla* left Fez, the Cherarda attacked. About noon, a group of horsemen probed the left side of the square. It was not a serious attack, and was easily repulsed by rifle fire and Pisani's 80-millimeter gun. However, Sidi Mohammed panicked and Mangin was forced to take command. The war minister calmed down when he saw the Cherarda horsemen flee. He even ordered his servants to make tea, but bundled up his things quickly when Mangin, breaking with tradition, ordered the square to march off in pursuit of the retreating Cherarda.

For the next five days, the *mehalla* penetrated farther into Cherarda country, pillaging, skirmishing, looting. On March 7, it came to rest on Jebel Tselfats, about thirty miles northwest of Fez. Trenches were dug along the four sides of the square. The ground was soon covered with bones and excrement. The air smelled foul. And then it began to rain.

The inclusion of a strong contingent of French officers and NCOs in the Cherarda *mehalla* had been a personal triumph for Lieutenant Colonel Mangin. "How can you ever hope to control the tribes until you have a strong army?" he had asked Moulai Hafid. "Once you control your own land, once you can guarantee order in Morocco, the bankers will be satisfied that their loans are secure and the French troops will withdraw from the Chaouia." It was a transparent lie. But the Sultan had become so unsettled by the pressures of office that he may have failed to notice the falsehood. In the autumn of 1910, a delegation of influential tribal chiefs had even traveled to

Tangiers to ask the French to intervene on their behalf with Moulai Hafid. The French had, of course, refused. But the impertinence! The idea of a *mehalla* with real muscle appealed to Moulai Hafid. He was caught in a power struggle between, on the one hand, Madani el Glaoui and Mohammed el Mokri, who had divided the makhzan posts between their two families; and on the other, the tribes, who were being forced to pay the outrageous levies of this "Berber makhzan." This was at the root of the Cherarda revolt: the Cherarda were a *jaysh*, or Arab, tribe which traditionally had provided men for military service in lieu of taxes. Now, desperately short of cash, the makhzan began to demand money even from those tribes which before had been exempt, with predictable results. Faced with this simmering revolt, Moulai Hafid had had no choice in November 1910 but to hand the sharifian army over to Mangin with a dismissive "Do what you want with it!"

Mangin knew exactly what he wanted to do with "this barbarous mass"—impose discipline. Discipline had never been considered necessary for the *mehalla*. Its strength lay above all in the "superstitious fear which it inspires." Fighting was a last resort. The arrival of the *mehalla* customarily served as a starting point for negotiations between the makhzan and the tribes. The Sultan's emissaries formed alliances, bribed chiefs to desert their tribal allies, set the tribes fighting among themselves and, eventually, collected tribute. "It is a well-known principle that when the tribes are fighting among themselves, the makhzan is at ease," Mangin told his mission, ". . . [and] it is this imperfect military state of affairs which we must transform into a regular military organization." He found the precedent for the force which he wished to create in the Armée d'Afrique. Its disciplinary regulations would be applied to the letter: rebellion, desertion with arms, pillage, the stripping and murder of the wounded—all were henceforth to be punishable by death. Soldiers would be paid a daily stipend, thereby eliminating the need to steal or to own a shop or practice a trade to supplement often nonexistent army pay. The army's notorious indiscipline was to become a thing of the past.

Mangin's first task was to eliminate the less reliable elements among the 5,547 *askar* who made up the Sultan's army. Each *tabor* was called into the courtyard of the palace where, in small groups, they were taken into an interior enclosure and asked to stack their rifles against the wall "for verification." This was the signal for the entry of two hundred hand-picked Moroccan troops who pushed the disarmed *askar* through a back door into the street. In this way the entire army was disarmed, and only four thousand of the better soldiers asked to sign a reenlistment contract. But this did little to solve the issue of discipline. Mangin's main problem was that he had too few French officers and NCOs to carry out the reforms he desired. The French could merely administer the *askar*, while the caids remained in effective command. Military posts in the *mehalla* were distributed on the basis of the spoils system among the friends of the vizier. No one entered public service out of a sense of duty or patriotism in Morocco. Military service, like government, was a business venture. The selling of arms and other matériel from the Sultan's depots was a long-established practice among caids and *askar* alike: a stock-taking carried out by French officers in October 1910 revealed that the army was short 1,491 rifles and many cartridges, 3,000 uniforms, 477 saddles, 388 horses and 114 mules. Pay offered another source of graft. On campaign, a *mehalla* could fend for itself. However, in periods of inactivity or when soldiers were stationed in Fez, the *askar* were forced to practice a trade or to steal to feed themselves and their families. When the famished *askar* became a public nuisance, the Sultan reluctantly opened his treasury and distributed money to his caids to pay their soldiers. The caid kept as much of this money for himself as he dared, allowing an absolute minimum—in practice, very little—to filter down to the *askar*.

The lack of regular pay, Mangin concluded correctly, was the cause of sharifian military indiscipline and of the endemic desertion. The French undertook to pay the equivalent of five English pence per day, directly to the *askar*. The caids, of course, were furious at having been cut out of their major source of income. It was all very well for the French to pay the *askar*. But who would pay the caids? Certainly not the Sultan. Conflicts between the French and the caids were not long in coming. One incident will serve as an example. After Mangin had paid the military musicians personally, the chief of the music, Sharif el Mrani, formed up his men and demanded half of their pay. This was a reasonable enough request by the standards of the *mehalla*, but the men naturally complained to Mangin. Mangin, in turn, complained to the vizier, who obliged el Mrani to restore his men's pay and forbade him to punish those who had complained. El Mrani waited for two days and, on some small pretext, ordered that the grumblers be given the bastinado. Mangin again intervened and el Mrani was forced to flee for refuge to the Mosque of Moulai Idris. Soon, that mosque contained a whole array of caids seeking refuge on similar grounds. Most eventually sent presents to one of the viziers, paid a fine and left the mosque. But the no-nonsense attitude of the French left much bad blood between the mission and the caids.

The new code of discipline left the *askar* bewildered. Few of them had a military vocation, but were instead in the army because of a family quarrel, a murder, a debt, or because an ill-disposed caid had made it impossible or inadvisable for them to live at home. They remained in the army both because they had little alternative and because the pillage of the *mehalla* offered a livelihood. Patriotism and loyalty to the Sultan or to the *tabor* were virtually unknown. But Mangin persisted in his attempt to impose order on the army, in spite of the fact that military reform could only follow a thorough transformation of makhzan attitudes to government. Mangin, however, was a soldier, and as such maintained a naïve faith in the value of military discipline and of the paternal attentions of the officer for his men, a mixture of coercion and concern, force and justice. This came as an unpleasant surprise to those most directly concerned. The *askar* who reenlisted in November 1910 had been enticed by the prospect of regular pay. But they had not foreseen that the *roumi* would take such an intransigent attitude toward the traditional perquisites and established practices of their trade, not, that is, until January of 1911, when two *askar* were actually shot for desertion. The intention was to "*encourager les autres*"; the results were quite the opposite.

The Cherarda expedition consequently also proved to be a failure. Rather than mastering the revolt, the expedition succeeded only in inflaming it. By attempting to discipline the *mehalla*, the French had deprived it of its major force — terror. The swarm of men who had earlier moved toward the douars and villages of the dissidents like locusts now gave place to a relatively orderly and ill-armed square which lumbered to the Jebel Tselfats and sat down. If the *mehalla* did not move, it could not loot. In that case, why should the tribes submit? Moreover, all the marginal tribes who might have been counted upon to attach themselves to the *mehalla* and do much of the serious fighting and intimidation now deserted it. The *mehalla* thus lost its screen of irregular cavalry and its scouts, while the ranks of the rebels swelled and the *mehalla* was besieged in its own camp. As if this were not bad enough, it rained incessantly in March. Each day the makhzan camp sank deeper into the mud.

The Cherarda *mehalla* had achieved nothing. Nothing, that is, unless one suspected as did le Glay that between them Mangin and Gaillard had arranged things so as to remove the bulk of the army from Fez. To a degree, le Glay was right. The Cherarda expedition came about, in fact, as the result of two conspiracies, one Moroccan, the other and more important one, French. Detestation of Madani el Glaoui had evoked a coalition of tribal discontent. On February 25, 1911, a number of chiefs, including those from the Beni M'tir and the Zemmour, met at Agourai, a small village south of Meknes, to plot el Glaoui's overthrow. It was decided that on March 14, the day when the tribes traditionally traveled to Fez to offer gifts to the Sultan, el Glaoui and el Mokri would be assassinated during Friday prayers. Moulai Hafid would be kidnapped and taken to the territory of the Beni M'tir, where the conspirators would offer to lead a *jihad* on his behalf. The Cherarda and the Beni Hassen were later included in the plot. It is almost certain that Madani's spies had informed him of this conspiracy. Perhaps that is why he had his tax gatherers squeeze the Cherarda so that they revolted prematurely, thereby compromising the plan.

This tribal conspiracy against Moulai Hafid played into the hands of Mangin and Gaillard. According to le Glay, they pressed for a punitive expedition against the Cherarda and intentionally kept the *mehalla* inactive on Djebel Tselfats to encourage the Beni M'tir to besiege Fez. By the second week in March, that is precisely what had happened. A noose of tribes led by the Beni M'tir had been drawn around the city. Communications with the coast were cut. Tribal leaders made contact with Abd el-Aziz, in retirement in Tangiers, and attempted to entice him to reclaim his throne. Aziz declined. Their choice of rebel sultan, therefore, fell on another of Moulai Hafid's brothers, Moulai Zayn. On April 19, the *ulama* of Meknes declared Moulai Zayn the new sultan. Moulai Hafid was now perilously close to the fate that had overtaken his brother.

The French had learned their lesson since 1908. Then, Lyautey had argued that French troops should have intervened to save Abd el-Aziz and declare a protectorate. This time his advice would be followed. The trouble, as Gaillard and Mangin were well aware, was that public opinion in France was not prepared for a Moroccan protectorate. Indeed, it was positively hostile to it. A French takeover must be initiated with circumspection. They had not manufactured the siege of Fez; Madani had done that. But they intended to profit by it. This was easy enough to do. The press notices virtually wrote themselves: The Sultan who wishes to cooperate with France and modernize his country is besieged in his holy city by a rebellion of fanatical tribesmen, while the bulk of his forces are engaged in putting down a revolt elsewhere. The lives of Frenchmen, indeed, the fate of civilization in North Africa, are in danger. Only France can save them. Dr. Felix Weisgerber, a Frenchman of Alsatian origins and the Moroccan correspondent of France's most influential newspaper, *Le Temps*, could be counted upon to do his bit. Gaillard would bombard the Quai d'Orsay with appeals for help, echoed by Edouard de Billy from Tangiers. Mangin would badger the Ministry of War in rue Saint-Dominique.

The most important act of the conspiracy, however, was to be played out in Paris. Gaillard's efforts to create a crisis in Fez would be in vain if the government refused to order a relief column. That was, after all, what had happened to Gordon at Khartoum: Gladstone had declined to be stampeded, the general and his garrison had been massacred and the Sudan was lost to Britain for over a decade. Might not the same thing happen if France, which was far less procolonialist than Britain, also refused to send a rescue party? It all depended on the right combination of political circumstances in Paris. Already in January Prime Minister Aristide Briand had denied the commander of the 5,500 troops in the Chaouia, General Monier, permission to lead a punitive expedition against the Zaer after members of that tribe had ambushed a French patrol and killed a Lieutenant Marchand. Gaillard and Mangin had taken a great gamble. If it came off, they would quite rightly credit themselves with the responsibility for the incorporation of Morocco into the French Empire. If they failed and the rebels took Fez, they might pay with their lives. Mangin left the Cherarda *mehalla* and returned to Fez, leaving Major Edouard Brémond in charge at Djebel Tselfats. Brémond was not optimistic; his men were almost out of ammunition and, without pay since February, were turning mutinous. Sitting in his bell tent, his feet in mud up to his ankles, the ubiquitous cigarette dangling from his lips, Brémond began to write letters of adieu to his friends in France.

In Paris, the leader of the colonial party, Eugène Etienne in company with Henri de Marcilly, the new director of the Moroccan desk at the Quai d'Orsay, calculated the possibilities of a giant step forward in Morocco. Seldom had the political climate been more favorable for a colonialist coup. The government of the Radical Socialist Aristide Briand had been toppled in the first days of March following the death of the war minister, General Brun. The fall of the Briand ministry marked something of a milestone in the political history of the Third Republic. Under Briand and his predecessor

Clemenceau, the French Republic had achieved something like ministerial stability—only two governments in five years, almost a record; but it was one that deputies were not keen to repeat. French parliamentarians disliked stable ministries for the simple reason that it deprived so many of them of the chance to hold ministerial office: all that talent going to waste on the back benches, all those clever men unable to extend their influence and distribute favors to their constituents and clients through this or that ministry. Above all, they were denied the healthy pension that automatically went with a government portfolio. It was considered a contravention of the republican spirit that ministerial office should be the preserve of such a small group of men. The collapse of the Briand government found them resolved to replace him with a man more to their taste.

Ernest Monis was just such a man—gray, faceless, a true second-rater. Without any real following of his own, he was obliged to pick his cabinet in such a way as to appeal to the varied, and often contradictory, interests of the Chamber of Deputies. His choices for the ministries of war and of foreign affairs proved to be of great importance. To the rue St.-Dominique went Maurice Berteaux—wealthy, elegant, a left-wing Radical with pronounced demagogic tendencies.

Berteaux had set his sights on the Elysée Palace, but so far his wealth, charm and oratorical talents had not advanced him very far along the road to the presidency. Now, at last, he had a ministry. He was in a position to be useful to people, to buy gratitude by distributing favors. And whose gratitude could be more worthy of purchase than that of Eugène Etienne, whose colonial party, although unofficial and unacknowledged, was coherent, unified and one of the most important forces in the Chamber?

The new minister of foreign affairs, Jean Cruppi, was unlikely to hinder him. On the contrary, Cruppi was a complete innocent in international relations. The look of disdain which he always wore behind his mustache and pince-nez masked a profound absence of talent. Cruppi was not ministerial timber. He and Monis were like two lost boys in a political wilderness. Berteaux became their first consul.

Berteaux wanted to be useful to Etienne, but early in March the situation in Fez had yet to be clarified. General Monier was still bleating on about the need to punish the Zaer for the death of Lieutenant Marchand. During his brief visits to the war ministry, between political meetings and speeches, Berteaux devoted most of his attention to that problem. In early April, however, the insistent reports from Morocco began to penetrate the inner sanctum of the ministry: "The tribes which support the makhzan are on the verge of defecting," Gaillard wrote on April 2 in the first of a series of messages that would soon become a daily litany of predicted disaster. He was supported by de Billy in Tangiers: "The situation in Fez is extremely precarious and the gravest results are possible." Henri de Marcilly deposited these dispatches each morning on the desk of his boss and personal friend Cruppi, while Etienne gently nudged Berteaux toward action. On April 17, Cruppi, Berteaux and Etienne met to discuss the situation in Fez. Like most politicians, Berteaux procrastinated: let Moroccans save their own sultan. He wired Monier to help Moulai Hafid raise a *harka* in the Chaouia to relieve Fez. But this clearly would not satisfy the colonialists. They wanted a French column to precipitate the protectorate. On April 20, Monier demanded permission to occupy Rabat and Kenitra, a town near the mouth of the Sebou only a hundred miles from Fez, from which he might launch a relief force. When news reached him that the Cherarda column had been recalled to defend the endangered capital, Berteaux finally allowed himself to be persuaded.

Etienne was an accomplished political tactician, and the Fez expedition must stand as one of his most impressive accomplishments. What one must most admire is his perfect sense of timing. When the cabinet was finally called on April 23 to rubber-stamp Berteaux's decision, few of the ministers were in Paris. In fact, Paris had been emptied of politicians; it was the Easter recess. The first word received by Joseph Caillaux, the man who would soon inherit the resulting international crisis, was in the copy of the *Times* he picked up at breakfast in his London hotel. He was thunderstruck. What would be Berlin's response? This very question had been put to Cruppi on April 23. But why ask Cruppi? What did he know of international affairs? Cruppi produced a reply which Jules Cambon, the French ambassador in Berlin, had received from Bethmann-Hollweg two days earlier. The German Chancellor had clearly been placed in a Catch-22 situation: "I will not tell you no, because I do not want to take the responsibility for your compatriots," he told Cambon. "But I do not encourage you." Did this reply contain a hint of menace? The only man who might tell them, Théophile Delcassé, was spending Easter in Tunisia with President Armand Fallières. The rump of the council of ministers decided that they could not shoulder the blame for the deaths of their compatriots in Fez. The expedition would go ahead.*

---

*Berteaux never lived to harvest the whirlwind that his decision produced. At the end of May, he and Prime Minister Monis visited the Paris suburb of Issy to inaugurate the start of the Paris–Madrid air

There remained only one further detail for the colonialists to arrange: For appearance' sake, French intervention in Fez should be at the request of the Sultan. Moulai Hafid proved uncooperative at first. But his lack of money combined with the unsettling effects of his two years in office made him vulnerable to Gaillard's persuasive powers. The increasing strength of the tribal insurrection against him did the rest. On March 12, the Beni M'tir raided the douars south of Fez and settled in for a long siege at their camp at Ras-el-Ma, eight miles southwest of the city. On the twenty-second, the Ait Youssi joined the rebellion and carried out *razzia* up to the very walls of Fez. A sortie against the rebels at Ras-el-Ma collapsed in disorder on March 26 when the *mehalla*, without its French instructors, panicked at the first sound of firing, suffering twenty dead and fifty wounded. The artillery was extricated only with difficulty by Pisani and Ben Sedira, who had returned from the Cherarda *mehalla* to Fez. More tribes joined the siege in April. By the middle of that month, Moulai Hafid had a rival at Meknes; his brother Moulai Zayn offered himself as sultan. Gaillard now spent many hours closeted with Moulai Hafid at the palace in an attempt to persuade him of the advantages offered by French cash and French force. The wily Algerian Benghabrit was also sneaked through the siege lines into Fez and spent most of April 7 with the Sultan discussing the advisability of a protectorate. Finally, on May 4, Moulai Hafid agreed to request French intervention. But the request was by this time a mere formality—the preparations for the French march on Fez were already so well advanced that the request had to be backdated to April 27 to make it appear as if it had preceded, rather than followed, the French movement.

This was a great triumph for the colonial party. It was also a great gamble. Its success depended upon two factors: first, Monier must reach Fez before it fell to the dissidents. Second, and more important, the German government must stand by while the Armée d'Afrique invaded Morocco.

---

race. As the official party crossed the runway, the motor of a plane which had just taken off was heard to sputter. Guiding his faltering aircraft back to earth, the pilot swerved to avoid a squadron of cavalry and came down in the middle of the official party. Monis was badly injured. Berteaux was horribly mutilated by the propeller and killed. The Monis government thus became the only government in the Third Republic that did not fall, but was fallen upon.

CHAPTER XVI

THE RESCUE

"Monier tu dors, ta colonne va pas vite;
Monier tu dors, ta colonne va pas fort."*

Captain le Glay, slight, bespectacled, impish, sang these impromptu words as he accompanied himself on a shluh mandolin. The reference to the snail's pace of General Monier's rescue column was calculated to annoy Major Edouard Brémond. It succeeded. He could hear the bearded, bearlike Brémond cursing him in the next tent. "My superiors are tragic actors," le Glay wrote in his diary. "They want to remain so to the bitter end."

General Monier did indeed seem in little hurry to lift the siege of Fez and rescue his compatriots. He was a very deliberate man, cautious and thorough. To the French soldiers in Fez, however, he seemed hesitant, even plodding. To be fair to Monier, the delays were not entirely of his own making. Monis, Cruppi and Berteaux insisted until almost the end of April that the principal effort of relieving Fez should be assigned to a "flying column" of Moroccan troops. By this, they meant the thousand *goumiers* which had been raised by French intelligence officers in the Chaouia together with a *harka* which Moulai Hafid had called up from Marrakech. The *goumiers* were eager enough to march, but the men from the Haouz showed little enthusiasm. Only five hundred badly armed men arrived in Casablanca. Over half of these deserted almost immediately and of those who remained, only eighty agreed to join the expedition. Monier argued that it was folly to rely on Moroccans to lift the siege of Fez. A relief must be made up of ten thousand French-led troops with another ten thousand in reserve. (Monier would take no chances on failure.) This exchange of communications with Paris via Tangiers and Oran took time. Only on April 23 did Paris agree to bring the French army of occupation to twenty-two thousand men and authorize Monier to occupy Kenitra, about thirty miles north of Rabat.

---

*"Monier you are sleeping, your column's only creeping:
Monier you're asleep, your column's off its feet."

Monier's operation was a model of staff-college thoroughness, and staff-college torpor. His troops set out from Casablanca on March 26 northward along the coast. They were preceded by *goumiers* and by thousands of hastily printed tracts designed to reassure the population:

O believers, men of disorder have risen among you. They have intoxicated you with the odor of powder and have afterward deceived you with their lies. They have shown you our ships full of soldiers and guns. They told you that this was the realization of a premeditated plan of conquest, that our soldiers are going to occupy your territory and place you under their yoke. Calm your spirits, O Moslems, and listen to the truth. Yes, we have landed a great number of soldiers and guns, but not to conquer lands, for we have enough. What we wish, for upon this we shall never give way, is that our European brothers who live among you no longer have their lives and property threatened. To end these outrages and this violence, His Sharifian Majesty has called upon the *harkas* of his tribes who have rallied in great numbers. And we are here only to offer our guns to support the defenders of order and of the traditional authority of the country.

And so it continued, lie upon lie, concluding with threats against anyone who opposed them. As a piece of native-affairs handiwork it was both naïve and tactless. It could have convinced no one, least of all the population of Rabat, which watched the army approach in silence. As Monier had been forbidden to enter the town, a portion of the curtain wall was demolished. The troops marched through the breach to the Bou Regreg River, to be ferried the three hundred yards to the north bank by a hastily assembled armada of small boats. A brief pause in the old pirate haunt of Salé, a gleaming collection of geometric shapes across the Bou Regreg from Rabat, and the French column plunged into the Forest of Mamora to reemerge at Kenitra.

Kenitra stands on the left bank of the Sebou four and a half miles from the sea. When the French first saw it in 1911, it was a medium-sized town surrounded by high white walls which rose out of the sandy, treeless plain. This was to be the staging post for the march on Fez. Its great disadvantage lay with the fact that it had no seaport. Mehedya, at the mouth of the Sebou, was no more than a collection of thatched huts on a broad sandy estuary; the great Atlantic breakers made it virtually impossible to unload men and supplies. So Monier settled down at Kenitra to await their arrival via Casablanca.

Monier's temporary immobility both annoyed the government and offered a sitting target for the Moroccan raiders. Had Lyautey been in charge, the relief column would certainly have been organized differently—a few battalions of Algerian and Senegalese riflemen stiffened by mounted legionnaires and *chasseurs*, with spahis and mounted *goumiers* on the flanks, two thousand to three thousand men in all. Add a few 75s for luck, everyone pack rations for twelve days, and off! Monier, however, was more cautious. He calculated that he would need at least six thousand men to defend Fez. To this, add another three thousand to secure his lines of communication to Kenitra, plus several thousand more to hold the dogleg to Casablanca. The Chaouia, of course, must be defended, a contingency plan established and men set aside to meet every possible emergency. This was something which could not be done overnight. Monier put all this in his reply to Berteaux's telegram of April 28 urging him to get moving.

Monier's immobility added to his problems. The Moroccans, who at first had been overawed by the presence of so many troops, began to take courage once they saw how the French coagulated around their base of supply. They began to strike the French at their most vulnerable point—the cumbersome supply columns that spread through the Forest of Mamora between Salé and Kenitra—first hesitantly, then with increasing boldness.

The Forest of Mamora is not an impenetrable wood. Five times the size of the Forest of Fontainebleau, its well-spaced trees of cork and wild pear and almost total absence of undergrowth give it the appearance of an immense park. In the spring of 1911, with a carpet of irises, hyacinths and narcissus, and the wild pear in bloom, it must have been delightful. But few Frenchmen ventured to enjoy it, for Mamora had become the base of operations for those resisting the French incursion.

It was the problem of the South Oranais all over again. Men who should have been preparing to march on Fez had to be detached to protect the convoys, secure posts, punish the douars of the raiders. As Monier delayed, the government became more nervous. Fed on a steady diet of grim reports sent by Gaillard via Tangiers, Paris began to bombard Monier with demands for action: "The formal orders of the government are that the requirement to arrive in Fez to save the European colony must take priority over every other consideration," Berteaux wired Monier on May 10. "Carry out your military action in compliance with this directive." Berteaux's telegrams had, by now, achieved an almost hysterical tone. And no wonder. For almost a fortnight, Monier had treated the war minister with Olympian disregard. "The day has finished without your having replied to my telegrams," became the familiar opening sentence of the war minister's daily communications in the first week of May. Nor could Monier be persuaded to act by the urgent message brought by messengers from Mangin dated May 5: "Our situation is critical. Do not lose a minute. Low on food and money; artillery munitions sufficient for two more battles; population hostile, soldiers doubtful, surrounded by tribes who attack with vigor."

At last, at 4:30 on the morning of May 11, the day Moulai Hafid's request for French intervention arrived (unknown to Monier) at Tangiers, a French force commanded by Colonel Brulard made up of 92 officers, 3,700 men, 1,150 mules and horses and 400 camels left Kenitra marching east. Brulard had only his compass to guide him. Knowledge of the line of march was based almost exclusively upon what could be gleaned from Moroccan sources. The general plan was to follow the broad valley of the Sebou to its confluent with the Wadi Mikkes, turn south along the Mikkes until it crossed the main Fez–Meknes road and approach Fez from the west. It was not the most direct route, but it avoided the mountains and the many hostile tribes which a straight line of march would have encountered. Monier planned to establish three posts between Kenitra and Fez. Brulard's assignment was to find a suitable spot for the first post and then to await the arrival of the second supply echelon of 55 officers, 1,700 men and innumerable camels carrying firewood led by Colonel Henri Gouraud. A third echelon led by Colonel Dalbiez with 60 officers and 1,850 men was to follow.

Brulard's march took him along a sandy track which snaked eastward through flat country. To his right he could distinguish the skirt of the Forest of Mamora. He placed a strong flank guard on that side. These soldiers held off a few attacks in the morning, mainly halfhearted ones which cost him only three wounded *goumiers*. A courier bearing a message from Mangin to Monier delivered it to Brulard by joining a dissident attack and throwing down his rifle as he approached the French lines. This message, however, was confusing. It asked the general to pass through Meknes "to return this town to the makhzan and disperse the Beni M'tir." Either Fez was in imminent danger of capture or it was not. Perhaps this is why Brulard paused for twenty-four hours at the end of his first day's march at Mechra Remla, where he was joined on the following day by Gouraud's men.

On the morning of May 13 after a night march, the combined columns arrived at the village of Lalla Ito. The rebel tribesmen who defended this collection of mud houses joined by garden walls were quickly dispersed by a few bursts of shrapnel. The new occupiers were now besieged in their turn: throughout the night of May 13–14, tribesmen which Gouraud estimated at 1,500 crawled through the high grass on the south face of the French encampment to attack legionnaires who manned the narrow slit trenches there. At first light, a combined sortie of legionnaires, tirailleurs and Zouaves cleared the attackers; ten Moroccan dead were found and three wounded captured who, to their utter astonishment, were given medical treatment.

At 3:30 on the morning of May 15, Brulard led twelve infantry companies, two mounted batteries and seven squadrons of cavalry out of Lalla Ito for a surprise attack on the Moroccan camp at the edge of the forest. By the time the French arrived before the dissident camp, however, daylight gave them away. The Moroccans had already begun to strike their tents and drive their animals into the forest before the first shells burst over the camp. Brulard unleashed his *goumiers* and spahis, who charged into the camp from each flank. The *goumiers*, their eyes bright in the presence of so many things to steal, began to attach bunches of chickens tied together by the legs to their saddles and drive the sheep toward Lalla Ito as the disgruntled owners expressed their displeasure by sniping from the trees.

The strike at the Moroccan camp discouraged further attacks on Lalla Ito. A few old men and women now came forward to sell poultry and eggs. Tribesmen arrived to look, to talk, to trade, but as yet none asked to submit. On the sixteenth, Brulard set his ponderous advance in motion once again. This had now established a regular pattern: a column would strike out before dawn and march until midafternoon, when it would establish a defensive position and await the arrival of reinforcements over the next forty-eight hours, before pushing ahead again in the same manner. Lalla Ito was designated as one of Monier's three permanent posts, as was Sidi Gueddar two days' march to the east. Soldiers were assigned to defend them, intelligence officers began to make contact with the surrounding tribes, and foraging parties were sent out to bring in provisions. This took time. More, it took men. These posts became the "devourers of men" of which Lyautey had complained in the South Oranais.

On May 18, Monier had to reorganize his remaining forces by dividing them into two columns under Brulard and Dalbiez, which would alternately march and bring up the supply column. On the nineteenth, the French again set out dragging the cumbersome araba wagons up the slopes of the Cherarda and down again to the Sebou through countryside deserted by its inhabitants. On the twentieth, a messenger arrived with a penciled note from Mangin: "Mon Général, the Sultan believes it absolutely necessary that you march *very rapidly* to Fez." Fires appeared on the hills and rumors of a night attack ran through the French column, but the night was calm. At first light on May 21, they again marched. Yet another note arrived from Mangin: "If you do not march very *rapidly*, you will perhaps unfortunately arrive too late!" By nine o'clock, they had crossed the Meknes bridge and spread out over the plain of Fez. On their right, the heights of Ras-el-Ma and the rebel camp could be seen and, by ten-fifteen, the walls of Fez were visible.

At this point, let us turn back and see what had happened in Fez since March. The departure of the Cherarda *mehalla* at the end of February had virtually denuded the city of its defenses. Two hundred *askar*, 450 black troops of the Sultan's guard and fewer than 2,000 tribesmen under two caids, Ben Djilali and Ben Aissa, made up the sum total of the garrison. "The few troops we have are entirely demoralized," Mangin wrote to Tangiers. Ben Djilali and Ben Aissa were unreliable, he continued. In fact, Ben Djilali had already sold 1,200 rifles to the dissidents. The Cherarda *mehalla* was too small to subdue the Cherarda, but Mangin reasoned that it kept a large number of dissidents occupied. Le Glay, as usual, disagreed with his superior: the Cherarda *mehalla* had simply inflamed the revolt against the Sultan. Morale in Fez deteriorated seriously following the ignominious defeat of a sortie by the garrison against Ras-el-Ma on March 26. The Europeans briefly considered a mass flight, but decided that the turbulent state of the country made that course of action unwise. Prices in Fez began to rise as food became scarce, hoarded, it was whispered, typically, by Jews out to make a profit. On April 2, a substantial attack was mounted against the makhzan camp at Dar Debibagh by three thousand tribesmen. Mangin ordered his cavalry to draw the attackers to within artillery range, where Pisani and Ben Sedira put them to flight.

For the moment, Fez could be defended by well-directed artillery. But the key to the city's defense was money: Moulai Hafid was barely able to pay his own troops. The French had to pay the Cherarda *mehalla* themselves; on April 11, an official of the French legation in Tangiers arrived at Djebel Tselfats at the head of several mules laden with eleven thousand duros. The merchants who had refused to extend credit to the *askar* now produced their goods. Even the Cherarda came in to sell their produce to the famished "*mehalla* of the Christians."

In Fez, the Sultan's position continued to deteriorate. On April 9, a portion of his tribal levies defending the Dar Debibagh defected and joined an attack led by the Beni M'tir. The same thing occurred three days later, when their replacements mutinied and rushed to within two hundred yards of the makhzan trenches before being turned back by Mangin's artillery. The noise of the engagement brought the population to the rooftops and, or so the French believed, to the verge of revolt. Desperate, Moulai Hafid ordered the return of the Cherarda expedition. But that, for the moment, was quite impossible: the torrential rains that had turned the camp on Djebel Tselfats into a quagmire had also swollen the wadis that blocked the way home. Only on April 21, after Mangin sent him a sharply worded order, did Major Brémond order his men to break camp.

The expedition was very low on ammunition; an attempt to resupply them from Fez on April 14 had been turned back by the Cherarda. For the first two days of the return march, they met little opposition. By the twenty-fourth, however, news of the *mehalla*'s march had drawn the Cherarda out of their douars. The French instructors and their apprentice soldiers were soon surrounded by clouds of horsemen. The next two days witnessed a running skirmish. Only with difficulty did the French officers keep their fragile army from splitting in fear. At one point, le Glay obliged one of his men to release a young girl whom he had captured in a douar. The *askar* cursed him as the prisoner clung to the Frenchman's stirrup. The *mehalla* marched forward over a carpet of flowers, under a pelting shower of badly aimed but neverthe-less deadly bullets, until, on the twenty-sixth, it came within sight of Fez. Dr. Philipp Vassel, the German consul, and his wife rode out to meet them dressed, as were all Europeans now, *à l'arabe*. Brémond greeted the German coldly. Le Glay, characteristically, was utterly charming and kissed Frau Vassel's hand. The first thing the *askar* did on returning to Fez was to change uniforms and buy combs, a strange purchase, le Glay thought, as, like all good North African Moslem men, they had shaved their heads.

The arrival of the Cherarda *mehalla* did little to strengthen the Sultan's position. Their ammunition was exhausted. Nor did their contact with the population of Fez, which Mangin reported as being "heart and soul with the rebels," improve their discipline. Besieged on Djebel Tselfats, every *askar* instinctively realized that only discipline guaranteed their survival. Now, Gaillard reported on May 7, they were becoming surly and mutinous. Lack of pay had pushed many to return to brigandage. This undermined the fragile discipline of the army even further. The Sultan's seemingly hopeless position had done the rest: "Their superiors tell me that they consider Moulai Hafid's cause as lost," Gaillard reported, "because the blockade is unbreakable and the town can hold out no longer than fifteen days. . . . The tribes have massed around Fez forces which the Sultan's *mehallas* are not capable of defeating." The morale of the *askar* was so precarious that the French instructors ceased to remain with them in their camp at night for fear of assassination.

Part of the problem was Monier's total silence. Occasional *rekkas* (couriers) could take a message through to Kenitra, but none were returned to Fez. It was rather like placing messages in bottles and casting them into the sea. The route to Taza was open and this way Gaillard was able to remain in touch with General Georges Toutée in Oudjda. But Toutée had been forbidden to cross the Moulouya, while he was as much in the dark as Paris of Monier's movements. "The total absence of news from Tangiers as well as recent orders has placed us in the greatest confusion," Gaillard complained in one of his one-way messages.

The Europeans still found ways to keep going. The British consul, James McIver Macleod, a "painfully dour if immensely worthy" Scot of Presbyterian persuasion, organized Sunday services in his dining room. These were regularly attended by French diplomats and instructors, whether out of boredom or out of respect for the Entente Cordiale. Macleod would punctuate his interminable sermons delivered in broad Scots to an uncomprehending congregation of French Catholics by periodically calling out a number. This was a reference to a hymn that Mrs. Macleod had copied out on a large sheet of paper. The harmonium would build up wind and Gaillard, sitting in the front row, would sing with great enthusiasm in his heavily accented English. Macleod never detected the sarcasm. Nor, apparently, did he ever detect his subordinate, the young Henry Selous, flirting with his two daughters in the back of the room.

On May 11, the most serious attack yet was launched on the west wall by three thousand Berbers laden with scaling ladders, hatchets and gasoline, but they were turned back before they reached the outer line of trenches. Simultaneously, a commando unit of fifty Hayaina rushed the *mechouar* where most of the munitions were stored. The raid was foiled when the gates were slammed in their faces. Two days later, the besieged French heard that the rescue force had yet to leave Kenitra. This news brought the already demoralized Moulai Hafid to the point of nervous collapse. He withdrew completely into his palace, leaving affairs of state entirely in the hands of Gaillard.

By May 15, ammunition for the 75s and 80s was so low that le Glay pulled some old 37s out of the Sultan's arsenal, which was more like a museum than an armory. On the eighteenth, the Beni M'tir brought some Krupp cannon into line against Fez. These guns were so badly served, however, that the French had little difficulty in countering their fire. But the French artillery ammunition was now virtually exhausted. Morale improved on the nineteenth, when a *rekka* brought news that Brulard had reached Lalla Ito. He had rolled the message into a cartridge case, placed it up his rectum and passed through the insurgent lines by pretending to be an idiot. In fact, the attack of the eighteenth proved to be the parting shot of the Beni M'tir. The approach of the French in force had, as usual, exposed the fragile nature of the tribal coalition. The dissidents melted away from Ras-el-Ma.

The relief of Fez excited great controversy in 1911. Even today that controversy is not settled. The Germans and the anticolonialist lobby in France claimed that Fez was never in danger—that the rescue mission was an act of deliberate deception produced to precipitate a protectorate. Against this, one must place the official French view which maintains that, had Monier delayed his arrival much longer, he would have found the Europeans in Fez headless corpses and the Jewish mellah a smoldering ruin.

Where does the truth lie? Probably somewhere in between. As we have seen, Gaillard and Mangin certainly took advantage of the siege to stimulate an atmosphere of crisis. The dispatch of the *mehalla* against the Cherarda served little strategic purpose, at least after mid-March, and it was probably, as le Glay maintained, kept away from Fez to make the Sultan's position appear more precarious in the eyes of Europe. By the time it was recalled in early April, however, there is every indication that the French diplomats and soldiers did believe that they might perish like Gordon at Khartoum. In a real sense, their position was very different from that of the English general a quarter of a century earlier. In the Mahdi, the men of the Sudan had found a leader who was able to weld them into one, steel-hard force. No such leader existed to infuse the loose coalition of tribes that gathered on Ras-el-Ma with a common spirit. British sources reported that the tribes would never invade Fez, out of respect for the holy sanctuary of Moulai Idris. This was inaccurate; in 1912, they not only invaded Fez, but also seized banners that decorated the shrine as trophies of war. But it is true that the tribes did not detest Fez as a source of wickedness in the same way as the desert men had reviled Khartoum. The Berbers hated el Glaoui and the *roumi* who sought the subjugation of their country. The real danger for the Europeans in Fez lay not in the siege itself but in the possibility of a general uprising by the population of Fez, and, more particularly, of the *askar* (as later events were to prove). Even the cynical le Glay would admit that, as the French column approached Fez on May 20–21, the *askar* were on the verge of mutiny: a rebellion in one of the artillery batteries was suppressed only by the energetic action of Pisani, while *askar* of different units had to be mixed to prevent the growth of conspiracies. They were constantly harangued by agitators. In 1912, the *askar* would listen. In 1911, they hesitated; le Glay silenced one Fassi, who came to incite his battalion to massacre their instructors, by throwing a bucket of water over him.

For the present, however, Fez was "saved." The French force advanced over the plains to the west in midmorning on May 21 in somber lines of infantry flanked by spahis in their red capes. Mangin rode out to meet them in his jellaba and was almost fired upon by legionnaires. The viziers also walked to meet the advancing column in a white-draped line. The liberators approached Fez with shouts and singing. The Fassis merely watched in stony silence as the Algerians, Senegalese, legionnaires and French filed along the walls, flags flying and bands playing to their bivouac at Dar Debibagh, almost two miles from the city. The markets which had been empty suddenly filled as if by magic with provisions.

On the following day, Monier walked between two hedges of his troops into the palace. Moulai Hafid, a Legion of Honor cross pinned to his jellaba, greeted the general effusively and demanded that he punish the Beni M'tir. That had to be postponed. Monier ordered operations to clear his lines from the coast to Fez and to open another communication route through Zaer country to the Chaouia. On the night of June 4–5, a force of 1,500 Beni M'tir mounted an attack on the French camp at Dar Debibagh. Henri Gouraud, one of the army's most promising officers, was ordered to organize the retribution. The Beni M'tir stronghold at Bahlil was set as his objective. But, as he soon learned, Moroccans did not think in terms of strongholds. They preferred to fight in open country. Dynamiting the casbah at Bahlil proved largely an empty gesture: only two men refused to surrender, and perished in the explosion.

Monier's next target was inevitably Meknes and the court of the pretender, Moulai Zayn. It proved a straightforward operation. On the eighth, two columns under Brulård and Gouraud set out from Fez marching west. Again, the Beni M'tir preferred to oppose their approach in open country rather than from behind the extensive walls of Meknes. After clearing some feeble resistance off the last ridge before the town, the French placed an explosive charge against the Aguedal gate of the palace and blew it in. Moulai Zayn surrendered, acknowledged Moulai Hafid as sultan, and was marched off to house arrest in the royal palace in Fez. The legion also demanded that Meknes send them a hundred women as spoils of war. This order was later canceled by Monier, but only temporarily; Meknes was soon to become the largest brothel in North Africa run exclusively for the Armée d'Afrique.

These operations had been carried out without authority from Paris. The general's orders were to save the Europeans in Fez and to prop up the throne. These were the limits imposed on the French by the 1906 Act of Algeciras. Conquest of new territory was definitely an infringement of that agreement. Not surprisingly, therefore, the new war minister, Adolphe Messimy, was disturbed to read of Monier's operations in the press: his commander in chief in Morocco had clearly slipped the leash. On the twelfth, a telegram reached Monier forbidding him to take Meknes. By that time, Monier had not only taken Meknes, he had left it to a garrison of legionnaires and marched north around the western edge of the massif of Zerhoun toward the holy city of Moulai Idris. As they pushed their guns through the marshy ground past the square outlines of the Roman camps which stood sentinel for the ancient town of Volubilis, tribesmen came down from their villages to sacrifice a bullock and ask for the *aman* of submission. At the town of Moulai Idris, Monier met the major chiefs of the Zerhoun. This visit proved an astute move. Not only did it help to pacify an important tribe whose mountain territory commanded the route between Fez and Meknes, it also reassured the leaders of Islam that the French had no plans to convert them forcibly to Christianity. If the French were to succeed, they must lay the ghost of the *jihad*. Already, on the night of May 20–21, as French troops approached Fez, the muezzin of the Mosque of Moulai Idris in Fez, the most sacred in Morocco, had diplomatically announced to the faithful that in a dream he had seen the saint embrace General Monier.

French troops had lifted the siege of Fez. But in doing so the colonialists had created an international crisis of such dimensions that it is no exaggeration to say that it almost advanced the outbreak of the Great War by three years. The first hint that the inexperience of the Monis ministry in international affairs combined with the acquisitiveness of the colonial party might have created a serious diplomatic incident came in early June when the French ambassador in Berlin, Jules Cambon, attended the races at Grünewald. One of the advantages of the diplomat's profession was that it could be practiced in agreeable surroundings. As Cambon navigated through this sea of plumes and spiked helmets, he was congratulated by the Prussian crown prince on the French seizure of Fez. But, the German added ominously, "you have . . . only to give us our share." "I am convinced that we will be obliged to buy our liberty," the ambassador reported to Cruppi on June 10. Cambon was not wrong. On July 1, the German ambassador entered the office of the foreign minister of only two days, Monsieur Justin de Selves, to present the bill: "German firms, especially in Agadir, are worried by tribal disorder. . . . They have asked the Imperial Government for protection. . . . We have dispatched a warship."

The new prime minister, Joseph Caillaux, was stunned for a second time. He had inherited an international mess from Monis. Pushed by Germany, Spain had occupied Larache on June 8 and El Ksar on the following day. Already Spanish troops and French *goumiers* had exchanged shots. Now, Germany had laid her cards on the table and in the process demonstrated that she could manufacture crises as well as France. Berlin demanded her slice of the sharifian cake in the form of the Sus, the land south of the High Atlas which included Agadir. Caillaux could not give way on this point, for to do so would undermine the Entente with Britain. As in 1905, Germany was again playing a dangerous game, and she knew it. There was a powerful faction at the imperial court, led by the crown prince, which wanted a war with France sooner rather than later. France's ally Russia was slowly recovering from her mauling in the Russo-Japanese War of 1904–5. Even Britain was beginning to prepare her army for continental intervention. Now was the time to strike, these men reasoned, before the Entente became too strong. Even Caillaux did not rule out the military option. In the presence of President Armand Fallières, he asked the French army's new commander in chief, General Joseph Joffre, if the French army would have the 70 percent chance of victory in a war with Germany that Napoleon had considered the prudent margin. The corpulent Joffre thought and then answered, quite simply, "No." "Then we shall negotiate," Caillaux concluded.

On November 4, 1911, France and Germany signed an accord giving the French complete freedom in Morocco in return for territorial concessions to Germany in the Congo and the Cameroons. The "Moroccan question" was, at last, settled. But in the process attitudes on both sides of the Rhine had hardened. Europe was now more firmly than ever set on a course for war. That, however, is another story. France must concentrate on consolidating her gains.

CHAPTER XVII

THE MASSACRE

The conquest of Morocco had been characterized by friction between soldiers and diplomats from the very beginning. Their dispute was one of methods rather than goals. The diplomatic contingent was sensitive to the reactions of Europe, while soldiers thought exclusively in tactical terms. Soldiers regarded the diplomats as overcautious. The envoys of the Quai d'Orsay found their military colleagues reckless, even foolhardy. The march on Fez exacerbated, rather then cooled, this conflict. Before May 1911, each group worked from their own enclaves—the soldiers from Ain Sefra, Oran and, since 1907, Casablanca, while the diplomats reigned supreme in Tangiers and Fez. By calling in the soldiers to lift the siege of Fez, however, the diplomats Gaillard and Regnault had introduced them onto the center stage. The generals no longer nibbled away at Morocco from the periphery, from the Chaouia and the South Oranais. They had now stormed—from outside—the fortress that the diplomats had attempted unsuccessfully to suborn from within: the makhzan.

Arguments over methods of conquest, however, masked an even more fundamental gulf between the two camps, and that was a social one. In Britain and Germany, soldiers and diplomats were more often divided by intelligence than by social milieu. This was not the case in France. The two professions recruited essentially from two separate social classes. It is no exaggeration to say that in France of the Third Republic, the Quai d'Orsay had become the last bastion of the aristocracy. Men of good family, Jesuit education and conservative political views were denied jobs in the other state bureaucracies, whose recruitment was carefully regulated by the bourgeois republic. They shunned the world of business and finance as vulgar. The diplomatic service offered these men a comfortable and respectable existence in the service of France.

The atmosphere in the French army was far more bourgeois. There were, of course, aristocrats in the French army, but these tended to concentrate in the fashionable cavalry garrisons around Paris and in the horse-breeding country of the Basse Normandie. Unlike those in England and

Germany, aristocrats in France never managed to stamp their social personality on the army, as the young Lyautey discovered to his disgust. The French officer corps before 1914 was neither very aristocratic nor was it particularly Catholic. Rather, it was bureaucratic, largely because it had absorbed the "meritocratic" methods of promotion through examination and administration favored by its republican masters. Lyautey's complaints about the aloofness of officers and their ignorance of their "social role" centered on the fact that the aristocratic, Catholic paternalism which he favored was not prominent in the new army of the republic. The French officer corps was not a closed shop. The Napoleonic tradition of the "career open to talent" meant that over half of its members had been promoted from the ranks. This lower-level social recruitment combined with a pay structure that was derisory by British and German standards to create a very egalitarian atmosphere in the French officer corps; officers of equal rank and superiors addressing subordinates used *tu* in preference to the more formal *vous*.

Outside of France, the army was more bourgeois still. In this respect, the Armée d'Afrique and the colonial army bore a certain resemblance to the Indian army, which attracted British officers too poor to keep up with the aristocratic life-style which ruled army messes in England. But the French army in the colonies had a far more grizzled, rough-and-ready quality than did the relatively poor but respectable Indian army. It served largely as a catchall for metropolitan army misfits—homosexuals such as Lyautey, men escaping unhappy love affairs or paternity suits, men without the brains or connections to stake out an honorable career in France, men who had quite simply grown bored waiting for the next round of the German War. For this reason, officers in France dismissed their colonial colleagues as "a collection of hooligans." It was not surprising, then, when the soldiers and diplomats met in Fez, that differences in their professional outlook and social origins would set them quarreling.

Monier and Gaillard were soon feuding over how to organize and govern Morocco. This was the most recent episode in a long debate between the colonialists and the imperialists. The colonialists argued that a colony should be governed through the native hierarchy, the invisible hand behind the throne. The imperialists were partisans of "direct administration"—the uniform application of the laws of empire. In fact, there was no clear military-diplomatic divide on this question. The Quai d'Orsay supported the colonialist argument because the Act of Algeciras bound them legally to support the authority of the Sultan, not override it. They, therefore, joined company with colonial soldiers such as Gallieni and Lyautey who had become champions of "indirect" methods of administration in Indochina and Madagascar. Lyautey argued that the colonial power should prop up the natural social hierarchy, build upon a firm foundation of custom and authority, rather than undermine it and perhaps transform local chiefs into maquisards.

The imperialists were to be found principally in Africa, and more particularly among the soldiers of the Armée d'Afrique. Their views were based partly on experience, partly on temperament. For over forty years, between the conquest of Algiers in 1830 and the Franco-Prussian War of 1870–71, Algeria had been ruled as a military colony. The young Third Republic had given Algeria over to civilian administrators, but the habit of direct administration lived on in the army in the form of the Arab bureaus, which ruled the recently pacified regions of the Moroccan frontier and on the desert fringe, and in the native regiments themselves—the spahis and tirailleurs. French officers saw themselves as the elder brothers of their North African soldiers and of the populations who fell under their control. It was their duty to guide and command people who, in a social sense, were still in a state of adolescence. To rule through the local hierarchy, at least in Africa, was to perpetuate a system notorious for its brutality and injustice. It would be the denial of the "civilizing mission" which they had taken upon themselves. Only they could guarantee the rule of law through the application of a uniform, imperial administration and code of justice. In fact, this debate—over which much ink was spilled—was largely an artificial one. Once in power, the imperialists proved to be simply bureaucrats concerned with administrative uniformity, while colonialists never allowed their native charges the wide measure of self-rule that they had promised in theory. If these discussions had an object, it was to distract the attention of politicians at home from colonial realities.

They might also serve as rallying points for quarrels whose content was as much personal as political. This became immediately apparent as soon as the French garrison had settled into the Dar Debibagh. Gaillard, the experienced Moroccan hand with extensive contacts in the makhzan and among the tribes and with a pocket full of money to influence events in the way he thought best, was well placed, he believed, to lay the foundation for "indirect" rule through the Moroccan hierarchy. Monier could not have been more at odds with his diplomatic colleague over this question. He had governed the Chaouia without help from the Moroccans and he intended to do the same in those areas of Morocco which he now controlled. Besides, he had given his word of honor as a soldier to the Beni M'tir and the Zerhoun that the Sultan would treat them fairly. His intelligence service began to appoint caids, administer justice and arbitrate tribal disputes without reference to the Sultan or to his viziers. Very quickly, two parallel hierarchies developed, one loyal to the Sultan and through him to Gaillard, and the other established outside of Fez by the army. The problem was complicated by the fact that no one had defined the respective authority of Gaillard and his boss Regnault, and General Monier. Each answered to a different minister. While major disputes could perhaps be settled ultimately by the council of ministers, the remainder of the arguments and differences between the two men continued unresolved, poisoning relations and weakening the French position in Fez.

Throughout the winter of 1911-12, resentment against the French grew. Both the colonialists and the imperialists were at fault. The diplomats, eager to modernize the makhzan administration, ended the tax exemptions which many of the *jaysh* tribes and the religious groups had traditionally enjoyed. For his part, Monier brought pressure on the Sultan to dismiss Madani el Glaoui. On May 26, Glaoui was sent a message telling him not to accompany Moulai Hafid to Friday prayers: "He has dropped me. May God drop him," Madani replied. Monier defended this and other instances of the army's interference in Moroccan politics by claiming that officers were obliged to intervene so as not to accept responsibility for the "abuses" of makhzan officials.

On one issue, however, Gaillard won a clear victory—the reorganization of the sharifian army. Monier was naturally suspicious of an independent army trained and stiffened by French officers and NCOs but under the command of the Sultan and his *allef*, or vizier for war. Like so many other French soldiers, Monier admired the bravery and fighting qualities of the Moroccan tribesmen. Here was excellent raw material which should be incorporated into the regular native units of the Armée d'Afrique, first as *goumiers*, then as tirailleurs and spahis. To allow them to be formed into an independent military force would not only perpetuate the traditions of indiscipline which characterized the *mehalla*, it was also positively dangerous in Morocco's semipacified state. Where, for instance, would its duty lie in a conflict between the Sultan and the French? He lost the argument. On August 15, the government ordered the French to train an army of six thousand men under the authority of the Sultan.

Goumiers, the Quai d'Orsay had complained, did not fall under the authority of the makhzan and so were incompatible with their notions of "indirect rule." But more important, the organization of a strong sharifian army would allow the repatriation of French troops. The government favored this, as it would silence critics who argued that Morocco absorbed too many French troops at a time of great international tension in Europe. The Quai d'Orsay warmed to the idea, as it would remove its rival from Morocco. In Paris, the notion of a sharifian army caught fire in the government; in January 1912, the council of ministers presided over by Raymond Poincaré adopted plans for an army of 13,000 Moroccans and an imperial guard of 2,000 blacks under the command of General Brulard. The first of the 51 officers and 171 NCOs designated to lead this new army had already begun to arrive in Fez in the autumn of 1911.

By the spring of 1912, the Sultan and his viziers were resigned to the inevitability of a protectorate. Germany, Morocco's last hope in Europe, had been bought off with the Cameroons. The French army occupied, and administered, large sections of the country. Morocco's finances were controlled by the Banque de Paris et des Pays-Bas. Sign they must.

The diplomatic mission led by Regnault set out from Tangiers with the draft treaty on March 16, 1912. Eugène Regnault was a man very much attached to his creature comforts: his baggage contained 576 bottles of Vichy water, 1,000 bottles of wine, 300 bottles of champagne and 34 of cognac, 310 tins of potted meat, 21 terrines of foie gras, 50 kilos of dried vegetables, 440 pounds of potatoes, pasta, cheese, 100 pots of jam, coffee, tea, 49 pounds of bonbons, 54 packets of toothpicks and a magnificent fireworks display. When this well-fed mission followed by its enormous caravan arrived in Fez on the twenty-fourth, the makhzan had prepared a respectful welcome: they were guided through a hedge of *askar* formed along the walls of the Aguedal while at the Bab Segma a large crowd of Jews cheered and their orchestras played "La Mère Michèle," which they believed to be the French national anthem. Once the predominantly Jewish Fez Djedid quarter of the city had been crossed, however, the welcome was decidedly less spontaneous. The vast area of the Bou Djeloud was deserted. At the foot of a mosque, the pasha had assembled a troop of prostitutes whose ululations were meant to give the impression of the population's explosion of joy at the arrival of the French. When this brilliant cortege of plumed and bemedaled diplomats plunged into the narrow, teeming streets of old Fez on their way to the Glaoui palace, which had been prepared as the new French embassy, they were ignored. In front of the Dar el Glaoui, Regnault dismounted and declared himself satisfied with their welcome. Dr. Felix Weisgerber, who had accompanied the mission replied: "Well, *monsieur le ministre*, you are not difficult to please."

Once arrived, the diplomats presented the treaty of protectorate for the Sultan's signature with almost indecent haste. Given the pompous talk about the virtues of "indirect rule" which had echoed through the corridors of the Quai d'Orsay for over a year, the conditions of the treaty caught Moulai Hafid completely unawares. Hunched on a gilded reproduction Louis XVI settee, flanked by Gaillard, Regnault and the Algerian Benghabrit, Moulai Hafid now learned the awful truth. He had, of course, expected to hand over foreign policy to the French. But he had not expected this: administration, justice, financial agreements and the army were also to be taken from his control. The Sultan was to have no say in negotiations over the status of Tangiers. Worst of all, there were no guarantees for the future of Islam. This was a particularly foolish omission on the part of the French, given the widespread belief among Moroccans that the *roumi* intended to convert Morocco to Christianity by force. The protectorate would leave the makhzan no more than a hollow shell, a Potemkin village of a government, all façade and ceremony with no real substance. The Sultan would now become a political eunuch on a level with the bey of Tunis. It was ignominious. Moulai Hafid became depressed and truculent, he hesitated and argued. But finally on March 30 he signed.

One of the conditions, indeed virtually the only condition, upon which Moulai Hafid had insisted during the negotiations was that news of the treaty be made public only when he had reached Rabat. This was wise, given the popular outrage which news of the treaty would certainly provoke. Perhaps Regnault or Gaillard could not resist the temptation to leak the news to the press, for the Parisian daily *Le Matin* soon announced the signing. The Quai d'Orsay was furious. But it is unlikely that the news could have been kept secret for long in any case. Indeed, it is more likely that whispers in the palace had been heard on the streets long before *Le Matin* went to press. (Why the French assumed that *Le Matin* was ever read in Fez is not clear.) Besides, Monier's departure for the coast with the bulk of the French garrison as soon as his intimidating presence was no longer required was indication enough that the diplomats had accomplished their mission.

To those familiar with Morocco, such as Dr. Weisgerber, the mood in Fez in early April was heavy with menace: Moroccans no longer smiled, hastened to distance themselves from their European friends and even pretended not to recognize them. Children and lunatics, however, expressed their feelings more forcefully, by spitting and cursing. The wildest rumors floated about the streets, fed by the secret plans which Regnault and the Sultan were making for their departure. The Sultan was a prisoner, it was said. The French planned to kidnap him and take him to Rabat. On April 12, a Moroccan friend warned Weisgerber not to leave with the Sultan and Regnault on the seventeenth (even the departure date was common knowledge), for the tribes planned to attack the party, seize the Sultan, tear up the paper upon which the treaty was written and launch a *jihad*. The situation was very serious. Monier's departure had reduced the French garrison at Dar Debibagh to two understrength battalions of Algerian and Senegalese tirailleurs, a squadron of spahis, one four-gun battery, a machine-gun section and a handful of communication troops—barely 1,500 men in all. This was hardly enough to put down an uprising in Fez, especially if the loyalty of the five thousand *askar* wavered. But these warnings were brushed off by the diplomats. Plans were set in motion to depart on April 17; the Sultan and Regnault would leave Fez separately, meet at Ras-el-Ma and together make their way to Rabat.

On the night of the sixteenth, however, rain fell in torrents. The prospect of sodden tracks, swollen wadis and swamped campsites was too much for Regnault, who ordered the departure postponed. This was not made known to the *askar* who assembled on the morning of April 17 in the Casbah Cherarda as usual to collect their daily pay. It was singularly unfortunate that the military mission had chosen this day of all days to introduce a reform that, in the atmosphere of mistrust which reigned in Fez and which could not but contaminate the *askar*, was bound to have unhappy consequences.

The reorganization of the sharifian army had begun surprisingly well; surprisingly, that is, because most of the French officers assigned to train the *askar* had been drawn from the metropolitan army and not from the Armée d'Afrique, which was more experienced in dealing with Moslem soldiers. The officers who volunteered for the job appear to have found it a challenge and, on the whole, to have carried out their duties conscientiously and with tact. There had been some cases of friction: the notoriously bluff Major Brémond had offended his soldiers, who were worried that the particular conjunction of Venus with the moon on one evening announced a catastrophe, by remarking that the glories of Arab astronomy had declined into superstition. Given the importance which the *askar* assigned to celestial movements, it was even more insensitive of the French to plan so many important events on April 17, a day of a partial eclipse of the sun.

The first priority of the military mission in the early autumn of 1911 had been that of barracks. The sharifian army had none. The *askar* slept where they could—in the corridors of the palace, in rented rooms, in the fonduks or with prostitutes, much as most regular soldiers in Europe had done until well into the nineteenth century. Consequently, the Casbah Cherarda, which stood just outside the walls to the north of Fez, was requisitioned, the three hundred families who occupied it expelled and the bulk of the sharifian army installed. In this way, French officers felt, they could keep an eye on their men, insulate them from the unfortunate effects of constant contact with the population and better ensure discipline.

While the appropriation of the Casbah Cherarda caused some resentment in the city, the soldiers settled in with little trouble. Most were probably delighted to have a roof over their heads. The real problem occurred with the messing arrangements. When the old royal army had been disbanded in November 1910 and the best elements reenlisted in the new army, the men had been promised a daily pay of four billiouns, the equivalent of five English pence, out of which they purchased their own food in the market-place and messed where they liked. Four billiouns for these men was a small fortune—enough to eat, pay for a prostitute and purchase a bottle of *mahia* from the Jews in the mellah. The trouble, according to the military doctors who examined the *askar*, was that more money was put toward prostitutes and *mahia* than went for food. Cases of malnutrition became more common. The solution? Withhold half of the *askar*'s pay and give it to him in kind. This system had already been introduced in two *tabors* in the Gharb. But the Gharb was not Fez. The substantial number of prostitutes in the red-light quarter of Moulai Abdallah were loath to accept a cut in their incomes, and they told the *askar* so—again, and again, and again. Their complaints and taunts must have worn the nerves of the Sultan's soldiers thin, for when Lieutenant Metzinger formed up his *tabor* on the morning of April 17 and announced the new reform, his men mutinied. This was the spark applied to the dry straw which Fez had become in April 1912. About fifty *askar* ran into the streets where they met other soldiers. In this way, the revolt spread to other battalions which had, until that moment, accepted the new system without violent complaint.

Ironically, the safest place for a French soldier to be when the mutiny erupted was with his own *tabor*. Many of these officers and NCOs survived, like Lieutenant Metzinger, who was seized by his men and bundled into a quiet spot. After nightfall, his *askar* put him in Moorish dress and smuggled him into the French camp at Dar Debibagh. His closest brush with extinction came when *askar* from another *tabor* who had just delivered their own officer safely to Dar Debibagh attempted to take him away from his escort and murder him. A patrol of Algerian spahis persuaded a group of sharifian artillerymen to give up one of their NCOs by requesting "their Christian to kill." When Captain Fabry arrived at his *tabor* at 12:45 p.m., he was told: "Run, Captain! By order of the Sultan we are killing all officers."

Those who were not with their men were less fortunate. The mutinous soldiers first ran to the palace, where they begged the Sultan to intervene on their behalf with the French: "We are soldiers of the Sultan, not of the French!" they shouted. Moulai Hafid was decidedly nervous as he listened to their excited complaints about pay and their fears that the French would make them carry knapsacks, which they regarded as beneath their dignity as warriors. "Take us with you when you leave Fez," they begged. The Sultan eventually shoved these deputations back onto the streets, where the mutiny had by now become a full-scale revolutionary *journée*, with "the lowest elements of the towns people" joining the *askar*. Any French soldier found outside was pursued by a mob and murdered. Women on the rooftops kept up a chorus of ululations. From their vantage points, some women even pointed out the quarry to the packs of pursuers. One or two soldiers bolted upstairs onto the roofs in an attempt to escape, only to be brought down by the large stones kept there to hold down washing. The victims were stripped and hacked to pieces.

The fact that the mutiny had broken out near lunchtime no doubt saved the lives of many Europeans. Henry Selous had just left the British consulate at one o'clock for the rather grandly named Hôtel de France where he regularly dined, when he was called back to decipher a telegram. In this way, he was denied an interesting afternoon. A mob arrived at the bottom of the blind alley where the pension was located and began to pound the bolted door with the butts of their rifles. The proprietress and a Spanish Franciscan attempted to speak to the rioters through the door, only to be killed by bullets that splintered the wood. The remaining sixteen diners retreated to the top of the stairs and greeted the intruders with a hasty volley as they broke through the door. The siege lasted until nightfall, when the Europeans were able to creep away over the rooftops.

Several officers were surprised and killed in their houses. One captain was murdered by his servant as a mob broke in the door. The telegraph station was attacked and four of the five soldiers who manned it were killed after putting up a defense that lasted two hours. Adjutant Pisani with a handful of faithful *askar* held off repeated attacks on his artillery barracks before making his escape to Dar Debibagh in the early morning of the eighteenth, taking with him the breech-blocks of his guns. Elsewhere, four officers trapped by a mob in their house enlarged a bull's-eye window on the first floor and slid to the street along knotted sheets, followed by a shower of plaster brought down upon them by bullets. The last man slipped through the window feet first, firing at the assailants, who had hacked their way through the ceiling. Once in the street, the Frenchmen jumped into a sewer entrance, hoping to follow it to the river and escape. They had gone barely a hundred yards, however, when the water, swollen by the recent rains, reached the roof of the sewer. By swimming several yards underwater, they were able to reach another air pocket. But this lasted only a few yards before it too disappeared, and they had to retreat. They resigned themselves to waiting until nightfall. But when they approached the sewer entrance again, they discovered that men were lowering a lantern on the end of a rope in an attempt to locate them. They retreated into the sewer and spent the night up to their necks in the freezing water, surrounded by enormous rats, their bare feet cut by fragments of glass and pottery. At daybreak, they again approached the sewer entrance but could hear firing. This continued all day and kept them in their hiding place. Finally, on the morning of the nineteenth, after thirty-six hours in hiding, two officers crawled out into the now-deserted street. Just as they emerged, an armed Moroccan turned the corner. The two officers overpowered and disarmed the man, who protested that he was a friend who had been sent to lead them to safety. Two of the officers agreed to follow him. The other two, fearing a trap, elected to return to their freezing hole. Thirty minutes later, a second Moroccan arrived with a paper signed by General Brulard.

The French casualties of eleven officers and eight NCOs killed on April 17, along with nine European civilians, would certainly have been higher had the rioters not turned their attentions on the mellah. As usual when disorder threatened, the Jews sealed off their quarter. After an hour-long assault, however, the gates gave way with a groan, allowing a torrent of looters to flood the mellah. The Jews made for their traditional refuge in the Sultan's palace, but not before forty-three of their number were massacred. The menagerie of the palace soon offered the sad and bizarre spectacle of cages full of terrified Jews next to those filled with wild beasts. Weisgerber found the mellah

> nothing more than a pile of ruins. Shattered furniture, broken kitchen utensils among which lie the bloated and hideously mutilated bodies of men, women and children, surrounded by bands of rats. Along the collapsed walls, several dogs, too full to move, content themselves with showing their teeth. A scroll of the law, torn and soiled, remains in a black pool of coagulated blood which emits an appalling smell.

General Brulard, acting commander of the Fez garrison in Monier's absence, set about organizing a center of resistance around which the Europeans could rally. Dar Debibagh was safe enough. A cordon was thrown around the "diplomatic quarter" of Fez el Bali to include the Glaoui Palace, the French and British consulates, the Auvert Hospital and the wireless station. This offered the advantage of being accessible through the Bab al Hadid on the south wall. For the moment, however, his perimeter could be defended only by hospital orderlies and convalescent soldiers. The diplomats raised the flag and sent their servants out to bring in provisions, which they did by joining the pillage.

Brulard ordered Major Philipot, who within seven years would be a lieutenant general in command of an army on the Western Front, to reinforce the perimeter with troops from Dar Debibagh. After floundering beneath the walls of the Aguedal under the fire of the mutinous *askar*, the major redirected his tirailleurs around the south wall to enter the perimeter through the Bab al Hadid gate. It was not an easy march. One of his companies was pinned down beneath the walls of the mellah and suffered thirty-five dead and seventy wounded before it could disengage. Furthermore, the packets of tribesmen who had begun to gather in preparation for the kidnap attempt on the Sultan planned for the seventeenth had lined the crests to the south of the city. Only by wading up the waist-deep Wadi Zitoun could Philipot protect his men both from the snipers on the walls of the mellah and from the Berbers to the south. He reached the Auvert Hospital by late afternoon with two companies. These began immediately to patrol the streets of the perimeter, erect posts on the roofs of the consulates, and seal off the narrow lanes with barricades.

Brulard next attempted to occupy strongpoints, especially gates. One patrol of fifteen Senegalese holding the Bab Bou Djeloud had been promised aid by a caid who had remained faithful. Eventually, the caid and his men arrived. Taken off their guard, the Senegalese were fired upon by the Moroccans, who then fled, leaving nine of the blacks dead and four wounded.

Colonel Taupin took up positions on the hills south of Fez and began a slow bombardment of the town. This, combined with energetic patrolling from the diplomatic quarter, cleared Fez el Bali of rioters by the eighteenth. Concentrated in Fez Djedid, they became even more precise targets. This gave the edge to the French and convinced most Moroccans that the revolt was doomed. Notables began to arrive at the French headquarters in the Auvert Hospital to give assurances of loyalty. On the afternoon of the eighteenth, a battalion of legionnaires arrived from Meknes. Some of the *askar* began to surrender. Others scattered into the hills. On the twenty-first, General Monier returned to Fez with twenty-three companies of infantry, three squadrons of cavalry and several artillery batteries which he sited in commanding positions to the north and south of the city. The roofs of Fez were now aflutter with improvised tricolored flags, a plea to Monier not to shell their houses in retribution. As Henry Selous made his way home, he passed the pasha of Fez Djedid riding in the direction of the hospital followed by two mules bearing the decapitated and mutilated remains of the nineteen French instructors who had perished in the mutiny.

CHAPTER XVIII

THE SECOND SIEGE OF FEZ

Hardly had Monier sighted his guns on the city when he and Regnault began to exchange recriminations. For months the two men had fought a silent duel for influence in Morocco which had gradually poisoned relations not only between them but also between the Quai d'Orsay and the War Ministry. Now their feud went public. Regnault and Gaillard were categorical about who must shoulder responsibility for the revolt. The French officers of the military mission with their rigid adherence to European military conventions had failed to demonstrate the imagination and flexibility which the delicate task of training the Sultan's soldiers required. As evidence of this, Regnault particularly emphasized their decision to impose the knapsack. Also, he chided, what was the intelligence service doing? Was it not their duty to feel the pulse of the country, to predict the mood of revolt? But how could one expect French soldiers, who were unable to divine the thoughts or to gauge the morale even of the *askar*, with whom they were in daily contact, to predict the larger currents of opinion running through Fassi society?

It is worth considering the army's defense in some detail, as the judgment that the Fez revolt was primarily the responsibility of the military mission has been widely accepted as the final verdict. First, General Brulard argued in defense of his mission, the question of the knapsack was an irrelevance. True, the storehouses contained several crates of knapsacks, but the mission had never planned to issue these to the *askar*. They had been ordered by Moulai Hafid in December 1910, when it was his intention to equip his army in a European manner. After the decision of August 1911 to reorganize the sharifian army, the French had introduced the *barda*, which consisted of a tent-half into which the *askar* rolled their kit. The introduction of the *barda* had, it is true, provoked some desertions, but it had been generally accepted by the *askar*. Besides, Brulard pointed out, even if the infantry believed that they were to be issued with knapsacks, it was never an issue in the cavalry *tabors*, which had spearheaded the revolt. They were in daily contact with Algerian spahis and saw very well that they carried neither *barda* nor knapsack.

This said, however, it does appear that the *tabors* thought they were to be issued knapsacks. Lieutenant Metzinger noted that during one training march with his men just before the mutiny, the *askar* frequently chanted: "O Harrab [instructor], you will never allow us to become beasts of burden and carry packs. We are not mules." If this belief was widespread, and the French had no intention of issuing knapsacks, then they should have made their intentions clear. While the question of knapsacks cannot be considered the primary cause of the revolt, as Regnault maintained, it did provide a source of misunderstanding between the *askar* and the instructors.

The question of withholding pay for food has been considered in the last chapter. This forms the most serious, and in the final analysis the most plausible, charge against the soldiers, no matter how well intentioned that reform was. Brulard countered, however, that to blame the revolt on the decision to withhold pay was to confuse the symptom with the disease. In the first place, this system had been introduced a fortnight earlier in two *tabors* in the Gharb without causing serious problems. The *askar* in Fez had known for some time that this reform was to be introduced. Second, only one *tabor* revolted when the new pay scheme was announced at 11 a.m. on April 17. The remainder grumbled, but agreed to await the arrival of their caids. It was the arrival of the caids, Brulard maintained, that touched off the revolts in the remaining *tabors*: Relations between the caids and the officers and NCOs of the mission were not good. Many of them were upset by the political situation in the country. They feared for their positions in the new army. Consequently, they adopted equivocal attitudes and undermined discipline by refusing to enforce it.

Some historians have cited the decision to make French the language of command as one cause of discontent fueling the revolt. This is unlikely. The language of command in the sharifian army was English, dating from the days when Moulai Hassan had relied chiefly upon English instructors to train his *askar*. Why should the *askar* have seen any real inconvenience in changing from one *roumi* language to another? The number of commands was relatively small, and they could be quickly mastered even by the most slow-witted *askari*.

Lastly, Brulard concluded, one must not underestimate the instinct to pillage which had been an integral part of Moroccan military tradition. An army recruited principally from among the criminal classes could not be transformed into a legion of citizen soldiers overnight.

To be sure, the soldiers had made tactical errors. But had not the decisions of the diplomats been strategic mistakes of the highest order? The soldiers had resisted the idea of a sharifian army from the beginning. The reorganization had been imposed by the Quai d'Orsay, which now rounded on the soldiers and accused them of causing a revolt. The instructors were remote from their men. But how could it be otherwise when there were only one French officer and four NCOs for every 550 *askar*, and these spent the bulk of their day verifying accounts so that the caids would not cheat their men? Few of the instructors spoke Arabic, and so had to rely on their caids or on the classical (and to the *askar* incomprehensible) Arabic of interpreter Reynier. Knowledge of the thoughts, moods and opinions of their men was at best secondhand or deformed by the interpretations of the caids. The *tabor* of the only instructor who did speak Arabic, Lieutenant Ben Sedira, did not mutiny. Nor was it fair to charge the intelligence service with being blind to the signs of revolt when Regnault had expressly forbidden them to operate within Fez. Monier argued that Gaillard operated his own intelligence service: "The consul of France who has resided in Fez for ten years, should he not have been informed first through his numerous relations?" The diplomats had mishandled the negotiations over the protectorate. By maintaining a shroud of secrecy, by ignoring reports that the country was in a state of great agitation, they had allowed the wildest rumors to circulate and political tensions to build up beyond the danger mark. The army may have struck the match, but the diplomats had provided the fuel.

The anchor of the *Jules Ferry* clattered down the side of the ship and disappeared into the blue-green sea. Only a republic could name its warships after faceless "frocks," as the soldiers disrespectfully called their frock-coated political bosses in Paris. But Lyautey did not think of that now as he surveyed the low silhouette of Casablanca. The place had changed beyond recognition since he had last visited it in 1908. Then, it had been a bleached Arab casbah surrounded by the shallow trenchworks and triangular white tents of the French military camp. Now it looked like a boom town in some sand-blown Klondike: new buildings had been nailed together along hastily laid-out streets which still bore the deep ruts of the winter rains. The town was full of men (Greeks and Lebanese most noticeable among them) who had flocked to Morocco in search of quick fortunes. In the town's two cafés, Jews clutching maps circulated among the tables attempting to interest newcomers in the purchase of land titles, some of which were valid. Indeed, land speculation seemed to be the town's major industry—few officers above the rank of captain had not been offered choice pieces of property by makhzan officials over dinner.

Perhaps it worried Lyautey. He had entertained visions of returning to command a medieval kingdom. But for the moment his mind slipped back to that Sunday dinner two weeks earlier in the Versailles house of Alexandre Millerand. The garden had been cloaked in the light-green shades of late April. Lyautey, called in from his headquarters at Rennes, where he commanded the Tenth Corps, had been in excellent form. The war minister and Prime Minister Raymond Poincaré had let him talk and, had they still entertained doubts about his appointment as Morocco's first resident general, these were vanquished by what was, even by Lyautey's normally high standards, a masterful performance. It was, of course, bad luck for poor Eugène Regnault. But he had been amply compensated with the Tokyo embassy. Besides, Moroccans were warriors. They needed a soldier to lead them, not some bloodless diplomat.

The Quai d'Orsay had taken this very badly and insisted that their man St.-Aulaire be assigned as Lyautey's permanent secretary. Lyautey had resolved the problem of a potential spy in his entourage with a characteristic combination of charm and intimidation: he placed St.-Aulaire in the middle of a circle of staff officers and told him, "My dear St.-Aulaire . . . Those idiots in the Quai d'Orsay sent you here to mess me about. You and I are going to be thick as thieves. Who is going to be messed about? It is those idiots in the Quai d'Orsay. Is that a deal?" And, of course, it was. Lyautey kissed the diplomat on both cheeks, shook his hand, and bound him for life.

In 1909 Lyautey had also acquired a wife, the thirty-eight-year-old widow of a colonial army colonel who had two sons, both officers. Why he had decided to marry at such a late stage in his career is unclear. His letters make only the most fleeting of references to her. They had first met in Oran, and again later in Casablanca, where she had been active with the Red Cross. Now that his life had acquired a certain stability and status, he must have felt the need for a wife who would organize the social side of his existence. By all accounts, she presided over his receptions and dinner parties with elegance and efficiency. The available evidence seems to indicate that Lyautey and his wife were linked by esteem rather than passion. "She is independent and used to an active life which will not suffer too much, I hope, from the perpetual upset of mine," he wrote to Louise Baignières.

In Casablanca, Lyautey met Colonel Gouraud. The two men became friends immediately. Gouraud had already acquired a reputation in the army as the man who had captured Samory, the black chief who had for so long resisted the French in the Western Sudan. The son of a doctor who had a fashionable practice in Paris' Faubourg St.-Germain, the tall, bearded Gouraud was far more naval than military in appearance. At the head of two battalions of tirailleurs, Lyautey and Gouraud marched to Fez via Rabat and Meknes.

As Lyautey rode along, he must have been reminded of a similar journey which he had made nine years earlier from Oran to Ain Sefra. Then, he had traveled along a thin line of French posts, each inert, vulnerable, folded in on itself. The situation in May 1912 of those posts which Monier had created to link Fez with the sea was similar: "The line of posts is a taut wire which can snap at any moment," he wrote. If Lyautey had one recurring nightmare, it was that the French would meet in Morocco the same sort of popular resistance that had driven the Emperor Napoleon III's troops from Mexico a half-century earlier. He had no wish to emulate Marshal Bazaine. It was so easy to conquer a country; the art lay in holding it.

It would not prove an easy task. Opposition to the French was well nigh universal. The notoriously fickle Fassis were known to sympathize with the tribesmen who were gathering under the leadership of the pious sharif Si Mohammed el Hajjami, who had liberated a few rusty old guns from Bou Hamara's arsenal at Taza and assigned some of the mutinous askar to work them. To the southeast, the Beni M'tir were again active. The two groups had exchanged turbans to seal their alliance and begun to coordinate plans for an attack on Fez. Lyautey and his escort arrived in Fez on May 24. They were greeted by a company of disarmed askar and by Eugène Regnault, who tried his best to stifle his disappointment behind a diplomatic smile. Had Lyautey arrived even twenty-four hours later, he would have been denied entrance, for the second siege of Fez slammed shut behind him.

That the French in Fez were in great danger, greater perhaps than during the mutiny a month earlier, was not immediately apparent. Lyautey had learned in Paris that Monier and Regnault had long ceased to see eye to eye. Indeed, he had been appointed in part to override that rivalry. But he had not been prepared for the total breakdown of communications which he discovered upon reaching Fez.

The mutiny of the askar had cracked the façade of politeness which Monier and Regnault had maintained only with difficulty through the winter of 1911–12. Disagreement between them over the causes of the revolt masked even more fundamental differences over how it should be repressed. Monier wanted to teach Fez a lesson, and sighted his guns on the city; but Regnault refused to agree to a bombardment. Nor did he support the general's imposition on Fez of a fine of 1.5 million francs. In this, Regnault had been backed up by the Quai d'Orsay and the dispute, as usual, had been transported to Paris. As a consequence, the French administration in Morocco had been virtually paralyzed. More than four hundred of the mutineers scattered into the hills. A hundred or so others were caught, court-martialed and, eventually, shot by firing squad. But it was a laborious process. Day after day, the Fassis watched those caught up in the French net being led out of town to the place of execution. This was a bad method, Lyautey later told Henry Selous: Justice in the colonies should be swift and brutal—a week or so of bloodletting, and then hand-shaking all round. That would have cleared the air. But Monier's dilatory justice, his strict curfew and his fines had increased anxiety and resentment among the Fassis. House-to-house searches were threatened and anyone caught with a weapon, the general promised, would be harshly treated. As virtually everyone in Morocco owned a weapon of some description, the result had been virtual panic. When Selous returned to his flat after the mutiny, he found his table covered with an odd assortment of weapons ranging from rusty Spanish bayonets through flintlocks to Martinis and Lebels. Where better to deposit incriminating evidence than in the house of the first secretary of the British consulate?

By the time Lyautey arrived in Fez, differences between Monier and Regnault had grown so acute that the two men, and their staffs, could agree on nothing—even on whether or not Fez was actually in danger. Monier said things were very bad indeed: the tribes around Fez were in great turmoil, the sharifian army was utterly disorganized, and he had only 32,000 troops and 5,600 *goumiers* west of the Atlas with which he must defend the Chaouia, Rabat, Kenitra, the Gharb and Fez. Lyautey must have smiled inwardly as he heard his old St.-Cyr classmate rattle off this catalogue of difficulties. Thirty-two thousand troops and 5,600 *goumiers*! With those numbers and a little imagination Lyautey could conquer the whole of Africa!

Regnault, on the other hand, was absurdly optimistic. He had no reason to be. Both Weisgerber and Gaillard had warned him that it could only be a matter of days before the tribes would lay siege to Fez once again. The Berbers had forewarned the Fassis that their attacks would be directed only at the French. Regnault brushed aside these warnings. Probably he wanted to give no credence at all to reports the truth of which would require a larger role for the army and thereby enhance the status and power of his archrival Monier. However, Lyautey was not blind. Sitting in his dress uniform—white breeches, black thigh boots, his tunic bulletproof with medals and his white-plumed bicorn resting on the table—as he prepared to pay his first official call on the Sultan, he dashed off a rapid message to Albert de Mun: "We are camped in enemy country."

The diplomats carried on as if the French embassy at the Dar el Glaoui were in the middle of London or Vienna. A garden reception for the new resident general in the afternoon was followed in the evening by an official dinner of welcome. Around 10 p.m., as Lyautey was making his excuses to leave, the guests heard the explosion of a 75 followed by the high staccato of a machine gun. Lyautey was calm. The defense of Fez was the task of Monier. He retired to his new residence in what was once the palace of Menebbhi, asked one of his staff officers to read some poetry to him and, eventually, went to bed.

Few other French soldiers slept that night, however. A substantial number of tribesmen, which the French put at fifteen thousand, besieged the eastern curve of the wall between the Bab Ghissa in the north and the Bab F'touah to the south. Monier's task was not an easy one. The walls of Fez were far more picturesque than defensible: buildings blocked access to large sections of them, while the interior ramparts had crumbled away in many places. Consequently, Monier elected to defend the gates. Artillery and machine guns kept the attackers at bay almost everywhere except at the Bab Ghissa. There, a section of Algerian tirailleurs had to contend with the plunging fire of the assailants who occupied the tombs of the Merinides on the hill above them while infiltrators, ensconced in the minaret of the Mosque of Bab Ghissa, sniped at them from behind. The Algerians suffered seventeen dead and twenty-five wounded before they were relieved by a company of legionnaires, who cleaned out the mosque, placed a machine-gun nest in the minaret and kept up a steady fire on the Merinides. Near the Taddert barracks, more tribesmen breached the wall before being driven out of the city by a battalion of reinforcements rushed from the Dar Debibagh. The evening had ended in a stalemate, but the French had lost thirty-eight dead and eighty-five wounded.

For the next two days, the tribesmen drank tea, discussed plans, sealed more alliances and awaited more rifles. They did not attack. Lyautey, however, was far from inactive. "The general situation remains very serious," he wrote to Albert de Mun. And so it was. The French garrison in Fez numbered four thousand troops. In a good defensive position, they could easily hold off twice their number. But Fez was not a good defensive position. The walls, as we have seen, were more of a hindrance to the defenders than a breastwork. The 2,600-foot Djebel Zalagh towered over the town to the north. To the south and east, the gardens and low, marshy ground which flanked the Wadi Zitoun and the Wadi Fez provided ample dead ground for an attacker. Virtually anywhere one chose to look, the walls were not only breachable but easily breachable. And, of course, the most important question: what would be the attitude of the one hundred thousand Fassis? Might they not be persuaded, if they saw things going badly for the French, to turn on the garrison and massacre them? This would be very much in keeping with the reputation of this "murderous city."

Lyautey was only too well aware that feeling against the French was running very high. Since the uprising of April, Monier had piled humiliation upon humiliation. The Fassis could not have been too pleased when homeless Jews were billeted on them. The merchants especially were furious at the indemnity which Monier had imposed upon the town, for it was they who would pay it and they had not rioted. Nor had the ceaseless executions calmed spirits. It was like watching an endless stream of blood flow from beneath a closed door.

Lyautey elected to mend his bridges with the Fassis. For the next forty-eight hours, he ceaselessly courted the notables gathered for him by the British consul James McIver Macleod. He listened to their complaints, reassured them, charmed them. The rioters who remained in captivity were freed. The important *ulama* and their students in the Qarwyin Mosque were placed on government stipends on condition that they refrain from political activity.

Lyautey credited his conquest of the *ulama* with sabotaging the tribal attack that was finally unleashed on the twenty-eighth. Mohammed el Hajjami's *jihad* was denied the support of the most important religious body in Morocco. The attack came, as anticipated, from the north. Early in the afternoon, tribesmen could be seen gathering on the Djebel Zalagh. About 4 p.m., they suddenly boiled down the hill. Aerial bursts of shrapnel appeared like wads of cottonwool above them. Soon, the entire French line from the Casbah Cherarda in the west to the Bab F'touah in the east was engaged. Several groups of Moroccans penetrated the city by wading up the Wadi Fez to reach the Mosque of Moulai Idris, where they seized trophies—sacred robes and banners—to serve as symbols of resistance. But Lyautey had done his work well. These men found every door in Fez bolted against them. Their calls for a *jihad* echoed unanswered. Outside the walls, the 75s and machine guns ground down the attack. At the Bab Ghissa, where the French had suffered heavy casualties barely four days earlier, Moroccans fell in heaps to the machine gun, whose bullets plunged into their ranks from the minaret of the mosque. After an hour, they drifted away, leaving almost a thousand bodies on the field.

The major Moroccan attack had been broken, but Lyautey was taking no chances. He shifted his headquarters from the Menebbhi palace to the Auvert Hospital. There, he assembled all of his official papers, as well as those of Regnault, and placed next to them a four-gallon can of gasoline. The tribesmen would chance no further attacks on Fez for the next two days. But they remained close by, numerous, threatening, assassinating couriers and crawling in small groups through the gardens and olive groves to the south and east of the city to snipe at the French posts.

On June 1, in the gray light of dawn, Colonel Gouraud assembled a strike force of five battalions of tirailleurs and legionnaires, several squadrons of cavalry, six 75s and six 65-millimeter mountain guns outside the Bab Si Bou Jida. If Lyautey had received intelligence that el Hajjami had set his own *harka* in motion on that morning, he does not mention it. At 5 a.m., Gouraud's force moved off along the foot of the Djebel Zalagh in a north-easterly direction toward the Berber camp. As they topped a rise and gazed over the plain of the Sebou, the French saw advancing toward them in the early summer sun almost fifteen thousand men massed under the green banners of Islam. Gouraud knew exactly what to do: he aligned his twelve guns on the crest of the ridge, waited until the Moroccans shouting their war cries came within range, and blasted them into singed gobbets of humanity. The Moroccan mass shattered like a ball of mercury under pressure; some fled to the rear, others hunkered down behind what meager cover they could find on the plain, still more moved by the flanks to the cover of other hillocks. These were cleared with coordinated advances of infantry and artillery. Gouraud then formed his infantry in a two-and-a-half-mile front, cavalry on the flanks and artillery to the rear, and marched methodically toward the camp. Against this sort of machine precision, the Moroccans could not stand. A few resisted on the last ridge before their camp and inflicted a handful of casualties on their attackers, among them the Englishman William Redman, who had been incorporated into the French military mission. El Hajjami's camp was a mass of confusion, made worse by the steady pounding of the artillery. Here and there where a chief attempted to rally a few men around him, a well-placed shower of steel balls ended all resistance. The camp was burned. Gouraud bivouacked for the night on high ground a little to the south, and on the morning of June 2 marched back to Fez to an enthusiastic reception from Lyautey. Even the Sultan came to review the troops, who were marched through Fez Djedid to erase the memory of a similar procession of dead French soldiers. Five days later, Gouraud received his second star of brigadier. For the next two months, Lyautey employed him to smash other pockets of tribal resistance in the north, for the resident general himself was preoccupied with another serious threat in Marrakech.

CHAPTER XIX

MARRAKECH

Challenges to the sharifian throne traditionally came from beyond the Atlas. Great tribal movements which welled up in the Tafilalet had swept away dynasties in the course of Moroccan history. Viewed in this light, the challenge posed by a new pretender, el Hiba, appeared full of promise. Indeed, the French feared that Morocco might have at last produced the Mahdi who would unite the fragmentary resistance into one unified national movement. Tall, bearded, swathed in the blue cloth of the Sahara nomads, el Hiba's credentials as a resistance leader were impeccable. His father, Ma el Ainin, had achieved legendary status among his people for his opposition to the French in Mauritania. When Ma el Ainin died in October 1910, el Hiba had succeeded to his father's *baraka*. As rumors of the Fez mutinies were digested and inflated in Morocco, feeling grew that it was once again the duty of the people of the trans-Atlas to purify the Dar el Islam—to expel corrupt caids, annul taxes not sanctioned by the Koran and drive out the infidel. Few of the men who streamed out of the desert to proclaim el Hiba sultan at Tiznit in the summer of 1912 had ever seen a European. They certainly did not possess the remotest notion of modern firepower; ivory-encrusted muskets made up the bulk of their weaponry. They trusted to the sanctity of their cause and the *baraka* of their chief.

By July 1912, Lyautey may well have regretted ever having accepted his Moroccan posting. The situation he had been bequeathed by Regnault and Monier can only be described as a shambles. The north was in an uproar. This occupied most of his troops. The disgrace of Madani el Glaoui had set off a chain reaction which had placed Marrakech in the hands of men unfavorable to the French: el Mtouggi and his creature Driss Mennou, the new pasha of Marrakech who had supplanted the deposed Thami el Glaoui, the brother of Madani. The three great Atlas lords—Glaoui, Mtouggi and Goundafi—were at daggers drawn. Unless they could be persuaded to pull together and support the French, el Hiba would spill over the passes of the High Atlas onto the plain of Marrakech. They must do it, for Lyautey certainly did not have the men to hold Marrakech against the new revolt. If el Hiba took Marrakech, he might infect the powerful, and nervous, Zaian confederation of the Middle Atlas. The Chaouia would then be brought under serious pressure by a unified resistance movement.

As if el Hiba and Marrakech were not enough to occupy the new resident general, the Sultan was uncooperative. Lyautey complained that Moulai Hafid had "gone on strike." It was rather more like a "go slow." Moulai Hafid had almost certainly decided to abdicate. By refusing to cooperate with his new masters—delaying the appointment of caids, the signing of correspondence, of agreeing to anything which might ease the task of the French—he hoped to show that, even as a figurehead, his cooperation was vital. In this way, he might strike a better bargain when the time came to turn in his umbrella. Lyautey even accused Moulai Hafid of encouraging el Hiba. The resident general offered no proof to substantiate his charge, but there is every reason to believe that it was well founded.

The second siege of Fez broken, Lyautey bundled Moulai Hafid off to Rabat and installed him in the royal palace there. Now began the hard bargaining between the Sultan, the Algerian Benghabrit and St.-Aulaire over the terms of abdication. It proved a long and trying task. The Sultan, at once "barbarous and refined," alternated between flights of rage and troughs of despair. St.-Aulaire's one nightmare was that Moulai Hafid would escape to the hills and assume the leadership of a *jihad*. This would expose the protectorate as an empty treaty and present the French with still more problems. To guard him, however, was impossible, as rumors would have quickly spread that Moulai Hafid was a prisoner. Thus, on many evenings Moulai Hafid crept from his palace into the town. St.-Aulaire could simply hold his breath and hope that the morning would find him again in residence. There were ways of keeping him at home. Knowing the Sultan's weakness for champagne, which he, declaring himself above koranic law, drank at every meal, St.-Aulaire proposed a comparative study of the different producers. Mealtimes now presented the spectacle of the Sultan and St.-Aulaire sitting cross-legged at a low table, shoveling couscous with their fingers and sipping from glasses of Veuve Clicquot, Taittinger, Moët et Chandon, and the rest, courtesy of the French navy.

The military review of Bastille Day, 1912, was of great symbolic importance to the French, as it would offer the first public acknowledgment by the Sultan of his new links with France, in the eyes both of his own people and of the world. St.-Aulaire's task was to persuade him to attend. Moulai Hafid was ironical: "I have never understood very well why France regards as the most glorious event in its history the storming by rebels of its principal casbah and the murder of the caid who commanded it. Was this not a defeat for your Sultan and his makhzan?" He agreed to attend, however, after St.-Aulaire added a verse to the "Marseillaise" praising the virtues of Moulai Hafid, which was duly sung by the soldiers on the reviewing stand. The Sultan admitted that he was much impressed by the French. But he remained puzzled as to why they had not married their greatest man, Napoleon, to their most eminent woman, Joan of Arc. Indeed they had, answered St.-Aulaire, and the fruit of that union was General Lyautey.

Negotiations over the abdication were extremely delicate. In the first place, the Quai d'Orsay and the resident general disagreed over this issue, as on hundreds of others. Long telegrams poured out of Paris which Lyautey simply ignored. Moulai Hafid must go—about this there could be no argument. It was the manner of his going that was important. If he abdicated suddenly, as he threatened to do almost daily, each time negotiations hit a snag, it might provoke an adverse reaction both in Morocco and abroad. Who would replace him? Abd el-Aziz was too compromised in the eyes of his own people and, Lyautey believed, too attached to the English to bring out of retirement and replace on the throne. Of the other princes of the blood, no one who would prove suitably docile was immediately obvious. Moulai Hafid wanted to abdicate in favor of his four-year-old son. This was clearly unacceptable. The transfer of power must be smooth.

The second question was what to do with Moulai Hafid once he had abdicated. He had chosen Tangiers as his place of retirement. But St.-Aulaire feared that he might escape from their control in that international city. A pilgrimage to Mecca was proposed. That, said St.-Aulaire, would simply strengthen his *baraka*. The only place was France. Benghabrit described the pleasures of Paris in glowing terms. The Sultan succumbed. "But," he added, "I shall go as sultan while a caliph represents me here in my absence." The prospect of the mischief which Moulai Hafid might cause as the reigning sultan among the opposition deputies and anticolonialist press was too great to contemplate. He had quickly learned through reading daily translations of *Le Temps* and *Le Matin* that his most powerful allies were to be found in Paris: "Why does your president of the republic not give Monsieur Jaurès the bastinado?" he asked St.-Aulaire.

Most of the negotiations, however, were taken up by tedious arguments over money and property, and here the bald acquisitiveness of Moulai Hafid reached megalomanic proportions. In general, he adopted the view that any property was his to dispose of as he wished as absolute monarch while any outstanding debts were the responsibility of the state. He defended this principle with great tenacity and ability, "and had a classical Arabic quotation at hand—often most skillfully misquoted—to prove his every argument." The imperial palaces were stripped of their furniture, their mosaics and even an Italian marble staircase which was sent to decorate the new residence Moulai Hafid had ordered constructed for himself in Tangiers. However, he refused to accept responsibility for bills, even for the most trivial sums spent on the most frivolous items. These negotiations were prolonged; they were often conducted in the palace gardens with the Sultan seated on a mattress attended by his old black nurse and a white Berber woman who was his soothsayer. Moulai Hafid's attention would often be diverted by "his elephant, or his llamas or a group of cranes that would come wandering out of the shrubberies."

On July 30, Lyautey arrived in Rabat from Fez with a plan to break the deadlock. His choice as successor to Moulai Hafid was Moulai Yousef, the Sultan's brother and the pasha of Fez. Moulai Hafid would abdicate in his brother's favor and, after a brief stay in France, would be allowed to settle in Tangiers with a pension of fifteen thousand pounds ($75,000) per year. If the Sultan demurred, the resident general let it be known that while in Fez he had gathered enough sworn evidence of Moulai Hafid's misconduct—in particular, that he had pocketed the salaries of his officials—to blacken his name. Did this frighten the Sultan? It is unlikely. The Sultan could not steal because everything belonged to him—any Moroccan could have told Lyautey that. What might have worried Moulai Hafid more than Lyautey's naïve attempt at "counter-blackmail" was his threat to cut off Moulai Hafid's funds. After another ten days of haggling, the Sultan agreed to abdicate and sail for France upon Lyautey's promise of a check for one million francs to pay for his pleasures in Paris. However, when August 11, the day appointed for his departure, arrived, the Sultan declared that the sea was far too rough. The bar at the mouth of the Bou Regreg was impassable. The following day, he made the same observation, although the sea was calm. Lyautey contemplated using force to transport Moulai Hafid to the *Du Chayla* which swung at anchor beyond the bar. The situation at Marrakech had deteriorated drastically, and he really had little time to waste with this fickle despot. But he needed the letters of abdication. These were the only things which would bestow legitimacy upon Moulai Yousef, the only documents that the *ulama* would recognize. Lyautey became nervous, irritable, paced the floor of his office and barked at his staff. At two o'clock in the afternoon, a messenger arrived, out of breath, with a note from Major Henri Simon of the intelligence service: "The Sultan is going toward the harbor."

Lyautey and St.-Aulaire found Moulai Hafid already at the quai by the Bou Regreg. He chatted calmly with the two Frenchmen as caravans bearing his wives, concubines, servants, secretaries and black guards arrived and were loaded into the boats and rowed over the bar by fierce-looking boatmen dressed in turbans, embroidered waistcoats and balloon trousers. What happened next is disputed. Several accounts hold that Moulai Hafid handed Lyautey the letters of abdication, took out his umbrella of authority and broke it over his knee before embarking. More plausible is the account of St.-Aulaire, which has Lyautey and Moulai Hafid playing cat-and-mouse, one with his check, the other with his letters of abdication, until, in the confusion caused when a wave hit the rowboat, the treasures were exchanged.

The ex-Sultan arrived on board the *Du Chayla* in an advanced state of seasickness. The captain, an old sea dog who was a trifle perplexed by the exotic fauna now crowded onto the decks of his ship, pointed a finger at Moulai Hafid, laid out like a rag on a mattress: "What do I do with that one," he asked, "fling him into the sea or give him champagne?" St.-Aulaire suggested the second alternative. Moulai Hafid sailed off to France and, temporarily, out of Moroccan politics.

The steady advance of the new resistance leader el Hiba in the south had preoccupied Lyautey even before he had departed from Paris in May 1912. And well it might. The erect figure of el Hiba, only his eyes visible from behind his veil of blue cloth, surrounded by an equally imposing retinue of thirty blue-clad bodyguards, all his brothers, rode from casbah to casbah in the Sus sweeping up warriors into what was to become a *harka* twelve thousand strong. He also dragged behind him eight ancient Portuguese cannon pried from the walls of Tiznit. Lyautey placed his faith in the three great caids to hold the High Atlas against el Hiba. Major Verlet-Hanus, one of Lyautey's most talented intelligence officers, was dispatched to Marrakech to strengthen the resolve of the Atlas lords and of Driss Mennou, the pasha of Marrakech. Dr. Weisgerber visited Si Assa Ben Oman, the caid of the Abda, to enlist his support. What the two men discovered offered little comfort. A serious feud was brewing between the disgraced Glaoui clan and the Mtouggis. So far, the conflict had been confined to the kidnapping of young boys from each clan's extensive male harems and to the random murder of their tribal followers. But it offered a sad pointer to the future of the *politique des grands caids* which Lyautey hoped to construct. Besides (and this was made clear to both Frenchmen), el Hiba did not represent a localized tribal rebellion like that which the French had defeated at Fez. It was a revolution, and the caids were powerless to halt it.

What could Lyautey do? St.-Aulaire suggested that he seize Marrakech. Lyautey rejected this advice. In the first place, he had strict orders to confine operations to the Chaouia. This in itself presented no great obstacle to a march on Marrakech. Lyautey had long since learned to be contemptuous of Paris' appreciation of Moroccan affairs. He was quite prepared to indulge in a little "patriotic indiscipline." But he was desperately short of manpower and was too proud to go, kepi in hand, to the war minister and ask for more troops. However, Lyautey did possess one trump card: Colonel Charles Mangin.

On the surface, Mangin appeared the complete antithesis of Lyautey. While the resident general was slightly built, nervous and possessed a quick, lively intelligence, Mangin's heavy face and thick, barrel-like body gave him a dull, brutish appearance. This was deceptive—Mangin did not lack intelligence—but a keen ambition combined with a career spent campaigning in the harsh conditions of Africa south of the Sahara had made him insensitive, even callous; it was no accident that the men who were to serve under Mangin on the Western Front nicknamed him "the Butcher." By the time he arrived in Morocco in 1912, Mangin was already a name to be reckoned with in colonial army circles. Like Lyautey, he made a virtue of indiscipline; indeed, he had spent the greater part of his two years at St.-Cyr confined to barracks. Upon graduation (near the bottom of his class) in 1888, Mangin had joined the colonial army. There, he found greater scope for his energies. The Western Sudan was a brutal school of war, and Mangin, at the head of his beloved Senegalese, was involved in many of the campaigns of conquest. He was even reprimanded as a lieutenant for distributing young girls captured during a raid to his troops as "free wives." In 1896, he had joined Marchand's epic tramp across Africa to Fashoda and the historic confrontation with Kitchener on the Nile. Like Lyautey, he was well connected in colonialist circles in France. In 1910, he had attracted attention with the publication of his book, *La Force noire*, in which he called for the massive conscription of black troops to bolster France's flagging manpower reserves. His pleas went unheeded until 1917. In that year, Prime Minister Clemenceau, faced with the French army mutinies (caused in part by Mangin's wasteful offensives) and the possible collapse of the Western Front, called for the mobilization of the vast human resources of France's colonial empire. By 1918, almost one million blacks and Arabs were occupied in defending France, either in the front lines or in the war factories. Mangin claimed later that this number could have been quadrupled had he been taken seriously in 1910.

That Mangin's pleas fell on deaf ears in Paris was partially Lyautey's doing. The resident general, like most other French generals, found the Senegalese the most interesting troops in an army in which exotica were the rule: the tirailleurs were followed by a swarm of "free wives," known collectively as Madame Sénégal. Each black woman was wrapped in a single piece of brightly colored cloth, carried the obligatory iron cooking pot and, in many cases, a small child on her hip as well. The Senegalese bivouac was always the most popular in any French camp and attracted large numbers of curious Moroccans. As a spectacle, the *tirailleurs sénégalais* were splendid. As a fighting force, however, Lyautey thought them "an enormous bluff . . . recruited in haste, malingerers, without cohesion or stamina." This was not mere racism. The blacks, like the Algerians, were recruited increasingly by dubious methods—chicanery, fraud or simply a case of chiefs and caids sending into the army men unable to bribe their way out. It must also be remembered that Lyautey was scarcely more complimentary about the foreign legion; for him, they were little more than a band of German desperadoes—"People speak of sixty thousand men in Morocco," he complained, "forgetting that I have only twelve thousand Frenchmen."

Mangin was told to patrol the frontiers of the Chaouia accompanied by influential members of the royal family in an attempt to isolate southern tribes like the Doukalla, the Rehamna or the Zaian confederation from the popular enthusiasm for el Hiba. On August 12, Moulai Hafid abdicated. The negotiations, Lyautey believed, had been prolonged intentionally to allow el Hiba to seize Marrakech while the sharifian throne was vacant. On August 15, the pretender crossed the Ameskroud pass over the High Atlas with the blessing of Mtouggi, who controlled it. His camel-mounted warriors entered Marrakech on the eighteenth.

Most of the Europeans in Marrakech had left for Safi on the eleventh. A small group of six French soldiers and diplomats, however, had remained behind in the hope of effecting a last-minute reconciliation among the great caids that would prevent Marrakech from falling to el Hiba. By the evening of the 14th, it was obvious that this was impossible. They made preparations to escape north but had traveled nine miles when they were ambushed by a party of Rehamna tribesmen who forced them to return to Marrakech and place themselves under the protection of Thami el Glaoui.

The situation in which the notables of Marrakech now found themselves was unenviable. To the north, the threat of French intervention hung over them like the sword of Damocles. Few who had bothered to consider the future of Morocco could have doubted that the French were now far too deeply committed to allow Morocco to slip away from them. On the other hand, the movement that el Hiba had touched off was too powerful to resist in the short term. Consequently, they all maneuvered for position, slipping into that equivocal posture which would make responsibility so difficult to assign when events came to be analyzed. El Hiba, el Mtouggi, Driss Mennou and Thami el Glaoui negotiated for possession of the Frenchmen. Lyautey even contacted Thami el Glaoui through a Marrakech Jew named Joshua Corcos in an unsuccessful bid to ransom the captives. Finally, on August 23, Thami el Glaoui handed five of the Frenchmen to el Hiba. A sixth, a Sergeant Fiori, the brother of an influential Algerian deputy, he concealed in his house and permitted to maintain contact with Colonel Mangin. It was the best possible compromise: Glaoui kept a foot in the French camp while el Hiba now held the hostages who he believed would convince Lyautey to call off his campaign.

In this, el Hiba had miscalculated. If Lyautey hesitated to unleash Mangin, it was only because he wanted to build up his forces to a respectable level before marching on Marrakech. Also, he felt that the political ground had not been prepared, either in Paris or in the south. A small *harka* under one of el Hiba's brothers was sent against Mangin in mid-August. The colonel surprised the desert men in their camp and inflicted moderate losses. The Moroccans repaid the compliment two days later with a largely ineffectual attack on Mangin's bivouac. Mangin then took the offensive and broke the *harka*. He begged Lyautey for permission to march on Marrakech. But for the moment, Lyautey held his headstrong subordinate in check.

It is probable, as St.-Aulaire suggests, that Lyautey's eventual decision to seize Marrakech was prompted by a wire from the War Ministry strictly forbidding him to do so: "I put the telegram in my back pocket and I sit on it," Lyautey said, doing just that. "I shall only receive it in a few hours' time after I have sent another wire to Mangin." There was little to gain by further delay. Even if the French withdrew to the Chaouia, he had no guarantee that el Hiba would release the hostages. A retreat would simply encourage other tribes to join forces with him in the face of apparent French weakness. Lyautey also knew that el Hiba's position in Marrakech was crumbling. The blue men had outstayed their welcome. Few of them were housebroken, and their wild desert ways outraged even a town that was very close to the life of nomadic pastoralists. Shopkeepers were forced to accept their debased Saharian money. Government officials were forbidden to collect any taxes that were not sanctioned by the Koran. The caids were frightened that el Hiba might undermine their influence in Marrakech. The final straw came when el Hiba, no doubt under pressure from his followers, ordered all unmarried girls in Marrakech to be wedded to his men. Lyautey's wire of September 4 to Mangin read simply: *"Allez-y carrément"*—"Go ahead!"

Mangin's five thousand troops, divided into a "fighting square" and a convoy square of 1,500 mules and 2,000 camels, broke camp at three o'clock on the morning of September 5 and marched south all day under a torrid sun. The few wells along the route of march were quickly drunk dry, and the troops suffered horribly from thirst. At 2 a.m. on September 6, Mangin's force resumed its march. At first light, the colonel distributed water to his men before continuing to Sidi Bou Othmann. There is nothing special about Sidi Bou Othmann; it is a dark, flat plain entirely denuded of vegetation. But on the morning of September 6, it was crowded with el Hiba's *harka*, between ten and fifteen thousand men, some mounted, others on foot, milling beneath their banners along a front of two and a half miles.

The Moroccans must have thought Mangin mad. There before them was a small square, half a mile long on each face, which contained no more than a third of their number, marching resolutely toward them. They would surely be swallowed whole by the Moroccan mass. The Moroccans rushed at their quarry and, for what seemed an interminably long time, the two lines closed on each other in silence. Mangin admired the restraint of his enemy. His soldiers were tense. When, at last, the Moroccans opened fire at 1,600 yards, a sense of relief ran through the French square. Mangin waited. When el Hiba's men were about half a mile distant, he opened up with the full force of his twelve 75s, eight machine guns and 1,200 Gras rifles. The effect was catastrophic. The Moroccans, many of whom were armed only with sticks and stones, reeled but, incredibly, kept their cohesion. Their line folded like a crescent around the now-halted French square. Mangin redistributed his artillery, and the carnage continued. The 75s tore bloody gaps in the Moroccan lines while el Hiba's antique guns, served by a Spanish renegade, fired too high or else drove their shells into the parched earth without exploding. By nine o'clock, the Moroccans had had enough. They crawled away, leaving two thousand dead on the plain and thousands more wounded in what was the worst single defeat suffered in the history of the conquest. Mangin sent his four hundred horse toward el Hiba's camp, virtually deserted as the remnants of his army fell back on Marrakech. Mangin counted two dead and twenty-three wounded.

El Hiba had been smashed. Few would now believe in his *baraka*. As his beaten *harka* streamed out of Marrakech toward the south, the inhabitants set their dogs on them. But the fate of the hostages still hung in the balance. It was impossible for Mangin's army to continue: his troops had marched forty-seven miles and fought a major battle all in the space of thirty hours. They were desperately short of water. He sent a message ahead threatening to raze Marrakech to the ground if "a hair on the head of our compatriots" was harmed. He then set about assembling a light column of *goumiers*, spahis and a section of 75s under the command of Major Henri Simon for a dash to Marrakech. It was a dangerous mission. If el Hiba's men rallied, or if Marrakech proved hostile, this force could easily be surrounded or made to retreat. Possibly the Moroccans, seeing the French arrive in such feeble strength, might slaughter the hostages.

The light column set out around midday along a route well marked by the paraphernalia of a routed *harka*—abandoned tents, disemboweled sacks of wheat and dead horses. Before them in the distance the small finger of the Koutoubia minaret poked from a blue-green lake of date palms. The light column advanced rapidly, but each man was nervous; every rock, every hillock might conceal an ambush. A few weak attempts to halt the column were brushed aside by the 75s. One heavily defended hill, however, had to be bypassed, leaving a large group of Moroccans lying across their line of retreat. Then the vital artillery caisson shattered a wheel. The 75 shells were distributed among the horsemen and the column continued. At eight o'clock in the evening, they arrived at the fringe of the palm grove. Men and animals threw themselves into the muddy Wadi Tensif and drank until they nearly burst.

Major Simon's plan was to storm the royal palace, where the hostages were imprisoned, but it was clearly too late to attempt that. He ordered his men to form a square and they settled in for a very uncomfortable night. As they carried no baggage, they had neither rations nor blankets to protect them against the surprisingly cold night. Major Simon had also to decipher the conflicting messages that he received from Marrakech. He was an experienced native-affairs man, but the intrigue set off among the caids in Marrakech by the French victory was so complicated that even those most involved must have been taxed to understand exactly what was happening. At first light, as instructed by a messenger from Driss Mennou, Simon fired two shells from his 75. He then followed the wadi around the difficult and ambush-infested palm grove toward the Bab Doukkala. The artillery and the rough ground slowed the pace. The French also acquired an escort of several hundred horsemen who followed at a respectful distance but whose intentions were not entirely clear. Soon, evidence of a town began to appear— walls encircling irrigated gardens, fig, orange and olive trees, and fields of mint which gave off an exquisite perfume. They also heard gunfire coming from the direction of the town, evidence of a struggle between the partisans of Glaoui and those of el Hiba. Simon fired two more shells to encourage the Glaoui men. The sound of the firing ceased as the French column came under the city walls. Above them, the parapets were bristling with armed men. Who had won? Were these men friend or foe?

As Simon's men hesitated, a group advanced toward them. At their head was Algerian Lieutenant Kouadi, one of the hostages, who carried a letter from Major Verlet-Hanus informing them that the French hostages were safe. The two shells fired by Simon's 75 at first light had been the signal for the Glaoui men to seize the prison where the hostages were held and defend it against el Hiba. The light column galloped through the town toward the Glaoui palace. Most of the men they encountered in the streets were armed, but chose to flatten themselves against the walls rather than resist the impetuous ride of the rescue party. At the Dar Glaoui, Simon discovered the consul Maigret in the process of shaving off his three-week-old beard.

At two o'clock in the afternoon, Mangin's column arrived. They filed beneath the walls in a cloud of dust to their campsite in the gardens northeast of the town. Some of the officers ventured into Marrakech for a closer look at the capital of the south. What they saw disappointed them. Marrakech appeared to be in ruins; the deserted streets were choked with piles of rubbish and dead animals. At some of the larger intersections squatted groups of Moroccans who observed the French in silence. Only in the mellah did the conquerors receive an enthusiastic welcome: "Thousands of these unfortunates crowded onto the terraces or along the tops of the walls to shout hurrahs and ululations."

On October 1, the dun-colored staff car of the resident general, a machine gun mounted on the hood, bounced into Marrakech, the first automobile ever seen in the Haouz. Lyautey was preceded by a thousand horsemen carrying red-and-white banners. He climbed down to inspect a guard of honor of five hundred hastily recruited Moroccan police dressed in pink breeches, gold jackets and turbans who presented arms in a variety of grotesque positions while a Moroccan band played some excruciating military music. The resident general certainly knew how to make an entrance. The weather was delightful and the snow-capped peaks of the Atlas stood out majestically against the deep-blue sky. But the purpose of Lyautey's visit was not mere ceremony, as much as he reveled in it. As he stood on the terrace of the Dar Makhzan with the Glaouis, Mtouggi and Goundafi watching the monotonous fantasia beneath, he explained that he was prepared to forget their equivocal conduct over the hostages in return for a pledge of cooperation. Lyautey needed their support as much as they needed his goodwill. He simply did not have the troops to spare for the south. His plan was to rely on the Atlas lords to hold the Haouz and the High Atlas while he secured the Middle Atlas and opened the Taza corridor. Lyautey had elected to sacrifice principle to expediency, although he tried to convince himself of the opposite. It would simply require playing "native politics" on a grand scale and for considerably higher stakes, setting one caid against the others, not becoming indebted, keeping the three families on relatively equal terms, "always restraining their appetites to safeguard the population." In this sort of double game, however, the caids would teach the resident general a trick or two. Their obscure quarrels and political maneuvers proved incomprehensible and impenetrable to the straitlaced soldier from Lorraine. Gradually, Thami el Glaoui would vanquish his two rivals and carve out a position of power in the protectorate second only to that of the Sultan himself.

As the dust thrown up by the lines of horsemen dried their throats, the caids agreed to cooperate. Thami el Glaoui was reinstated as pasha of Marrakech and the *politique des grands caids* was launched, a policy which more than any other would serve to bring the protectorate into disrepute and soil Lyautey's reputation as a colonial administrator. Before leaving Marrakech, however, Lyautey gave his blessing to the other side of the colonial coin— Marrakech's new French colony. His attitude toward colonists was ambivalent. In principle, he would like to keep them out. And no wonder. Perhaps he was conscious of the irony as he lifted a glass of champagne to the "ordinary avant-garde of civilization" which crowded before him, a collection of prostitutes, sellers of alcohol and other low camp followers who had crawled to Marrakech in the wake of the victorious French army. The French protectorate in Morocco had been baptized in blood and champagne.

CHAPTER XX

THE ZAER

For some weeks now the intelligence officer at Camp Marchand had done little but listen to the buzzing of flies or look out onto the empty pink plateau which stretched away eastward, a mass of hillocks and folds, to the jagged peaks of the Middle Atlas beyond. Camp Marchand stood like a tatty sentinel on a piece of high ground between two wadis, now bone-dry in the baking heat of July 1912, where the Chaouia meets the land of the Zaer. For the past four months, morale in the collection of rotten tents and straw-roofed hovels had stood at rock bottom. To the north, the events of Fez and the "cleanup" operations of Gouraud, Brulard and Dalbiez had caused not even the tremor of a night attack on Camp Marchand by the dissident Zaer. To the south, the "terrible" Colonel Mangin was obviously preparing a big push on Marrakech. The officers who had abandoned comfortable garrisons in Hanoi, Dakar or Oran for the prospect of a little action in Morocco felt cheated. Sheer bad luck had brought them to this slum of an outpost, this collection of "canvas rags, rat holes and fleas' nests."

But now the torpor of Camp Marchand appeared to be lifting. For the last few days, convoys of supplies escorted by battalions of Senegalese, Algerians, colonial marines and *joyeux* had climbed onto the plateau. The camp was now a hive of activity, as over two thousand troops massed for the conquest of the Zaer. This expedition was long overdue. For the French, it had taken on the atmosphere of a Christian *jihad*, a crusade launched to avenge the death of a Lieutenant Marchand, whose name lived on at the camp. The circumstances of Lieutenant Marchand's martyrdom two years earlier had been forgotten in the fog of indignation and moral fervor. According to one unofficial, but probably correct, version, in 1910 Marchand had led a police *goum* of ten Algerians in search of a Zaer named Wild Taika

---

Much of this chapter is based upon three articles published in 1913 in the *Revue des deux mondes* by a French officer, General Ibos, writing under the pseudonym of Pierre Khorat. Ibos never names the actual officers involved, referring to them simply by their rank or function. Lyautey was annoyed by the articles, which were critical of his "native politics."

who had escaped from French custody after shooting a man who, he claimed, had stolen his cattle. Wild Taika was followed to his douar in the unpacified Zaer country northeast of the Chaouia by Marchand's *goumiers*. When the Algerians failed to find Wild Taika, they began to molest his wife, whereupon the fugitive emerged from his hiding place in a neighboring tent, shot Marchand and two of his soldiers, and fled.

This was the origin of the Zaer column which was now gathering at Camp Marchand. For two years, Monier had bombarded Paris with requests to be allowed to avenge Marchand's death, only to have them refused. A less principled commander—Lyautey, for example—would have unleashed a *razzia* on the offending tribe, planted a few posts in Zaer country and quietly, effortlessly, stretched the circumference of French occupation. But Monier was a product of the old school who believed that orders from the government must be obeyed. Lyautey was burdened with no such outmoded notions. His reputation as a commander, like the French colonial empire itself, had been built upon the delicate use of the *fait accompli*, before which governments, as had so often been proven, were powerless to act.

The "pacification" of the Zaer had put the French intelligence officer back in business. Since the Fez mutinies the year before, the intelligence service had come in for a good deal of criticism. Its officers were Arab bureau men, trained in Algeria, who knew little of the Moroccan tribes. Since 1907, they had been employed principally in investigating claims made by Europeans and their protégés against Moroccans in the Chaouia. Consequently, when Monier set them to govern the Gharb, their lack of knowledge meant that they listened to the wrong people, made unwise appointments and antagonized nearly everyone. Lyautey, however, was a committed partisan of "native politics." The intelligence officer was the essential element in his "organization on the march."

The outer office of the native-affairs bureau, so long empty, now filled with Moroccans. Several of the faces were familiar to this student of local politics: there was Bou Amar, who wanted to become caid of his faction, who were now with the dissidents. Across the room from Bou Amar and staring at him blackly sat Caid Said who, according to rumors, had been rejected by his people after Bou Amar had encouraged them to side with the *siba*. There was Bou Haza, lately of the dissidence. A trip to Casablanca with its thousands of *roumi* had convinced him of the inevitability of a French victory, from which he hoped to profit. This view was shared by the one-eyed Moussa, who proudly answered to the nickname of Francis I, be-

stowed upon him by the officers of Camp Marchand because his profile resembled that of the monarch of the Field of the Cloth of Gold. Piratical instincts had drawn the majority of this crowd, who, one by one, expressed
the simple desire "to eat up the neighbor." No intelligence officer could make
good Europeans out of these men. But he could certainly make them bad
Arabs.

This was the raw material—caids without authority, men with ambitions
for power, traitors, spies, or those who offered their services to the French
out of a desire to avenge a dead brother or recoup a herd of sheep lost in a
razzia—from which the intelligence officer must construct a "native policy."
Upon whom would his choice fall? Said was obviously the most worthy man,
the one who embodied legitimacy and whom justice should reward. But in
this case the intelligence officer decided to place his money on Bou Amar.
He was in the business of realpolitik, not one in which favors were handed
out on the basis of sentiment or justice.

Bou Amar had promised to deliver a douar of a hundred souls, but in
the early dawn of the following morning, as the *joyeux*, Senegalese and
spahis assembled for the hunt, he appeared with only fifteen men, ragged,
dirty and of a distinctly unwarlike appearance. French suspicions deepened
when, after two hours of rapid marching, the small force reached the
appointed place of rendezvous with the douar which wished to abandon the
siba for the safety of the French camp. For miles around, the countryside was
empty. "You have lied to us, Bou Amar!" the intelligence officer shouted.
"Where are your partisans? Is it with these fifteen flea-ridden warriors that
you intend to force your douar to come with us?" The *joyeux*, who disliked
being disturbed at the best of times, were in a filthy mood and would surely
have lynched Bou Amar had there been a tree within thirty miles to throw a
rope over. Some of the officers began to fear a trap. But a force of 250 men,
two 65-millimeter guns and 20 spahis should be able to fight its way back to
camp with little difficulty. After more of Bou Amar's mumbled assurances,
the unit's commanding officer decided to forge ahead. They crossed another
six miles of parched highlands to a point of vantage where they might better
survey the vast emptiness of the countryside. Still there was nothing. The
intelligence officer called Bou Amar a liar. The commanding officer made
more concrete threats, to which the angry gesticulations of the *joyeux* added
credence. The Senegalese began to caress their amulets in expectation of an
attack. The gunners stood impassively by their mules, waiting for the order to
assemble their 65s. Reluctantly, the officers agreed to allow Bou Amar to go

in search of his douar. The column stacked their rifles, opened their tins of sardines and settled down for a long wait.

After several hours, the intelligence officer was awakened by the sound of distant firing. An artillery corporal rushed up to announce that a group of people, preceded by their herds, was approaching. The officers climbed to the rocky point where the two 65s stood guard. There, they could see the mass of people and animals—men on horseback followed by their wives, children, sheep, camels and donkeys swaying beneath impossible burdens— flowing toward them like a river. Bou Amar had succeeded in separating his douar from the dissidents. One hundred and thirty tents brought in without a shot fired. Even the *joyeux* appeared reconciled at this victory. Bou Amar, only yesterday an obscure intriguer, would have his caidship.

The intelligence officer of the force would also have his reward—chief intelligence officer in the 1,500-strong Zaer column and, afterward, a post in the newly subdued territory. The Zaer column itself proved to be a walkover. The tribes could never assemble more than five hundred rifles at any one moment, so that after desultory fighting on the first night around the French camp, the column settled into a leisurely military promenade. Douar after douar offered a young bull for slaughter as a prelude to the request for the *aman*, the formal symbol of submission, and piled an ancient assortment of weapons at the feet of the colonel (the more modern models were secreted away). Intimidation was the easy part. The occupation must be made to stick.

The intelligence officer became the power broker of the new order. Each time he emerged from his tent, he was besieged by the swarm of hopefuls who followed in the wake of the column, many of them the same men who had sat in his office at Camp Marchand: "Don't forget that Sheik Mohammed, of the Ouled Moussa, stole thirty of my sheep last year!" "Remember you promised to make me caid of the Ouled Daho, in the place of that old rogue Hammani!" and so on. A dishonest man could become rich in this job. An honest man must try to unravel their disputes, distinguish legitimate complaints from attempts to settle old scores, reward the right men. It was an impossible task. He could give a dazzling demonstration of French power. Justice was far more a case of hit or miss.

The combat officers regarded their colleague with mixed feelings. The marines disapproved of him. They preferred the more exciting methods practiced south of the Sahara. Others argued that times had changed. The worsening situation in Europe had created a vocal group of deputies, not all of them left-wing, who argued that it was folly for France to commit large numbers of troops in Morocco when the real threat lay on the Rhine. "Public opinion will not tolerate murderous battles here," they said. "The last two fights cost us twenty dead and fifty wounded, and half of these were French. It will take only a few more fights like that to make Morocco as unpopular as Tonkin and Madagascar." Here was the essential truth: "native politics," what today we would call "hearts and minds," had been developed *not* because it had proved its worth as a military doctrine, but because it made colonial conquests more acceptable to public opinion at home. Big battles with heavy losses perhaps made dramatic reading and earned promotions for ambitious commanders and decorations for their subordinates. But they also drew fire from the substantial body of "dissidents" in the Palais Bourbon. Lyautey realized this and ordered that battles must be avoided.

"Native politics" in the final analysis boiled down to an appeal to the naked self-interest of those prepared to attach themselves to the French cause, and to blatant economic warfare. Make yourself master of the fields and pastures, ferret out the hidden silos in which the Moroccans store their grain, and the tribes will submit. This was the sort of expedition in which the intelligence officer specialized. A spy arrived with the promise to locate the silos of the dissidents. Two companies of infantry and a machine-gun section were soon on the march followed by a horde of *goumiers* and their families—old men, children and women—fired with the holy task of "eating up the neighbor." They arrived at a hillside, indistinguishable from any other hillside, covered with low dwarf palms. The intelligence officer deployed his two companies to keep the disgruntled owners of the silos who, even now, could be seen gathering on the horizon, at arm's length.

At a signal, the Arabs settled among the scrub like a flock of starlings and began to prod the earth with their knives. After a few minutes, one of them let out a whoop, the announcement that he had discovered the chimney of a grain silo. Some of his friends moved over to help him. Clods of earth were pushed aside by agile fingers until, at the bottom of a hole three feet deep, a thick mattress of rotten straw was revealed. The sweating figures rested a few moments and, with a look of anxiety, began to remove the straw. "Wheat or barley?" asked the intelligence officer. The nauseating odor that rose from the excavation told its own story: "Barley! Barley!" the Arab cried, delighted, as he knew that a supply of wheat had recently arrived in the camp from Casablanca. "It belongs to you," the intelligence officer said. "Take it to the administration lieutenant and he will pay you for it"—at a price, he might have added, far above the market rate, an extra incentive to join with the invaders and a way to collapse the markets of the dissidents.

The first silo uncovered, the remainder revealed their hiding places in quick succession. The intelligence officer spent the next hour or so arbitrating the inevitable disputes over ownership. But the timid attacks of the owners of the silos, while never serious, had obviously cooled the ardor of the diggers. *"C'est fini!"* they insisted, and the intelligence officer led these "rabbits" back to the camp in disgust. One could not expect courage from *goumiers*. All one could hope was that the profits which they made by selling grain and wood to the French camp would excite enough envy among the dissidents to draw them within the orbit of French influence.

It worked with some. Small groups of Moroccans began to arrive, on foot and without arms, to ask for the *aman*. "We are the children of the government and the colonel is for us a father," their spokesman explained, before severing the front legs of a young bull and leaving it to bleed to death at the feet of the French officer. Then, when the moment was judged opportune, he added: "Because the colonel is just and merciful, will he deliver us from our caid! He has a big stomach and it is because of him that we are dissidents." An argument erupted as the caid defended himself by heaping abuse upon his former charges. The colonel decided in favor of the caid. The argument vanished in a feast of couscous, in which partisans and dissidents complimented each other on their bravery in battle like actors playing out their roles, and reconciled their differences—if indeed, out of sight of the French, they had ever had any differences. For French officers, such events were a revelation. As many dissident douars took care to place one or two of their sons in the *goumiers* as an insurance against surprise, the reconciliations took on the air of a family reunion—which, in a real sense, they were. Many of the French officers now began to understand why the *goumiers* often fought with so little enthusiasm or why, in the heat of a melee, the bullets that zipped over their heads seemed sometimes to come from the direction of their own partisans. At least one well-known intelligence officer had perished at the hands of his own *goumiers*. In any case, the image of the conquest which Lyautey peddled at home—namely, that France did not conquer Morocco, but merely turned the natural hostility of the tribes against their neighbors—was an oversimplification. Many of the douars which asked for the *aman* were simply the other half of a family which had already submitted. Even when real hostility existed between two tribal groups, armed partisans could not be counted upon to do anything but waste great quantities of bullets and *razzia* a few women and sheep.

The French tactic when subduing a territory was to settle the douars in the shadow of their post and disperse them once the territory had been brought under their control. On occasion, douars might be persuaded to come in, as was the case with Bou Amar, if for no other reason than to be able to extort vast sums of money from the garrison for eggs, chickens and goats. The majority, however, submitted only when confronted with a *force majeure*. The difficulty for the intelligence officer was to locate the transient pastoralists. If he sent out small patrols, they might easily be ambushed. Partisans were unreliable for reconnaissance either because they were reluctant to divulge the locations of douars in which they had relations or because, as notorious cowards, they refused to venture too far from the security of the French posts. A "reconnaissance in strength" by French forces would be quickly detected and the douars might simply move to avoid it.

In the final analysis, the intelligence officer had to rely principally upon informers. In a textbook operation, the informer would locate a douar within a night's brisk march from the post, a maximum of around twelve miles. When dawn broke, the nomads would find themselves under the guns of a battalion of infantry and a section of artillery, with *goumiers* and spahis blocking their line of retreat. If the elders refused to parley with the French and attempted to flee, then a few aerial bursts from the French guns would bring them to their senses.

But how many things could go wrong! Informers were usually unreliable, drawn principally from among men who held a grudge against their faction for some injustice, real or imagined. Their absence was often a signal to the douar to shift its location, so leaving many French expeditions to wander aimlessly over the *bled*. Or, as often happened, the French arrived well after daylight, having become lost in the dark, mapless terrain, giving the douar time to make its escape.

One may wonder also how many times a weak commander, or a marine officer educated in the Western Sudan, simply allowed his men to raid the douar rather than bring it in intact. Statistics obviously do not exist, but it is probably safe to suppose that the *razzia* was the preferred method of subduing a territory. The more farsighted officers opposed the *razzia*, not because it alienated the very people whom the French hoped to win over, but because discipline disintegrated in the looting spree that followed. It also became very difficult to herd the sheep and goats which made up the principal part of the booty back to the camp, especially if one was harassed by tribesmen. Captain Charles Kuntz's legionnaires overcame their lack of expertise as herdsmen by perfecting a very passable imitation of bleating sheep which kept their four-footed charges together.

"Native politics" became the official dogma of the Moroccan conquest. It developed *not* because it had met with any real success on the ground, but because it projected a better image of the conquest in Paris. Most of Lyautey's subordinates acknowledged that their chief's new methods were simply a sham. That is one reason why he was an unpopular commander. It was also the reason why he had so many discipline problems with commanders who burned to distinguish themselves in battle and, in the process, attracted the hostile attentions of the Paris press and of Jean Jaurès. Of no one was this more true than of Charles Mangin.

CHAPTER XXI

CONSOLIDATION AND DEFEAT

Charles Mangin's victory at Sidi Bou Othmann made him the toast of Morocco. In the messes, officers debated whether the conquest would be an affair of weeks or months. Then, the resident general slammed on the brakes.

Lyautey was not terribly confident in the autumn of 1912. There were now two Moroccos, he wrote, "one which we occupy" and the other, "much more important, constituted by the Berber masses, profoundly shaken, fanatical, warlike." The coast was relatively secure, from Kenitra in the north to Safi in the south. Essaouira was occupied by French troops. But in the hinterland behind the town, the powerful caids of Anflous and Guelloui had "defected" and gone over to the *siba*. Marrakech was, in the bureaucratic jargon, under the "indirect" rule of the great caids of the Atlas. In the north, the narrow corridor which tied Meknes and Fez with the coast was vulnerable to rumblings among the Rif tribesmen to the north and the restive Beni M'tir and the only partially pacified Zaer to the south. The spur of unpacified territory to the west of the Middle Atlas around Khenifra was a particular worry. This was the land of the Zaian confederation, reputed to be the most redoubtable warriors in a country of redoubtable warriors. 1913, Lyautey decided, would be the year in which the new protectorate would be consolidated as a prelude to extending it. There was much to do: organize a civil administration, design and make a start on the construction of a new capital at Rabat, build roads and extend the railway. The tribes must be given time to accept their new sultan, Moulai Yousef. Lyautey ordered the suspension of new military conquests.

The resident general's directives were greeted with disbelief, then with anger, by his command. They were astounded that he would halt a conquest in full flood. Lyautey had reckoned without the recklessness of Mangin and the spirit, found especially in the marines, which he typified. Lyautey, the *enfant terrible* of the South Oranais, who for years had provoked his superiors to the extreme limits of patience, had now to face a sullen mutiny within his own ranks.

Lyautey's differences with Charles Mangin began with the occupation of Marrakech. When Colonel Gouraud had broken the second siege of Fez, Lyautey rewarded him with a promotion to brigadier general and the command of the Fez region. Mangin, by contrast, was judged too "impulsive" and "undisciplined" for an independent command. Left alone in Marrakech, he would have pursued el Hiba over the Atlas into the Sus. Lyautey had assigned the pursuit of el Hiba to Thami el Glaoui because he wanted to clear Marrakech of the armed thugs in the pay of the great caids. Glaoui was given two Krupp 77s, two French 75s and sent to drive el Hiba back into the desert. Keeping his options open to the last, however, Glaoui's *harka* managed to raise much dust and burn vast quantities of powder with little result.

Mangin found his commander's policy shortsighted. El Hiba had not been eliminated. He had merely shifted his activity farther south. Taroudant, a red-walled city nestled among gardens of fig, orange and lemon trees, had become his new stronghold. The snow-covered wall of the high Atlas stood as a barrier to a French incursion from the north, while Taroudant itself lay across the important junction of caravan routes from the south, the Tafilalet in the east and Agadir on the Atlantic coast. Until el Hiba was driven from Taroudant and destroyed, the High Atlas and the Sus would remain unstable. Glaoui's intentionally ineffectual pursuit had boosted el Hiba's prestige and prolonged his influence, for it had demonstrated that the great caids were not yet committed to the French. Lyautey's faith in the value of "native politics," "indirect rule" and *harkas* organized under "loyal" caids led to chaos. Many of the caids who had asked for the *aman* after Sidi Bou Othmann, now began to reconsider their positions as the French forces drifted northward. Two such caids were those of Anflous and Guelloui, to whom Lyautey had assigned the task of keeping order in the mountainous country between Essaouira and Agadir.

Essaouira is a unique town in Morocco. It is also a vulnerable one, and at no time was it more so than in the winter of 1912–13. Essaouira had been founded in the eighteenth century as a trading center for Europeans seeking to tap what was then a lucrative trans-Saharan trade in gold, ivory and slaves. The fact that Sultan Mohammed ben Abdallah had given the task of designing the town to a captive French engineer accounts for its relatively European appearance—high angled walls in the style of Vauban, and wide, regular streets so unlike the twisted mazes of Arab casbahs.. As the Sultan intended Essaouira to be inhabited principally by Europeans and their Jewish agents, he had deliberately sited the town on a remote part of the coast at the end of a long, sandy peninsula jutting into a bay that had previously been a pirate haunt. Approached from Safi or Marrakech, Essaouira appears silhouetted against the dunes, the bay and the islands that form a breakwater against the Atlantic. To the south, the foothills of the High Atlas roll to the sea, a country of low, irregular mountains covered by spiny argan trees, each small peak and crest surmounted by blind windowless farms built for defense.

It was along the track that wound south from Essaouira to Agadir on December 16, 1912, that a force of 300 French Zouaves and a *tabor* of 180 Moroccan policemen were ambushed by tribesmen loyal to the caids of Anflous and Guelloui. For ten days the French force was besieged. Its food and water were soon exhausted. Resistance would surely have collapsed had it not been for the heavy rains which swept in from the Atlantic. An amphibious rescue operation was launched from Casablanca, but because of heavy seas, it was forced to stand off Essaouira for four days. Once landed, General Brulard fought his way at the head of three companies of *chasseurs alpins* fresh from France and one of Zouaves to the point twenty miles south of Essaouira where the soldiers and police were trapped. The return trip was equally difficult: the column, laden with sixty-seven wounded, was harassed all the way back to Essaouira.

The hinterland behind Essaouira was now in revolt. The French, however, held several advantages. First, Essaouira was a secure base of operations which could be supplied by sea. Second, in General Franchet d'Esperey, a future marshal of France, the French had a commander of great ability. Third, for the first time the French used aerial reconnaissance. In this way, they could locate the large *harkas*, like that which gathered in the palm groves near Essaouira in early January 1913. By a skillful use of converging columns, Franchet d'Esperey was able to break up the *harka* and secure his major routes of communication. The Moroccans retreated to their hilltop casbahs, from which the French were forced to winkle them out one by one. By the end of January, operations concentrated on the casbah of Anflous; it was taken, after bitter fighting, on the twenty-fifth.

The campaign around Essaouira in the winter of 1912–13 stoked army discontent with Lyautey's reliance on "native politics" and "indirect rule." Most of this opposition centered on Mangin, who made no secret of the fact that he considered his superior's methods not only timorous but also potentially disastrous. He publicly requested a transfer back to France. Lyautey refused. He might yet require Mangin's undisputed military talents. But more, to ship him home under a cloud after Sidi Bou Othmann would simply have swelled the numbers of those who were already complaining that the colonel had been shabbily treated.

To read Lyautey's letters or the sycophantic memoirs of some of the officers who served on his staff, one would inevitably conclude that Lyautey was a popular general. On the contrary, he was intensely disliked by his command. To a certain extent this was inevitable: colonial soldiers, a rather rough-and-ready lot, could not help but resent Lyautey's patrician airs and theatrical gestures. They also saw his insistence on "native politics" and "indirect rule" as overly cautious. He was forever lecturing them: "In Africa, one defends oneself by moving." What twaddle! The French advanced in Morocco as they had advanced in the Western Sudan—by the sheer weight of their firepower. Why try to adapt to the mobility of the Moors when all one had to do was form a square and allow the enemy to break himself in futile frontal assaults?

The fact that Lyautey's tactics had proved unsuccessful had made little difference to his career, which particularly irked his subordinates. Lyautey was always able to cover his failures with a clever smokescreen of propaganda. Above all, they saw him as a hypocrite: He claimed to be a straightforward military man, a respecter of traditional values and hierarchies against the greed and depredations of the horrible Third Republic. In fact, nothing could have been further from the truth. His career had been built on his political connections. He collaborated openly with a regime he claimed to despise and was prepared to use his political friends to ride roughshod over the chain of command. On the other hand, while he pretended to be open-minded and tolerant of the opinions of subordinates, in practice he dealt ruthlessly with anyone who opposed him. Lyautey's ability to circumvent a routine-ridden military bureaucracy may not have been a bad thing. But for officers without access to influential deputies and journalists, who served out their lives in obscure positions and remote garrisons, who battled their way up the military hierarchy and never got very far, for whom military life retained all of its servitude and little of its grandeur, Lyautey appeared a fraud—a spectacular fraud, but a fraud nonetheless.

Lyautey persisted in his plan for consolidation of the protectorate in 1913. He particularly wanted to avoid an early confrontation with the Zaian confederation under its powerful patriarch Moha ou Hammou. Mangin was given the job of organizing a screen of friendly tribes between the Chaouia and Zaian territory along the Wadi Oum er Rbia. It was a strictly political mission in which Mangin was to make full use of his intelligence service under Major Henri Simon, the doyen of intelligence officers in Morocco. In no circumstances, Lyautey told Mangin, was he to cross the Oum er Rbia. He might as well have set a wolf to guard a flock of sheep.

Across the Oum er Rbia in front of Mangin's forces lay Casba Tadla, a large market town which served Moha ou Said as a capital. For Mangin, the strategic importance of Casba Tadla was obvious. Like Khenifra farther north, it lay across the main route which linked Fez and Meknes with Marrakech. The crenellated walls and bastions of its seventeenth-century fortress towered over the sinuous Oum er Rbia at the point where it was crossed by a bridge of ten unequal arches. Across the river on the left bank, a slender minaret covered with a fine pattern of interwoven stonework rose from the blocklike houses. It was an objective Mangin could not resist. On March 25, 1913, he crossed the wadi at night and fell on Moha ou Said's camp early the next morning, scattering the enemy. Casba Tadla was occupied without opposition, as were several smaller settlements. Lyautey was furious, and ordered his subordinate back to the French side of the Oum er Rbia. In tactical terms, this order was unwise. The Moroccans loved nothing better than to attack a retreating column. Their douars were not at risk. Their women and herds were safe. They were spared the need to judge when to cease resistance and request the *aman*. Consequently, Mangin's rear guard was hard-pressed and lost thirty-three killed and sixty-three wounded.

By May, it had become apparent that Mangin and Lyautey would never agree on a strategy for the Oum er Rbia. "Hold your positions," the resident general ordered on May 2. "I said and I repeat that when you want to carry out in a country serious and long-lasting political work, you cannot achieve it by a fixed date," he repeated on May 24. He urged Mangin to "talk" to the Moroccans, to send Simon to split the factions. He dispatched his chief of staff, Colonel Pellé, to reason with Mangin, all to no avail. Mangin had been educated in another school. Simon's methods were too slow. Nor did Mangin believe that they could be made to work. The only way to bring Moha ou Said into submission was to take the fight to his side of the Oum er Rbia. Finally, on June 6, Lyautey gave in to the hectoring of his subordinate. Against the advice of Franchet d'Esperey, Lyautey gave permission to Mangin for a march on Casba Kisba.

Franchet d'Esperey's objections were several. Not only were the warriors of the Middle Atlas formidable fighters; but the tactics which had worked in the flat country of the Chaouia and at Sidi Bou Othmann might prove inadequate for the more mountainous country around Casba Kisba. Mangin brushed aside these warnings. On June 7, he formed his 4,200 troops and fourteen guns into the usual attack square and convoy square, and marched toward Casba Kisba. His squares were invulnerable. But his cavalry screen under Major Picard impetuously left their infantry support too far behind and were badly mauled by Berbers firing from behind the cover of rocks. Mangin was forced to abandon twenty bodies, precious trophies which brought even more tribesmen into the attack. The French were soon marching through a country in which every bush and rock seemed to conceal an enemy rifle. On June 10, as his rear guard passed through a narrow defile, it met a hail of fire from the heights which cost him another twenty-two dead. In all, Mangin's three-day promenade had cost 77 dead and 170 wounded, small beer by the standards of Verdun and Passchendaele, but for the French in Morocco heavy losses indeed. The French could, of course, replace their casualties. But they would bolster the cause of the resistance, as would Mangin's abandonment of Casba Kisba. Lyautey sent Franchet d'Esperey to Casba Tadla to remonstrate with Mangin. Fully aware that his career was at stake, Mangin put on an impressive display: the garrison was turned out in their dress uniforms to greet the general when he arrived on June 17. Franchet d'Esperey seemed to be in a good mood when the two men disappeared into Mangin's tent for a hard talk. Yes, his losses had been severe, Mangin admitted, but those of the Moroccans had been higher still. He denied vehemently that he had disobeyed orders. The officers struck a compromise: Casba Tadla would become a permanently occupied French post if Mangin, his reputation now slightly tarnished by his losses around Casba Kisba, would go quietly to France.

The auguries for 1914 were good, Lyautey believed, for the two projects which he had planned for that year: the junction of eastern and western Morocco by the capture of Taza and the occupation of Moha ou Hammou's capital at Khenifra. Lyautey's plan for Taza was simplicity itself: as soon as the winter rains ceased, Taza would be taken by a coordinated pincer movement—General Baumgarten advancing from M'soun in the east to link up with Gouraud marching from Souk el Arba de Tissa, northeast of Fez. "Native politics," as practiced throughout the winter by both generals, had not advanced the French one inch closer to Taza. On the contrary, Gouraud had been virtually besieged at Souk el Arba de Tissa and was obliged to strike northward against the Tsoul and Branes tribes in early May to clear his flanks before marching on Taza.

On May 10, Gouraud and Baumgarten set off simultaneously. Gouraud organized his nine battalions into three squares which easily held off the swirling attacks of the Ghiata horsemen to seize Amelil. Baumgarten reached Taza in one night's forced march, taking the garrison by surprise and occupying the town virtually without firing a shot. It proved a disappointing prize. Seen from a distance, the crenellated walls of red brick set on a bluff which dominated the Taza gap appeared picturesque. On closer inspection, however, the town proved to be a tumbled-down ruin occupied by miserable creatures who for too long had been subject to the tyranny of the ruling Ghiatas. At Amelil, Gouraud had to contend with a strong force of Tsoul tribesmen who had established themselves on the low hills to the north. On May 12, he attacked, driving them from crest to crest for almost six miles before returning to Amelil. Four days later, Gouraud and Baumgarten met at Meknassa Tahtania, three miles from Taza. The Maghreb was now French from Tunis to the Atlantic. Lyautey arrived on May 17 to celebrate the event with a review of six thousand troops on the plain outside the town.

The conquest of the Zaian confederation proved a far more difficult operation. By 1914, the spur of Zaian territory which jutted out from the Middle Atlas had been occupied on three sides. To the south, Casba Tadla was in French hands. To the west, the Zaer country had been pacified and French posts created at Oued Zem, Christian and Oulmes. To the north, General Henrys had pushed out from Meknes to occupy Ito and Ifrane. On the map, then, the operation appeared to pose few difficulties. Columns could be thrown out from three directions to converge on the Zaian capital at Khenifra. In 1914, Khenifra was not a beautiful town, but it had a certain presence. Even its color conveyed something of the character of its Zaian inhabitants, with a massive square casbah dominating a blood-red plain that ran south and west to the wall of the Middle Atlas, "a red city in a red land." The gardens and orchards that surrounded the town and the quaint muleback bridge that spanned the clear, swift-flowing Oum er Rbia did little to temper the fierce appearance of the capital of the Zaians.

The Zaians were a tribe of nomad pastoralists who took their flocks to the mountains in summer and returned to winter on the plain of Khenifra. Like most pastoral peoples, they were fiercely independent, but Moha ou

Hammou had drawn the factions into a nominal unity. Moha ou Hammou had become chief of the Zaian confederation in 1877, at the age of twenty. A man of great simplicity, great wealth and hospitality, he had dominated his people through his political sagacity and military force. His popularity had made him one of the most influential men in Morocco since the time of Sultan Moulai Hassan. This was little appreciated in the French camp. The problem lay with the intelligence service. Since 1912, many young officers had volunteered for native affairs because they knew that the service was especially favored by the resident general. Intelligence officers were far more likely to be noticed than were those in charge of the convoy guard. Ambitious, inexperienced, eager to please, they often drew up unrealistic or overly optimistic reports based on unreliable information. Moroccans told them that the Zaians would welcome the French with open arms. These opinions they passed on uncritically.

The Zaians were slow to react to the French offensive. This was quite understandable. It took time for the news of the arrival of a French column to reach the outlying douars and for men to leave their flocks to staunch the invasion. It was not, generally speaking, until the third day of an operation that the French would encounter serious opposition. For this reason, the march on Khenifra was prepared in secrecy. The French must strike in haste, all the more so because they had elected to divide their forces into three separate, and dangerously weak, columns. As d'Amade's experience in the Chaouia had proved, this tactic allowed the Moroccans, if alerted in time, to concentrate on one of the columns. The rationale for divided forces in this instance lay in the fact that the columns could converge on Khenifra from three different directions, confusing the defense and moving more rapidly than would one mammoth column. The operation was well planned by General Henrys and, on the face of it, succeeded brilliantly. On June 10, the three columns set out from near Casba Tadla in the south, Christian in the west and Lias in the north. Within two days, they had seized Khenifra. The inhabitants and their flocks fled in panic into the mountains.

All the same, the operation had an unsuitably Napoleonic flavor about it. "Seize the capital . . . nerve center of administration . . . psychological importance . . . resistance will collapse"—all the clichés one learned at the staff college were inappropriate in Morocco. This should have been obvious after Settat, Casba Tadla and Casba Kisba, when the seizure of towns had failed to dampen resistance among pastoral peoples. On the contrary, the occupation of a point on a map often proved a liability. This was certainly true of Khenifra in June 1914. Once in possession of Khenifra, the French fell into a dangerous lethargy. Their "capital" was occupied, but the Zaians remained inviolate in their mountains. The expected pursuit, the *razzias* and death, did not follow. The French did not even destroy the crops which the Zaians had left unharvested in the Khenifra valley. Perhaps they were hungry? As French troops began to withdraw, the Zaians recovered their courage. Perhaps God did not intend the French to occupy Khenifra. They began to creep back into their valley. French wood-and-water parties were ambushed and supply convoys attacked. By the end of July, the French had taken over a hundred casualties. The morale of the newly raised Moroccan spahis was the first to crack; they began to desert, sometimes after murdering their Algerian NCOs. The remainder of them were disarmed, and their horses distributed among Algerian tirailleurs.

News of the outbreak of war in Europe reached Moha ou Hammou almost as soon as the French commander at Khenifra, Colonel Laverdure, was informed by wire that his garrison would be stripped of two battalions. When, on August 4, the troops under Major Blondiaux marched out of Khenifra for Casablanca and France, they were immediately attacked and lost sixteen killed and fifty wounded before they got clear of Zaian territory. Khenifra was now tightly encircled and was to remain so for another two weeks. The siege was broken by a combination of luck and sheer accident. In preparation for the arrival of a vital supply column on August 20, a detachment of troops was sent on the night of the nineteenth to storm Djebel bou Moussa which dominated the road into Khenifra. To their surprise, the French found the hill unoccupied. When, at daybreak, the Zaians realized that the strategic position had gone by default, they launched a massive assault. The result was a bloodbath: two hundred Zaian dead and countless wounded. As night fell, the valley of the Oum er Rbia echoed with "an unforgettable concert of cries and lamentations" as the women came in search of their men.

As if by magic, the siege dropped away. The Zaians had lost heart and Moha ou Hammou was reluctant to see his prestige diminished by further attacks. For their part, the French stayed put. Lyautey had ordered that for the duration of hostilities in Europe, the conquest must be held and not extended. Unpacified tribes were not to be provoked, the *siba* was to be left in peace. A strange live-and-let-live attitude developed between two enemies who days before had been locked in mortal combat. With winter approaching, Moha ou Hammou even brought his camp down from the mountains to el

Herri, seven miles from Khenifra. There, several islands of tents containing perhaps three thousand people spread over the plain, as they had done every winter for centuries.

In the autumn of 1914, Morocco west of the Atlas was held by only eighteen battalions. Those French officers stranded in Morocco were exceedingly bitter, and none more so than Colonel Laverdure. It must be remembered that the Great War which broke out in 1914 was expected to be brief. This was the first war in Europe since 1871, and Laverdure felt that he had been unfairly excluded. To this stroke of ill luck was added the humiliation of a formal order forbidding him to strike at Moha ou Hammou's camp. It was unbearable, especially for an *officier soudanais* brought up in a system where impetuous conduct was not only rewarded, it was *de rigueur*.

On the night of November 12, Laverdure divided virtually the entire French garrison into four groups of one or two companies, each with its own artillery and cavalry. The Zaians awoke on November 13 to the sound of 75 shells ripping through their tents. In the utter panic which followed, Moha ou Hammou was saved by two of his sons, who led him to safety. The rout of the camp was the signal for a *razzia* by the Algerians and *goumiers*, in which two of Moha ou Hammou's wives were captured. By the time the officers had restored discipline and gathered their troops for the return march to Khenifra, however, the Zaians had rallied, their numbers swelled by others who had rushed to join them. Laverdure's force was cut to pieces, probably because they had exhausted their ammunition. Thirty-three officers and almost seven hundred men were slaughtered, their bodies stripped and mutilated. The skeleton garrison at Khenifra attempted a sortie to disengage Laverdure's men, but their numbers were too few. Only a handful of men who had been wounded in the initial attack on the camp returned to the safety of the town. The Zaians captured eight guns, ten machine guns and seven hundred rifles. It was the worst defeat by far the French had ever suffered in Morocco.

Lyautey was almost panic-stricken. Laverdure's catastrophe threatened to puncture the hard outer shell of Moroccan defense. He blamed the rue St.-Dominique for the débâcle: they only promoted and decorated officers for heroism in battle, ignoring the slow, delicate but important tasks of the intelligence service. He need not have worried. Moha ou Hammou did not exploit his victory. General Henrys arrived in force to plug the gap. At Khenifra, Moha ou Hammou's two wives were exchanged for the bodies of Laverdure and five other officers.

The conquest of Morocco was grinding to an end, though this was not apparent to the participants. Another, far larger conflict was already casting its shadow. The Khenifra defeat enraged Lyautey. His anger was not directed at Moha ou Hammou. On the contrary, he ordered the Khenifra garrison to seek no reprisals. The Zaians and the French settled back into the uneasy truce which was to last for the duration of the Great War.

With Colonel Laverdure beyond criticism, Lyautey vented his anger on the *officiers soudanais*. Their obsession with the pitched battle had almost unraveled what was certainly one of his most brilliantly successful coups. In late July 1914, the government had informed Lyautey that if war broke out in Europe, he was to withdraw his soldiers from virtually all of occupied Morocco. Small garrisons were to be maintained in the coastal towns and along a line stretching from Kenitra on the Atlantic coast, through Meknes, Fez, Taza to Oudjda in the east. "The fate of Morocco will be decided in Lorraine," the order declared superciliously. Lyautey was, of course, aware of that. What he was prepared to resist, however, what he had always resisted, was that the fate of Morocco should be decided in Paris. He dismissed the bureaucrats there as "idiots."

On July 30, Lyautey met his four regional generals in Rabat. They all agreed that a French withdrawal to the coast would precipitate a general uprising in Morocco and might even destabilize Algeria and Tunisia. The course of action upon which they agreed was the exact opposite of that ordered by Paris: they would indeed withdraw from occupied Morocco, but outward to the mountains rather than to the coast. "We shall hollow out the carcass and leave the shell," Lyautey said. The ultimate success of this tactic depended upon one crucial factor: the attitude of the Moroccans within the pacified territories. The task of convincing them to remain loyal to France fell principally upon the generals.

That they succeeded in their tasks was remarkable given France's new weakness in Morocco and what the Moroccans understood of her weakness in Europe. A very few of the caids, such as el Glaoui, had newspapers translated and were reasonably aware of the relative strengths of the European powers. Even so, what they read could not have reassured them. It could only have reinforced the general view in Morocco that the German tribe was stronger than the French tribe and likely to win the coming fight. Still, the German tribe was very far away while the French were on the spot. Gouraud was told by the notables of Fez to maintain sufficient troops in Morocco and to keep their struggle with the German tribe short. Mtouggi told General Lamothe in Marrakech simply: "You hold the sea. We will hold the land." Because of the success of his strategy, Lyautey was able to return thirty-seven battalions of infantry, nine squadrons of cavalry and six batteries to France, more than requested by the government. These were replaced in large part by territorial battalions. The arrival of the older men much impressed the Moroccans, for soldiers who had survived into their thirties and forties were thought to be warriors of great skill.

With the outbreak of war, the military conquest virtually halted. General Lamothe crossed the High Atlas into the Sus to help Glaoui put an end to a brief revival of el Hiba's fortunes in 1916. In the Rif, a new pretender, Abd el Maleck, gave some cause for concern in 1917. In 1917 also, a section of the Middle Atlas south of Taza was occupied without opposition. Expansion was halted because the French were thin on the ground. But the conclusion that Lyautey had virtually lost interest in further expansion is irresistible. After 1919, he formalized this attitude by dividing the country into "useful Morocco" and the rest. For Lyautey, military conquest had never held any fascination for its own sake. Even in the South Oranais after 1903, he had been far more interested in organizing pacified areas than in military operations. Now, he threw himself into public works with a vengeance: harbors and roads were built, often with German prisoner-of-war labor, markets were established, infirmaries and schools created. A great fair was established at Fez at which the wooden horses of the merry-go-round were a special favorite of former dissidents. In the words of one historian of the protectorate, much was done for Moroccans, but little was done by them. Morocco under Lyautey became virtually a socialist state. He would show his visitors the "new" Morocco with the delight of a child, even when, as in 1924, disaster threatened in the Rif.

Moroccan notables who supported the French occupation did reasonably well out of it as their positions were now relatively secure and no longer subject to the mercurial whims of the Sultan or the conspiracies of his viziers. Thami el Glaoui offers probably the best example of a Moroccan who profited spectacularly from his association with the French. In the Middle Atlas, Moha ou Hammou met a sad end. Zaian resistance to the French fragmented when a quarrel over succession broke out in his family. Three of his sons—Hassan, Amacoq and Bouazza—offered their services to the French, who allowed them to organize their own *goumiers*. In 1922, Moha ou Hammou was killed during a skirmish with one of his son's *harkas*.

Moulai Hafid's career after his abdication was characteristically bizarre. He had set sail for Europe in 1912 aboard the *Du Chayla* convinced that he was under arrest. His apprehensions were calmed somewhat when at Gibraltar he and his entourage were transferred to a P & O liner. While on board, the ex-Sultan visited the cabaret, where he witnessed a magic act put on by a young woman. Moulai Hafid was particularly impressed when she filled an apparently endless number of glasses from one small teapot. When he tried to buy this teapot from the young woman, however, she refused. He was very disappointed: "It would have been so useful when one was traveling."

Despite his regal reception at Marseilles, Moulai Hafid did not immediately abandon his suspicions of his hosts. He only reluctantly entered the train for a trip to the fashionable spa town of Vichy in central France, and was visibly nervous when the carriages began to gain speed. When, with a loud whistle, the train plunged headlong into the darkness of the first tunnel, Moulai Hafid panicked, grabbing the arm of the French officer next to him and demanding that the train be stopped. His fear quickly spread to his servants and harem. Their shouts and screams ceased only when the train emerged from the tunnel into the daylight. "You will kindly tell them not to do that again," he ordered. When it was explained that the train must pass under the hills, Moulai Hafid replied: "Then the train must stop and I will walk over the top and join it again on the other side."

At Vichy, the ex-Sultan's passion for animals caused some consternation at the Hôtel Majestic. On a visit to a local farm, he purchased twenty-seven white Charolais cows. On his instructions, the farmer delivered them that very night to the hotel car park, where they were to be seen "meandering in and out of smart motor cars, lowing gently into ground-floor windows." It was also Moulai Hafid's habit to take early-morning walks. On one of these he met a dog seller who sold him a small mongrel puppy at the end of a piece of string. The small dog so amused Moulai Hafid that he called his servants together and told them to scour the town to buy more dogs. When one of the servants asked how he was to know which dogs were for sale, he was told that every dog at the end of a piece of string could be purchased. As they spoke no French, they were instructed to bring both the dogs and the seller to the hotel, where a bargain would be struck. The garden of the hotel was soon filled with irate ladies, indignant at having been kidnapped by Moulai Hafid's servants while walking their dogs.

Moulai Hafid subsequently returned to Tangiers, where he resumed his tedious negotiations with the French over bills and property. When the war broke out, he was enticed by Germany to cross the straits to Spain and, from there, to preach resistance to the French in Morocco. These activities inevitably brought protests from Paris, so that the Spanish government eventually interned him in the Escorial Palace near Madrid. He made up with the French after the war, and died at Enghien-les-Bains, near Paris, in 1937.

Morocco turned out to have been the crèche for some of France's most successful Great War generals. Franchet d'Esperey became a marshal of France. Charles Mangin also continued his controversial career after 1914, this time as the protégé of General Robert Nivelle. The failure of Nivelle's *bataille de rupture*, which had been approved by war minister Lyautey, briefly eclipsed Mangin. But he reemerged at the head of an army in 1918. An impetuous *officier soudanais* to the last, he fell afoul of Clemenceau in the postwar years by distributing secret army funds to Rhenish separatists in the hope of fragmenting Germany. He died in 1925. Gouraud, on the other hand, became one of Clemenceau's favorites. He replaced the lackluster d'Amade at the head of the French contingent in the Dardanelles in 1916, where he lost an arm to a Turkish shell, and recovered to replace Lyautey as resident general the following year. In 1918, Gouraud commanded the Fourth Army on the Western Front. He died at Granville in Normandy in 1946. Perhaps the greatest success story of the conquest was the Moroccan Division, which became the most decorated French unit in the Great War.

That so many colonial men performed well in the Great War was a source of consternation and annoyance in the metropolitan army. Since the Franco-Prussian War, when *"africains"* such as Bazaine, Canrobert and MacMahon had led the French army to disaster, it was received wisdom in France that Africa was a poor school of war. The experience of a few "nigger bullets" was no substitute for the scientific study of war as it would be fought in Europe, as taught in war-college kriegspiels and rehearsed in autumn maneuvers.

The fallacy of this view seems to lie with the fact that colonial officers never believed that warfare in Africa would in any way resemble that which they might one day meet at home. The one rule of warfare for colonial officers was that there were no rules, that every situation was different and must be confronted with flexibility and imagination. Colonial officers were required to make rapid decisions under pressure, think on their feet, react to each new situation as it arose, not spend hours cramming for some examination based on rote learning and historically derived formulas. How many preconceived notions, how many elaborately developed theories of warfare, perished in the firestorm of 1914.

That the distinction between colonial and continental warfare became quasi-official in the years before 1914 was largely the work of Lyautey. The French had been fighting colonial wars since the invasion of Algeria in 1830. General Thomas Bugeaud, a veteran of the Peninsula and the Chouan uprising of 1831–32 in the Vendée, had taught the army the value of light, mobile units when faced with an elusive foe. It was Gallieni, however, who in the 1890s developed the doctrine that would become known in the post-1945 world as "hearts and minds"—the combination of civic action and military operations which served as the basis for counterinsurgency strategy in the third quarter of the twentieth century. For Gallieni, as for the British in the Malayan emergency of the 1950s, this tactic worked reasonably well because he was able to organize an indigenous population to resist domination by a foreign group in its midst—in this case, the Chinese. The Vietnamese no doubt preferred to be left alone. But when forced to choose between Chinese bandits and French soldiers, they chose the latter.

Lyautey was not an original thinker, as he himself admitted. His talents essentially lay in the field of public relations and propaganda. It was Lyautey who elevated "native politics" to the level of a general principle. As a doctrine of warfare, it rested on two basic assumptions: first, that the native society was riven by deep divisions which could be exploited by the invading European power, and second, that the native people preferred prosperity to independence. In the Moroccan situation, neither assumption was safe to make. Moroccan society was certainly divided, but its members retained a firm sense of belonging to the Dar al Islam. To believe that Moroccans were prepared to welcome the French simply for the privilege of trading at their (heavily subsidized) markets, was quite simply naïve.

When the events of the conquest are examined, it becomes clear that "native politics" seldom proved effective. Most officers considered *goumiers* more trouble than they were worth and positively resisted, as arming insurrection, the distribution of rifles to factions of tribes for a brief campaign. As a military force, *goumiers* were effective only if closely supported by regular French units, and then only for limited operations. The French moved forward by the sheer weight of their firepower. Time after time, Moroccan resistance broke against French squares. Only when this happened, did Moroccans begin to seek a compromise.

If "native politics" failed as a military doctrine, it was brilliantly successful as a piece of colonialist propaganda. That "hearts-and-minds" techniques did not produce the miraculous results claimed for them by Lyautey must have come as something of a shock for French soldiers in Algeria, Americans in Vietnam and Portuguese in Angola, Mozambique and Guinea.

Brilliant propaganda also papered over many of Lyautey's failings as a colonial administrator. Lyautey was determined that Morocco should not become another Algeria; there "direct administration" and "proletarian colonization" had deprived the indigenous population of any real stake in society. In both respects, events took a direction which he was unable to control. By the very terms of the protectorate, responsibility for virtually every important ministry, except perhaps that of Islamic education, passed into the hands of French functionaries—cautious, blinkered, ignorant of the world which they governed. "Is not the wisdom of God manifest?" Moulai Hafid remarked to Walter Harris after his exile to Tangiers. "Has He not given intelligence even to a dog? A little less, it is true, than to the elephant. But a little more than He bestowed upon the French administration." The postwar years also witnessed a large influx of colonists who brought with them racist attitudes and who bought up the best land, stimulating the rural exodus as numbers of new landless Moroccans flocked to the cities.

The caids were still responsible for the Moroccan population in tribal areas, and it was they who benefited most from the French occupation. While only the most ardent nationalist would claim that Morocco before the protectorate was a happy society, it is true that it had achieved a sort of primitive equilibrium. The venality and abuses of the caids traditionally had been limited by the fact that the people they governed were armed and quite prepared to revolt. The first act required by the French upon pacification was that the population be disarmed. This left them defenseless before the caids, who were now even more powerful because they were backed up by the French. Each caid had a native-affairs officer assigned to him to ensure that justice was done. But this proved an inadequate safeguard. How could a young lieutenant or captain, with an imperfect command of the language and only the most rudimentary understanding of the native society, hope to hold his own against a caid superior both in years and in cunning? In any case, if the caid and the native-affairs officer were at loggerheads over an issue, the Moroccan simply had to wait until the officer's two-year tour of duty was completed and he was transferred elsewhere.

But Lyautey's ideas on administration were a product of more than simple abhorrence of the Algerian example. He sought to shape Morocco to conform to his own aristocratic political ideals. He maintained a faith in hierarchy and authority long after they had been abandoned by conservatives in France as unworkable. In Morocco, Lyautey had acquired a feudal society. He wished to preserve the social framework of "old" Morocco and guide it toward enlightened rule. In this respect, he was a peculiar breed of colonialist. While others were eager to demonstrate the benefits which colonial expansion offered to the homeland in terms of trade or troops, Lyautey seldom felt the need to give the conquest of Morocco a *raison d'être* beyond providing a backdrop against which he, and by extension France, could perform his great deeds.

Yet he did not belong entirely to the eighteenth century. He sought to modernize Morocco's economy. He also wanted to draw the new Moroccan intelligentsia into the civil service. He saw more clearly than others that it was these people who must be integrated into the social and political framework of the protectorate if it was to survive. The greatest indictment of Lyautey's period as resident general was that, while himself above corruption, he tolerated abuses both by the caids and by settlers. "You cannot create a colony with virgins," he said in his own defense.

For Lyautey, Morocco became a refuge from a France he regarded as a lost cause, a great land inhabited by an unworthy people. In 1917, he was recalled to Paris to serve—briefly—as war minister. A colonial who had spent the best part of the preceding twenty-five years outside of France, Lyautey would seem an odd choice to lead the rue St.-Dominique; but the government was desperate. Three years of war had bled the country and polarized opinion both in the army and in parliament, and victory was as elusive as ever. Having remained abroad, Lyautey was virtually the only military chief not to have been caught up in the increasingly acrimonious debate between "easterners" and "westerners," those who would concentrate on the Balkans and those who wanted to beat the Germans in Western Europe. His colonial outlook should have put him in the camp of those who sought a victory through a Balkan strategy. But for a series of complicated reasons, the left had captured this "eastern" camp. Conservatives remained wedded to achieving victory on the Western Front. Lyautey found himself called upon to gather support for yet another costly offensive against impregnable German positions. Coming only weeks after the dreadful slogging match at Verdun had mercifully ended, it was too much. Lyautey had no faith in the plan put forward by General Nivelle for a concentrated offensive to "rupture" a narrow segment of the German line. The only thing to rupture, he was sure, would be French morale.

Lyautey might have fought for another solution. But to be fair to him, his room for maneuver was desperately limited. To have opposed the Nivelle offensive would have been to play into the hands of the left, which would have demanded even more troops to swell the army of their darling, General Maurice Sarrail, at Salonika in northern Greece. The issue was complicated further by the fact that the British Prime Minister, Lloyd George, supported Nivelle to the hilt, not because he had any faith in his plan, but because he was eager to put his commander-in-chief, General Douglas Haig, under French command, in order to control him better. But the political atmosphere in Paris in the late winter of 1917 was dreadful, and this must have affected Lyautey deeply. The Russian front was on the verge of collapse. The Americans had not yet come into the war. The spirit of the *union sacrée* which had united all parties from left to right in the early days of the war had by then broken down into bitterness and acrimony. Lyautey was a man who required respect. He was accustomed to a court of admiring subalterns, not disrespectful left-wing deputies out to make a name for themselves by insulting the great and powerful. When Lyautey stood up to speak in parliament on a relatively minor question, he was heckled by the left. His patience snapped and he stormed out of the Chamber to return to his self-imposed exile.

The settling of accounts with the Third Republic he so detested was delayed by the sweeping right-wing victory in the 1919 elections. In 1921, he was made a marshal of France. But the victory of the left-wing *cartel des gauches* in the elections of 1924, which coincided with a serious rebellion by Abd el Krim in the Spanish zone of the Rif, brought a marked change of fortune.

When, in 1925, Abd el Krim's troops attacked along a broad front held by small French posts, they were almost everywhere victorious. Although this attack had long been predicted, news of the outbreak of hostilities threw Rabat into a panic. Lyautey was now an old man of seventy-five. His health was poor and he was virtually deaf. Nevertheless, he demonstrated the foresight and strength of character which had saved Morocco for France before. Against the almost unanimous advice of his staff, he ordered that Taza be defended. Heroic resistance by colonial troops at Taza limited Abd el Krim's advance to manageable proportions.

The French government dispatched War Minister Paul Painlevé to tour the Rif front in June. It was during this visit that, according to St.-Aulaire, Lyautey sealed his own fate. The aging aristocratic general and the thrusting republican politician were temperamentally incompatible. As they stood at an observation post on the southern slopes of the Rif from which they could see some entrenched French soldiers under fire on a neighboring hill, Painlevé asked Lyautey: "Shall we not carry the greetings of France to those brave soldiers?" The old general turned to his aide-de-camp and said in a clearly audible voice: "What a bloody fool!"

Painlevé returned to Paris and recommended that military operations be handed over to Marshal Pétain, the hero of Verdun. Lyautey quite rightly saw Pétain's appointment as commander-in-chief as the signal that the government no longer had confidence in him, and he resigned. On September 5, 1925, he boarded an ordinary packet steamer at Rabat. The trip to France was significant for Lyautey if only because it caused him to modify somewhat his violent Anglophobia. In 1922, the young Jacques Millerand visited him in Rabat in the company of his father, Alexandre Millerand, the president of the French Republic. To his amazement, he found hanging on his bedroom wall in the resident general's palace a picture of a man, horribly mutilated, his eye sockets empty. Early the next morning, Lyautey burst in to explain: "You are perhaps surprised to see this photo," he said, using the familiar *tu* form of address. "It usually hangs in my bathroom. But as I gave my apartment to your father, I didn't want to leave it. Do you know what it is? A Boer tortured by the English. Every morning, while washing, I look at it to remind myself of the hatred I have for those pigs."

The British nevertheless held Lyautey in great respect. Forewarned, they sent two warships to escort his steamer through the Strait of Gibraltar. At Marseilles, there was no official welcome. He descended the gangplank, a lonely old man in civilian clothes, and boarded the train for Paris.

How can we assess Lyautey? It is difficult to know the real man because he was such an actor. He appears on balance a rather *papier mâché* character, a *grand personnage* surprisingly devoid of substance. He offered himself as an inspiration for a generation of young people eager to dedicate themselves to an ideal, yet he single-mindedly pursued his own interests. He claimed to be an enemy of bureaucracy, but under Lyautey Morocco became a bureaucrats' paradise: three times as many Frenchmen were employed to govern Morocco as Englishmen were used to rule India with forty times the population. He talked in lofty terms of leaving the "natural social hierarchy" undisturbed, which meant in practice that he was prepared to tolerate corruption remarkable even by oriental standards. El Glaoui was allowed to rule Marrakech like a Mafia boss, down to control of the city's twenty-seven thousand prostitutes, who had to pay him a percentage of their earnings. For other Moroccans, however, Lyautey did very little: as late as 1940, only 3 percent of Moroccan children were attending a school. His failures as a general have already been discussed. These were disguised, however, by his immense charm, his fluent style and a small army of writers and politicians whom he seduced into acting as his public-relations agents. His quiet admonitions that they were being overly generous in their praise were interpreted as evidence of modesty and pushed them to even greater heights of eulogy, which was almost certainly what he had intended. Still, Lyautey added color to what was otherwise a rather faceless and boring army, and that must count for something.

The ingratitude of the Third Republic and the policies followed by his successors in his beloved Morocco embittered Lyautey's last years. His replacement was an ex-governor general of Algeria, who standardized many of the practices of "direct administration." The Rif was subdued in 1926 and Abd el Krim exiled to the island of Réunion in the Indian Ocean. The Middle Atlas, the Sus and the Tafilalet were, one by one, brought under the protectorate. In his native Lorraine, Lyautey busied himself organizing his papers. He was a patron of the Boy Scouts of France and, it was rumored, in contact with extreme-right-wing groups. Questioned about the place where he made his name, he always replied: "Morocco? Never heard of it." In the summer of 1934 he died, and was buried with full military honors in Rabat. His creation did not long survive his death. In 1956, the protectorate was ended. El Mokri, grand vizier in 1912 when the Treaty of the Protectorate was signed, was also present to see it ended, aged 105.

Chapter I   The ROAD *to* ZOUSFANA

page 6 *"lived and died."* Rohlfs, *Adventures in Morocco*, 8.
    made his escape. W. Harris, *The Land of the African Sultan*, 310–13.
    "as fertile as a garden." Rohlfs, *Adventures*, 19.
  10 *preparing it in Morocco.* C. Andrew, *Théophile Delcassé and the Making of the Entente Cordiale*; J. J. Cooke, *The New French Imperialism, 1880–1910*; E. Burke, *Prelude to Protectorate in Morocco, 1860–1912*.

Chapter II   EUROPEANS *in* AFRICA

  12 *"into one boat."* Colville, *A Ride in Petticoats and Slippers*, 20.
  13 *onto the beach.* W. Harris, *The Land of the African Sultan*, 6.
    posting in 1910. Selous, *Appointment to Fez*, 13.
    "dung and dates." Madame St.-René Taillandier, *Ce Monde disparu*, 153–54.
    a performing ape. W. Harris, *Land of African Sultan*, 15.
  14 *still-wriggling body.* Ashmead-Bartlett, *The Passing of the Shereefian Empire*, 213.
    "all to himself." St.-Aulaire, *Confessions d'un vieux diplomate*, 77.
  15 *eye on the inheritance.* Robert Kerr, *Morocco After Twenty-five Years*, 126–27.
    from the Arabian Nights. W. Harris, *Land of African Sultan*, 16.
    a profit margin of 150 percent. Kerr, *Morocco*, 267.
    wrote Harris. W. Harris, *Land of African Sultan*, 14.
  16 *wrote Madame St.-René.* Madame St.-René Taillandier, *Ce Monde disparu*, 188.
    charging boar. St.-Aulaire, *Confessions*, 75.
  17 *extinguish all conversation.* Madame St.-René Taillandier, *Ce Monde disparu*, 161–71.
    British visitor noted. Parsons, *The Origins of the Moroccan Question*, 13.
    "dine together twice weekly." Madame St.-René Taillandier, *Ce Monde disparu*, 158.
  19 *old tricks.* Parsons, *Origins*, Appendix F.
    King Orélie-Antoine actually existed. Cunninghame Graham, *Mogreb-El-Acksa*, 34.
  20 *the Moor paid.* Meakin, *Life in Morocco*, 248–51.
    "upon the worms." Drummond Hay, *A Memoir*, 37.
    1895 to 1905. Nicolson, *Lord Carnock*, 118–19.
  21 *should be well treated.* Miège, *Le Maroc et l'Europe, 1830–1894*, vol. II, 566–67.
    won French protection. Miège, *Le Maroc*, 550.
    "cruel in business." Cunninghame Graham, *Mogreb-El-Acksa*, 34.
  22 *was largely respected.* R. Le Tourneau, *La Vie quotidienne à Fez en 1900*, 149.
    to buy him out. Parsons, *Origins*, 67–68, 573–74.
  23 *"Master the Sultan."* Drummond Hay, *A Memoir*, 169.

page 24 *inspired fear.* W. Harris, *Land of African Sultan*, 192–94.

25 *curiously flavoured.* Drummond Hay, *A Memoir*, 273.

"expense of the mission." Kerr, *Morocco*, 50–51.

26 *war and the administration.* Scham, *Lyautey in Morocco* . . . , 49–51.

the desired effect. L. Harris, *With Moulai Hafid at Fez*, 155–57.

27 *crowned heads of Europe. Ibid.*, 214.

to collect their due. Ibid., 96.

Tattenbach thanked him profusely. St.-Aulaire, *Confessions*, 150–51.

28 *brought for settlement.* Meakin, *Life in Morocco*, 220–21.

"governing classes"? Nicolson, *Lord Carnock*, 129.

"any European invader." Ibid., 119.

Chapter III   The COUNTRY

29 *at least half correct.* Drummond Hay, *A Memoir*, 6.

30 *converting to Islam.* Rohlfs, *Adventures in Morocco*, 12.

"company of believers." Ibid., 19, 27.

31 *"maledictions on the Christians."* Caillé, *Travels* . . . , vol. II, 26.

" 'God be praised.' " Rohlfs, *Adventures*, 28, 189.

32 *vile and base people.* Leo Africanus, *A History and Description of Africa*, 185–86.

a nation of one-handed men. Caillé, *Travels*, vol. I, 87.

"They combine . . . all possible vices." Ibid., vol. I, 99.

Moors had yet to discover. Erckmann, *Le Maroc moderne*, original manuscript in AHG.

told Cunninghame Graham. Cunninghame Graham, *Mogreb-El-Acksa*, 116.

33 *unveiled, unprotected, unabashed.* Meakin, *Life in Morocco*, 87.

"clothes were generally torn." Rohlfs, *Adventures*, 195.

stick their tongues through this. Lemprière, *A Tour Through the Dominions of Morocco*, 142–44.

34 *"are continual."* Meakin, *Life in Morocco*, 80.

seeing other women. W. Harris, *The Morocco That Was*, 156–7.

were not confined to Europe. Rohlfs, *Adventures*, 42.

a wife for her son. Le Tourneau, *La Vie quotidienne à Fez en 1900*, 195–96.

Rohlfs maintained. Rohlfs, *Adventures*, 43.

rigid segregation of the towns. W. Harris, *Tafilet*, 40.

35 *hope of remarriage.* Rohlfs, *Adventures*, 44.

not the cause or effect. Meakin, *Life in Morocco*, 43, 45–46.

37 *"behalfe of their women."* Africanus, 183.

redeemed his reputation. Erckmann, 118.

in defense of the Berber. Cunninghame Graham, *Mogreb*, 126.

killing of a visitor's dog. R. Bidwell, *Morocco Under Colonial Rule*: . . . , fn. 301.

"to protect him afterwards." Segonzac, *Voyages au Maroc, 1899–1901*, 96.

38 *Walter Harris wrote.* W. Harris, *The Morocco That Was*, 232.

list of forgotten supplies. Meakin, *The Land of the Moors*, 412–13.

"powders for the natives." Colville, *A Ride in Petticoats and Slippers*, 13–14.

"advisable for great bustard." W. Harris, *The Land of the African Sultan*, 36.

39 *sending the rider sprawling.* Colville, *Ride in Petticoats*, 118.

might actually come to pass. Ibid., 201–02.

page 39 *wrote Meakin.* Meakin, *Life in Morocco*, 43.

 usually led to bloodshed. E. Westermarck, *Ritual and Belief in Morocco*, 485–86.

 40 *after much splashing and shouting.* Colville, *Ride in Petticoats*, 68–70.

 41 *"cursing through the darkness."* Rankin, *In Morocco with General d'Amade*, 88–89.

 "reassuring noise." St.-Aulaire, *Confessions d'un vieux diplomate*, 92.

 42 *of couscous daily.* Colville, *Ride in Petticoats*, 214–15.

 impossible to replace in Morocco. W. Harris, *The Morocco That Was*, 230.

 "do what I could for him." Colville, *Ride in Petticoats*, 224.

 thirty pounds blood money. Drummond Hay, *A Memoir*, 104.

 spilled down his front. Ibid., 90.

 43 *foul prisons of Fez.* St.-Aulaire, *Confessions*, 42.

 vanishing reputation of former power. W. Harris, *Land of African Sultan*, 77.

 "fertility of the earth," Rohlfs wrote. Rohlfs, *Adventures*, 253.

 44 *bought with little difficulty. Ibid.*, 103.

 a gullible peasantry. W. Harris, *Land of African Sultan*, 57.

 45 *sanctuary was finally reached.* Rohlfs, *Adventures*, 254.

 the tribe would be blessed. Segonzac, 83.

 parodies of French military costume. Rohlfs, *Adventures*, 95–96.

 46 *that he returned safely home.* Segonzac, *Voyages*, 85.

 the butchery continued. W. Harris, *The Morocco That Was*, 279–81.

 laid offerings at his feet. Rohlfs, *Adventures*, 108.

 "As hungry as a pilgrim's flea." Ibid., 250.

 47 *other arrangements.* Parsons, *The Origins of the Moroccan Question*, Appendix F.

Chapter IV   FEZ

 48 *orange, pomegranate and palm trees.* Madame St.-René Taillandier, *Ce Monde disparu*, 244.

 49 *has caused the fall.* Colville, *A Ride in Petticoats and Slippers*, 141.

 50 *cordial hatred exists on both sides.* Meakin, *Life in Morocco*, 16–17.

 "the Jew is at home." Charles de Foucauld, *Reconnaissance au Maroc, 1883–4*, 395.

 into the medina. Ibid., 396.

 brazen fearlessness through gardens. L. Harris, *With Moulai Hafid at Fez*, 93.

 51 *a servant's life in Morocco.* Ashmead-Bartlett, *The Passing of the Shereefian Empire*, 234–35.

 stampeded for drier ground. Le Tourneau, *La Vie quotidienne à Fez en 1900*, 58.

 52 *too close to the bone. Ibid.*, 41, 298.

 defeat the men of Fez. W. Harris, *Tafilet*, 359–60.

 53 *canary in a cage.* Le Tourneau, *La Vie quotidienne*, 243.

 in some other way was deformed. Meakin, *Life in Morocco*, 179–80.

 54 *cannot come into the house.* Forbes, R. *El Raisuni*, 222.

 55 *lay recovering at their feet.* Rohlfs, *Adventures in Morocco*, 83.

 "not in the stomach." Ibid., 88–89.

 patient would agree to swallow it. Ibid., 358–59.

 palace lions. W. Harris, *The Morocco That Was*, 330–31.

 "the card to the sore." Ibid., 325.

 he simulated a fantasia. Veyre, *Au Maroc dans l'intimité du Sultan*, 89.

page 57 *he followed the operation. Ibid.*, 141.

58 *extravagances of the Sultan.* St.-Aulaire, *Confessions d'un vieux diplomate*, 66.

60 *"great victory for peaceful penetration." Ibid.*, 121.

with their knives. Ibid., 73-74.

61 *with his secretaries.* Nicolson, *Lord Carnock*, 118.

62 *biting his lower lip.* Rankin, *In Morocco with General d'Amade*, 186-87.

individual European states. AHG, C 20.

"Eiffel Tower?" Veyre, *Au Maroc*, 106.

his was no good. W. Harris, *The Morocco That Was*, 150.

"the Nazarene." Ashmead-Bartlett, *Passing of Empire*, 22.

63 *disappointed in him.* Nicolson, *Lord Carnock*, 145.

Chapter V   TAGHIT

71 *"pointless to remain."* Sir John Drummond Hay heard similar sentiments from veterans of the 1844 Battle of Isly. *A Memoir*, 80-81.

too exhausted to pursue. Revue de Paris, October 15, 1903, 699-714. Archives historiques de guerre, Algérie, 15. Blaudin de Thé, *Historique des compagnies méharistes.*

did not notice them. Caussin, *Vers Taza*, 32-33, 72-74, 76.

73 *No Moroccan bodies were found. Bulletin du Comité de l'Afrique française*, 1903, 316-17. Arnaud and Cortier, *Nos confins Sahariens*, 154-55.

Chapter VI   The CALL

74 *counts for something.* H. Lyautey, *Vers le Maroc*, 7.

75 *suitable for general exhibition. Ibid.*, 6.

76 *decisions of great lucidity.* See, for instance, M. Paléologue, "Comment le service de trois ans fut rétabli en 1913," *Revue des deux mondes*, May 1, 1935, 71-72.

prickly and arrogant. Catroux, *Lyautey le Marocain*, 67.

77 *raiders into Morocco.* Aperçu sur la situation de la frontière de la subdivision d'Ain Sefra, *Vers le Maroc*, 15-28.

78 *a good plan.* H. Lyautey, *Vers le Maroc*, 14.

Lyautey succumbed. Maurois, *Marshal Lyautey*, 16-17.

79 *part college, part seminary.* Beaufre, *1940, The Fall of France*, 15.

80 *in that year.* Hanrion, *Saint-Cyr, neuf années de commandement*, fn. 43.

blue (cotton) for exercises. Beaufre, *Fall of France*, 15.

punishment and chivying. Ibid.

of the carriages. Hanrion, *Saint-Cyr*, 72.

81 *remained a "barbaric country."* Heidsieck, *Le Rayonnement de Lyautey*, 58.

84 *until his death.* Le Révérend, *Un Lyautey inconnu*, 176, 184, 186-88.

85 *by metropolitan officers.* The French army had three principal divisions: the metropolitan army, which included 90 percent of military personnel, was stationed in France; the Armée d'Afrique, principally made up of volunteers and native regiments, was responsible for the Maghreb; the colonial army, the old marines, was transferred from the navy to the War Ministry in 1900. Made up of volunteers, both French and native, it was responsible for Africa south of the Sahara, Madagascar and Indochina. Both

individual professional soldiers and entire regiments could be seconded to another army for the duration of a campaign.

page 85 *sticking pins into rats.* Zeldin, *France, 1848–1945*, vol. II, p. 819.

   86 *"where there are still chiefs."* H. Lyautey, *Vers le Maroc*, 8.

   87 *"break my neck." Ibid.*, 17.

   88 *quite inadequate brakes.* C. Andrew, "The French Colonial Movement During the Third Republic: The Unofficial Mind of Imperialism," *Transactions of the Royal Historical Society*, 1976.

   89 *melted back across the Atlas.* Dunn, *Resistance in the Desert*, 194.

   90 *"our North African empire." Petit Journal*, June 14, 1903.

   91 *"digested."* H. Lyautey, *Vers le Maroc*, 32.

Chapter VII   The ROGUI

   93 *pulled the trigger.* L. Arnaud, *Au Temps des mehallas*, 156.

   94 *given to the shrine, and left. Ibid.*, 156–57.

   95 *the interest of the picture.* General Domingo Badia, *The Travels of Ali Bey*, 178.

      south of Taza. Burke, *Prelude to Protectorate . . .* , 62.

   96 *the sanctity of Bou Hamara.* L. Arnaud, *Mehallas*, 161–62.

      to occupy his grave. Maitrot de la Motte Capron, "Le Roghi," 514–76.

      its capital at Taza. L. Arnaud, *Mehallas*, 162–63.

      friendly and very noble. Du Tallis, *Le Maroc pittoresque*, 79.

   97 *"a horrible brazier." Ibid.*, 65, 75, 80.

      lead to his downfall. Burke, *Prelude*, 64.

      sheer invention. Usborne, *The Conquest of Morocco*, 130–31.

      to smash Bou Hamara. L. Arnaud, *Mehallas*, 163.

   98 *an arsenal at Fez.* Parsons, *The Origins of the Moroccan Question*, 21–22.

      before they reached the battlefield. Maitrot de la Motte Carpon, "L'Armée chérifienne," 26.

      were actually blind. Erckmann, *Le Maroc moderne*, 244.

      fire from the hip. Parsons, *Origins*, 22.

   99 *four thousand on the ground.* Rankin, *In Morocco . . .* , 189–90.

  100 *"grimaces on the face of the enemy."* Maitrot de la Motte Capron, "L'Armée chérifienne," 28.

      who accompanied these expeditions. Weisgerber, *Au Seuil du Maroc moderne*, 58.

      "than by the enemy." AHG, C24, December 18, 1910.

      bother of battle. Maitrot de la Motte Carpon, "L'Armée chérifienne," 26.

      traveling to the souq. Bidwell, *Morocco Under Colonial Rule*, 293.

      "as they pleased." Rohlfs, *Adventures in Morocco*, 114–15.

      no two of which were alike. Parsons, *Origins*, 22.

  101 *"how to shoot."* Veyre, *Au Maroc dans l'intimité du Sultan*, 156.

      faster than it had come. L. Arnaud, *Mehallas*, 167–70.

  102 *serpent under the apple tree.* Madame St.-René Taillandier, *Ce Monde disparu*, 235.

      promptly reinstated him. L. Arnaud, *Mehallas*, 129–32.

      in honor of Colonel Maclean. Ibid., 212.

  103 *to the attackers. Ibid.*, 174.

      waited with bated breath. St.-René Taillandier, *Les Origines du Maroc français*, 105–06.

      was never established. Ibid., 109; Arnaud, *Mehallas*, 182.

page 104 *expedition in May.* St.-René Taillandier, *Les Origines*, 120.

for sale in the marketplace. L. Arnaud, *Mehallas*, 194.

career of Bou Hamara. St.-René Taillandier, *Les Origines*, 143.

to capture Oudjda. Ibid., 212-13.

105 *dealing with the makhzan.* Burke, *Prelude*, 65.

Chapter VIII   EL RAISUNI

106 *"Why don't we do as he?"* L. Arnaud, *Au Temps des mehallas*, 217, 223.

108 *"does not feel himself a man."* Forbes, *El Raisuni*, 35.

109 *"its punishment eternal." Ibid.*, 151-52.

"respect due to his birth." W. Harris, *The Morocco That Was*, 181-82.

110 *"within three hours of Gibraltar."* Nicolson, *Lord Carnock*, 148.

111 *"slow thinking Moor."* Harris, *Morocco That Was*, 193.

112 *conditions would be met.* St.-Aulaire, *Confessions d'un vieux diplomate*, 102.

114 *they nonetheless acceded. Ibid.*, 103.

touchstones of the protectorate. Ibid., 188-89.

becoming ungovernable. Nicolson, *Lord Carnock*, 153.

115 *whip bit deeper.* St.-Aulaire, *Confessions*, 110-11.

116 *a constant reminder!* Forbes, *El Raisuni*, 78, 105.

like everyone else. Harris, *Morocco That Was*, 199.

117 *violence of 1906-07 must be placed.* Burke, *Prelude to Protectorate . . .* , 91.

build the monument. Documents diplomatiques, affaires du Maroc, 1901-12, vol. III, 9, 13-29.

120 *a gigantic bluff.* Harris, *Morocco That Was*, 202-07.

"paid no attention to us." Forbes, *El Raisuni*, 82.

121 *back to Tangiers. Ibid.*, 86-96.

Chapter IX   *The* LYAUTEY METHOD

123 *strike them from behind.* E. Arnaud and M. Cortier, *Nos Confins Sahariens*, 213.

124 *secret encroachments into Morocco.* H. Lyautey, *Vers le Maroc*, 301.

dismissed them as ambush bait. Ibid., 72.

played their flutes. E. Arnaud and M. Cortier, *Nos Confins*, 117.

127 *not a man, not a horse, missing.* H. Lyautey, *Vers le Maroc*, 324-29.

raids into the Guir. Ibid., 329-30.

128 *following their own interests. Ibid.*, 20-21.

dominating the desert. E. Arnaud and M. Cortier, *Nos Confins*, 70-73.

129 *only one that worked there. Ibid.*, 103-04.

openmouthed with disbelief. Ibid., 84.

250 miles from their bases. Ibid., 78.

130 *Moslem religious brotherhoods.* Catroux, *Lyautey le Marocain*, 125.

legionnaires are good diggers. Ibid., 18-19.

131 *"Moscova, Lützen, Bautzen." Ibid.*, 122.

spanked the wind. H. Lyautey, *Vers le Maroc*, 194.

132 *true friendships of his life.* Catroux, *Lyautey*, 87-88.

page 133 sake of a few rifles. Dunn, *Resistance in the Desert*, 143.

"diplomatically" rebaptized Berguent. H. Lyautey, *Vers le Maroc*, 77.

could excite jealousy. *Ibid.*, 81.

134 back to Algeria. *Ibid.*, 81–82.

Paris could have his resignation. *Ibid.*, 90.

"anxious hours of my life." *Ibid.*, 96.

135 Combes and General André. *Ibid.*, 114–15.

Chapter X   1905: *The* COUP *de* TANGER

139 launch Marchand across Africa. Cooke, *The New French Imperialism*, 81–97.

144 Moroccan customs receipts. St.-Aulaire, *Confessions d'un vieux diplomate*, 91–101.

strength of that support. Burke, *Prelude to Protectorate* . . . , 80–85.

to withdraw. Nicolson, *Lord Carnock*, 161.

in the decade before 1914. For another view, which interprets German policy as rational response to Delcassé's attempt to disrupt the status quo in Morocco, see J.-C. Allain, *Agadir, 1911*, 28–38.

145 purely "platonic." *Ibid.*, 165.

Germans had to give way. St.-Aulaire, *Confessions*, 162.

146 "static to a dynamic state." Nicolson, *Lord Carnock*, 199.

Chapter XI   CASABLANCA

147 "methodical provocation." Burke, *Prelude to Protectorate in Morocco, 1860–1912*, 91.

148 for sale in the market. *Documents diplomatiques, Affaires du Maroc*, 1901–12, vol. III, 216–17, 229–30.

150 Bouzid did nothing. Ashmead-Bartlett, *The Passing of the Shereefian Empire*, 23–25.

to bend to French will. AHG, C 20, August 27, 1905.

151 provided by the engine. Rankin, *In Morocco with General d'Amade*, 3.

the crisis had passed. Ashmead-Bartlett, *Passing of Empire*, 28–31.

"by delaying it." St.-Aulaire, *Confessions d'un vieux diplomate*, 177.

153 "Jaurès' gob." *Ibid.*, 178–79.

exceeded their orders. A. Adam, *Histoire de Casablanca*, 103–37.

155 Casablanca erupted. Ashmead-Bartlett, *Passing of Empire*, 38–45.

"small risk to ourselves." *Ibid.*, 63.

156 "according to their ugliness." L. Harris, *With Moulai Hafid at Fez*, 61.

covered his body. *Ibid.*, 60–61.

157 "monstrous erection." C. Hourel, *Mes Aventures marocaines*, 39.

159 my only company. L. Harris, *With Moulai Hafid*, 62.

back to Algeria. AHG, C 20.

allowed to go home. Moore, *The Passing of Morocco*, 35.

Chapter XII   *The* CHAOUIA CAMPAIGN

162 the next casbah. Montagne, *Les Berbères et le Makhzen dans le sud du Maroc*, 327–37.

plain of Marrakech. *Ibid.*, 337.

page 163 *modernize the country.* Burke, *Prelude to Protectorate . . .* , 102.

out-of-date Egyptian newspapers. Ibid., 99–101.

164 *hands trembled visibly.* L. Harris, *With Moulai Hafid at Fez*, 85.

Hafid appeared "unbalanced." Gouraud, *Au Maroc*, 43.

165 *his new Sultan.* Maxwell, *Lords of the Atlas*, 99–101.

167 *dressing station at Casablanca.* Ashmead-Bartlett, *The Passing of the Shereefian Empire*, 77–100.

flats of their swords. Ibid., 101–09.

"leave the sea." Hourel, *Mes Aventures marocaines*, 39.

168 *selling their rifles.* Ashmead-Bartlett, *Passing of Empire*, 152–53.

symbol of Christian baptism. Burke, *Prelude*, 109.

174 *"It makes me laugh," he said.* St.-Aulaire, *Confessions d'un vieux diplomate*, 186.

175 *"organization on the march."* Maurois, *Marshal Lyautey*, 138.

he said to St.-Aulaire. St.-Aulaire, *Confessions*, 186.

176 *"I held it."* Azan, *Souvenirs de Casablanca*, 167, 181–90.

178 *"understood it not."* L. Harris, *With Moulai Hafid*, 64.

enemy's women. Forbes, *El Raisuni*, 173.

cross-channel neighbors. Ashmead-Bartlett, *Passing of Empire*, 134.

was to cease. AHG, 3H 72.

by constant retelling. L. Harris, *With Moulai Hafid*, 62–63.

180 *stench of burning tents.* Rankin, *In Morocco with General d'Amade*, 158–59.

cries of the children. Ibid., 154–62.

181 *rippled over the town.* Hourel, *Mes Aventures*, 123–24.

182 *at Settat and safety.* L. Arnaud, *Au Temps des mehallas*, 250–57; d'Amade, *La Campagne de 1908-9 en Chaouia.*

Chapter XIII   The BENI SNASSEN and BOU DENIB

184 *clever Lieutenant Catroux.* Catroux, *Lyautey le Marocain*, 125.

virtually dried up. Dunn, *Resistance in the Desert*, 116–19.

185 *not very popular either.* Kuntz, *Souvenirs*, 150.

"keep the security." Lyautey, *Vers le Maroc*, 276.

186 *fled if pressed.* Kuntz, *Souvenirs*, 20–21.

187 *"in confidence."* Guennoun, *La Montagne berbère*, 107, 137.

"to carry them out." Forbes, *El Raisuni*, 194.

188 *"stepping on a child."* Kuntz, *Souvenirs*, 168.

189 *sapping morale.* AHG, 3H 72, August 24, 1907.

191 *legionnaire shepherds.* Kuntz, *Souvenirs*, 114.

any man found armed. Ibid., 115.

congratulations of his government. Boulle, *La France et les Beni Snassen*, 36–65.

193 *French had been humiliated.* Kuntz, *Souvenirs*, 202–04.

set out for Colomb-Béchar. Dunn, *Resistance*, 223–34.

194 *"considerable losses."* Kuntz, *Souvenirs*, 250–51.

195 *empty-handed. Ibid.*, 252.

French in the East. Bernard, *Les Confins Algéro-Marocains*, 162–65.

196 *owl or the hawk.* AHG, Algérie 17, quoted in Dunn, *Resistance*, 235.

page 197 *return to Colomb-Béchar.* Kuntz, *Souvenirs*, 346–47.

198 *"twenty thousand men there," he thought. Ibid.*, 370.

Chapter XIV   A NEW SULTAN

201 *to waste it.* Ashmead-Bartlett, *The Passing of the Shereefian Empire*, 352–57. L. Harris, *With Moulai Hafid at Fez*, 205–06.

expense of the Chaouia campaign. St.-Aulaire, *Confessions d'un vieux diplomate*, 191.

202 *an end to it all.* L. Harris, *With Moulai Hafid*, 238.

Hafid the murderous tyrant. Burke, *Prelude to Protectorate . . . .*, 128–31.

203 *International Court at The Hague.* Martin, *Quatre siècles d'histoire marocaine*, 495.

204 *"our military mission."* AHG, C 22, Regnault letter of November 3, 1908.

"little by little." Ibid., C 24, note of December 18, 1910.

retreating mehalla. Ibid., C 22.

205 *"value of our civilization." Ibid.*, August 25, 1909.

206 *calls himself a Moslem.* Maitrot de la Motte Capron, "Le Roghi," 556.

five cartridges apiece. Le Glay, *Chroniques marocaines*, 9.

symbol of the Sultan's power. Le Glay, *La Mort du Rogui*, 25.

207 *fighting over the spoils.* AHG, C 22.

toward the northwest. L. Arnaud, *Au Temps des mehallas*, 274–75.

placid gaze of Moulai Hafid. Maitrot de la Motte Capron, "Le Roghi," 552–54.

lost their right hand. AHG, C 22, August 19, 1909.

208 *tortured and mutilated.* L. Arnaud, *Au Temps des mehallas*, 282.

mehallas on campaign. Maitrot de la Motte Capron, "Le Roghi," 552–58.

for his downfall. AHG, C 22, August 19, 1909.

209 *walked out and surrendered. Ibid.*, August 22, 1909.

fleeing women. L. Arnaud, *Au Temps des mehallas*, 276–77.

second shot. Le Glay, *La Mort du Rogui*, 21.

rescue him. AHG, C 22, August 22, 1909.

take him prisoner. Ibid.

"kill me." Le Glay, *La Mort du Rogui*, 31.

212 *give up her jewelry.* AHG, C 22, June 1, 1910.

released his prisoners. Ibid., August 3, 1910.

had been in 1907. Ibid.

Chapter XV   The FIRST SIEGE of FEZ

213 *their own caids.* Le Glay, *Chroniques marocaines*, 239–40.

214 *began to rain. Ibid.*, 13–36.

215 *regular military organization.* AHG, C 24, December 18, 1910.

a thing of the past. Ibid., November 1910.

into the street. Le Glay, *Chroniques*, 61.

reenlistment contract. AHG, C 24.

216 *a stock-taking . . . by French officers. Ibid.*

between the French and the caids. Ibid., C 22, September 1, 1910.

page 218 included in the plot. Azan, *L'Expédition de Fez*, 7-8.
to besiege Fez. Le Glay, *Chroniques*, 71.
219 badger the Ministry of War. *Ibid.*, 71-72.
his friends in France. *Ibid.*, 71.
220 their first consul. Caillaux, *Mes Mémoires*, vol. II, 65-67.
221 gravest results are possible. Messimy, *Mes Souvenirs*, 155.
"do not encourage you." Caillaux, *Agadir*, 93-94.
222 the French movement. Azan, *L'Expédition de Fez*, 76.

Chapter XVI   The RESCUE

223 "to the bitter end." Le Glay, *Chroniques marocaines*, 292.
226 first week of May. Azan, *L'Expédition de Fez*, 54-55.
led by Colonel Henri Gouraud. Gouraud, *Au Maroc*, 5.
227 sniping from the trees. Capperon, *Au Secours de Fez*, 80.
228 to the dissidents. Burke, *Prelude to Protectorate . . .* , 162.
dissidents occupied. Azan, *L'Expédition*, 19.
against the Sultan. Le Glay, *Chroniques*, 84.
229 verge of revolt. Azan, *L'Expédition*, 26-28.
·   Frenchman's stirrup. Le Glay, *Chroniques*, 129.
Frau Vassal's hand. *Ibid.*, 149.
shaved their heads. *Ibid.*, 189.
230 "not capable of defeating." Azan, *L'Expédition*, 54.
back of the room. Le Glay, *Chroniques*, 125-26.
231 an idiot. *Ibid.*, 244.
sanctuary of Moulai Idris. Bartow, *The Agadir Crisis*, 177.
232 bucket of water over him. Le Glay, *Chroniques*, 254.
in open country. Gouraud, *Au Maroc*, 45.
233 spoils of war. Kerr, *Morocco After Twenty-five Years*, 334.
embrace General Monier. Bidwell, *Morocco Under Colonial Rule*, 135.
234 Cruppi on June 10. Bartow, *Agadir Crisis*, 208.

Chapter XVII   The MASSACRE

238 colonial realities. Zeldin, *France, 1848-1945*, vol. II, p. 940.
239 treat them fairly. Azan, *L'Expédition de Fez*, 105-06.
traditionally enjoyed. AHG, C 24, Simon report, April 25, 1912.
"abuses" of makhzan officials. Azan, *L'Expédition*, 221-22.
240 "indirect rule." *Ibid.*, 225-26.
fireworks display. Charles-Roux and Caillé, *Missions diplomatiques françaises à Fez*, 226.
241 "not difficult to please." Weisgerber, *Au Seuil du Maroc moderne*, 269-70.
242 not to recognize them. *Ibid.*, 272-73.
declined into superstition. Le Glay, *Chroniques marocaines*, 70-71.
243 nerves of the Sultan's soldiers. Selous, *Appointment to Fez*, 129.
244 "killing all officers." AHG, C 24, Brulard report, May 12, 1912.
over the rooftops. Selous, *Appointment*, 141.

page 245 signed by General Brulard. H. Jacques, *Les Journées sanglantes de Fez*, 47–67.
   246 an appalling smell. Weisgerber, *Au Seuil du Maroc moderne*, 292–93.
      joining the pillage. *Ibid.*, 283–84.
   247 perished in the mutiny. Selous, *Appointment*, 144.

Chapter XVIII   The SECOND SIEGE of FEZ

   248 neither barda nor knapsack. AHG, C 24, Brulard report, May 12, 1912.
   249 "we are not mules." Selous, *Appointment to Fez*, 129.
      refusing to enforce it. Brulard report, *ibid.*
      fueling the revolt. Burke, *Prelude to Protectorate* . . . , 184–85.
   250 cheat their men? Brulard report, *ibid.*
      operate within Fez. AHG, C 24, June 6, 1912.
      "numerous relations?" *Ibid.*, May 17, 1912.
   251 bloodless diplomat. Poincaré, *Au Service de la France*, vol. I, 98–99.
      bound him for life. St.-Aulaire, *Confessions d'un vieux diplomate*, 20–21.
      to Louise Baignières. Le Révérend, *Un Lyautey inconnu*, 241.
   252 "can snap at any moment," he wrote. P. Lyautey, *Lyautey l'Africain*, vol. I, 6.
   253 cleared the air. Selous, *Appointment*, fn. 151.
   254 "in enemy country." P. Lyautey, *Lyautey*, 9.
      38 dead and 85 wounded. Selous, *Appointment*, 185.
   255 to Albert de Mun. P. Lyautey, *Lyautey*, 9.
      4,000 troops. *Ibid.*, 18.
      had not rioted. Burke, *Prelude*, 168.
      refrain from political activity. *Ibid.*, 198.
   256 bodies on the field. Selous, *Appointment*, 155. Usborne, *The Conquest of Morocco*,
      180–81.
      can of gasoline. Selous, *Appointment*, 154.
   257 dead French soldiers. Gouraud, *Au Maroc*, 182–93.
      resistance in the north. St.-Chapelle, *La Conquête du Maroc*, 136–50.

Chapter XIX   MARRAKECH

   259 "barbarous and refined." St.-Aulaire, *Confessions d'un vieux diplomate*, 251.
   260 the fruit of that union was General Lyautey. *Ibid.*, 252–53.
   261 prove his every argument. W. Harris, *The Morocco That Was*, 131.
      "out of the shrubberies." *Ibid.*
      blacken his name. St.-Aulaire, *Confessions*, 261.
      Moulai Hafid's funds. *Ibid.*
   262 by fierce-looking boatmen. P. Lyautey, "L'Abdication de Moulai Hafid," 615–18.
   262 over his knee before embarking. Usborne, *The Conquest of Morocco*, 188.
      second alternative. St.-Aulaire, *Confessions*, 262.
   263 ask for more troops. *Ibid.*, 265.
   264 "12,000 Frenchmen." *Ibid.*, 274.
   265 ransom the captives. Burke, *Prelude to Protectorate* . . . , 204.
      call off his campaign. Maxwell, *Lords of the Atlas*, 128–29.

page 265 *in the south.* St.-Aulaire, *Confessions*, 265.

"another wire to Mangin." Ibid.

266 *was crumbling.* P. Lyautey, *Lyautey l'Africain*, vol. I, 33–34.

wedded to his men. Burke, *Prelude*, 205.

267 *23 wounded.* Usborne, *Conquest*, 192–93; Bugnet, *Mangin*, 120–23; Cornet, *La Conquête du Maroc sud*, 38–39.

dogs on them. Bidwell, *Morocco Under Colonial Rule*, 108.

268 *three-week-old beard.* Cornet, *La Conquête*, 33–49.

"hurrahs and ululations." Ibid., 56.

269 *deep-blue sky. Ibid.*, 80.

"safeguard the population." P. Lyautey, *op. cit.*, 43.

270 *victorious French army.* St.-Aulaire, *Confessions*, 267.

Chapter XX   The ZAER

271 *"rat holes and fleas' nests."* P. Khorat, "Scènes de pacification marocaine," I, 666.

272 *and fled.* Kerr, *Morocco After Twenty-five Years*, 329–30.

antagonized nearly everyone. Azan, *L'Expédition de Fez*, 205–06.

273 *make them bad Arabs.* Forbes, *El Raisuni*, 103.

274 *his caidship.* Khorat, I, 645–82.

275 *"as Tonkin and Madagascar." Ibid.*, II, 128–29.

276 *orbit of French influence. Ibid.*, 129–33.

his own goumiers. Ibid., III, 660.

277 *looting spree that followed.* Gouraud, *Au Maroc*, 36.

278 *four-footed charges together.* Kuntz, *Souvenirs*, 112–13.

Chapter XXI   CONSOLIDATION and DEFEAT

279 *"fanatical, warlike."* P. Lyautey, *Lyautey l'Africain*, vol. I, 41.

280 *too "impulsive" and "undisciplined."* Bugnet, *Mangin*, 128.

great caids. P. Lyautey, *Lyautey*, August 1913.

with little result. Ibid.

281 *on the twenty-fifth.* St.-Chapelle, *La Conquête du Maroc*, 175–84.

potentially disastrous. Catroux, *Lyautey le Marocain*, 59.

undisputed military talents. P. Lyautey, *Lyautey*, 79.

283 *and 63 wounded.* Azan, *Franchet d'Esperey*, 26–70.

he repeated on May 24. P. Lyautey, *Lyautey*, 84, 99–100.

284 *go quietly to France.* Azan, *Franchet*, 68–70.

287 *in search of their men.* Said Guennoun, *La Montagne berbère*, 185.

Epilogue

289 *"idiots."* St.-Aulaire, *Confessions d'un vieux diplomate*, 283.

Lyautey said. Ibid., 277.

290 *"hold the land."* Bidwell, *Morocco Under Colonial Rule*, 108.

page 290 *a socialist state. Ibid.*, 24, 6.

291 *when one was traveling.* W. Harris, *The Morocco That Was*, 163.

"on the other side." Ibid., 167.

292 *walking their dogs. Ibid.*, 168-70.

293 *quite simply naïve.* Dunn, *Resistance in the Desert*, 224.

294 *hands of French functionaries.* A. Scham, *Lyautey in Morocco, Protectorate Administration, 1912-1925*, 48.

"the French administration." Harris, *The Morocco That Was*, 145.

295 *transferred elsewhere.* Bidwell, *Morocco*, 81-90.

297 *"What a bloody fool!"* St.-Aulaire, *Confessions*, 298.

"those pigs." "Jacques Millerand parle d'Alexandre Millerand," *L'Histoire*, No. 8, January 1929, p. 108.

SELECTED BIBLIOGRAPHY

Archives historiques de guerre, Château de Vincennes, série C, Maroc.

Adam, A., *Histoire de Casablanca*, Aix, 1968.

Africanus, Leo, *A History and Description of Africa*, New York, n.d.

d'Amade, General Albert, *La Campagne de 1908-9 en Chaouia*, Paris, 1911.

Andrew, C. *Théophile Delcassé and the Making of the Entente Cordiale*, London, 1968.

Andrew, L., and Kayna-Forstner, A. S., *France Overseas*, London, 1981.

Arnaud, Captain E., and Cortier, Lieutenant M., *Nos Confins Sahariens*, Paris, 1908.

Arnaud, Louis, *Au Temps des mehallas*, Casablanca, 1952.

Ashmead-Bartlett, E., *The Passing of the Shereefian Empire*, London, 1910.

Aubin, Eugène, *Le Maroc d'aujourd'hui*, Paris, 1913.

Ayache, Albert, *Le Maroc*, Paris, 1956.

Aymes, Lieutenant, *Comment on se bat au Maroc*, Paris, 1914.

Azan, Paul, *Souvenirs de Casablanca*, Paris, 1911.

_____, *L'Expédition de Fez*, Paris, 1924.

_____, *Franchet d'Esperey*, Paris, 1949.

Barbour, Nevill, *Morocco*, London, 1965.

Barthou, Louis, *La Bataille du Maroc*, Paris, 1919.

Bartow, Ima Christine, *The Agadir Crisis*, Chapel Hill, North Carolina, 1940.

Benoist-Méchin, *Lyautey l'Africain, ou le rêve immolé*, Lausanne, 1966.

Bernard, A., *Les Confins Algéro-Marocains*, Paris, 1911.

Berriau, Colonel, *L'officier de renseignement au Maroc*, Rabat, 1918.

Betts, R., *Assimilation and Association in French Colonial Policy, 1890-1914*, New York and London, 1961.

Bidwell, Robin, *Morocco Under Colonial Rule: French Administration of the Tribal Areas, 1912-1956*, London, 1973.

Blaudin de Thé, *Historique des compagnies méharistes*, Algiers, 1955.

Boisboissel, General Yves de, *Dans l'ombre de Lyautey*, Paris, 1954.

Bourdon, G., *Ce que j'ai vu au Maroc, les journées de Casablanca*, Paris, 1910.

_____, "Les Débuts du règne de Moulai Hafid," *Renseignements coloniaux*, supplement of the *Bulletin du comité de l'Afrique française*, 1908, p. 43.

Bugnet, Commandant, *Charles Mangin*, Paris, 1924.

Buisseret, Count Conrad de, *A la Cour de Fez*, Brussels, 1907.

Burke, Edmund, *Prelude to Protectorate in Morocco, 1860-1912*, Chicago, 1976.

Caillaux, Joseph, *Agadir*, Paris, 1919.

_____, *Mes Mémoires*, 3 vols., 1943.

Caillé, René, *Travels Through Central Africa to Timbuctoo and Across the Great Desert to Morocco, Performed in the Years 1824-28* (1830), 2 vols., London, 1968.

Capperon, Louis, *Au Secours de Fez*, Paris, 1912.

Catroux, General, *Lyautey le Marocain*, Paris, 1952.

Caussin, Captain, *Vers Taza, 1913–14*, Paris, 1922.

Ceccaldi, Captain, *Au Pays de la poudre*, Paris, 1914.

Charles-Roux, F., and Caillé, J., *Missions diplomatiques françaises à Fez*, Paris, 1955.

Colville, Captain H. E., *A Ride in Petticoats and Slippers*, London, 1880.

Cooke, J. J., *The New French Imperialism, 1880–1910*, Newton Abbot, 1973.

Cornet, Captain, *À la Conquête du Maroc sud, 1912–13*, Paris, 1914.

Cruickshank, Earl F., *Morocco at the Parting of the Ways*, London, 1935.

Cunninghame Graham, R. B., *Mogreb-El-Acksa*, London, 1898.

Denis, Pierre, *L'Evolution des troupes Sahariennes*, thesis, University of Rennes, 1963.

Dervil, G., *Trois grands Africains*, Paris, 1945.

Domingo Badia y Leblich, General, *The Travels of Ali Bey*, London, 1816.

Drummond Hay, Sir John, *A Memoir*, London, 1896.

Dunn, Ross E., *Resistance in the Desert*, London, 1977.

Erckmann, Jules, *Le Maroc moderne*, Paris, 1885.

Esperandieu, Pierre, *Lyautey et le Protectorat*, thesis, University of Paris, Faculté de droit, Paris, 1947.

Forbes, Rosita, *El Raisuni*, London, 1924.

Foucauld, Charles de, *Reconnaissance au Maroc, 1883–4*, Paris, 1888.

Gaulis, B. G., *Lyautey intime*, Paris, 1938.

Gellner, Ernest, *Saints of the Atlas*, London, 1969.

Gorrée, Georges, *Memoirs of Charles de Foucauld*, London, 1938.

Gouraud, General Henri, *Au Maroc, 1911–14, Souvenirs d'un Africain*, Paris, 1949.

————, *Lyautey*, Paris, 1938.

Grove, Lady, *71 Days Camping in Morocco*, London, 1902.

Guennoun, Captain Said, *La Montagne berbère*, Paris, 1929.

Hanotaux, G., *Mangin*, Paris, 1925.

Hanrion, General L., *Saint-Cyr, Neuf années de commandement, 1871–1880*, Paris, 1888.

Hardy, G., *Portrait de Lyautey*, Mayenne, 1949.

Harris, Lawrence, *With Moulai Hafid at Fez*, London, 1909.

Harris, Walter, *The Land of the African Sultan*, London, 1889.

————, *Tafilet*, London, 1895.

————, *The Morocco That Was*, London, 1921.

Heidsieck, P., *Le Rayonnement de Lyautey*, Paris, 1937.

Hourel, C., *Mes aventures marocaines*, Casablanca, 1952.

Howe, Sonia, *Lyautey of Morocco*, London, 1931.

Jacques, Hubert, *Les Journées sanglantes de Fez*, Paris, 1913.

Kerr, Dr. Robert, *Morocco After Twenty-five Years*, London, 1912.

Khorat, Pierre (pseudonym General Ibos), "Scènes de pacification marocaine," *Revue des deux mondes*, October 1, November 1, December 1, 1913.

Kuntz, Captain Charles, *Souvenirs de campagne au Maroc*, Paris, 1913.

Ladreit de Lacharrière, J., "Grandeur et décadence de Mohammed El Hiba," *Bulletin de la Société de géographie d'Alger*, 1912, pp. 473–86.

Landau, Rom, *Moroccan Drama*, London, 1966.

Lechartier, Captain, *La Colonne du Haut Guir en septembre 1908*, Paris, 1908.

Le Glay, Maurice, *La Mort du Rogui*, Paris, 1926.

————, *Chroniques marocaines*, Paris, 1933.

Lemprière, William, *A Tour Through the Dominions of Morocco*, London, 1813.

Lenz, Oscar, *Timbuctou*, Paris, 1886.

Le Révérend, André, *Un Lyautey inconnu*, Paris, 1980.

Le Tourneau, R., *La Vie quotidienne à Fez en 1900*, Paris, 1955.

Loti, Pierre, *Au Maroc*, Paris, 1890.

Lyautey, General Hubert, *Vers le Maroc*, Paris, 1937.

_____, *Paroles d'action*, Paris, 1927.

_____, *Du Rôle social de l'officier* (1891), reedited, Paris, 1931.

_____, *Du Rôle colonial de l'armée* (1900), reedited, Paris, 1920.

Lyautey, Pierre, *Lyautey l'Africain*, 4 vols., Paris, 1953.

_____, "L'Abdication de Moulay Hafid," *Revue des deux mondes*, 1953.

Maitrot de la Motte Capron, A., "L'Armée chérifienne," *Bulletin de la Société de Géographie d'Alger*, 1929.

_____, "Le Roghi," *Bulletin de la Société de Géographie d'Alger*, 1929.

Mangin, General Charles, *La Force noire*, Paris, 1910.

Martin, A. G. P., *Quatre siècles d'histoire marocaine*, Paris, 1923.

Martinière, Henri de la, *Souvenirs du Maroc*, Paris, 1919.

Mauran, Dr., *Le Maroc d'aujourd'hui et de demain*, Paris, 1909.

_____, *La société marocaine*, Paris, 1912.

Maurois, André, *Marshal Lyautey*, London, 1931.

Maxwell, Kenneth, *Lords of the Atlas*, London, 1966.

Meakin, Budgett, *The Land of the Moors*, London, 1901.

_____, *The Moors*, London, 1902.

_____, *Life in Morocco*, London, 1905.

Messimy, Adolphe, *Mes Souvenirs*, Paris, 1937.

Miège, Jean-Louis, *Le Maroc et l'Europe, 1830–1894*, 4 vols., Paris, 1961.

Millerand, Jacques, "Jacques Millerand parle d'Alexandre Millerand," *L'Histoire*, no. 8, January 1979.

Ministère des affaires étrangères, *Documents diplomatiques, Affaires du Maroc, 1901–12*, 6 vols., Paris, 1905–12.

Montagne, Robert, *Les Berbères et le Makhzen dans le sud du Maroc*, Paris, 1930.

Monteil, Vincent, *Le Maroc*, Paris, 1962.

_____, "Les Bureaux arabes au Maghreb, 1833–1961," *Esprit*, November 1961.

Moore, Frederick, *The Passing of Morocco*, London, 1908.

Nicolson, Harold, *Lord Carnock*, London, 1930.

Nordman, D., "L'armée d'Algérie au Maroc," in *Armées, guerre et politique en Afrique du Nord*, Paris, 1977.

Paléologue, Maurice, "Comment le service de trois ans fut rétabli en 1913," *Revue des deux mondes*, May 1, 1935.

Parsons, F. V., *The Origins of the Moroccan Question*, London, 1976.

Pellow, Thomas, *The Adventures of Thomas Pellow of Penryn, Mariner*, London, 1890.

Piquet, Captain Victor, *Campagnes d'Afrique*, Paris, 1912.

Poincaré, Raymond, *Au Service de la France*, vol. I, Paris, 1926.

Rankin, Lieutenant-Colonel Sir Reginald, *In Morocco with General d'Amade* (1909), London, 1931.

René-Leclerc, C., *L'Armée marocaine*, Paris, 1905.

Rivet, Daniel, "Lyautey l'Africain," *L'Histoire*, no. 29, December 1980.

Rohlfs, Gerhard, *Adventures in Morocco*, London, 1874.

St.-Aulaire, Comte de, *Confessions d'un vieux diplomate*, Paris, 1953.

St.-Chapelle, A. M. G., *La Conquête du maroc*, Paris, 1913.

St.-René Taillandier, G., *Les Origines du Maroc français, 1901–6*, Paris, 1930.

St.-René Taillandier, Madame, *Ce Monde disparu*, Paris, 1947.

Scham, Alan, *Lyautey in Morocco, Protectorate Administration 1912-25*, Berkeley, 1970.

Segonzac, Marquis René de, *Voyages au Maroc, 1899-1901*, Paris, 1903.

Selous, G. H., *Appointment to Fez*, London, 1956.

Simon, H., *Un officier d'Afrique*, Paris, 1930.

Stuart, G. H., *The International City of Tangiers*, London, 1931.

Tallis, Jean du, *Le Maroc pittoresque*, Paris, 1905.

Trouncer, Margaret, *Charles de Foucauld*, London, 1972.

Trout, Frank E., *Morocco's Saharian Frontiers*, Geneva, 1969.

Twain, Mark, *Innocents Abroad*, London, 1896.

Usborne, Vice-Admiral C. V., *The Conquest of Morocco*, London, 1936.

Veyre, G., *Au Maroc dans l'intimité du Sultan*, Paris, 1908.

Waterbury, John, *The Commander of the Faithful*, London, 1970.

Wazan, Emily, Cherufa of, *My Life Story*, London, 1911.

Weisgerber, Dr. Felix, *Au Seuil du Maroc moderne*, Rabat, 1947.

———, "L'Insurrection d'El Hiba," *Afrique française*, 1930, 595-600.

Westermarck, E., *Ritual and Belief in Morocco*, London, 1926.

Zeldin, T., *France, 1848-1945*, 2 vols., London, 1978-80.

INDEX